Working the Street

WORKING
THE STREET

Police Discretion and
the Dilemmas of Reform

M I C H A E L   K.   B R O W N

Russell Sage Foundation　　　*New York*

Library of Congress Catalog Number: 80–69175
Standard Book Number: 0–87154–190–4

For Vivian

Contents

List of Tables and Figures   ix

Preface   xi

Introduction   3

PART ONE
Bureaucracy and Political Choice

Chapter 1
Administrative Discretion and Public Policy   21

Chapter 2
Police Professionalism and the Bureaucratization of
Police Work   36

PART TWO
Cops as Professionals and Bureaucrats

Chapter 3
The Patrolman and the Community   55

Chapter 4
The Police Task and Organization   75

Chapter 5
The Dilemmas of Administrative Control   96

PART THREE
Working the Street

Chapter 6
Crime Fighting   135

Chapter 7
Nonenforcement: Minor Violations and Disturbances   182

Chapter 8
Police Discretion and Operational Style   221

Chapter 9
Coping with the Police Bureaucracy   246

PART FOUR
The Politics of Police Discretion

Chapter 10
Political Control of Police Discretion: The Dilemmas of
Reform   283

Appendix
Scale Construction   307

Notes   313
Bibliography   329
Index   339

List of Tables and Figures

TABLES

1.1	A Framework for the Analysis of Administrative Discretion	30
3.1	Average Felony Crimes by Department, 1969–73	67
3.2	Background Characteristics of Patrolmen	70
5.1	Sergeants' and Watch Commanders' Attitudes Toward Supervision	105
5.2	Perceived Supervision Problems (Mean Scores)	106
5.3	Departmental Expectations (Mean Scores)	112
5.4	Criteria for Promotion (Mean Scores)	117
5.5	Mean Rankings for Departmental Criteria for Promotion	118
5.6	Perceptions of Supervisors' Behavior	120
5.7	Perceived Limits on the Exercise of Discretion	125
6.1	Observed Field Incidents by Department	140
6.2	Patrolmen's and Supervisors' Attitudes Toward Priorities of Law Enforcement	146
6.3	Patrolmen's and Supervisors' Attitudes Toward Aggressiveness and Crime Fighting	164
6.4	Breakdown of On-view Incidents by Department	168
7.1	Patrolmen's and Supervisors' Attitudes Toward Enforcement of Minor Violations	184
7.2	Patrolmen's and Supervisors' Evaluations of the Attitude Test	200
7.3	Patrolmen's and Supervisors' Attitudes Toward Order-maintenance Incidents	210
8.1	Typology of Operational Styles	224
8.2	Operational Style by Department	239
8.3	Operational Style by Attitudes Toward Supervision	241
9.1	Patrolmen's Responses to Discretionary Incidents	250

9.2   Average Adult Arrest Rates for Selected
      Misdemeanors, 1972–73   259
9.3   Supervisors' Responses to Discretionary Incidents   262
9.4   The Drunk Driving Incident   268
9.5   The Dispute Between Neighbors   270
9.6   The Family Dispute   272
9.7   The Disorderly Juveniles   274

FIGURE

5.1   Perceptions of Influence by Patrolmen   100

Preface

IT WAS NOT so long ago that the police were a walking Rorschach test for what ailed American political life. Citizens signaled their feelings by pasting expressions of support on the bumpers of their cars or by making the term "pig" an integral part of the political lexicon of the times. The police were both a part and a reflection of the political upheaval of the 1960s. In the racial crisis of that decade they became catalysts for the major black revolts and were symbols of the deteriorating relationship between blacks and whites in the cities. They also served in the effort to curb discontent over the Vietnam war—whether openly controlling anti-war demonstrations or clandestinely infiltrating the anti-war movement. But the police became controversial not only because of what they did, but because their actions were a manifestation of more deeply embedded conflicts in American society. As the protracted social and political conflicts of this era stripped away the veneer covering race relations, and as the legitimacy of political authority crumbled, the police became unwilling symbols of both the need for change and the need for order.

Passions over the police were at a fever pitch ten or twelve years ago when the idea for this book was first conceived, but they have never abated entirely, and events in the late 1970s in Houston, Philadelphia, Los Angeles, and now Miami have rekindled them. Revelations of a pattern of violence directed toward minorities in all four cities have raised anew questions about the way minorities are treated by the American system of criminal justice. The violence in Miami in the spring of 1980, however, marks a more disturbing development, for Miami appears to signify that the underlying conflicts of the 1960s have reemerged and that once again the police are the catalysts in a widening gyre of social conflict. The background of the Miami riots—continued fiscal stress upon local governments, incipient conflict between blacks and Hispanics in a time of economic distress, and increased political conflict over a shrinking economic pie—may be indicative of things to come.

I had two aims in writing this book. One was simply to understand what it is police officers do, how they do it, and why. Such questions, of course, are at the heart of the continuing political controversy over the police. But if it is important to know whether the police are consistently brutal or uncivil toward citizens, or whether they routinely violate civil rights, then simply to catalog the activities of the police is misleading, for it obscures the totality of the police experience and what it comes to mean to policemen. Counting the number of times a patrolman swears at a citizen may permit generalizations about how civil the police are, but it reveals nothing about why they feel compelled to do it nor what part such events play in their development as public officials who must, of necessity, wield broad powers of discretion.

To understand the police experience means to look at their choices as they do, seeing the reality they confront not as we might wish it to be but as they encounter it. I have sought to do this by looking at the dilemmas and moral choices police officers face on the street, and by detailing the organizational pressures that impinge upon them. It is unfortunate that so much of the writing on the police has been guided by the presumption that what is wrong with the police is the men (and now women) who become police officers, and that if they were somehow different—better educated, more sensitive to the ambiguities and strains of urban life, even more middle class—all would be well. The belief that the men and women attracted to police work are prone to authoritarianism may be comforting to some but it is erroneous. I would be the last to deny the significance of personality for police work, but any discussion of the relevance of personality must take into account the strains of police work and the demands placed upon police officers by the bureaucracies they serve.

To see the street with its cast of characters, its temptations, and its dangers as police officers see it, is to write neither an exposé nor an apology. There is very little that I could say about the police that would be more shocking than the revelations that have appeared in the media over the last ten years. Also I do not think that a close look at the external social and organizational forces that shape the choices of police officers will suggest that they could not behave otherwise. I am often amused that many of the same people who chide liberals for defending ameliorative social policies toward minorities on the grounds that the social and cultural environment of blacks and Hispanics has limited their opportunities are also quick to defend the police on similar grounds. The police, they often suggest, are the real victims, who must act as they do because of the people they confront. The fact, of course, is that the police always have some choice in any situation, and the essential thing is to understand why some alternatives are consistently preferred over others.

This brings me to my second concern in writing this book: to understand what it is the police have become. Whatever else one might say about the behavior of the police officers in Miami, Houston, or Philadelphia, or even those who aroused such concern a decade ago, these officers bear only a superficial resemblance to the police described by the Wickersham Commission in the 1930s. Between the time the Wickersham Commission investigated the state of American police departments and the outbreak of civil disorder in the 1960s, the American police had become professionalized. For example, the Los Angeles Police Department was one of the most corrupt and lawless departments in the country in the 1930s, but by the time of the Watts revolt in 1965 it was regarded as the epitome of police professionalism.

For the last thirty years, professionalism has been the "holy grail" of the police fraternity, the preferred solution to corruption, hostility between citizen and police officer, and the rising crime rate. The reformers have assumed that well-educated, well-trained, and well-paid men and women will do what is necessary to protect and serve the community. The only remaining difficulty is that the police—as Jack Webb used to put it on the television series, *Dragnet*—"must recruit from the human race." But given the continuing abuses of police power and the hostility between the police and minorities, one might legitimately ask whether this professionalism is all that the reformers presume it to be. In any event, I am skeptical that any study of the modern police can claim to explore fully the dimensions of the police experience without recourse to a first hand account of it.

My own conception of the problem has been shaped by a recognition that the professionalization of the police is but part of a broader process of reform and modernization that has engulfed local government over the last ninety years. The governmental reforms engineered by the Progressive movement at the turn of the century have become the widely accepted solution to the economic and political forces impinging upon the nation's cities. But where reform has triumphed it has also succeeded in insulating many of the ongoing political decisions of municipal government from the conflicting currents of local politics. The decline of the political bosses has led to the rise of the modern power-brokers, the public servants who staff public bureaucracies throughout the country. In New York City, as Robert Caro has shown in his superb biography of that city's premier public servant for forty years, the corrupt politicians of Tammany Hall were replaced by the power-hungry Robert Moses. This is perhaps one of the chief legacies of urban reform: the emergence of a highly bureaucratized system of government in which administrators and street-level bureaucrats are the true politicians of our age.

The police, more than many other municipal agencies, have probably had greater success in achieving the bureaucratic autonomy that is implicit in reform. And this, I think, is why they are worth studying. To explore the world of contemporary police officers is not just to ask how they cope with the pressures and strains of their work or why they make the decisions they do, it is to explore the ambiguities and limits of reform. In the wake of Miami this issue has taken on a particular urgency. If nothing else, events there demonstrate once again the flaws in the Progressive vision of professionalism and the limits to reform. There is a compelling need to think afresh about how the police can be improved, and how they can be made accountable for their actions.

But, however necessary the required change is, we should not delude ourselves that tinkering with the police—developing new mechanisms of internal control, recasting police officers as "social workers with guns"—will somehow solve the police problem once and for all. The problem of the American police is ultimately bound up with deeper questions about the course of justice in American society and the racial crisis that lies at the heart of the American experience. Anthony Bouza, Bronx borough commander of the New York Police Department, in an interview several years ago, was moved to ask, "to the degree that I succeed in keeping the ghetto cool, to the degree that I can be effective—to that degree, fundamentally, am I deflecting America's attention from discovering this cancer? . . . The fact of the matter is that we are manufacturing criminals. . . . We are very efficiently creating a very volatile and dangerous subelement of our society. And we are doing it simply because we don't want to face the burdens and the problems and the responsibilities that their existence imposes on any society with conscience. . . . And I am very well paid, almost to be the commander of an army of occupation in the ghetto. And that is a great tragedy."

If anything, Bouza's reflections are more accurate today than they were in 1978. To suggest that our police problem is but a small part of a much deeper social conflict, though, is not to invoke a liberal cliché ("if only poverty could be eliminated, there would be no problem") but to caution against making the police a scapegoat for our unwillingness to face up to the inequalities of American society. There are doubtless many police officers who would just as soon be nothing more than members of an army of occupation, but to eliminate them will not resolve matters. In some ways willfully denigrating the police only makes things worse. To do so is perhaps comforting, for it absolves us of any responsibility for what happens in the ghetto. The truth of the matter, however, is that the police—the way they are deployed and the way they often behave—mirror the social relations of American society. Until those relations change we will continue to have a police problem.

I have accumulated more than my share of debts in the six years that this book was in preparation. The initial field research and survey were aided with a graduate research fellowship provided by the Law Enforcement Assistance Administration. Portions of this book previously appeared in the *Journal of Voluntary Action Research.* I am also grateful to the Russell Sage Foundation for its assistance in this project.

The field research was as successful as it was because of the generous assistance I received from the three participating police departments. I would like to acknowledge the cooperation of the many police officers who endured the survey and who allowed me to share their company as they worked the streets of Los Angeles. They may not agree with all of my conclusions, but they should know that I learned a thing or two from them in the course of my research. And I would like especially to thank George Beck, Deputy Chief of Police, Los Angeles Police Department; Jay Stroh, Chief of Police, Inglewood, California; and Louis Sunyich, Chief of Police (now retired), Redondo Beach, California, all of whom gave generously of their time and assistance.

Many other people provided invaluable assistance along the way. James Fisk, a former Deputy Chief of the Los Angeles Police Department and now one of five police commissioners in Los Angeles, was instrumental in helping me to get this study off the ground. He also proved to be a helpful sounding board for many of my ideas on police discretion during the formative stages of this book. John C. Ries, my dissertation advisor, provided thoughtful criticisms of the manuscript. Rick Shingles was a source of encouragement and timely advice. Donna Bahry, Vivian Brown, David Paris, Michael Schtazberg, and Walter J. Szczepanek all provided numerous criticisms and suggestions from which I greatly benefited. Steve Erie read the manuscript more times than he or I can remember, and if the book is not as good as it could be, it may be because I stubbornly refused to take advantage of all his suggestions.

My most profound intellectual debt is owed to my friend Harold Brackman. Harold's sage and incisive comments on an early version of the manuscript enabled me to deepen the argument and to shape a flawed manuscript into a readable book. A free copy from the author is hardly adequate payment for his labors.

And finally I owe more than I can express to Vivian Brown—not just for her assistance in restraining my impulse for rococo phrases, but for generously tolerating the grumpiness that long hours of writing seem to bring out in me and for believing it was worth doing.

Working the Street

Introduction

Politics and the Police

THIS BOOK is a study of patrolmen, the lowliest but most significant of policemen. It is about the routine decisions patrolmen make as they work the street, as they manage their task of coping with crime and disorder: a decision to stop and "shake" two black kids walking down the street; a decision to let a drunk driver meander on his way; a decision to forcibly break up a fight between a man and his wife; a decision to pull the trigger to stop a suspected "felon" as he recedes into the darkness. Much of the book is devoted to describing and explaining how, when, and why patrolmen wield their awesome powers of coercion and with what effect.

My intention is not merely to illuminate how working cops confront and grapple with the uncertainties and moral dilemmas of their work nor to assess how justice is administered on the streets. A study of police discretion can tell us something about the workings of public bureaucracies and the way in which the structural characteristics of these bureaucracies shape political choice. An analysis of the exercise of discretion by patrolmen provides a glimpse into the problematic relationship between politics and administration and the attendant problem of democratic control. It poses questions about the scope, use, and political control of the power of administrative discretion.

Police discretion—the day-to-day decisions of policemen—is tantamount to political decision making, for the role of the police is based upon the legitimate use of coercion. The significance of this fact extends beyond the narrow responsibility for enforcement of the criminal laws: coercion both defines the role of the police and lies behind or is instrumental in the accomplishment of most police functions. It is the use of coercion that unites the otherwise disparate activities of the police; it is present in both the act of enforcing the law and in that of peacekeeping. This is not to say that the police always rely upon coercion; only that their role is defined by the necessity of mediating or controlling situations which require, as Egon Bittner has put it, "remedies that are non-negotiably coercible."[1] Broadly, then, we may define the role of the police as the coercive regulation of social behavior among the members of a community in the interests of the protection of life and the preservation of order.

It is not just that the police wield coercive powers that is of interest; rather, that they do so selectively. Arthur Woods, a New York Police Commissioner during the Progressive era, once likened policemen to judges: they have to decide "whether or not a law is violated and therefore whether to take official action."[2] Discretion is an inescapable element of police work, and it arises from two factors: the ever-present reality of scarce resources and the ambiguity of the law. Police departments are required, like other public organizations, to carry out their functions with limited public resources. Policemen must set priorities and allocate their resources accordingly. The administrator must decide how to deploy his men and how to divide up the annual budget allocation, while the patrolman or detective must decide how to allocate his time and energy. Control of the purse strings enables a police administrator to create and nurture specialized units that can direct their efforts to a particular problem. Traffic enforcement is very different in a department that has a specialized traffic unit than in one that does not. But many of the most important decisions are made by patrolmen, working the streets, singly or in pairs, at all hours of the day. And here one of the most important questions is how one's time away from calls shall be used.

The choices of working cops are rarely made on the basis of clear-cut legal standards. Far from meeting the standards of specificity and clarity required by the principle of *nulla peona sine lege,* the law as it unfolds to the average street policeman is unarguably ambiguous. What, for example, constitutes disturbing the peace? When is a man drunk and in violation of the law? When he has passed out in the street, when he is seen staggering down the street, or when he merely responds to a patrolman's interrogations with a slurred voice? What is the difference between a misdemeanor and a felony assault? A felony assault is frequently defined in practice by prosecutors as an assault in which the victim sustains a "traumatic injury." But what is a traumatic injury? The law defines only the outer limits of discretion, and tells a policeman what he may not do—rarely what he should do.

The reasons for this ambiguity are commonplace. Legislators cannot anticipate all of the daily problems of law enforcement nor can all of the ambiguities be eliminated through successive drafts of the law. Yet, much of the ambiguity is a consequence of the legislative process, reflecting either intentional gambits or the passions of legislators and the vagaries of the deliberative process. In either case, the result is to expand the powers of discretion the police possess. For example, statutes are often made all-encompassing in order to preclude the existance of "loopholes" which would allow offenders to escape.[3] Most gambling statutes are written in such a way that both commercial and social gambling are against the law, though it is normally assumed that the laws were written to prevent the local Mafia from running crap games rather than to stop little old ladies from giving bingo prizes at the church social. Yet, as a practical matter, if this distinction is drawn, it is the police who draw it. Frequently, then, the police must interpret the law's intent and the circumstances under which it applies. One of the difficulties this poses for the legal system is that some laws may be used by the police to harass people.

Next, consider laws that are normally intended to accomplish desired social objectives rather than to prevent criminal behavior per se. These include "non-support" laws, which are designed to ensure that child-support payments are met. How far and under what circumstances the desired objectives are attained is a matter largely decided by the police. Is society better served if every husband who defaults on his child-support payments is carted off to jail? Or is this matter better handled through referral to a social agency? Whatever the answer, the point is that the police presently decide these questions.

Thus, the police have crucial policy-making powers by virtue of their power to decide which laws will be enforced and when. At issue is not simply the legality of these decisions, but the routine use of the legitimate means of coercion in society. The day-to-day choices of policemen affect the meaning of law, order, and justice within American society. Decisions to abrogate constitutional safeguards diminish individual liberties. Decisions to employ coercion—to stop and interrogate, and to arrest—determine who will or will not be held accountable to the courts, and thus what is legally acceptable behavior. Finally, the use of social distinctions based on class and race in enforcement and in maintaining order by the police can significantly affect the outcome of criminal justice proceedings. It matters not at all if the criminal courts are color-blind, as some investigators contend, if the police routinely employ such invidious distinctions.[4] All of these police decisions are political in the sense that they influence, if not determine, the impact of formal social controls and the allocation of justice.

To say that the police, through their discretionary choices, determine the meaning of law and order, is largely to say that patrolmen determine the meaning of law and order. It falls to patrolmen to decide when to take action, how to apply vague legal standards to specific circumstances in a heterogeneous society while adapting to changing social mores and values, and how to fashion a working set of priorities. For better or worse, the societal goals to which police action is directed are served by the intelligence, whims, caprice, desires, and craftsmanship of patrolmen.

It may appear preposterous to assert that patrolmen have the power to determine the course of justice; patrolmen obviously do not make the laws nor do they set policy within a police department. Indeed, the contemporary view holds that much of what patrolmen do is not connected with law enforcement and justice at all; rather, they are all-around social workers who keep the peace and provide services. Patrolmen direct traffic, manage domestic disputes, administer stern warnings to wayward juveniles, find lost children, talk suicidal people down from rooftops, and perform a variety of incidental administrative chores. Such a view obscures their coercive role and the political consequences of their decisions. Patrolmen make most of the arrests for major felonies, all decisions to stop and interrogate, and decisions not to enforce the law or take action, particularly in the context of assaults.[5] If and when the police deny legal protection to individuals, abridge due process, or employ distinctions of race and class, it is patrolmen who do so. In short, patrolmen are profoundly involved with the most significant questions facing any political order, those pertaining to justice, order, and

6

equity. They necessarily trade in the recurring moral antinomies that accompany political choice, and through the exercise of discretion patrolmen define and redefine the meaning of justice.

Given the significance of police discretion for the allocation of justice within American society, it is crucial to understand what determines the routine choices patrolmen make. Part of the answer is to be found in an understanding of the beliefs patrolmen hold toward their jobs, the law, and the events and people they confront on the street. Choice is possible for a patrolman only if he can impose order on the raw, turbulent world that is his fare eight hours a day. Patrolmen do not react to each incident as though it were unique; they draw distinctions, they generalize—in short, they fashion a coherent set of beliefs to guide their actions. These beliefs structure their perception of events and their definition of the situation, and provide the norms and standards that influence their judgment of alternative courses of action. Ironically, then, police discretion, often justified as a way to take account of the unique and mitigating elements of an incident, requires the use of beliefs and decision-making rules to structure action.

What counts in the exercise of discretion is a patrolman's sense of priorities and his considered reflections on the conflicts and requirements of his task. The decision to arrest, the decision to stop and interrogate an individual, or the decision to ignore a family dispute is partly the result of a succession of choices a patrolman has already made. How he believes his time free from calls should be utilized, how strictly he believes minor violations should be enforced, his views on service and order-maintenance activities, the depth of his preoccupations with controlling crime, and even his day-to-day mood are not, strictly speaking, discretionary decisions. But these decisions shape his choices on the street.

If a patrolman's beliefs are significant in understanding police discretion, how are we to characterize these beliefs? Are they to be described in terms of a "working personality," a more or less common set of beliefs which derives from the reaction of patrolmen to intrinsic characteristics of the police occupation (the presence of danger, social isolation, and [perceived] public hostility), as Jerome Skolnick has suggested?[6] Or, alternatively, do they reflect deeply ingrained attitudes, such as authoritarianism, which are a consequence of being socialized into a working-class ethos?[7] While there may be some truth in both of these views, they obscure the dissimilarity among patrolmen. What immediately strikes the observer of patrolmen is their diversity. Patrolmen from much the same background, who have undergone roughly similar experiences, and who share a wide range of political and social attitudes handle the same kind of incidents differently. Some believe that every drunk driver, regardless of mitigating circumstances, should go to jail; others will arrest a drunk driver only as a last resort. Patrolmen react in fundamentally different ways to the pressures and demands of their occupation, and rather than a common set of values and beliefs, what we find, I shall contend, are highly distinctive approaches to police work.[8]

Much of this book describes the beliefs of patrolmen and shows their relevance to the way they wield their powers of discretion. But if one focused solely on the encounters between patrolmen and citizens, and merely described the strategems that patrolmen employ on the street and the beliefs that guide their actions, a central fact of life on the street would be omitted. A patrolman is not free to act solely on the basis of his personal beliefs. It is often forgotten that the role of a patrolman is characterized by a fundamental duality: he is both an autonomous official who responds to the needs of a community as he deems necessary, with the power to determine the fate of the citizens he encounters, and a bureaucrat subject to the coercive inclinations of administrators. Though patrolmen have greater latitude in performing their task than most operatives in public bureaucracies, they are nevertheless enmeshed in a system of hierarchical controls and work-group pressures.

But how are a patrolman's decisions and behavior affected by the system of administrative controls in a police department? Oddly enough, despite the importance that numerous authors have attached to bureaucracy in understanding police behavior, there are few clear-cut or satisfactory answers to this question. Perhaps the most thorough treatment of the matter to date is James Q. Wilson's study of eight police departments.[9] If Wilson suggests, for a variety of reasons, that police administrators may have only limited control over the behavior of patrolmen, he argues that they can affect discretion by manipulating the beliefs of patrolmen. In his view, the beliefs of patrolmen derive from a set of expectations communicated to them by police administrators that define broad norms of conduct and reflect distinctive administrative styles. Wilson identifies three such styles—Legalistic, Watchman, and Service—and then goes on to show how these administrative styles lead to different patterns of decision making.

Introduction

Despite Wilson's clear explanation of discretion and the impact of bureaucratic controls, his argument is flawed by a questionable assumption. He argues that the choices of patrolmen are consistent with the expectations of the chief of police, but this assumes precisely what is most problematic: whether patrolmen will, in fact, conform to the expectations of administrators. Moreover, his evidence, consisting largely of arrest rates, is far from conclusive.[10]

The virtue of Wilson's study is that it focuses on the right problem in the analysis of police discretion, namely, the way in which the dynamics of bureaucracy influence the behavior of patrolmen. It is thus a reasonable point of departure. But there are other questions that ought to be asked. What is the structure of administrative controls within police departments? What kinds of cues and incentives are actually conveyed to patrolmen? How do they perceive the expectations of the chief of police and other administrators? Do the extremely authoritarian hierarchical controls in police departments have any bearing on the exercise of discretion, and if so, what? To what extent do sergeants and watch commanders influence the way patrolmen exercise their discretion? Is the chief of police as omnipotent as so many students of the police have assumed? Are there work-group norms, shared by patrolmen, that shape their choices on the street? Is the impact of administrative controls influenced by the size of the department?

If we wish to understand how bureaucratic controls affect the exercise of discretion by patrolmen, we must look at the way patrolmen respond to the demands of administrators and the consequences for discretion. Yet it would be folly to treat patrolmen as ordinary bureaucrats. Their behavior, even in highly professional departments, cannot be understood on the basis of the rule-oriented behavior that is characteristic of so many public bureaucracies. Their task is far too complex and uncertain for that. What must be recognized is that patrolmen lead something of a schizophrenic existence: they must cope not only with the terror of an often hostile and unpredictable citizenry, but also with a hostile—even tyrannical—and unpredictable bureaucracy. The core argument in this book is built around the idea that police discretion is to be understood in terms of an enduring conflict between the uncertain requirements of police work and the demand of administrators for control. This conflict affects both the structure of administrative controls within police departments and the behavior of patrolmen. Ultimately, police discretion turns on the way patrolmen adapt to the contradictory requirements of behaving as autonomous professionals who perform an uncertain and arduous task and as bureaucrats subject to the restraints imposed by a multitude of administrative controls.

My purpose in this book, then, is to fashion an explanation of police discretion that takes account of the impact of bureaucratic controls on the behavior of patrolmen. It is written largely from their perspective at the bottom of the bureaucratic ladder. My concern with police bureaucracies must be understood in light of the emergence in late twentieth-century America of a professionalized police and the implications of this for police work and the political control of police power. For the theoretical and empirical significance of this study finally turns on an attempt to assess the impact of police professionalism on contemporary police work.

The Police and the Reformers: New Variations on an Old Theme

How are we to control the police? How are we to prevent abuses of power and obtain a measure of political control over police discretion? This question resurfaced in America in the context of the civil strife of the late 1960s. The catalysts were the decisions of President Lyndon B. Johnson to pursue an extended war in Vietnam and to go beyond the initial civil-rights victories of the early sixties to wage a war on poverty, which produced not the beneficent results that he had hoped for—American power standing fast overseas and the elimination of poverty—but instead intense social and political conflict. Events could not be contained. Criticism of the decision to expand the war in Vietnam led to criticism of American foreign policy since World War II; the decision to embark on a war on poverty and the riots in American cities focused attention on the urban crisis. The police were important figures in both conflicts. The conduct of the police in handling demonstrations against the Vietnam War during these years became a matter of controversy as did the relationship between the police and the poor black and Mexican-American residents of the inner city. The police were regarded either as the symbols of an oppressive and illegitimate political order or as the lone guardians of order, the bulwark against anarchy.

Introduction

It is profoundly ironic that the police were the center of controversy at this time, for serious questions were posed about the use of
police power after the police had undergone extensive professionalization and after many of the abuses of police power had presumably
been curtailed. The evolution of the American police can be characterized as an effort to professionalize the police along lines initially
laid down by nineteenth-century reformers. The thrust of the reform
effort was to insulate the police from politics through civil service
reforms, to put police work on a technical basis, and to bring about
greater control over the police through the imposition of legal and
administrative controls.[11] But the questions about the scope and use
of police power that animated the nineteenth-century debates on
the police were never resolved. Much as the reformers might wish,
politics was never really separated from the administration of police
work; it was only submerged under the rhetoric of professionalism.
The tumultuous years of the late 1960s reopened all the old questions,
and the debates over the use of police power during this period
punctured the rhetoric of police professionalism and brought politics
—with a vengeance—back into police work. But how could it be
otherwise? As in the nineteenth century, the police were at the
center of many of the raging political controversies. The larger public issues which vexed people during this period brought to the fore
the enduring problems of the exercise of police power that any free
society must face. Just as the Irish migration, the subsequent ethnic
and class conflict in nineteenth-century American cities, and the
slavery issue raised questions about the use of police power one
hundred years ago, so the contemporary plight of blacks and Mexican-Americans and the Vietnam War raised similar issues a decade
ago.

Central to the controversies in both eras were allegations of police
brutality, race and class discrimination in law enforcement, violation
of civil liberties and suppression of rights to protest government
actions, desire for zealous enforcement of puritanical laws, and the
placement of seemingly arbitrary restrictions on the police in their
literally never-ending war on crime and disorder. Yet in all of these
controversies the *right* of the police to exercise discretion in the
application of their coercive powers was never seriously questioned.
Rather the questions have always concerned how, when, and according to what standards the police exercise their discretion.

Widespread antipathy toward the police has subsided, but an
unease remains. According to public opinion polls, blacks (and other

minority groups) continue to believe that the police are routinely guilty of misconduct. More relevant than public opinion polls, however, is the disquieting evidence of police misconduct. If the police are now reasonably honest and less likely to engage in the widespread brutality characteristic of the depression years when the Wickersham Commission conducted its investigation into police actions, neither do they approach the ideals of professionalism. There is widespread corruption in putatively professional police departments, evidence of brutality and substantial lawbreaking by the police themselves, and a persistent incivility in relations between police and public.[12] Contemporary criticism extends beyond these traditional issues to questions about police effectiveness in coping with crime and disorder, their preoccupation with crime control when much police work consists of providing services, and the matter of equal or differential law enforcement.

If the civil strife of the late 1960s reopened the question of the use of police power, the nineteenth-century debate on the police continued to define the contours of any discussion of the police in American society. In this debate, both issues of the effectiveness of the police in controlling crime and public disorder and issues of political control over police discretion were inextricably linked to the question of centralized versus local control. The nineteenth-century reformers argued for centralized control over police actions, and for impersonal and uniform enforcement of the law. Implicit was the idea of the police as professional elites, separated from the particularistic influences of the local community, who would strive for equal and strict enforcement of the law. Political control was to be obtained through centralized administrative control. In contrast, local politicians, not all of them connected with political machines, emphasized the need for the use of police power to be tempered by the mores and values of a particular community. Control over police discretion was predicated on the idea that the police had to be part of the community rather than above it.[13] The debate continues today but with an ironical twist: it is now the reformers who advocate decentralization and those favoring the status quo who advocate a professional police. Contemporary reformers argue that professionalism has not resulted in a fair, equitable, and humane approach to social problems, as an earlier generation of reformers assumed it would. Rather, the professionalization of local government has served only to centralize decision making and to insulate professionals from client pressures and demands through bureaucratic autonomy. The professional bureaucracies of local government are not only unresponsive to external pressures, especially by the poor and downtrodden, but they are also incapable of effectively responding to a changing social and political environment. The police are only the most important manifestation of this development.[14]

The "new" reformers argue that the cycle of bureaucratic dysfunctions that leads to abuses of police discretion and a lack of responsiveness can be broken only through radical decentralization of governmental functions and by allowing citizens greater control over the formulation and implementation of policy in police departments. Under a decentralized system, it is argued, citizens will be better able to articulate demands, will know more about the individuals who serve them, and consequently will be able to gain more effective control over police discretion. From the standpoint of administrators, decentralization will facilitate greater internal control over patrolmen and increase their knowledge of the community and citizen demands. Decentralization ultimately means control over police discretion on the basis of shared values between the police and residents of a community.[15]

In contrast, those who prefer the status quo are far more sanguine about police professionalism. Professionalism has brought about decided improvements in police behavior: it has greatly minimized brutality and corruption, has worked subtle and beneficial changes in the values of policemen, and has made the police more efficient and effective in what they do. This is not to deny that serious problems remain; rather the argument is that greater accountability is to be obtained through continued professionalization of the police, and any radical attempt at decentralization would only make things worse.[16] Often, then, the suggestion is that things could be improved by requiring more education and better training for cops, and by devising mechanisms to respond to complaints and achieve greater internal control over patrolmen.

Yet the more astute students of the police as well as a few police officers themselves have begun to express reservations over some elements of the model of police work fashioned over the last eighty years. In particular, these individuals have begun to question the wisdom and effectiveness of such extant doctrines as "preventative patrol" and to wonder if the police have become far too isolated from the communities they serve. This has led to a reevaluation of the police function and a call to de-emphasize crime fighting in favor of the service and order-maintenance role.[17] It has also led, in a few departments, to attempts to decentralize operations through team policing in order to reestablish contact with the residents of a community or neighborhood and to improve the effectiveness of police work.[18] These responses represent not an abandonment of police professionalism but an attempt to modify it to take account of its most serious shortcomings.

Both of these critiques and others are predicated on the assumption that police professionalism is either a complete or partial failure. Yet it is not at all obvious what impact professionalism has had on police work, especially on police discretion, nor what kinds of reforms would bring about greater accountability and control over the police. The theme stressed in the most recent works on the police is that police professionalism has led to the bureaucratization (in the Weberian sense) of police departments and the emergence of a style of police work that is impersonal, strict, and detached from community and political pressures. The crude, often violent beat cop who was intimately tied to the political machine has been replaced by the spit and polish of efficient, impersonal professionals who are tied to quasi-military administrative structures. Yet no profound and deep-seated change such as the reform of the police proceeds unimpeded and without its share of unintended outcomes. What, we should ask, are the limits of police professionalism and the consequences for the exercise of discretion by patrolmen? In what ways and to what extent have the values of working policemen been changed by the onslaught of professionalism? In what sense has police professionalism made the police not just more efficient and effective in controlling crime (though there is some doubt about this) but more accountable as well? Accountability in a professional police force rests on the strength of hierarchical and professional controls over police discretion. But to what extent has professionalism, through the proliferation of bureaucratic rules and an authoritarian style of command, actually led to centralized control over the behavior and decisions of patrolmen? Does the effect of administrative controls differ in small as compared to large departments as the decentralizers presume? If so, how, and with what effect for police discretion?

Thus, an explanation of police discretion that takes account of the impact of bureaucratic controls and an assessment of the impact of police professionalism are two sides of the same coin. Serious students of the police and would-be reformers who fail to understand the pressures and constraints of police work and how the bureaucratization of police work under the guise of professionalism has affected

14

police discretion, run the risk, in my judgment, of greatly oversimplifying the problem of accountability. This is true of both those who advocate continued professionalization of the police and those "antiprofessionals" who seek decentralization. My intention in this book is to set forth the empirical analysis that will both provide an explanation of police discretion and allow an evaluation of various strategies for reform.

The plan of this book may be described as follows. In Part One, I develop a theoretical framework for the analysis of administrative discretion and apply it to the police. Chapter 1 develops the logic behind the framework, and in chapter 2 I use the framework to develop a preliminary assessment of the impact of police professionalism. Part Two explores the nature of a patrolman's relationship to the community in which he works and to the department. In chapter 3, I discuss the implications of the separation between police and community that is a consequence of professionalism. In chapters 4 and 5 a theoretical model of the structure and impact of bureaucratic controls on patrolmen is developed and evaluated on the basis of data collected from the three departments that are the subject of this study. In Part Three, I develop the analysis and explanation of police discretion. Chapters 6 and 7 are devoted to describing how patrolmen use their discretion in crime fighting and in handling minor violations and disturbances. In chapters 8 and 9, I turn to the matter of explanation. Chapter 8 explores the implications of a patrolman's beliefs for the exercise of discretion, and chapter 9 evaluates the impact of administrative controls. Part Four returns to the issues I have raised here and evaluates four different proposals for reform.

A Methodological Preface

The analysis in this book is based on a study of three professional police departments in Southern California. Two of these are small departments, each with fewer than one hundred policemen; the third is the Los Angeles Police Department (LAPD), a department that has the reputation of being one of the most professional in the country. One of the small departments, Inglewood, faces a rather serious crime problem; the other, Redondo Beach, serves a complacent community with a moderately low crime rate. In LAPD, I selected a high-crime division (Rampart) and a low-crime division (Northeast) for study.

These three departments are not representative of American police departments, but they do reflect, perhaps more precisely than a more inclusive sampling, all the dilemmas and consequences inherent in police professionalism. The research design permits a comparison between two small departments and a large department, and between two high-crime and two moderately low-crime areas. This allows an evaluation of the impact of administrative controls in small and large departments, and provides for a crude control of the effects such things as the crime rate and the complexion of the community have on the behavior of patrolmen. My logic in regard to the latter is that if department policies or expectations, for example, are *relatively unimportant* in determining the choices of patrolmen, one would expect, given the research design, that there would be few, if any, differences between the two high-crime areas and between the two low-crime areas in the kinds of decisions patrolmen make, but significant differences in the choices made between the high- and low-crime areas regardless of department. On the other hand, if departmental policies and expectations were *relatively important,* one would expect the converse. There is no pretense that this research design takes account of all the exogenous factors that could conceivably affect the behavior of patrolmen. But it does allow for a reasonable assessment of some rival explanations.

Three kinds of data are used throughout the study: data obtained through participant observation of police work; data obtained from the departments, for example, arrest rates; and survey data based on an interview schedule administered to patrolmen and field supervisors (sergeants and watch commanders) in all three departments. For the participant-observation phase of the study I spent about five months riding in patrol cars in all three departments. I rode in Redondo Beach and Inglewood for two and one-half months during the fall and winter of 1972–1973 and in the two divisions of LAPD during the summer of 1973. There were no restrictions set by any of the departments, and I always selected the officers and the beat. The majority of observations took place during night watch, the 4:00 P.M. to 12:00 A.M. shift, though I rode day watch and morning watch a few times for purposes of comparison. One of the reasons I concentrated on one shift was to facilitate the development of rapport between myself and the policemen I was studying which would enhance the validity of my observations. The field observations are not based on a sample of shifts, but I believe these data are a fair representation of the activities of patrolmen. Night watch is usually the busiest shift and provides the opportunity to observe a wide variety of calls and decisions. There are more calls for service than on morning watch (midnight to 8 A.M.) and more crime related activity than on day watch. The real problem with these data has to do with the possibility that patrolmen toned down their behavior in my presence (one patrolman admitted as much at the end of the night). This, of course, is a difficulty of any participant-observation study, and I attempted to minimize it by cultivating the necessary trust and riding for an extended period of time.

While riding I concentrated on two tasks. First, I closely observed each situation that patrolmen became involved in and then probed for their reasons for making a particular decision. Second, I conducted informal, open-ended interviews with patrolmen about their attitudes and feelings toward police work, crime, citizens, and the department. Many of the quotations used throughout the text are taken from these interviews. The case histories that appear in chapters 6 and 7 are also drawn from the field observations.

The questionnaire was administered to all patrolmen who agreed to answer it in the small departments (there were three refusals in Redondo Beach and none in Inglewood), and to a random sample of patrolmen in the two divisions of LAPD. Altogether, 198 patrolmen were interviewed. In addition, a total of 57 field supervisors were interviewed. This included every field supervisor in the small departments and all but two or three in the two divisions of LAPD. The interviews were conducted in the station at either the beginning or the end of an officer's shift of duty. Throughout, I attempted to minimize distortions and biased responses by taking stringent steps to assure the confidentiality of the results and to make patrolmen aware of the purposes of the study.

I have attempted to combine the use of participant observation and survey research for two reasons. The first has to do with the question of validity. While I have taken all the normal precautions with these methods, the reader is still entitled to be rather skeptical of the behavior of patrolmen when being observed by an outsider and of the responses of patrolmen to a questionnaire administered by an outsider. The field observations, interviews, and aggregate data, however, provide *alternative* measures of police attitudes and behavior, and I think it is possible through cross-checking the findings of one method with another to strengthen the overall validity of the analysis.[19] Cross-checking the interview responses with the field observations provides a way of detecting distorted or dishonest responses. The chief criterion I use throughout to evaluate the adequacy of the survey responses is their consistency with the field observations. In turn, the interview data prevents one from drawing rash conclusions on the basis of the field observations. And both the survey responses and the field observations can be checked against aggregate data such as arrest rates. Such comparisons are hazardous, if not crude, but I believe that a more thorough understanding of the police hinges on such a procedure.

My second reason for proceeding as I did was a desire to combine the depth made possible by extended participant observation with the ability to generalize that can be obtained only through a comparative study of three departments using survey and aggregate data. Participant observation is touted for its utility in developing insights and hypotheses, and the survey is regarded as more rigorous methodologically because it affords the opportunity explicitly to test hypotheses and draw causal inferences. Yet both have disadvantages: participant observation often precludes generalizing and does not lend itself to evaluating hypotheses, while the survey can verge toward superficiality. But there is no reason why these approaches cannot be combined. Employing both methods in a study of several organizations may yield far better results than either used alone.

Yet it would be foolhardy not to admit that there is a deep-seated tension between these two methods. There are discrepancies in the results obtained between the two methods, discrepancies that cannot always be resolved. If I am often inclined to place more weight on the field observations than on the survey responses, it should be remembered that both are subject to bias. There is also tension in shifting the level of analysis from the way patrolmen behave on the street to a comparison of the three departments. This is sometimes messy, but it is necessary. Whatever discomfort the reader may feel, he or she should know that this procedure at least keeps me honest.

PART ONE

*Bureaucracy
and Political Choice*

In a modern state the actual ruler is necessarily and unavoidably the bureaucracy, since power is exercised neither
through parliamentary speeches nor
monarchial enunciations but through the
routines of administration.

Max Weber

Chapter 1

Administrative Discretion and Public Policy

THE FATE of the modern police is emblematic of a broader trend in industrial societies: the bureaucratization of these societies and the concomitant reliance upon the administrative apparatus to achieve desired social goals. In a very real sense, administration has supplanted politics. With the expansion of government, the centrality of the bureaucracy for public policy is considerably augmented, and the political arena becomes an administrative arena. Key political issues are resolved less through the deliberations of elected officials than through the routines of administration.

The politics of bureaucracy is largely a politics of administrative discretion. But in what sense can administrative discretion be construed as political? Political decisions, which are conventionally defined as the "authoritative allocation of values for a political system," have always referred to those decisions which alter the course of public affairs in fundamental ways.[1] Examples of political decisions would include the decision to launch a war on poverty in 1964; a decision to create a national health insurance system; or a decision to decriminalize marijuana. To understand the genesis of these decisions, political scientists have traditionally investigated the process of decision making within the legislative branch or by political executives such as the President. Yet a preoccupation with these decisions and institutions overlooks the reality that men not only make laws but also implement them.[2]

Rather than critical decisions which effectively determine political action, key political decisions might be more aptly viewed as watersheds, as the culmination of one kind of decision-making process and the beginning of another. The first, policymaking, encompasses what is conventionally defined as politics—the pulling and hauling of groups within the legislature and executive branch. The second, the exercise of administrative discretion, encompasses the process of implementation and actually continues the political struggles of the first, albeit within the context of an administrative organization and the framework of a policy decision. A policy decision may structure the ensuing process of implementation but it does not determine the outcome of a program; that hinges on the politics of implementation. The power of administrators derives not merely from their ability to influence the outcome of legislative decisions, but from their control over the process of implementation. Administrative discretion has significant political consequences because the act of discretion admits of varying degrees of action and inaction, and because administrators have the power *not* to enforce the law or to refuse to implement a specific part of a program. The decisions of administrators determine in individual cases who will benefit, who will be deprived, who will be affected by a law or program, and how strictly the law will be enforced. On the one hand, the exercise of discretion, while it may have a determinant effect on the outcome of a program, may not seriously alter or contravene the intentions of the legislature. On the other hand, it may confer upon administrators the power to reshape or otherwise modify policy decisions.

If administrators clearly have the capacity to make public policy either through resolving ambiguities in the legislation or by refusing to implement all or part of a policy, their ability to do so depends largely on their autonomy. "A public officer," Kenneth Culp Davis has argued, "has discretion [the ability to make policy] whenever the effective limits on his power leave him free to make a choice among possible courses of action or inaction."[3] The range of discretionary choices open to an administrator may be highly structured and limited to very few alternatives due to the specificity of the legislation and the overseeing activities of elected officials. Or administrators may have considerable freedom to decide when and how to act. The greater the degree of autonomy an administrator has, the greater the potential for reshaping policy decisions through the exercise of discretion. I do not assume that even if an administrator possesses a great deal of autonomy in implementing a policy, he will in fact reshape the policy; he might choose to act in strict accordance with the provisions of the legislation. But given the ambiguity of most legislation and the complexity of governmental activities (the conflicting policy imperatives confronting administrators, multiple pressures from interest groups, and uncertainties about the impact of a program), some discrepancy between the initial legislation and the way it is implemented is inevitable. This is true of both administrators and street-level bureaucrats. The latter are public service workers who possess a substantial amount of discretion in implementing social policy, and their routine decisions are, as Michael Lipsky recently observed, tantamount to policy decisions.[4]

How are we to understand administrative discretion and explain the actions of administrators or street-level bureaucrats? The first thing to recognize is that the question cannot be reduced to a pat formula that treats bureaucrats as self-interested politicians and views administrative decisions as the outcome of a process of organizational bargaining and manipulation.[5] There may be some virtue in recognizing that administrators and street-level bureaucrats such as the police act on the basis of self-interest, but they are not ordinary politicians. Rather, they operate within the confines of an administrative structure in which obligations and responsibilities are delimited and action is subject to control through a system of authority and through external constraints such as the law. The political choices of administrators, and especially street-level bureaucrats, reflect not only individual goals but also the dynamics of organization. To say, then, that power in modern societies is exercised through the routines of administration is to do more than assert that administrators wield enormous power. It is to ask how the routines of administration shape political choice.

I argue that the exercise of discretion by administrators and street-level bureaucrats is to be understood in terms of the way in which the structural characteristics of bureaucracies influence the implementation of public policy. In implementing a policy or law, administrators grapple with both the intricacies of the policy itself and with the pressures, constraints, and dynamics of the complex network of social relationships that characterizes any formal organization. In the case of street-level bureaucrats, this amounts to arguing that their discretionary choices, and hence public policy, depend on the impact of the pressures and incentives generated by a complex system of administrative controls and on the way in which they adapt to these. In some instances, the dynamics of this process may involve nothing more than the use of organizationally derived decision rules to guide the implementation of policy.[6] In other instances, though, the nature and impact of bureaucratic pressures may be more subtle. Donald Schon has demonstrated how internally generated pressures for organizational stability shaped public policy in regard to the blind. Schon discovered that although the clientele of agencies serving the blind had changed from individuals with the single impairment of blindness to individuals with multiple handicaps, the blindness system responded by adopting mechanisms to screen out those individuals with multiple handicaps. The reason the blindness system manipulated their clientele rather than changed the range of services offered is to be found, according to Schon, in the "dynamic conservatism" of the blindness system.[7]

The beginning of wisdom in the analysis of the implementation of public policy lies in realizing that many decisions are a response not to the nature of the clientele, the demands of interest groups, or even the intent of the policy, but rather to internally generated bureaucratic pressures. This applies most forcibly to street-level bureaucrats in general, and to the police in particular. In order to see why, it will be necessary to define further the concept of administrative discretion and the nature of the factors that limit the discretionary choices of street-level bureaucrats.

A Theoretical Framework for the Analysis of Administrative Discretion

To analyze and explain the exercise of administrative discretion involves determining the criteria administrators use in implementing a policy or statute and the impact of political, organizational, and environmental constraints on that process. An elaboration of this statement will provide a theoretical framework for the analysis of police discretion. I begin with a more precise elucidation of the concept of administrative discretion.

Discretion, I have argued, must be distinguished from policymaking. Policymaking is the act of choosing the norms—framing a law for example—to guide future actions, and necessarily involves unusual or non-routine choices. Administrative discretion, by contrast, is the act of making choices in light of policy norms, and involves routine but adaptive choices. In the act of discretion, although the decision maker accepts a framework of values and goals, some aspects of the decision process are unspecified or contingent on circumstances and thus up to the judgment of the individual.[8] To clarify the distinction between policymaking and discretion, consider the example of a steersman on a ship. The decision of what course a ship will take between two points is a policy decision; but the decisions made by the steersman to maintain course while taking account of weather conditions and the like are discretionary decisions. More broadly, administrative discretion may be defined as the regulation of social and political processes in light of institutionalized political (legal) norms.

The discretionary choices of administrators are of two kinds: *procedural* and *substantive.* Procedural choices are those which structure the administrative context of discretion. They include decisions to create specialized units to implement programs, the formulation of rules and procedures to guide administrative discretion, budgetary decisions, and even decisions about training procedures. These choices influence substantive decisions; a decision to create a juvenile bureau in a police department has enormous consequences, as James Q. Wilson has pointed out, for the way juveniles are treated.[9]

Substantive choices may be categorized as either *allocative* or *regulatory.* Allocative decisions have distributional consequences and determine the level of services among groups, classes, and geographical areas. Regulatory decisions are those that pertain to the enforcement of a rule or law and consist of two broad choices: the decision to intervene in a particular set of circumstances; and the decision of what action to take, that is, whether to resolve the matter in a formal way through court action or through an informal settlement. The decisions of the police are of course regulatory choices. An analysis of the exercise of discretion by patrolmen must explain why patrolmen decide to intervene in a particular situation, and why they enforce or do not enforce the law.

This definition of discretion implies the legitimacy of policy decisions, and thus some consonance between the act of discretion and the imperatives of the policy mandate. Most policy decisions are either delegated to ongoing administrative organizations or necessitate the creation of a new organization. In either case, the policy mandate establishes or modifies the organization's responsibilities, its legitimate sphere of action or domain—the population served, the range of services provided, and the manner in which they are provided—and the obligations of those individuals occupying positions of authority within the organization.[10] The legitimacy of administrative policies and actions is contingent upon confining discretionary choices to the preestablished domain or at least justifying such choices in terms of the policy mandate.

The policy mandate bounds but does not determine discretionary choices. The implementation of any policy or law is a process in which choices are profoundly influenced by the desires, ambitions, and idiosyncrasies of the people involved, by the structure and goals of the administrative organization, and by the character of the political and work environment.

Discretionary choices will be based on the presumed (that is, interpreted) objectives of the policy mandate and the objectives, interests, needs, and whims of the individual decision maker. The act of discretion is structured by the decision maker's belief system.[11] No decision maker grapples with the complexity of the world by treating each situation as unique; rather, events and actions are judged in light of prior values, a knowledge of comparable situations, and a pre-defined set of alternatives. Individuals abstract out of a particular set of experiences criteria, principles, and rules which serve as signposts in future but similar situations. No matter how chaotic, how unique a set of circumstances they encounter, decision makers approach them on the basis of their learned responses to reasonably similar situations. As a result, a discrete set of values and facts are woven together and form a perceptual net which guides individual decisions. In this analysis I shall refer to these perceptual nets as either belief systems or the *operational style* of an administrator.[12] While the content may vary greatly among individuals, these belief systems are highly coherent structures characterized by selectivity, consistency, and stability.[13]

An operational style is not a set of rules and formulas which are more or less mechanically applied to decision making. It is a general set of beliefs which are only loosely related to actual decisions but which influence a decision maker's perception of events, his judgment of the intentions of individuals in a particular situation, and his evaluation of alternative courses of action. We may distinguish two types of judgments characteristic of the content of operational styles: value and reality (empirical) judgments. Value judgments contain the normative structure of a belief system and reality judgments establish the causal connections among events.

An operational style is an important determinant of the way an administrator or policeman will respond to events and is an important variable in explaining discretionary choices. But what are the sources of the values and beliefs contained within an operational style? One explanation is that the content of an operational style reflects personality attributes and the process of preadolescent socialization. In this view, personality may be said to operate upon decisions through an operational style.[14] But operational styles may also be shaped by organizations, and one might say, in fact, that administrators control the choices of subordinates by influencing their beliefs.

Whatever the dictates of his operational style might suggest in a given situation, an administrator or street-level bureaucrat is not entirely free to act in any way he chooses. The degree of autonomy an administrator possesses clearly varies. The freedom of action enjoyed by the police, for example, is far greater than that possessed by municipal librarians. The nature of the limits (or lack of limits) on an administrator's autonomy depends upon the factors that affect the *latitude* of administrative discretion.

The latitude of discretion is initially affected by the form of the policy mandate, and the salient distinction here is between specific and vague policy mandates. It is obvious that a highly detailed and specific policy mandate may severely limit an administrator's discretion, though such policy mandates are typically the exception. Even if a policy mandate is specific this still does not preclude the exercise of discretion (a fact invariably forgotten by those who advocate more precise policy mandates as a way of controlling the action of administrators). An administrator must interpret the circumstances to which the policy applies; limited resources and time preclude the full implementation of every policy; and an administrator may decide not to implement or enforce a policy for other reasons (for example, community pressure or conflicting goals). Thus, the specificity of the policy mandate by itself is not sufficient to completely constrain an administrator's discretion.

The latitude of discretion really depends upon the extent to which an administrator's decisions are controlled or otherwise influenced by external actors or institutions. There are two kinds of constraints which may impinge upon and limit the exercise of discretion: *environmental* and *organizational*. By environmental constraints I refer to those exogenous actors, institutions, and social forces that administrators must consider in implementing a policy or that serve to limit administrative autonomy.[15] Some of the most significant institutional constraints here are those that are part of the broader political system. In addition to legislative decisions which structure administrative discretion (the policy mandate), these include procedural rules and norms (constitutional and administrative law) that specify appropriate procedures for the implementation of a policy; legislative, judicial, and executive actions designed to ensure conformity to the policy mandate; and attempts by various interest groups to influence administrative action. For street-level bureaucrats, this also includes the characteristics of their work environment: the objective characteristics and demeanor of clients, the adequacy of organizational resources, and broader characteristics of the community such as cultural traditions. The salience and impact of these environmental constraints often depend on more deeply rooted social and economic phenomena such as the rate of social and economic change, and the level of class or group conflict.

Organizational constraints refer to the system of administrative rules, policies, and managerial controls designed to ensure conformity to administrative directives. These include organizational structure (degree of centralization, division of labor); types of organizational controls (rules, incentives, recruitment and training procedures); and the behavior of administrators and supervisors. The impact of organizational constraints depends on the ability (and often the desire) of administrators to rationalize organizational processes, to bring under administrative control the decisions and behavior of subordinates.

Since policy mandates are delegated to administrative agencies, the impact of environmental constraints, particularly those that derive from political institutions, is largely contingent on the relationship between a public organization and its environment. In a case study of two police departments, Michael Ban found that the impact on the decisions of policemen of Supreme Court rulings like Mapp v. Ohio, designed to bring police actions into conformity with the Constitution, depended less on the inclinations of individual policemen than on the institutional autonomy of the police department from local politics and civic leaders, and on the ability of police administrators successfully to resist demands to honor such rulings.[16] The autonomy of administrative decision makers, then, depends on the autonomy of the organization, on the extent to which it is structurally independent of external control, and on the ability of top-level administrators to manipulate and control environmental constraints. While all administrative organizations seek a measure of autonomy from their environment, the degree of autonomy attained is frequently contingent on broader social and political forces, on the evolution of the structural characteristics of the political system. Municipal reform has clearly led to greater administrative autonomy for local governmental agencies than was true when city departments were inextricably linked to big city political machines. This has had significant consequences for police discretion.

The salience of environmental constraints, however, also depends on the level of organization to which one is referring. The latitude of discretion for middle managers is wholly dependent on organizational constraints while that of organizational elites and street-level bureaucrats is not; the latter two will, in some degree, be directly influenced by environmental constraints. Organizational elites are responsible for mediating between the agency and the broader political and social environment, and they are called upon to negotiate policy mandates and worry about the acquisition of organizational resources. It falls to street-level bureaucrats to manage environmental uncertainties that confront the agency in the implementation of a policy or program; they deal directly with the agency's clients. Thus, the role of organizational elites and street-level bureaucrats is characterized by a *duality,* a situation in which the individual mediates between the organization and its environment. One consequence of this duality is that occupants of such roles are likely to have broader powers of discretion than other members of the organization.[17]

Yet there is an obvious and important difference between organizational elites and street-level bureaucrats. The latter, unlike organizational elites, are enmeshed in a system of rules designed to govern their behavior, and subject to watchful supervisors and a host of training and indoctrination programs predicated on ensuring conformity in beliefs and values among organizational members. The significance of the duality inherent in the role of a street-level bureaucrat is that it limits the impact of administrative controls but does not afford the kind of autonomy that an organizational elite possesses. There is a paradoxical quality to a street-level bureaucrat's relationship to an administrative organization, for he is both autonomous and controlled. This paradox is the root of many of the conflicts and moral dilemmas faced by street-level bureaucrats.

TABLE 1.1

A Framework for the Analysis of Administrative Discretion

The Latitude of Discretion	Decision Makers	Types of Discretionary Decisions

A. Environmental Constraints
  1. *Political:* Policy mandate established by legislature; actions by courts to assure conformity to procedural and statutory rules; actions by political executives to assure conformity to policy mandate; political structure which establishes context for relationship between administrative organizations and political institutions.
  2. *Contextual:* Culture; degree of social conflict or consensus; size and heterogeniety of community; character of clientele.
B. Organizational Constraints
  1. *Administrative Structure:* Division of labor; degree of centralization
  2. *Organizational Controls:* Formal rules; incentive systems; recruitment and training; information systems to monitor performance.
	A. Administrative Elites
	Broad powers of discretion; influenced by political, environmental, and organizational constraints, and mediate between these; in position to structure and manipulate organizational constraints, though the ability to do so may be limited (depending on circumstances) by power of subordinates.
	B. Managers and Supervisors
	Limited powers of discretion; almost wholly influenced by organizational constraints. However, implementation and effectiveness of administrative controls depend on their decisions.
	C. Street-level Bureaucrats
	Broad powers of discretion in many cases; latitude of discretion depends on scope of responsibilities, tasks, and impact of organizational constraints. Influenced by organizational and environmental constraints, and at operational level mediate between these.
		A. Procedural
		  1. *Organizational Structure:* Defines responsibilities of subunits, allocates tasks, etc.
		  2. *Program Rules:* Establishes policies to guide the implementation of programs.
		B. Substantive
		  1. *Allocative:* Allocation of budgetary resources to various subunits.
		  2. *Regulatory:* Encompasses decisions to intervene, whether or not to resolve a violation formally or informally, and choice of tactics.

The central concepts in the theoretical framework advanced here are displayed in table 1.1. Any inquiry into the process of administrative discretion requires an answer to two questions: what are the criteria, the values and empirical judgments, that an individual brings to bear in the implementation of a policy mandate; and what is the impact of organizational and environmental constraints upon discretionary choices? My concern now is to consider the implications of this framework for the exercise of discretion by street-level bureaucrats.

Administrative Discretion in Street-level Bureaucracies

The key to understanding the exercise of discretion by street-level bureaucrats lies in the dialectical relationship between the act of individual choice and the impact of organizational constraints. My orienting hypothesis is that the discretionary choices of street-level bureaucrats are largely shaped by the values and beliefs of the decision maker *and* the goals, incentives, and pressures of the bureaucracy. The decision rules, values, and priorities of operational discretionary choices are determined by the joint impact of the bureaucratic requirements for stability and the maintenance of integrity, and by the need for street-level bureaucrats to adapt to these organizational pressures while performing an arduous and difficult task.

Yet I do not presume conformity of discretionary choices with either organizational rules or externally imposed decision rules, procedural or substantive. The assumption is rather one of the continuing possibility of conflict between the values and beliefs of the street-level bureaucrat and the organization. The interesting question in the analysis of administrative discretion is to understand the conditions under which a decision maker must or will conform to organizational constraints. The discretionary powers of street-level bureaucrats can be controlled to the degree that a public agency structures belief systems relevant to the task and narrows the latitude of discretion. In many governmental agencies, discretionary choices about how to allocate organizational resources and distribute services are governed by the elaboration and use of uniform decision rules. This process involves reducing organizational activities (and decisions) to a stable, predictable, consistent pattern through the development of a pattern of mutual (role) expectations—some of which are formalized in rules and procedures and some of which are sustained on the basis of shared understandings and values—among the members of an organization. There is both an obtrusive and unobtrusive side to this process. On the one hand, behavior may be overtly structured through "programs" or rules which define appropriate and inappropriate actions in a given situation. Such rules are supplemented by a system of authority relationships and managerial controls that serve to control behavior through a variety of incentives and sanctions. On the other hand, the cumulative effect of these and other mechanisms such as the structure of communications, training programs, and indoctrination is to unobtrusively mold individual belief systems.[18]

Throughout the twentieth century the work and decisions of local officials have become increasingly rationalized—subject to more extensive administrative control and characterized by the systematic application of technical expertise. This results largely from half a century of municipal reform and, more generally, from the modernization of American society.[19] Yet if the bureaucratization of local government has left no municipal agency untouched, the capacity of city administrators to bring the actions and decisions of street-level bureaucrats under their control is still problematic and varies greatly among public agencies. There are discernable limits to the process of routinization in organizations, and hence limits to the impact of organizational constraints on discretionary choices. These limits are not merely due to the intractability of the human spirit, to the inability of whole persons to fit neatly into well-defined organizational roles and, as a result, to the continuing dialectic between the demand for routinization and resistance to it. The ability of city administrators to shape the belief systems of individual street-level bureaucrats and the degree of administrative control over specific decisions depend also on the ability of an organization to control environmental and task-related uncertainty.

The chief uncertainties confronting a public organization arise from the ambiguities and conflict surrounding the elaboration of the policy mandate and organizational goals, and from the limits to the rationalization of the organizational task. Organizational goals refer to the broad statements of purpose that identify the rationale of the organization, the task, the legitimate means to accomplish that task, and those individuals, social groups, and institutions that may be relevant to the accomplishment of the task. Rarely, though, is there complete agreement about the goals of a public agency. The goals of public agencies develop through a complex social and historical process that reflects political struggles—both among influential participants within the organization and between organizational elites and external groups—attendant to the formation of the organization and the development of policy mandates affecting the operation of the agency.[20] The existence of goal conflict in public agencies is due less to the differing interpretations of organizational goals held by agency members than to the effort by different political interests to have public agencies serve different ends. Public agencies, consequently, may be expected to serve more than one master. Welfare departments, for example, are expected to serve the poor and to prevent fraud; police departments are expected to control crime but not at the expense of constitutionally guaranteed liberties.

The limits to the rationalization of the organizational task depend on both the technology used by organizational members and the nature of the task.[21] We may distinguish between those technologies that are based on scientific knowledge and are highly rationalized (that are calculable) such as engineering and medical technology, and those that are based largely upon experience and intuitive judgments and consequently have a low degree of rationalization. In general, the greater the degree of rationalization in a technical process, the more certain and predictable the outcome. The predictability of a technical process can be increased either through a deepened understanding of the task on the basis of scientific knowledge that permits increased rationalization, or through modification of the task itself—for example, by selectively recruiting a clientele. For two reasons, however, there are definable limits to the process of technical rationalization. Some organizations—the police, prisons, schools —may be captive to a clientele and unable to make changes, other than minor ones, in the nature of that clientele. Second, the task may be such that notwithstanding our blind faith in technology, there is little if anything that can be done. Crime is obviously a rather intractable social problem that does not admit of easy solutions.

The more intractable the sources of uncertainty, the greater the limits on routinization within an organization. A public organization in which the goals and range of responsibilities are not subject to intense political conflict, and which performs a relatively routine task such as distributing library books or maintaining streets, is able to reduce the latitude of discretion to a narrow set of alternatives

33

defined by organizational rules. The criteria applied in different circumstances reflect decision premises largely set by management. In contrast, a public organization confronted with more or less intense political conflict over what it does, and which must attempt to provide satisfactory solutions to intractable social problems, will face immense difficulties in rationalizing organizational decision making. Consequently, the latitude of discretion is rather broad and the criteria used to judge different events may be a manifestation of the personal values of the decision maker as much as the priorities and expectations of administrators.

The work environment of many street-level bureaucrats is uncertain, often volatile, and, most significant, enmeshed in politics. As they are engaged in the distribution of services or the regulation of social behavior, street-level bureaucrats are subject to the contending claims of political groups and interests. What they do has demonstrable political consequences. This is especially so in the case of the police who, by virtue of their coercive role, are drawn into an antagonistic relationship with society. The police are expected to protect people, to be fair and impersonal, and to uphold the law as well as enforce it; but they encounter hostility, requests to temper enforcement to mitigating circumstances, and demands that they break the law to preserve order. The police must continually reconcile conflicting moral and political imperatives, and consequently their relationship to the public is characterized by ambivalence and hostility.

The uncertainties of the street-level bureaucrat's work environment preclude extensive rationalization of his task, and hence limit the impact of organizational constraints. At the same time, though, the continuing political and social pressure to rationalize public agencies means that street-level bureaucrats will be subject to renewed efforts to bring their activities under control. In short, street-level bureaucrats are caught between the rationalizing tendencies of local governments and the uncertainties of their work environments. This contradiction constitutes the major dynamic affecting the behavior and discretionary choices of street-level bureaucrats; it shapes both their judgments of fact and value and their latitude of discretion. While I believe this contradiction is applicable to many street-level bureaucrats, it is most apparent with the police.

The proposition that police discretion is to be understood in terms of a contradiction between the uncertainties of police work and the increasing rationalization of police bureaucracies is the leading thread of my analysis. If this development reflects a broader trend in American society toward the rationalization of public affairs, the specific roots of this contradiction lie in the municipal reform movement and the effort to professionalize the American police. In order to understand the implications for police discretion, we must explore the changes in police work wrought by professionalism.

Chapter 2

Police Professionalism
and the Bureaucratization
of Police Work

THE POLICE wield their powers of discretion in specific historical circumstances. The values and beliefs they bring to bear in their work—their conception of their duties and responsibilities, their understanding of the law, their ideas of how strictly the law should be enforced and when it should be enforced, their conception of order —and the political and organizational arrangements within which they function depend on the relationship of the police to society at any given time. The eighty-year effort to professionalize the police has wrought fundamental changes in the relationship of the police to the society they are charged with protecting. Professionalism has changed the institutional matrix within which the police operate and thus the basis of the legitimacy of their authority.

The most notable thing about a policeman, as Michael Banton has taken great pains to argue, is that he is a member of the society in which he enforces the law. "Being members of the society themselves," Banton argues, "policemen share the same values as the other members. . . . This means that the police will use their discretion in ways which diverge from the ideal of perfect justice but which conform to the pattern of social control."[1] This has two implications.

First, societal prejudices and values will influence the way the law is enforced. What policemen learn as members of society carries over and affects their routine discretionary choices. But the effect of social values and prejudices on a policeman's decisions depends on the degree of involvement of policemen in society. Isolation from or at least separation between policemen and society minimizes the salience of broader social values for police discretion.

The second, more subtle, implication of Banton's argument is that the police must function within the prevailing moral consensus of society. As instruments of formal social control, the legitimacy of police authority depends on the character of their relationship to society. The police cannot rely solely upon their coercive powers to obtain obedience to the laws and to maintain order—or rather there are limits to their ability to do so. They must depend, to some degree, upon informal patterns of social control to maintain order, and thus must operate within the bounds of prevailing values in order to maintain their moral authority. Perhaps the most interesting consequence for police discretion is that the ability of the police to enforce the laws rigorously is limited. It leads, in other words, to a predilection for leniency.

The ability of the police to sustain their moral authority is problematic. The moral consensus upon which the legitimate authority of the police is based is rarely as widespread as often presumed in an economically dynamic and socially heterogeneous society such as America. Legal rules reflect the outcome of social and political conflict within a society, the momentary victory of a social class or group in achieving its aims and asserting its will. The outcome of this process will not always be accepted as legitimate, as the long history of legislating morality demonstrates. Even attempts to enforce those laws for which there does exist widespread acceptance may be challenged at times when the basic foundations of the social order are called into question.

Moreover, the role of the police is broader than law enforcement; they are expected to serve as "peace officers," to provide a variety of services and to keep order within a community. Carrying out these activities while operating within the moral consensus of a society is as problematic as enforcing laws for which there is very little consensus. The interpretation of what constitutes disorder varies from community to community, and the attempt of the police to mediate disputes may ultimately be resented by both parties to the dispute.

Both as law enforcers and as peacekeepers, the police wield their coercive powers amidst deep-seated moral and political conflicts. They are often at the center of group and class conflict. The police are by and large deployed to protect society from the actions of specific groups, most often the lower classes (in fact, the development of the police in the nineteenth century was largely predicated on controlling the "dangerous classes").[2] The police are also caught between the contending moral claims of various social groups. The fate of "deviant" groups within a community often depends on the vigor with which the police enforce laws against those behaviors which offend the moral sensibilities of a community.

At the same time, the success of the police in maintaining order and mediating conflict depends on their ability to fashion a satisfactory relationship with the community being policed, one that sustains the legitimacy of their authority and either minimizes the occasions when they have to resort to force or provides the autonomy necessary to permit vigorous enforcement. As a result, there is an inescapable contradiction between a policeman's obligation to enforce the law and preserve order, and the necessity of acting within the moral consensus of the community being policed.[3] It is through the exercise of discretion that the police continually confront and adapt to this contradiction. Police discretion, then, is more than an operational necessity imposed by ambiguous laws and scarce resources, and more than a way of tempering the strictures of the law to mitigating circumstances. It is a necessary element in adapting to the social and political forces which impinge upon the police, and in sustaining the legitimacy of police authority.

Loyalty to the law and sensitivity to community norms and expectations are two poles on a continuum, both in the evolution of the police in America and in the individual adjustments that every policeman must make. The debate over the proper scope of police authority in nineteenth-century America turned on these polar conceptions of the police role. Broadly, one might view the evolution of the American police as moving from a concept of *personal authority,* rooted in the character of a policeman's relationships with the community being policed, to a concept of *impersonal authority,* which is tied closely to the legitimacy of the state and based on a concept of the police as dispassionate servants of society.[4] In the former, a policeman's authority derives from his sensitivity and responsiveness to community norms, while in the latter it rests on adherence to legitimately enacted legal powers and restraints.

These two concepts of authority imply different institutional matrixes and have different consequences for the exercise of discretion. The distinction most frequently advanced is one between the amounts of discretion a policeman possesses. Under a system of personal authority a policeman's powers of discretion are thought to be broad, subject only to the restraints imposed by shared values within a community. They are presumably more narrowly confined and more restrained by the law and bureaucratic rules in a system based on impersonal authority. But the difference is not so much one of the scope or amount of discretion, though it is quite clear that the police today are more restrained by legal restrictions than they were seventy years ago, as a difference in the kinds of constraints that impinge upon policemen and the consequences for the way they use their powers of discretion.[5] Banton's thesis that police discretion is to be understood in terms of a policeman's relationship to society needs to be interpreted in light of the historical evolution of the police. Baldly put, we have witnessed in the twentieth century the declining significance of community norms and expectations for police behavior, as a result of urban reform and the concomitant bureaucratization of police work. By seeking to bring police work under the control of centralized administrative organizations, reformers have sought to make policemen more impersonal, detached, and strict, and more responsive to legal and bureaucratic restrictions on their power, while making them less subject to external community and political pressures. But the irony of the effort to professionalize the police is that if it has served to insulate them from external political and legal controls, it has also served to maintain and in some ways widen their powers of discretion, and it has had only a marginal effect on the practices and values of working policemen.

The Origins and Elements of Police Professionalism

If there is a single point on which the police and their critics might agree it is that reform of the police through professionalism is the principal means by which the police can be made more effective, more efficient, and more accountable to the public. Yet it is a striking curiosity about police professionalism that the problem of discretion was never seriously considered by either the police or the reformers, though professionalism was ostensibly directed toward increasing public control over the decisions of the police. Indeed, for a long time many prominent police officials denied the reality of police discretion.[6] A professional police was supposed to enforce the law fearlessly and impersonally for all the public, though this begged the question of what "public" was served by fearless law enforcement. The reasons for the absence of any acknowledgment, much less discussion, of discretion lie in the historical origins of police professionalism and the way in which the concept of professionalism was applied to police work.

Professionalism as an attribute of an occupation and its practitioners is based on three related elements.[7] Professionals are experts; they apply the results of theoretical knowledge, acquired during an extended period of training, to a specialized area of human endeavor, and their actions and decisions are presumably governed by universalistic criteria. The authority of professionals rests on the claim that they alone are qualified to apply a particular body of knowledge. A second element of a profession is a devotion to service. Professionals, unlike self-interested entrepreneurs, are expected to be devoted to an ideal of community service rather than the attainment of material well-being. Huntington designates this devotion to service as the social responsibility of a profession and argues that it is this that distinguishes a professional from a mere technician.[8] The relationship between a professional and his client is to be governed by detachment and "affective neutrality," and a professional's decisions are to be based upon the client's best interests. Finally, all professions claim autonomy from external controls, on the presupposition that professions, through a code of conduct and the close scrutiny of a professional's conduct by his peers, are self-controlling, and that such autonomy is necessary for the application of professional knowledge to human endeavors. Among professionals, responsibility for one's actions is ensured by a system of collegial controls that differ from the hierarchical controls characteristic of bureaucracies. One consequence of the autonomy of professionals is that they acquire an identity of themselves as a special group set off from the rest of society, an identity frequently buttressed with a professional ideology.

Though the police might argue that police professionalism is based on these attributes, this claim is not entirely valid. The police are not independent professionals like doctors and lawyers, and there is substantial doubt about the claim to expertise that might underpin a professional police. Police work is based on an ideal of service, but their autonomy has less to do with acknowledged professional status than with the contemporary structure of municipal government. The modern police are closer to Amos Perlmutter's concept of "corporate professionals." Corporate professionalism is based on a "fusion between the professional and the bureaucrat—a fusion between group exclusivity and managerial responsibility."[9] As experts in the art of modern warfare, devoted to the service of the state, members of the military are professionals who stress their autonomy from conventional political controls (especially in wartime), their exclusiveness as an elite corps of officers, and the salience of their professional aspirations (not the least of which is the requisite professional status). At the same time, however, military organizations are characterized by a high degree of bureaucratization, and military personnel are presumably oriented toward the chain of command as much as toward their professional group. Two generations of reform have resulted in a comparable outcome for the police.

Though reform of the police was not really accomplished until after World War II by a second generation of reformers, the roots of police professionalism are to be found in the Progressive movement at the turn of the century. The Progressives sought to replace corruption-ridden political machines with strong executives and efficient nonpartisan government. Government would be run by trained professionals, experts in a specific field of endeavor, while authority and accountability would be centralized to chief executives who would be given wide powers to direct the operations of government. Politics, at least in its present manifestation, would be eliminated: patronage would be replaced with an all-encompassing merit system; areas of representation would be based not on the particularistic influences of the ward, but on the broader view of the whole city; and nonpartisanship would insure a deliberate and rational approach to city problems rather than politics as usual. Administration rather than politics held the key to the future.[10]

The central value in the Progressive vision was efficiency. Efficiency was a way of transcending politics, for it offered an alternative to political conflict. Social problems were thought to be technical rather than political in nature, and thus their resolution depended upon the ability of experts to bring their knowledge to bear. The application of expertise obviated the need for, and was thought to replace, political conflict. Just as many Progressives believed that the conflict between labor and management in the factory could be transcended through the application of Frederick Taylor's principles of scientific management, so they thought that efficiency in government would lead to a "harmony of interests" among diverse social and economic groups.[11]

Out of the reform movement emerged a concept of professionalism based on the ideas of discipline, the development and application of technical knowledge, autonomy for professionals to apply their skills, an emphasis on initiative in coming to grips with social problems, and above all on leadership of the competent. The Progressive concept of professionalism was elitist; professionals were guided by knowledge and standards that transcended the whims of the populace. In this respect it was seen as a brake on democracy; or, more precisely, as a way of reasserting the dominance of middle-class values over those of immigrant groups and the working class. But unlike the professionalism of doctors or lawyers, the Progressive concept provided for an additional measure of accountability. Accountability depended upon the presumption that authority would be wielded publicly and checked with the devices of "direct democracy"—the initiative, referendum, and recall. Implicit in this conception was the belief that elected (and appointed) officials could easily direct the machinery of government. Democratic government in the Progressive vision rested on subordinate compliance to executive authority; public officials were regarded as corporate professionals.[12]

Those Progressives preoccupied with reforming the police were concerned to separate the police from the vicissitudes of machine politics, upgrade their personnel, and narrow their responsibilities. These concerns were eventually translated into a coherent vision of police professionalism by a number of post-World War II policemen —among the most prominent being O.W. Wilson and William H. Parker. The link between the Progressives and the postwar generation of police reformers is August Vollmer, the single most influential policeman to apply the ideas of Progressivism to police work. While Vollmer may have been wrong on specific facts, the ideas he argued for are now accepted as the core of police professionalism.[13]

Professionalization presupposed a narrowing of the police function from the polyglot range of activities the nineteenth-century police performed, for if the police were to have any claim at all to be professionals they first had to establish a claim to expertise. Vollmer's solution to this problem was to insist that the role of the police in modern society is that of "the protection of society against crime and the criminal. It is the field of crime prevention."[14] While Vollmer consistently stressed the need for the police to adopt the most sophisticated technologies available to fight crime, he also evinced a clear preoccupation with order—though his comments are more veiled than those of William H. Parker who viewed the police as the thin blue line between order and anarchy. This preoccupation with order is linked to the idea that the police are required not only to apprehend felons but also to prevent crimes. Vollmer never clearly indicates exactly what he means by prevention, but it includes the notion of deterrence and the idea that the police must seek out crime. Commenting on traffic enforcement Vollmer said that:

> Where the force engaged in traffic enforcement is large enough and its activities are unceasing, a better order prevails; but no city can conduct a constant drive of the necessary proportions without drawing very heavily upon its treasury, and any let up whatever in the official vigilance is instantly reflected in a general disobedience of traffic rules. In short, fear of the traffic officer lasts just so long as the police pressure is generously and effectively applied. No sooner does it cease than traffic reverts to— and aggravates—its previous bad driving habits.[15]

With minor modifications this idea forms the basis of the theory of aggressive (preventative) patrol as a way of coping with crime. Thus an aggressive, competent, and professional police is the answer to the problem of crime in modern times.

If the control of crime is the most important objective of a professional police force, the single most deleterious factor that interferes with the performance of this function is politics. Like the Progressives, Vollmer and his heirs have insisted on a rigorous separation of police administration and local politics. Initially, this meant insulating the police from political influence through civil service regulations so they could presumably pursue lawbreakers with impunity. But Vollmer had more in mind. The separation of politics and police work was intended to insulate policemen from the vagaries of local politics, to enable them to act as neutral, dispassionate civil servants who could enforce the laws impersonally and equally. Vollmer's concept of the professional policeman was that of the detached public servant, standing above the community, utilizing his powers of coercion and expertise in the public interest.

Both the emphasis on crime control and the structural separation from politics presupposed organization, another element central to Vollmer's concept of professionalism. Technology was obviously of little use in fighting crime unless it could be organized. This meant the development of specialized units, more adequate record keeping, and the creation of a capacity to deploy policemen rationally in the fight against crime. Beyond this, what organization meant to professionals like Vollmer was the centralization of authority and strengthening of discipline in police departments. This initially stemmed from the need to root out corruption and break the ties between police departments and the machine; but it eventually broadened into an effort to rationalize the methods for controlling and disciplining policemen.

Yet many police reformers, especially Vollmer, were aware that greater organizational control over the activities of policemen would not necessarily resolve all fundamental problems of control. The analogy between the police department and the factory (or even the military) could be pushed only so far, for there are important differences in the tasks policemen and factory workers perform. The most obvious difference is that policemen simply cannot be supervised all of the time. And there are times when a policeman must be able to respond quickly to situations that are emotionally charged and where a life may hang in the balance. Recognizing these difficulties Vollmer and other reformers have concentrated on upgrading the quality and training of the men who become policemen. This includes the use of tests to screen out men with obvious psychological problems, beefing up training programs, and requiring college education—things that are now more or less the rule in most departments. Yet the determination of Vollmer and his successors to find the right kind of people to become policemen is curiously myopic. Gene Carte is close to the truth when he says that police professionalism always comes down to a search for the "perfect man." This preoccupation with the search for the "perfect man" is rooted in the belief that good personnel obviate the need for other reforms and other kinds of controls over police activity. "When we have reached a point where the best people in society are selected for police service," Vollmer argued, "there will be little confusion regarding the duties of the members."[16] What organization and technology cannot solve, good men will.

Crime fighting, the separation of police work from politics, the application of technology and organization to the police task, and the continuous effort to find and develop good policemen form the core of police professionalism. Born out of the pervasive corruption and ineffectiveness of nineteenth-century departments and the desire of reformers and businessmen to have consistent and efficient enforcement of the laws, the doctrines of police professionalism and the attendant reforms purport to resolve the dilemmas and conflicts of policing a hetrogeneous, urban-industrial society. Yet the model of professionalism adopted by the police, whatever its virtues (and there are some), avoided difficult problems. Nowhere in Vollmer's writings (nor in the writings of his successors) is there a concern for the ambiguities of the police role, for the social functions the police must carry out, or for the problem of discretion—which was more or less assumed out of existence—and the attendent problem of political control over police authority. Vollmer simply believed that once the police were professionalized other difficulties would take care of themselves. In times of social strife and conflict, however, this model could not—and did not—survive challenges to police authority. Reformers did not remove politics from police work; they only moved it out of city hall and into the police department.

The Impact of Police Professionalism: Police Bureaucracies and Police Discretion

There is no reason to entertain any illusions about the system of policing replaced by professionalism. Although the nineteenth-century departments were sensitive to the values of working-class immigrants and afforded them political leverage they would not have otherwise had, the police were rather ineffective in controlling crime or providing even a minimal level of services, and were frequently given to the worst abuses of their powers. On the other hand, even though professionalism has vastly improved the quality of police work and reduced the incidence of wanton violence, the broader implications of reform are less clear. In one sense, reform has well served the interests of the dominant middle class and the police. For the middle class it erected a system of policing that was more efficient than its predecessors and that assisted in bringing about their dominance over the tumultuous arena of city politics. For the policemen who were instrumental in bringing about reform, it served to enhance the status of the police and their image in the eyes of the public. But what have been the consequences for working patrolmen? How has reform changed their working lives and the way they use their powers of discretion?

Police professionalism has sought to change the values that inform the exercise of discretion, and are the basis of the legitimacy of police authority, by substituting formal legal and bureaucratic standards for those of particular communities. A police force based upon a personal concept of authority enhances the participation of policemen in the society they police. The crucial implication of this fact is, ironically, double-edged. It clearly means that the police will reflect the mores and prejudices of the community in the way they enforce the law. In the United States, this has been most apparent in the way the law has been enforced among blacks, with whom, for a long time, the practice of the police was to underenforce the law in the instance of an offense committed by a black against another black.

Yet the irony is that if police discretion often reflects some of a community's worst prejudices because the police operate within a community's moral consensus, policemen are nonetheless subject to the same *informal* social controls as other members of the community. Because a police officer is able to understand and appreciate subtleties of behavior, a citizen gains a measure of responsiveness that would not otherwise be possible. Thus to the extent that citizen and policeman are members of the same community and share common values, the former gains some informal control over the actions of the latter.[17] This is precisely the kind of control that was facilitated by the extreme decentralization of the American police in the late nineteenth century, where the intimate working relationship between the police forces and the political machines assisted in sustaining the cultural pluralism of American cities.[18] In police forces based upon an impersonal concept of authority, by comparison, the sole restraint upon the behavior of policemen derives from the force of administrative pressure to adhere to the law and organizational rules and procedures. The consequence, though, is not only to remove the police from the "informal control of community expectations but to reduce their moral authority," or, at the very least, make the legitimacy of their authority problematic.[19]

If the trend in twentieth-century America has been toward increasing separation between police and community, this development has not proceeded uniformly, and there are a number of factors that mitigate the separation and enhance a policeman's sensitivity to community values—the size and homogeneity of a community being only two of the more obvious ones. Yet one should not overemphasize such differences between communities. Aided by broader societal trends toward bureaucratization, reform has to a greater or lesser degree affected the operation of most American police departments. And to the extent that professionalism inculcates in policemen a distinctive set of values, it accentuates the differences between police and community—even in a small, homogeneous community. The chief implication is that the values and beliefs that guide police discretion are increasingly based on an ethos internal to the police, not on community norms, and reflect the pressures and incentives of police bureaucracies. In short, the greater the degree of professionalization, the greater the effect of internally derived values and organizational dynamics on police discretion.

At the same time, police reform has made the legitimacy of police authority more precarious. First, by severing the intimate connection between the police and the urban political machines, the urban reformers eroded the shared but particularistic moral consensus that often tempered police authority (especially in the case of urban ethnic groups) and the web of distributive politics that sustained order in nineteenth- and early twentieth-century American cities. By the 1960s, the police were confronted with the task of controlling discontent in the cities without the buffer of the urban political party.[20] Second, by placing crime control at the center of police work and cultivating a preoccupation with order, police reformers have created the very conditions that can undermine the legitimacy of police authority. The desire for aggressive police work greatly increases the capacity of the police to act lawlessly and without compunction. It inevitably deepens the division between the police and the people they presumably serve.

The key to understanding the impact of police professionalism lies, I think, in understanding that the reformers attempted to deal with the question of legitimacy by bureaucratizing police work. The autonomy from local politics sought by the reformers was predicated on the need to make the police efficient, effective crime fighters. But, as the reformers clearly recognized, this entailed the necessity of establishing stringent internal discipline within police departments. Such discipline was not merely necessary to eliminate corruption or to provide the trappings of efficiency and effectiveness in order to bolster the status of the police. It was necessary, the reformers believed, for developing a police force based on a set of universalistic and formalistic values responsive to the community as a whole. Autonomy from local politics and internal discipline are thus the twin pillars of police professionalism. The price of acting as a professional who addresses his clients in a community is to be a bureaucrat subject to the coercive inclinations of administrators.

The difficulty in all of this is that the vision of the reformers—the faith in subordinate compliance as a pillar of democratic control— breaks down within the department. Police reform has been predicated on bringing about a wholesale shift in the values and outlook of the American police and on imposing bureaucratic controls on police discretion, a shift described by James Q. Wilson a number of years ago as a transition from a police force based on a *system code* to one based on a *professional code*. [21] The values of the system code were particularistic. Authority relationships within the department were personalized and the legitimate authority of supervisors depended on adherence to shared values such as the pursuit of a "good pinch"; the task of law enforcement was treated as an instrument to further group ends, for example, to maintain respect for police authority; and the use of informers, the pursuit of graft, and the legitimacy of secrecy and violence prevailed. The values of the professional code, by contrast, are universalistic: authority relationships within a department are based on the legitimacy of rational-legal authority; the law is seen as a substantive end to be pursued and enforced impersonally; and there are express limitations on the use of informers, on discretion, and on the toleration of secrecy and violence.

I do not doubt that police professionalism has had profound consequences for the values, outlook, and actions of the police; but neither has it resulted in the wholesale change in values that Wilson and others assume has taken place nor in stringent administrative control over police discretion.[22] The reason for the limited impact of the professional code and the breakdown of discipline within professional departments lies in the continuing significance of the police culture. The police culture, as William Westley argued, is rooted in the centrality of coercion to police work and the consequent antagonistic relationship between the police and society.[23] One effect of the intrinsic cleavage between policemen and society and the attendant uncertainties of police work is to create and sustain a sense of isolation from the larger society among policemen which manifests itself as the "morale problem"—the difficulty for the police of finding a consistent and justifiable self-conception and assuaging feelings of public hostility. Confronted with what they feel is an ambivalent public, the police come to regard themselves as pariahs. Moreover, the uncertainties of police work serve to sustain, if not augment, the enormous anxiety and stress that come with making crucial decisions under conditions of great pressure and uncertainty. There is always a feeling among patrolmen that no matter what they do somebody will find fault.

The sense of separateness and the anxiety that accompanies decision making is relieved and exorcised through mutual support and trust between one another. Westley concluded that "the particular definitions of the public and of his conduct that the policeman develops out of this interaction assume a collective and cultural character because the police hold the experience in common, because of the strong consensual bond developed by the felt hostility of the public."[24] This is the basis of the police culture. The outward manifestation of the police culture is quite often defensiveness; inwardly, it legitimizes values and norms which help restore the loss of esteem and permit decisiveness in the face of uncertainty.

The pressures and stresses of police work that form the basis of the police culture do not abate under professionalism; if anything, they are intensified, partly because of new demands that are placed on the police and because professionalism accentuates and deepens the already existing isolation of the police from the public.[25] What the effort to professionalize the police has done is to graft a new set of values on the old. It has modified the marginal and less salient values of the police culture—those that interfered with the attainment of professional status—while reinforcing more central values. Exactly how professionalism has changed the values and beliefs of patrolmen and with what effect is a question that will be considered at length in the ensuing analysis.

More significant are the implications of the persistence of the police culture for a patrolman's relationship to the department, and the consequences for the exercise of discretion. The contemporary police may be described as corporate professionals precisely because they combine the task-related values of the police culture with the bureaucratic ethos of the reformers. But the values of the corporate group and the bureaucrat are incompletely fused; rather, professional police departments are characterized by an enduring conflict between the task-related values of the police culture and the bureaucratic values of police professionalism. For example, police professionalism has sought to impose the law, which is a universalistic set of standards, on the decisions of patrolmen, but this conflicts with the often pragmatic, instrumental criteria they feel compelled to use. Police professionalism enjoins the patrolman to be a bureaucrat rather than a judge, but the patrolman is often confronted with the need to be a judge whether he likes it or not. Finally, police professionalism has sought to impose a stringent internal discipline on patrolmen and to assert the salience of such goals as treating citizens courteously and minimizing public complaints about police behavior. The demand to control crime, however, mandates many of the practices legitimized by the police culture. Patrolmen are thus confronted with a conflict between honoring two very different organizational goals.

The palpable conflict in contemporary police departments between the values of the police culture and those of professionalism mirrors a more deeply rooted conflict between the immediate need of the police to control crime and preserve order and the more enduring need to sustain the legitimacy of their authority. The relationship between the police culture and professionalism is a contradictory, dialectical one. The bureaucratization of police departments, the demand for internal discipline, is limited by the police culture; but to the extent that the uncertainties of police work continue to sustain the ethos of the police culture, to the extent that police work demands deviations from the universalistic and formalistic values embedded in police professionalism—something that is assured given the preoccupation with crime fighting—there will be enormous pressure on administrators to reassert organizational discipline and to attempt to control the way patrolmen use their discretion. It would be a mistake simply to assume that the values of police professionalism are merely a mask that police administrators wear to fend off critics, a hollow shell that conceals the real nature of police work. It is precisely because professionalism is so closely tied to the question of legitimacy that police administrators must and do take the matter of discipline seriously. The professional autonomy demanded by reformers depends on it. The difficulty is that there are serious limits in the ability of police administrators to control their men.

In the preceding chapter I concluded that police discretion could not be understood in terms of the highly routinized rules typical of many public organizations. Rather, decision making in street-level bureaucracies is to be understood in terms of a contradiction between the work environment of street-level bureaucrats and the rationalizing tendencies of reform governments. This conflict is manifested in police departments as a conflict between the values of the police culture and those of professionalism, a conflict that affects the impact of organizational constraints on patrolmen and the values they bring to bear on the street. It leads, on the one hand, to a radical autonomy on the part of patrolmen which permits highly distinctive approaches to police work—operational styles—to flourish, and which has served, given the separation between police and community, to sustain if not broaden the wide latitude of discretion possessed by patrolmen. On the other hand, patrolmen are not totally autonomous, as they are caught between the demands of an uncertain and ambiguous task and a demand for conformity to the desires of administrators. Many of their discretionary choices as well as the salience of the moral dilemmas patrolmen confront turn on resolving this conflict. The task before us now is to explore the nature and depth of this conflict in the three professional departments that are the subject of this study.

PART TWO

Cops as Professionals
and Bureaucrats

Autocracy during office hours is the price
of democracy after hours.

Dwight Waldo

Bureaucracy is a circle from which no
one can escape. Its hierarchy is a hierarchy of knowledge. The apex entrusts the
lower circles with insight into the individual while the lower circles leave insight into the universal to the apex, so
they deceive each other reciprocally.

Karl Marx

Chapter 3

The Patrolman
and the Community

THE JOB of policing a community and, thus, the way the police wield their powers of discretion are undoubtedly affected by the social makeup of a community. The way a community setting shapes the exercise of discretion by a patrolman depends, partly, upon the actual problems of crime and disorder within a community. The kind of community in which a patrolman works may necessitate that he confront a variety of crimes and human maladies—from murder to drunkenness. Depending on the crime rate, it may also pose questions of personal safety. Most patrolmen readily acknowledge the relevance of the community setting: they expect to behave differently in the raw, turbulent environment of a black, lower-class ghetto than in the placid environs of suburbia. But a patrolman's behavior —his decisions—cannot be predicted from knowledge of the community environment alone. To assume otherwise is to assume that a patrolman's behavior is completely determined by the events and people he encounters—an assumption that even casual observation of patrolmen at work reveals as untenable. What is significant is what a patrolman learns about crime and disorder and the way he interprets his experiences on the street.

Just as important as the actual problems of crime and disorder are the community's vague, often ambiguous expectations of what the police should do about those problems. Expectations of what constitutes a tolerable level of order, how strictly the law should be enforced, and how juveniles should be treated, as these are manifested by the indigenous cultural milieu and communicated to the police by political leaders, community elites, and citizens, presumably influence police discretion. What the police actually do, though, depends on both their understanding of the community's expectations of the proper use of police authority and their own sense of what should be done. The link between what a community thinks should be done about crime and disorder and what the police actually do is always tenuous, but under police professionalism it has become even more so.

How a patrolman judges his experiences on the street and how he interprets the scope and limitations of his authority are a function of the way the police are organized in relation to the community. The professionalization of police work has served not just to inculcate in patrolmen a distinctive set of values and beliefs which sharpen the distinction between policeman and civilian. More fundamentally, it has changed the very character of the relationship between the two. A professional police force does not serve a community by responding to the unique and particular needs of its different segments; rather the police serve by controlling crime and enforcing the law in the community as a whole. The police are more than servants, they are professional servants. They stand above the community and assume the responsibility for interpreting and judging what are the serious problems of crime and disorder that a community faces and what should be done about them. As professionals, the police, as Everett Hughes once put it, profess; they provide services and remedies to the community in light of their expert understanding of crime and disorder. The community, for all practical purposes, is the client.

To fulfill the role of professionals requires autonomy. The ability to select priorities of enforcement according to professional judgments, to strictly enforce the law, and to utilize the aggressive tactics thought necessary to root out crime are contingent on departmental autonomy from political and community pressures. This of course is precisely why so many police reformers have insisted on limiting political control over the police. But the autonomy of a professional department, as we shall see, is never entirely complete.

What a patrolman in a professional department learns about a community is filtered through the lens of internally derived standards. Judgments of what constitutes disorder, of what the important crimes are, of how various incidents should be handled are based not on the demands of specific groups but on a patrolman's assessment of what is required. To what extent these judgments reflect the expectations of administrators or broader professional norms rather than the beliefs of individual patrolmen is an important question, and one that will be pursued throughout the analysis. For the moment it is sufficient to note that professionalism places the responsibility with the patrolman for determining when and what kind of police action is required. At the same time, the structural autonomy of professional police departments severely reduces the ability of citizens to influence departmental policies and practices. This extends both to judgments of what constitutes misbehavior or abuses of police authority, and decisions about priorities and tactics. That this inability to influence departmental priorities and practices should affect minorities and the poor more severely than the middle class is one of the enduring, if not unintentional, legacies of municipal reform.

To some, this description of the impact of reform on the relationship between the police and the community might appear to be overdrawn. Some policemen, who consider themselves professionals, might insist that police professionalism means responsiveness to the community. But it is not clear what responsiveness means in the context of police professionalism. It does not ordinarily mean that the police will refuse to enforce laws which some groups in a community find particularly offensive. In all probability, though, it does mean responsiveness to demands which accord with the ethos of professionalism. Thus, the question of how quickly patrolmen respond to calls for service is typically accorded greater significance than the question of priorities of enforcement.

Even so, not every contemporary police administrator would accept in its entirety the model of professionalism I have set forth, and even if they did, not every department is able to attain the autonomy necessary to implement it. In point of fact, there are several factors which mitigate the separation between police and community that is the consequence of professionalism. These can potentially increase a patrolman's sensitivity to the values of the community and his responsiveness to community demands and expectations. Three are important: the size of the community, the extent to which the police and the community share common values, and the attitudes of police administrators and the consequent department policies.

Size of the community (and by implication size of the department) is perhaps one of the more obvious factors that might decrease the separation between police and community, and one that is the subject of considerable discussion nowadays. In a small community a patrolman's knowledge of the needs and wants of the people and his understanding of their expectations of how the coercive powers of the police should be wielded are presumably enhanced. In a smaller community, citizens also presumably have greater access to the department to communicate demands or to complain about the way patrolmen are behaving. This access is often supplemented in a small community by an informal network of communications, especially in the willingness of local papers to report copiously on the activities of the police. Given these pressures, it is quite possible that in a small community the autonomy of the police may be far more precarious than in a larger, more heterogeneous community.

Shared values may also mitigate the separation between police and community. The more that policemen and citizens share common values, the more likely common definitions of order and criminality will be applied, a patrolman's understanding of what constitutes normal behavior within a community will be increased, and there will be more than a modicum of agreement on priorities. But many communities are not especially homogeneous, and socioeconomic differences may be overlaid (or replaced) with contrasting life-styles and sharp differences between generations. The police are usually in conflict with some groups in a community, and the question is often not one of whether the police are sensitive to the community but to which groups they are sensitive.

Finally, the degree of separation between police and community will depend on the structure of the department and administrative policies, matters that turn on the attitudes of police administrators. For example, departmental policies that regularly rotate patrolmen among the beats (or precincts) of a city inhibit the development of intimate knowledge of the residents and problems of a particular segment of the community. Recent innovations such as team policing are partly predicated on making patrolmen more aware of the needs and demands of specific neighborhoods within a community. Beyond this, though, it is the attitude of the chief of police that is crucial in determining how responsive the police will be to demands made by the community. His policies and preferences may be modified or even countermanded by subordinates, but he sets the tone and it is his interpretation of professionalism that counts. Indeed, the chief's vision of professionalism is far more decisive for the behavior of patrolmen than his specific preferences about the priorities of enforcement and other matters. The chief's interpretation of the relationship of the police to the community will be guided by his version of police professionalism, and by what he understands to be limits to the authority of the police. No chief of police can ignore the necessity of sustaining the legitimacy of his men's authority.

What a patrolman learns about the community he polices, and how he judges what he learns, is dependent on the degree of separation between policeman and community, a separation heightened by police professionalism but mitigated by the size of the community, by shared values between the police and the community, and by the attitudes of police administrators, especially the chief. Every department—and every policeman—must come to terms with the competing demands imposed by professionalism and the community milieu. The kind of accommodation reached between the police and community depends on the degree of departmental autonomy, the kinds of demands and people the police confront, and the values and beliefs of patrolmen about the communities they work in. The remainder of this chapter is devoted to discussing each of these elements of the relationship between the police and community in Los Angeles, Redondo Beach, and Inglewood.

The Relative Autonomy of Three Professional Police Departments

Of the three police departments observed in this study, the Los Angeles Police Department (LAPD) is the largest, with over 7,000 sworn personnel and about 3,000 patrolmen working the streets. In comparison, Inglewood, at the time of the study, had approximately 110 sworn personnel and from 62 to 70 patrolmen, and Redondo Beach had 65 sworn personnel and 37 active patrolmen. All three departments subscribe to the central tenets of police professionalism and reflect with varying degrees of emphasis a preoccupation with crime control, organization and training, and the necessity of maintaining the autonomy of the department from local politics. Yet there is a significant difference between the Los Angeles Police Department and the two smaller departments in their relative autonomy from the communities they police, and thus their ability to act as professionals.

The Los Angeles Police Department is regarded by many observers as the epitome of police professionalism. It is the legacy of William H. Parker, and even today bears the stamp of his personality. Parker is credited with professionalizing the department, which, until his reign, was as corrupt as any in the country.[1] Preoccupied with order, all of Parker's efforts and reforms were directed toward making the police the bulwark of order in an urban-industrial society.[2] In this Parker was to embellish as well as implement August Vollmer's design. His reforms were directed toward two objectives. First, Parker vigorously sought to limit external controls on the police and to assure the autonomy he believed necessary for the police to maintain order and curb anarchy. Known as an acerbic critic of those who sought to limit or even criticize the police, Parker is largely responsible for institutionalizing the heralded autonomy of the LAPD. Second, Parker sought to impose a stringent internal discipline on the department. His accession to power was marked by an increase in rules governing the minutiae of behavior, wider use of the Internal Affairs Division to investigate and prosecute officer misconduct, and the centralization of power and authority within the department.

Both of these structural reforms were fundamental to what Parker regarded as the role of the police in modern society. The responsibility of the police, he believed, was to promote the welfare of the community through the constructive use of the coercive powers of the police. The question that confronted the police was whether or not the actions of an individual or group were inimical to the welfare of society, and, if so, the police were obligated to move with all practicable speed and efficiency to remove the threat. Parker occasionally paid lip service to the notion that the police were subservient to the public, but the judgment of when someone's actions were inimical to the welfare of the community was a judgment to be made entirely by the police. Acquiring this judgment was the key, in Parker's opinion, to becoming a "perfect police officer in terms of a democracy."[3]

Parker's belief that the police should take the responsibility for defining threats to the community and the initiative in eradicating them is central to the doctrines of police professionalism. But the LAPD has succeeded more so than most American police departments in attaining the autonomy necessary to act on this belief. Long before law and order became a political issue in the late 1960s, the LAPD had already achieved considerable autonomy from local politics and was regarded as one of the more powerful of the administrative fiefs that make up Los Angeles's municipal government. The autonomy of the department has been sustained even after Parker's death and the Watts revolt in 1965 when the power of the LAPD and the uses it made of this power increasingly became a political issue. Moreover, all of Parker's successors, but especially Edward M. Davis, the chief of police from 1969 to 1978, have persevered in the belief that the LAPD and the LAPD alone is in a position to judge what the serious crime problems are and to act upon them. And they do so in the face of more vocal opposition than in the past.

In recent years, the LAPD has pursued a policy of aggressive enforcement at rock concerts and other gatherings of the "counterculture"; it launched a controversial attack on prostitution by deploying undercover policewomen; and it made extensive use of undercover narcotics agents in many of the city's high schools, a tactic that led to mass arrests of "drug pushers" during December 1974 and May 1975. By themselves these and similar incidents are not unique. Many big-city departments launched similar kinds of operations during this period, but no other department has done so quite as frequently and with as much success in fending off critics. All three incidents provoked substantial criticism of the department. The gist of much of the criticism was conveyed by one critic who, comparing the LAPD's enforcement policy at rock concerts to the mass arrests in the high schools, noted that "both were examples of police action beyond the dimensions necessary to keep our community free of crime. . . ."[4] The reactions of Chief Davis to such criticism vividly illustrate the model of professionalism upheld in the department, the belief that the police are in the best position to diagnose and act upon the ills of the community. As he said in defending the department's actions at rock concerts, ". . . In most places they [rock concerts] are allowed to go unpoliced and they become huge pot festivals where you can get stoned just walking through the place without even smoking. But this is the City of Los Angeles, and we're not going to give up any of it."[5] Thus, despite some difference in style and capabilities there was a notable continuity in the department's policies and actions between Parker's administration and that of Edward M. Davis. The ability to maintain this stance is largely a result of the department's autonomy.

The status of the department within Los Angeles city government is the formal basis of the department's autonomy. The chief of police is appointed, and can only be removed, under civil service procedures. While the mayor can influence the operation of the department, the formal authority for governing the department rests with a board of commissioners appointed by the mayor. There are only two points at which political officials can exert some control over the department—in the Police Commission and through the budgetary process—and in both the department has succeeded in acquiring considerable autonomy.

The Police Commission ostensibly sets policy for the department, but ever since Parker became police chief the commission has rarely been able to oppose the will of the chief. During Parker's tenure in office the commission was widely regarded as a "rubber stamp" for his policies. As one member of the commission from 1953 to 1966 recently commented, "We relied on Parker an awful lot, and maybe that's why we got the rubber-stamp image. But, you know, Parker was usually right—he wasn't wrong very often."[6] By and large the Police Commission has been just as unsuccessful in controlling Parker's successors.

Yet, there is one sense in which the charge of a "rubber stamp" police commission may be misleading. For the most part, there have been no deep differences on policing or tactics between the Police Commission and the last three chiefs of police. This was especially true during the tenure as mayor of the flamboyant but conservative Sam Yorty, when the Police Commission tended to support the department, even in the face of the criticism which erupted after the Watts revolt and the handling of anti-war demonstrations. This is partly because most of the commissioners represent the city's conservative business establishment and have accepted the assumptions and framework of police professionalism initially laid down by Parker. The commission appointed by Tom Bradley, Yorty's successor, has tried to assert more control over departmental operations and policies. They forced a revision in the department's shooting policy in the fall of 1977 after the shooting of an unarmed man, and two years later they openly challenged the department's report and exoneration of two patrolmen who shot and killed a woman. But whether they will be any more successful in controlling the department than their predecessors is an open question.[7]

One other indication of the department's autonomy is its ability to get what it wants in the municipal budgetary process. There are two reasons for the department's financial autonomy. First, it has been able to acquire fiscal independence by cultivating alternative sources of revenue, sources not easily controlled by the city council or the mayor. These include *in lieu* state subventions to the department, and, more recently, federal grants. These moneys are used for innovations or nonroutine appropriations such as "service betterment" programs, narcotics control, and officer support information systems.[8] Moreover, where possible the department has sought to remove or at least minimize the influence of elected officials over salaries. The adoption of the Jacobs Plan in the 1950s pegs salary increases to wage levels in private industry. The effect of this is to sharply limit the ability of the mayor and city council to control police expenditures.

The second reason for the department's financial autonomy is its effectiveness in getting reductions in the budget restored. The department's budget is carefully scrutinized by the staff of the City Administrative Officer (CAO), but cuts recommended by the CAO are as often as not restored by the mayor or the city council. This was certainly true during the Yorty years; but even when confronted with a more skeptical mayor in Tom Bradley and declining revenues since 1973, the department has still been able to get what it wants.

The success of the LAPD in dominating the Police Commission and in achieving financial autonomy is related to another factor: the salience of "law and order" as a political issue and the ability of a succession of chiefs, beginning with Parker, to appeal directly to the public for support. Lacking an explicit constituency to provide external support, the police rely upon a strategy of building the prestige and reputation of the organization and, when necessary, appealing to the most deeply rooted fears of the public. The LAPD has successfully pursued both strategies. From Parker on, it has worked to cultivate the image of an efficient, well-managed department, free of the vestiges of corruption. This not only reaps support from the business establishment, but also assuages the public, much of which is frequently far more concerned with the response time of individual patrolmen to a call than the way they use their powers of discretion. Yet the police also know that playing upon the most deeply rooted fears of the public—especially the fear of violent crime—is not without its political advantages. A police chief who warns the residents of a city, as Edward M. Davis once did, to "bar their doors, buy a police dog, call us when we're available, and to pray," usually gets his way when faced with impending budget cuts.[9] But more than fiery statements by the chief of police are involved; the department assiduously cultivates the support of numerous booster groups and assists them in lobbying before the City Council in support of departmental programs.[10]

The structural autonomy of the LAPD enables the police to fulfill the vision of professionals serving the community and to pursue a strategy of strict and aggressive enforcement of the law. It has also given the department enormous political leverage within Los Angeles and attenuated any semblance of external control.

If the policemen in Inglewood and Redondo Beach subscribe to the tenets of professionalism, they are unable to implement them fully. Indeed, the beliefs I have described as police professionalism are subtly modified in both departments, mostly because both departments are far less autonomous than the LAPD. The decisive factor that limits the autonomy of Inglewood and Redondo Beach in comparison to the LAPD is size, or more precisely, the proximity of the police to the community.

Both Inglewood and Redondo Beach are suburbs in the Los Angeles metropolitan area with council-manager forms of government. The chief of police in both departments is directly responsible to the city manager. Neither city manager at the time of the field observations appeared to exercise great control over the departments, and if there were the usual arguments over the budget, both chiefs usually got what they wanted.

Yet the role of the police is viewed somewhat differently in both of these departments. While neither the chiefs nor the patrolmen in the departments doubts the necessity of rigorously enforcing the law and aggressively suppressing crime, their view of their responsibilities is tempered by the realities of policing a small community. The most graphic illustration of the difference is the attitude of the chief in Inglewood toward enforcing drug violations at rock concerts, compared to the LAPD's. Inglewood is the site of a large arena, the Forum, which sponsors several rock concerts every year. When asked to compare the enforcement strategy in Inglewood with that of the LAPD, the chief responded: ". . . we don't have enough police officers, and neither does Chief Davis, to bust every pot smoker around, so the whole matter shakes down to a sense of priorities, a discretionary decision. With LAPD maybe it's pot, but with us the priority is providing the best protection for Inglewood residents."[11]

The chief's attitude reflects the necessity of coping with serious crimes with limited resources, and a sense of the limits on the police in a small community. In the context of a lengthy discussion of the relationship between the police and the community in Inglewood, the chief commented:

I'm playing to the audience, the community is different here. . . . I think that you're more exposed to the community because you have no place to go. You're set here, where in Los Angeles city you've got 400 some square miles. Here you're directly involved with citizens all the time. And I think that you have to take the tenor of the community to a degree into the operation of the department. Now, that's not saying there is politics or is it saying that there are special interest groups being given special attention. I'm just saying that you have to have a keener ear to the community because of the smaller sized area.[12]

If the chief accepts the fundamental tenets of police professionalism, he nevertheless feels obliged to be responsive—because of the department's proximity to the community—to what he believes are the community's expectations about the way the police should exercise their powers of discretion.

To a certain degree the same attitude prevails in Redondo Beach. The chief of police in Redondo Beach may exude the professional's preoccupation with crime and enforcement, but he also takes pains to emphasize that in a small community like Redondo Beach, which does not have a significant crime problem, a low-key style of enforcement is more appropriate. This does not mean that the police are not concerned with crime and enforcement, especially felonies, which are accorded the highest priority. Rather, they are obliged to be responsive to community demands. More than the other departments, Redondo Beach engages in extensive community relations activities, including ride-along programs and the like. While some members of the department regard this as an effective way of responding to the concerns of residents, others think the department is overly "P.R. [public relations] conscious."

There is a temptation to refer to these two small departments as communal departments, or departments that, despite the professional exterior, are based on a "personal" concept of authority, where the law is not enforced strictly and impersonally but selectively, in ways that are consistent with the values of the community.[13] But one should not overemphasize the responsiveness of either of these departments to community pressures. Both of the chiefs and most of the administrators and field supervisors in each department do not accept the idea that the police should tailor their policies and practices to every demand made by residents. Responsiveness in this context means, more often than not, providing a full range of police services as efficiently and effectively as possible, and minimizing complaints. Moreover, one could not say that these departments were equally responsive to all groups within the community. In each city a sizeable proportion of the residents were either black or Mexican-American, and in each there was some friction between the department and these groups. If these departments represented anyone, it was the middle-class majority. Thus, neither small department could be called communal, neither has consciously adopted a selective strategy of enforcement.

Yet neither department displays the professional orientation that characterizes the LAPD, the belief that the police and the police alone are in the best position to decide when and how to intervene. This is as much because they are constrained from doing so as because of anything else. In a sense, the police in these two cities are "responsive" in spite of themselves. The chief of police in Inglewood was alluding to this when he said that the police in a small community "have no place [else] to go." What he meant was that the police in a small community have neither the flexibility nor the autonomy to enforce the law just as they please. That is to say, the proximity to community pressures that is characteristic of a small department constrains its operations in a way that the operations of a larger department such as the LAPD are not. The underlying dilemma here is that the police in a small department cannot acquire the autonomy necessary to fulfill the requirements of police professionalism and still maintain the legitimacy of their authority. In other words, the drive of police professionalism to insulate the police from community pressures is partially attenuated in small police departments. As a result, many small departments are neither wholly communal nor professional; they embody elements of both, and to some degree the dilemma of balancing loyalty to the law with sensitivity to community pressures is more intense than in a larger, more autonomous department. This has some rather interesting consequences for administrative control and the exercise of discretion in Redondo Beach and Inglewood.

The Context of Police Work

In a sense, one cannot talk of the four communities—Redondo Beach, Inglewood, Rampart, and Northeast—as discrete, isolated entities. All are located in the Los Angeles metropolitan area, all partake of the culture and life-style of Southern California, and there are no differences in the law and political culture. Yet beneath the Southern California exterior there are some important differences in the kinds of problems and demands that patrolmen confront. As such, these four communities represent a broad comparison between two types of communities, a difference reflected in the attitudes of the patrolmen who work there.

Perhaps the chief difference, aside from size, between these four communities is the crime rate. Table 3.1 presents the average incidence of felony crimes reported to the police from 1969 to 1973. The data show that two of these communities have a moderately high crime rate (Inglewood and Rampart Division) and two have a moderately low crime rate (Redondo Beach and Northeast Division). With the exception of the rate for aggravated assault, the average rate for violent crimes (homicide, rape, robbery) and for serious property crimes (burglary and auto theft) is almost identical in Redondo Beach and Northeast Division. Burglary is regarded as the most serious crime problem by Redondo Beach patrolmen. Their feelings are mirrored in the statistics: between 1970 and 1973 the burglary rate increased from 175.0 per 10,000 population to 255.0. In addition to burglary, patrolmen in Northeast Division single out narcotics violations and juvenile gangs as significant problems. The presence of numerous juvenile gangs and frequent gang fights partly explain the higher rate of assaults in Northeast Division. Patrolmen in both communities, however, feel that despite the problems they work in slow, rather relaxed areas.

TABLE 3.1

Average Felony Crimes by Department, 1969–73
(Per 10,000 population)

Offense	High-crime Areas		Low-crime Areas	
	Inglewood	Rampart	Redondo Beach	Northeast
Homicide	.93	1.81	.74	.84
Forcible rape	5.08	9.10	2.90	3.60
Armed robbery	72.20	49.00	18.70	16.60
Aggravated assault	19.00	52.00	16.90	35.80
Burglary	243.70	277.60	204.80	190.40
Grand theft[a]	178.90	277.90	191.80	205.80
Auto theft	152.70	125.70	83.60	84.10

[a]Larceny greater than $50.00; figures are 1969–72 means.
SOURCE: Los Angeles Police Department, Statistical Digest, 1969–73, State of California, Bureau of Criminal Statistics, Redondo Beach Police Department; Inglewood Police Department.

The comparison between Inglewood and Rampart Division is not clear-cut, reflecting more than anything else the transitional character of Inglewood. Inglewood is undergoing change from an all-white, middle-class suburb, once a bastion of racism, to an integrated community. Yet the crime rate is only partly a manifestation of this change. Far more important is that the occurrence of crime in Inglewood has increased in recent years because of its location. Located in the southwestern and central area of Los Angeles, with easy access to major freeways, Inglewood is an ideal target for quick crimes such as the robbery of a liquor store by individuals who live elsewhere in the metropolitan area.[14] Moreover, Inglewood attracts a wide variety of transients because of the Hollywood Park Race Track and the Forum. Table 3.1 shows that the average five-year rate for homicide, forcible rape, assault, and burglary are higher in Rampart than in Inglewood, but the rates for armed robbery and auto theft are higher in Inglewood. Over this five-year period, however, the incidence of forcible rape, aggravated assault, armed robbery, and burglary in Inglewood all increased dramatically. In particular, the incidence of robbery in Inglewood doubled between 1969 and 1973, increasing from 46.0 per ten thousand population to 98.0 (the incidence of robbery in Redondo Beach, by comparison, remained about the same during this period); rape increased from 3.0 to 9.7; assault was up from 13.4 to 28.1; and burglary increased from 166 to 302. In 1973 the rates for forcible rape, robbery, burglary, and auto theft were higher in Inglewood than in Rampart Division. These are all serious crimes, though armed robbery is considered by many policemen to be the key indicator of a community's crime problem. Judging from this comparison, one would have to conclude that during the early 1970s Inglewood was facing an increasingly serious crime problem, more serious than either Northeast Division or Redondo Beach.[15]

Despite the differences in the range and seriousness of crime in these communities, all four areas are racially and ethnically heterogeneous and display wide variations in income distribution. Each has a sizeable minority population, though the proportion is greater in the two divisions of the LAPD than in either small department. In Northeast and Rampart, 44 percent of the population is either Mexican-American or black, as compared to 24 percent in Inglewood and 14 percent in Redondo Beach. Inglewood contains the highest proportion of blacks. The number of blacks in Inglewood has steadily increased since the mid-1960s, and by 1970 was estimated to be from 13 percent (U.S. Census estimate) to 25 percent (City of Inglewood estimate). It is doubtless substantially higher by now. Mexican-Americans are the predominant minority group in the other three communities.

At the same time, there is very little difference in the proportion of blue- and white-collar workers living in each community, and the unemployment rate and median years of education are almost identical. If each of these communities has pockets of poor people—Rampart is clearly the poorest with a median family income of $7,500 in 1970, a figure substantially below the other three—they are, on the whole, middle- and working-class communities.

There are two other demographic facts of some importance. Both Redondo Beach and Northeast have a higher concentration of juveniles than either Inglewood or Rampart. About 33 percent of the population in the low-crime communities is below 18 years of age compared to 23 percent for the high-crime communities. Second, the proportion of elderly people is slightly higher in Rampart than the other three areas. The concentration of juveniles in the low-crime areas and elderly people in Rampart poses somewhat unique problems for the patrolmen in these areas, a fact that must be remembered as we analyze the way patrolmen use their discretion.

In contrast to the racial and economic diversity of the population in these four communities, the patrolmen who work in them are largely white. About two-thirds come from working- or lower-class backgrounds, three-quarters served in the military before becoming policemen, and the median number of school years is slightly higher than that of the residents (see table 3.2). More important, perhaps, these patrolmen are by and large locals, men who grew up in the cultural milieu of Southern California. Over 50 percent of the patrolmen in these three departments were born outside of California, but 60 percent were raised either in the city in which they now work or in Los Angeles County. Finally, there are no significant differences in background characteristics between the patrolmen in these three departments.

This broad-brush comparison of the four communities provides some idea of the dimensions of the community context but conceals a fact of utmost significance for the patrolmen who work there. Each of these communities is residentially segregated; with the partial exception of Rampart, the minority and low-income populations are concentrated in specific areas of each community. One can move from the sedate, middle-class environs of West Inglewood, the Eagle Rock section of Northeast Division, and the affluent apartment dwell-

TABLE 3.2

Background Characteristics of Patrolmen

	High-crime Areas		Low-crime Areas		
	Inglewood	Rampart	Redondo Beach	Northeast	Total
ETHNICITY:					
White	89%	76%	100%	80%	86%
Black	3%	0%	0%	2%	1%
Mexican-American	3%	24%	0%	16%	11%
Other	4%	0%	0%	2%	2%
SOCIAL CLASS: [a]					
White-collar	38%	34%	38%	36%	36%
Blue-collar	62%	66%	62%	64%	64%
EDUCATION:					
Median School Yrs.	14.08	13.35	13.83	13.20	13.70
SERVED IN MILITARY:	60%	76%	74%	76%	70%
Number of Respondents	(62)	(51)	(34)	(51)	(198)

[a]Social class is measured by the respondent's father's occupation. White-collar includes: professional, managerial, sales workers, and clerical. Blue-collar includes: craftsmen, operatives, laborers, and service workers.

ers of South Redondo Beach to minority, working-class sections, where, according to patrolmen, the narcotics traffic is concentrated and fights, assaults, and robberies occur with some regularity. Patrolmen in these communities are well aware of these geographical differences. Redondo Beach patrolmen often said they disliked working the north end of town where the people were harder to deal with. Patrolmen in Inglewood regard the densely populated beats of the southeastern section of the city as the center of the city's crime problem, while Northeast Division patrolmen take a similar view of the Mexican-American community of El Sereno, south of the Pasadena Freeway. In each of these three areas, then, the extent to which there are shared values between patrolman and citizen depends on the area of the community a patrolman is working in.

Rampart, by comparison, is far more diverse than these three communities, more city than suburban. It is the most cosmopolitan of the four areas; an astounding number of ethnic groups live within the division boundaries—blacks, Mexican-Americans, Cubans, Russians, Filipinos, and Orientals. The combination of ethnic diversity and a somewhat higher concentration of poor people in Rampart means that patrolmen in this community are far less likely than patrolmen in the other communities to share a broad range of values with residents. But this difference between Rampart Division and the other areas is tempered by a pattern of residential segregation, which, if not as sharp as in the other communities, is nonetheless important.

If the differences between the high-crime and low-crime areas are distinct enough to permit a suitable comparison between different kinds of community environments, the reader should bear in mind that there are not only differences between these communities but also within them.[16]

The Beat: A View From the Patrol Car

The crime rate and demographic composition of the community portray only one side of the environment of police work. The other is the welter of perceptions and judgments of the patrolmen who work there. A patrolman learns much of what he knows about a community through the simple and obvious method of performing his task. By responding to calls for assistance, making traffic stops, arresting drunks, breaking up fights, or simply driving around and occasionally talking to people, he acquires an intimate but selective understanding of the community and its people. Experiences on the street are mulled over in the locker room or after work, and what results is a set of shared perceptions of the people, the community, and problems of concern to the police.

What a patrolman actually learns about the community he polices depends partly on the way he comes into contact with people in a community. The kind of knowledge a modern patrolman acquires is much different from that of his predecessor, the beat cop; it is, in many ways, more selective and perhaps less reliable. One patrolman, who had spent several years working as a beat cop on skid row, summed up the difference: "A cop needs information, you need to know who is good and who is bad, who are your friends and enemies. This is easier for a beat cop since he is in closer touch with the people." Regardless of whether this image of the beat cop is entirely true, the use of patrol cars places greater responsibility on the patrolman to learn about the people on his beat. Unlike the beat cop, he will not usually be stopped by people on the street, and his contact with residents, unless he takes the initiative, is fragmented and arbitrary. Modern patrolmen do not so much involve themselves with people as they observe them from a distance.

Police work is organized on a territorial basis in order to facilitate a quick and efficient response to calls for service and serious crimes. The boundaries of various beats in a professional department are based on the crime rate, work load, and geography. Patrolmen are responsible for all calls for service and all crimes in their area, though responsibility is a matter less of identification with a beat than of administrative efficiency. Knowledge of the beat may be compromised not only by departmental policies such as rotation, but by the independent actions of patrolmen. The tendency among patrolmen, particularly those that are highly aggressive, is to move around in order to be where the action is. Once they assign a man to a beat, police administrators are faced with the difficulty of keeping him there.

If the patrolmen in each of these communities tend to identify the same kinds of crimes—notably narcotics, burglary, and robbery—as serious problems confronting their departments, there are nevertheless important differences in the view that patrolmen take of each community and its problems. Patrolmen in the LAPD were observed to be the most detached about the communities they police, while those in Redondo Beach and Inglewood registered varying degrees of affection and disaffection.

Of all the patrolmen I observed, those in Redondo Beach displayed the most tangible sense of identification with the community in which they worked. If some patrolmen often voiced a feeling that the department should be doing more about burglary, narcotics, and traffic violations, no one believed the city confronted an insurmountable crime problem. Most lived in or near Redondo Beach, and regarded it as a pleasant community in which to live and work.

The police in Inglewood, by contrast, believe the city is under siege. They regard themselves at war, involved in an ultimately futile effort to stem the decline of a slowly sinking city. The increase in crime and what most policemen view as a more general deterioration of the city is attributed, more or less explicitly, to the movement of blacks into the city. While they do not make a point of it with every visitor, the Inglewood police are not reluctant to voice their feelings about blacks. One patrolman thought that the problems really began after the upheaval in Watts in 1965 when people presumably began to listen to the voices in the black community. Others are more straightforward, and suggest that blacks are not only inferior but prone to crime.

There is an ambivalence among Inglewood policemen. A deep-seated disaffection with the community is characteristic of most of them. Many Inglewood policemen once lived within the city boundaries, and have now moved to the suburbs; forty- and fifty-mile commutes were not uncommon at the time of the study. Yet these same policemen also point out that Inglewood is a good place to be if one likes action. A number of patrolmen told the author they chose to come to Inglewood because of the crime problem; they wanted to work in a city where there was some excitement and where police work involved more than the usual, mundane service chores. Thus, the frustration the police feel in Inglewood at being unable to cope with a rising crime rate is overlaid with an acute sense of disaffection. Consequently, many policemen have broken whatever ties they had with the community, and now look on the city as a place for some action and a chance to get the experience required to move elsewhere.

Unlike the extremes of affection or disaffection one finds in Redondo Beach and Inglewood, there is almost a cold-blooded detachment about policemen in the LAPD. Patrolmen in Northeast Division often voiced similar opinions to those in Inglewood: they believe the area is becoming "ghettoized", that it is slowly but surely deteriorating. This development is attributed largely to the migration of many Mexican-American families to the areas north of the Pasadena Freeway. But even if Northeast has its problems, and it is those patrolmen who grew up in the area who are most inclined to be despondent about the trends, most patrolmen see it as a rather slow and relaxed area to work in. It combines, they feel, some interesting crime problems with a slower pace; an officer can hustle or take it easy.

Patrolmen in Rampart exhibit a similar sense of detachment. The social diversity of the area is one of the central attractions for patrolmen working in Rampart. Known as a good division to get "street experience," it's fast enough to be interesting but not overwhelming. Patrolmen in Rampart are concerned about crime and the human maladies they deal with, but this is the concern of veterans, of men who have seen this before and will do what they can, but are not overly sanguine about the results. Unlike the police in Inglewood, there is no sense that the world is coming apart at the seams. There is little affection for the residents and their stake in the area; it is simply a good division to work in, especially if one is ambitious.

For the patrolman, the community presents a mosaic of dilemmas, opportunities, and limits that he must confront in carrying out his responsibilities and wielding his powers of discretion. How he meets these responsibilities depends on his relationship to the community, a relationship that is contingent on the autonomy of the department, the characteristics of the community he works, and his own judgments of what are the significant problems and opportunities. In all three of these communities there is a notable and enduring separation between policemen and community. Each department has a measure of autonomy from the community, though the LAPD is clearly better able to fulfill a professional role than either of the small departments. It is also apparent that there are significant differences between the values and outlook of the majority of policemen and those of specific groups in the community, namely, blacks and Mexican-Americans. But nobody in any of these communities was observed to be especially hostile toward the police. The most overt conflict between police and community is present in Inglewood, but this is due as much as anything else to the political sophistication of the black community and the frustration of the police. A similar split is observable in Rampart, especially in the poor sections, but it is muted because of the large number of illegal aliens in the area. Finally, while all of the patrolmen tend to emphasize the same problems, these problems are viewed differently in each area and considered to have different import.

Police professionalism enjoins the patrolman to act as an autonomous professional, to judge the needs of the community and his appropriate responses in light of an internally derived set of standards. The separation between policeman and community characteristic of these cities ensures that it is the operative values and beliefs of working policemen that will count in the exercise of discretion. But the patrolman does not confront the community as a completely autonomous professional; he is also a bureaucrat. I turn now to a consideration of the consequences of this for his behavior.

Chapter 4

The Police Task
and Organization

The right to discipline carries with it the power to control the conduct, actions and attitudes of the employees of an organization. When the right to discipline is vested with management, management has the essential tool with which to attain desired behavior from employees. . . . When employees are subject to disciplinary action from outside the organization, a fundamental rule of organization has been breached and the employee becomes confused, diffident, and inefficient.

Edward M. Davis

I'm getting jabbed in the ass by the public and jabbed in the ass by the department.

A frustrated patrolman

THE POLICE are often regarded as the epitome of the highly professional and bureaucratic agencies that are the legacy of municipal reform. Police departments are typically described as quasi-military organizations in which command and control is centralized, and administrators emphasize the legitimacy of hierarchical authority and rigid adherence to impersonal rules and regulations. Yet, it is also acknowledged that policemen wield broad powers of discretion and have substantial autonomy in carrying out their task. This paradox is rarely admitted, much less explained, by most observers of the police. The explanation lies in the structure of professional police departments, which is based on two distinct systems of internal control. One is bureaucratic, based on a system of hierarchical authority and impersonal rules; the other derives from the police culture and is based on a system of peer group controls. The coexistence of these two systems of internal control has led to an illusory centralization of power and authority while retaining a radical decentralization of the key decision-making powers within a police department, the exercise of discretion by patrolmen. Though these two systems of internal control overlap to some degree, they are a continuing source of conflict and tension within a police department. This conflict has important implications for the ways in which patrolmen use their power of discretion and for the ability of police administrators to control the actions of patrolmen. The roots and consequences of this conflict are the subject of this chapter.

Uncertainties of Police Work: The Development of an Occupational Culture

The function of the police is to regulate social behavior among the members of society in the interests of protecting life and property and preserving order, a role that entails the selective (or discretionary) use of coercive powers of arrest and force. The routine use of coercion sets policemen off from society. Often poised at the center of class and group conflict in a community, the police operate amidst deeply-rooted political conflicts. Not only are they frequently at odds with different groups, but policemen must continually balance ends and means as they grapple with intractable moral dilemmas. Moreover, because the police proceed forcibly, even belligerently, against perpetrators of crime, they frequently peel away layers of appearance and deceit from suspects and victims. Invariably, their actions are seen as offensive and unjust; and sometimes they are. Thus, if the police inspire admiration and even respect on occasion, they also bring forth fear, loathing, and resentment. Neither policemen nor citizens are likely to forget that the police are ultimately adversaries, the fire necessary to fight fire, the men delegated to perform some of a community's most obnoxious tasks.[1]

The pressures endemic to their coercive role converge to create an enduring bond of solidarity among the men who work the street, a bond that is reinforced by the necessity of working under conditions of great uncertainty and ambiguity. There are four additional characteristics of the police task, largely unmodified by the drive toward police professionalism, that serve to increase the uncertainty and ambiguity of working the street. One source of uncertainty stems from the ambiguity surrounding the identity of the clients of a police department. The putative clients of the police are the residents of the community they police. O. W. Wilson once suggested that the patrolman "must patrol his beat [and] be alert for conditions that may jeopardize the comfort, safety, and welfare of the people; and take action to correct improper conditions."[2] But what does this mean for a patrolman on a day-to-day basis? Who are the people whose comfort, safety, and welfare may be jeopardized by improper conditions? The answer to this question may be obvious when enforcing traffic laws; it is far less clear when mediating a family dispute or enforcing vice laws. These ambiguities are magnified where the proactive side of police work is concerned. In making frequent stops of individuals for purposes of investigation, it is not at all clear whose interests are being served. Thus, the determination of who the victim is and who the police end up serving, is a matter of some ambiguity and subject to a great deal of discretion. Under these circumstances, there is a tendency for the police to become their own clients, to define the moral standards attendant to law enforcement in light of their own values—a tendency enhanced by police professionalism.[3]

If the use of coercion is central to police work, the ever present reality of unpredictable violence is its counterpart. The actual threat of danger may be no greater than that in some other occupations, but its presence is a constant reminder of the coercive aspects of the police role: the thought that violence (or the threat of it) often begets violence. No one can observe patrolmen without appreciating their preoccupation with violence and their own safety. Most officers are aware that the chances they will confront a life and death situation is slight, but the possibility that they will is always there, and it is something most think they cannot afford to forget.

The depth of a patrolman's preoccupation with danger depends on its unpredictability. In "hot calls," where a patrolman rushes to the scene of a robbery with some certainty that the suspect is on the premises and armed, and in family disputes, a patrolman knows that violence is a distinct possibility. More uncertain are those innocuous situations, a traffic stop for instance, which make up much of the everyday activity of police work but which can explode in a patrolman's face. The expectation that violence will occur varies with the context of police work. Most policemen anticipate it as a matter of course in high-crime neighborhoods.[4] It is also related to the character of political conflict in a society. In the context of rising political extremism and polarization, such as the strife that accompanied America's involvement in Vietnam and the civil-rights struggles, the threat of danger assumes a new dimension: violence is no longer entirely contingent on the socioeconomic characteristics of a particular community, and therefore somewhat predictable; it is perforce more unpredictable and patrolmen are more inclined to approach any situation expecting violence.

Police work is a craft, and it relies heavily upon experience and intuition. The elements of this craft—the kind of information a patrolman relies upon and the strategies used to work the street and control people—are another source of uncertainty. Since many crimes occur in private, or at least out of sight of the police, and information as to the identity of the suspect is often sketchy and fragmentary, patrolmen face continuing difficulties in acquiring reliable information about the occurrence of crimes and the identity of those who commit them. In the absence of such information, working patrolmen must fall back on the most superficial and ambiguous of indicators: appearance, stereotypes, and the like. This invariably has its hazards.

A patrolman can never completely rely upon the legitimacy of his authority to obtain compliance; citizens can and will resist even the most innocuous of requests. A street cop cannot resort to an arrest every time someone questions his authority, though there are clearly those who believe they can. Patrolmen are thus confronted with the necessity of developing and relying upon crude but sometimes effective strategies to gain compliance. As one street-wise patrolman explained, a cop has to learn how to deal with people on the street. He has to know, "when to be firm, when not to be firm, when to take action, when not to take action; when to con people and act a little, and when not to. . . ." There is no unanimity among patrolmen about the best way to gain compliance; the only cardinal rule is that one must never lose control. As one officer bluntly stated, "we're not paid to lose." Patrolmen resort to a variety of strategies to gain compliance, but whatever the strategy they adopt they can never be entirely sure that it will work or that they will come out unscathed.[5]

Finally, a patrolman must routinely reconcile ambiguous and conflicting objectives. The conflicting moral choices patrolmen are called on to make derive from deeply rooted conflicts over the use of police power within American society. These conflicts are not resolved by administrators with neatly worded policies or even helped much by way of guidance from supervisors. Not only do patrolmen face the uncertainty that attends the resolution of any moral choice; they are never entirely sure how their decisions will be evaluated by police administrators.

It is one of the ironies of reform that police professionalism has accentuated the contradiction between ends and means that is at the heart of police work. The police have assumed the responsibility for using their coercive powers to eradicate crime, but as professionals they are expected to do so while upholding constitutional standards of due process. Even though the police often conclude that order is the higher value, professionalism makes it less easy to assert that people have forfeited their constitutional rights by committing a crime. The importance placed on the means policemen use to carry out their functions extends to the enforcement of minor violations and other facets of police work. If a citizen has violated a speeding law, he should be given a ticket but he should also leave with a smile on his face. The same applies to the peacekeeping duties of the police. Despite the reality that it is not always clear who caused a dispute, what legal statutes apply, or what can be done to resolve it, a patrolman will be expected to handle disputes in a way that precludes a complaint about his behavior.

By ignoring the reality of discretion professionalism also leads to a conflict between the need to enforce the law and treat citizens fairly and impersonally and the necessity of tempering decisions to the realities of the street. Administrators may believe that a patrolman should consider the unique aspects of an encounter, but he is still told to be fair and impersonal. What impartiality means in this context is rather ambiguous. When should a patrolman make an exception and consider the mitigating circumstances of a situation? Is justice always served by the impersonal but strict enforcement of the law? Whatever the answers are in the abstract, it is patrolmen who must grapple with these issues.

Given these ambiguities, it is not at all clear on what basis a patrolman's performance should be evaluated. Should a patrolman be judged by his ability to control crime (however that is measured), or the extent to which he upholds the Bill of Rights and maintains public confidence? But what does it mean to maintain the confidence and good will of the public if any action can potentially be judged as unjust or as harassment? Is a good patrolman one who dispassionately makes an arrest or issues a citation every time a violation has been committed? Or is he the officer who considers mitigating circumstances and sometimes ignores violations? Or failing to come to terms with these questions, should a patrolman be judged on a more mundane basis such as the extent to which he obeys organizational rules and meets preestablished production quotas? These ambiguities are exacerbated by the inability of administrators to precisely measure objectives and to directly assess the actions of patrolmen. They must inevitably rely upon very rough judgments about an officer's performance.

The centrality of coercion to the police role and the uncertainties of police work—the ambiguities over the clientele of the police, the presence of danger, the inadequacy of information on which to base decisions, the difficulties of obtaining compliance, and the necessity of reconciling contradictory moral and political imperatives—generate enormous anxiety and emotional stress for patrolmen. The various uncertainties of police work are interdependent and the effect ultimately cumulative; they lead to a series of recurring moral dilemmas which frequently admit to no satisfactory solution and to which every patrolman must adapt. In attempting to cope with these dilemmas a patrolman is invariably caught in the middle: he faces the uncertainties of the street as well as the uncertain reaction of watchful administrators. There is no way to escape the recurring stress and anxiety of police work, unless a patrolman chooses to avoid his responsibilities altogether.

Every encounter on the street is potentially laden with uncertainties, and in seeking to cope with them, patrolmen are often motivated by nothing more than the sheer need for survival. Yet in attempting to deal with the uncertainties of police work it is often the case that error compounds error. This is nowhere more apparent than when a patrolman faces a choice between protecting the indiscretion of a fellow officer or permitting administrators to hold the man accountable. After stopping two young Mexican-Americans, a couple of patrolmen arrested one of them on a traffic warrant. At the jail, though, the two patrolmen discovered that a mistake had been made: the young man did not fit the description of the man wanted for the warrant; all they had in common was the same name. The patrolmen offered to drive the young Mexican-American back to the spot where he had been originally stopped, but he refused, asserting that this was the fourth time he had been arrested on that particular warrant. Before releasing him, one of the patrolmen asked him to sign a statement to the effect that he had refused a ride back; the youth refused, and then the officer said he would have to return to the jail and refuse in front of a supervisor. At this point, with the handcuffs half off, the youth, out of fear and perhaps desperation, lurched toward the street. Almost simultaneously, the patrolman unlocking the handcuffs put him in a choke hold and choked him unconscious.

The sergeant in charge of the jail that night was summoned and informed of what had happened, though the patrolmen in their account altered the course of events slightly. The youth, they told the sergeant, was choked unconscious because it appeared he was going to strike one of them. One of the patrolmen suggested that perhaps they ought to consider arresting the young man for interfering with an officer. Looking like he had heard all this before, the sergeant replied they had made a mistake and should have released the youth regardless of whether he signed the statement. The patrolmen argued that they risked a personnel complaint if they let the man go without signing, but the sergeant insisted that they had made matters worse and, in fact, had no authority to order him to do anything once the initial mistake had been acknowledged. The sergeant went on to say that he was going to put the incident in his log and if a complaint was filed it would be investigated (though the sergeant attempted to persuade the young Mexican-American that it was all an innocent mistake). Exasperated with the sergeant's action, one of the patrolmen told him, "I'm getting jabbed in the ass by the public and jabbed in the ass by the department. . . ." The sergeant's somewhat fatalistic response was that every working policeman will inevitably get a "few beefs in his personnel package."

Though the two patrolmen overreacted and were guilty at the very least of excessive force, it was an honest mistake. More important, their action, facilitated partly by the fact that the youth was Mexican-American, was motivated by the rather uncomplicated need to "protect their ass," as they put it. One of them said later that he had been involved in a similar incident previously and had released the individual at the station, only to be the subject of a complaint later. These two patrolmen trusted neither citizens nor their supervisors, though both agreed that in this instance they had been unfortunate enough to have had to report the incident to a sergeant known for going by the book. Another sergeant might have handled it differently. But the significance of this incident is that the brutal treatment of the youth and the subsequent lie were motivated by two concerns: fear of what an innocent but angry young man might do and the potentially vindictive response of the department. In the crunch, these two patrolmen acted as if they could depend on nobody but themselves.

Faced with the manifold uncertainties of police work and the attendant moral dilemmas, patrolmen survive in the only way practicable: by relying upon one another. The ambiguities of police work thus lead to a bond of solidarity among patrolmen, a bond which is the basis of the police culture. One side of the police culture, a side which has perhaps been overly stressed, is that of policemen as pariahs, men who regard the public as hostile, fickle, and not to be trusted. But there is another, equally important, side to the police culture, and that is the solidarity among men of violence, a bond which permits fallible men to perform an arduous and difficult task, and which places the highest value upon the obligation to back up and support a fellow officer.

The police culture arises not just to cope with the vicissitudes of a hostile public, as Westley suggested, but also to meet the recurring anxiety and emotional stress that are part of police work. One of the functions of the police culture is to encourage decisiveness in the face of uncertainty. Patrolmen must be able to make judgments of extreme importance in emotionally laden circumstances, judgments which may be wrong, and even if they are not, may be criticized. The wherewithal to encounter continually the moral dilemmas of police work, to endure the frustrations and the sense of estrangement, and to still take action, depends upon the mutual obligations and solidarity that underpin the police culture.[6]

The police culture also serves to convey honor. Honor depends, as Hans Speier once observed, upon an awareness of the claim to honor and the willingness to pay it.[7] The circle of individuals both aware of and willing to meet the claim of honor for patrolmen is distinctly limited. Most patrolmen do not expect to be honored by either the public or the department. Patrol, as two officers observed, is the bottom of the heap: "You take all the crap, you are not trusted, you are expected to behave like a robot and never make mistakes. . . ." The circle of those aware of and willing to pay honor to patrolmen is all too often limited to their peers.

Loyalty is thus one of the core values of the police culture. As one patrolman expressed the matter, "I'm for the guys in blue! Anybody criticizes a fellow copper that's like criticizing someone in my family; we have to stick together." The police culture demands of a patrolman unstinting loyalty to his fellow officers, and he receives, in return, protection and honor: a place to assuage real and imagined wrongs inflicted by a (presumably) hostile public; safety from aggressive administrators and supervisors; and the emotional support required to perform a difficult task. The most important question asked by patrolmen about a rookie is whether or not he displays the loyalty demanded by the police culture.[8]

What does the obligation of loyalty mean to a working patrolman? In one sense, it denotes dependability, the willingness of an officer to do his share of work and not to stretch out (crime) report calls or other mundane tasks so that the burden of work falls on other officers. More significantly, the obligation for loyalty is a demand to defend, back up, and assist one's peers. An "officer needs help" call will bring all available patrolmen to the scene as back-up units. But there is a third meaning of loyalty, namely, the obligation to provide protection. The demand for protection is typified by the bond that exists between partners, a bond which is based on the norm of secrecy, the acceptance of the dictum that "whatever goes down in the car, stays in the car." Or as two patrolmen expressed it, "He'll lie for me and I'll swear to it." It was the force of this obligation that governed the behavior of the two officers who choked the Mexican-American youth and served to rationalize the fiction that the youth was preparing to strike one of them.

The survey data provide some insight into the extent to which the norm of loyalty is accepted among patrolmen. Eighty-three percent of the patrolmen interviewed in Redondo Beach, Inglewood and the two divisions of the LAPD agreed with the statement, "The most important obligation that a patrolman has is to back up and support his fellow officers" (there are no significant differences between the departments). Less striking but nonetheless important, 50 percent of the respondents said the only person they could trust and depend on in the case of a problem related to work was a fellow patrolman.[9] The responses to both questions, in turn, are highly related to the belief that aggressive and often illegal tactics are necessary to maintain order and that due process must occasionally be sacrificed if those who break the law are to be apprehended. Patrolmen believe the obligation to protect one another is necessary to meet the contradictory demands they confront and to cope with the unpredictability of the street. But whatever the justification in their minds, the bond of loyalty is regularly invoked to cover serious mistakes and misbehavior.

The effort to professionalize the police has not modified the value of loyalty or the penchant for secrecy and the willingness of patrolmen to cover the misbehavior of a fellow "copper." Patrolmen may be somewhat less likely to perjure themselves in order to cover the actions of a peer, though we really do not know for sure. More likely what has changed is the kind of behavior policemen will tolerate among their peers. Even so, the force of the norm of loyalty is such that it precludes all but limited external controls over the behavior of the police. The failure of civilian review boards and the courts to adequately control police behavior can be partly traced to the demand by the police culture for loyalty.[10]

The other core value of the police culture is individualism. The value placed on individualism is partly a manifestation of the adherence among patrolmen to the ideal of the inner-directed, aggressive street cop. But individualism also legitimizes the autonomy of patrolmen and thus is the essential counterpart to the value of loyalty.

Policemen are oriented toward action; the world is a place in which problems are solved by acting pragmatically and resourcefully. The inner-directed, aggressive policeman thrives on the chase, those instances in which it is clear where everyone stands, and the job is simply that of catching the bad guys. Far from being plodding subprofessionals, as the police have sometimes been characterized, they are calculating, manipulative men for whom the real lure of police work is the excitement. Policemen are not danger lovers but neither do they crave security; rather, they seek the awesome and unpredictable in a society where most men are reduced to the routine of the assembly line or paper-shuffling in a large bureaucracy.[11] No matter how dull or routine the job may seem at times, there is always the possibility that something will happen, that a robbery or burglary will take place. Joseph Wambaugh has captured this feeling better than anyone I know:

> Hollywood Division was a good place for police work. It was busy and exciting in the way that is unique to police experience—the unpredictable lurked. Ian Campbell believed that what most policemen shared was an abhorrence of the predictable, a distaste for the foreseeable experiences of working life. . . . No, policemen [were] not danger lovers, they were seekers of the awesome, the incredible, even the unspeakable in human experience. Never mind whether they could interpret, never mind if it was potentially hazardous to the soul. *To be there* was the thing.[12]

This feeling about police work is one that was expressed over and over in interviews and during the field observations. It contrasts sharply with the image of men motivated by the need for a secure job choosing police work as their profession. Doubtless some do prefer the security of the police occupation, but security is just as easily obtainable in other civil service positions. The recurrent impression obtained from talking with numerous patrolmen is that a good many of them left secure and well-paying white-collar jobs for the unpredictability of the street.[13]

The inner-directed policeman is a crime fighter; he values a "good pinch" and police work is viewed as a game of cops and robbers. Those situations that involve "real police work" are actively sought, for they allow a policeman to discharge his energy and validate the role of crime fighter. Skulking through alleys and back streets looking for miscreants and constantly monitoring the radio for the all too infrequent "hot calls" are the palpable manifestations of this role. A call that an armed robbery or burglary is in progress brings not just the assigned patrol car but any unit that is not otherwise occupied and can make it to the location in time. One night in Rampart, a call from the dispatcher that a fight was taking place between an unknown number of persons brought six patrol cars to the scene. But when it was discovered that the "fight" was a drunk who had passed out in an alley, responsibility was quickly turned over to the assigned unit.[14]

If the ideal of police work is the inner-directed crime fighter, the police culture does not require that every officer live up to this standard or work the street in precisely the same way. The values of the police culture derive from the hazards of police work and seek to minimize these hazards and protect group members. As long as a patrolmen accepts these norms and meets his mutual obligations to the group, he is free to use his powers of discretion as he sees fit. The same beliefs that lead policemen to attempt to minimize external control over their actions, operate within police departments to minimize second-guessing and allow each officer to exercise his independent judgment in each situation. Loyalty and individualism are thus opposite sides of the same coin: the police culture demands loyalty but grants autonomy.[15]

The connection between loyalty and individualism is most apparent in the relationship between partners. If loyalty means anything it means an obligation to the patrolman one works with. Besides the mutual obligation to back one another up, the relationship between partners is characterized by deference and reciprocity. Most situations can be acceptably handled in a number of different ways, and if a patrolman chooses to ignore a violation, his partner will normally acquiesce. Alternatively, if a patrolman decides to make an especially "shaky" arrest, his partner will probably go along (patrolmen who sharply disagree about how to enforce the law simply do not work together if they can help it). If the patrolman in charge (usually the driver takes charge) decides not to take action, he usually gives his partner the option of making an arrest. In those situations where there is a difference of opinion, the disagreement is often resolved in favor of making an arrest. Whatever the decision, the inclination is to defend it in any way possible; if an officer makes a particularly bad decision, he may receive some ribbing about it but it will be defended by his peers.

Two patrolmen responded to a disturbance call in an apartment building. The incident involved a minor dispute between a landlord and her tenant, who was quite drunk. The man lived on the third floor of the building; he had evidently lived there for several years, but he had a habit of losing the key to his apartment. What precipitated the dispute was the loss of the key again. The man wanted her to open his room with a pass key but she denied she had a key and refused to open the room. There matters stood when the police arrived. After listening to the landlord's story, one of the patrolmen decided that since the man could not get into his room and he was in the hallway of the apartment building which was, strictly speaking, a "public place," he would arrest him for being drunk. His partner acquiesced in the decision but took the trouble to point out that it was a "chicken-shit" arrest. In discussing this incident later on, however, this officer vigorously defended the arrest as necessary to prevent further trouble.

One key consequence of the autonomy legitimized by the norm of individualism is to foster the development of different styles of police work. Patrolmen establish their own priorities and adapt their work habits to these. For some this may mean a tendency to enforce "all" the laws, while for others it means a pattern of selective enforcement. There are also variations in the aggressiveness of patrolmen and different degrees of attachment to the service role of the police. The norm of individualism allows each patrolman to pick and choose as opportunities arise. Patrolmen as they ply their craft on the street are far more different from one another than many observers of the police have cared to indicate.

There is fairly strong evidence that patrolmen are rather individualistic. Not only were patrolmen *observed* to adopt rather different approaches to police work, but in response to the statement, "One of the most important unwritten rules among patrolmen is that each officer should be allowed to make his own decisions and enforce the law as he sees fit," 49 percent agreed and 49 percent disagreed. The preference for individualism is much stronger in the two small departments: 68 percent of the patrolmen in Redondo Beach and 55 percent in Inglewood agreed with the statement compared to 38 percent in the two divisions of LAPD. LAPD does have a reputation of "going by the book," and while I would not want to minimize the importance of these responses, they are partly contradicted by the field observations. Greater independence among patrolmen was observed in LAPD than in the small departments. Yet there was greater unanimity of opinion in LAPD about the way some incidents should be handled; in particular, patrolmen in LAPD are more inclined to say that in most cases an arrest should be made. I will return to the matter of these differences between the departments; the important point here is that in all three departments, a rather large percentage of patrolmen accept the legitimacy of the norm of individualism in the enforcement of the law.

The significance of the norms of loyalty and individualism for police discretion is that they serve to decentralize decision making radically within a police department. These norms not only grant patrolmen the freedom to fashion distinctive approaches to police work and to handle their job as they see fit. They severely limit the impact of hierarchical controls within a police department.

Police Bureaucracies: The Illusion of Centralization

Many observers of the police are fond of citing the quasi-military characteristics of police bureaucracies as the most notable feature of contemporary departments, and police administrators frequently attest to the superiority of this form of organization. Yet the analogy between police departments and the military, despite its appeal, is quite misleading. A quasi-military structure is not really suited to the requirements of the police task nor is it completely descriptive of the actual structure of a police department. Police work is organized in such a way that men working alone or in pairs carry out most tasks of the organization, and only rarely are they required to function as an organized unit—for example during a public disorder. Nor has specialization, which is characteristic of professional police departments, greatly altered the structure of police departments. Investigative units such as detectives, vice squads, and traffic and juvenile bureaus have been organized to handle specialized problems, but the bulk of police activity is still the result of the decisions and actions of patrolmen. The patrol division of any police department operates as a more or less autonomous subsystem within the police bureaucracy, with communications routed directly to patrolmen. These communications can be monitored from time to time by supervisors but they normally are not.

What is often considered distinctive about the quasi-military police bureaucracies (or any rational-legal bureaucracy) is the emphasis on command and control. While police administrators do exhibit a preoccupation with command and control—in fact one observer has characterized police departments as "punishment-centered bureaucracies"—the actual structure of the control system is far more complex than normally imagined. The emphasis on a quasi-military form of discipline in police departments must be considered in light of its historical roots. One of the reasons the military was turned to as a model for the police was that it appeared to provide for a system of control and discipline that would eliminate the most egregious abuses of authority and the misbehavior of the men then engaged in police work.[16] The professionalization of police departments has strengthened the concern for discipline without greatly altering the matters that will move a sergeant to reprimand a patrolman. The focus of bureaucratic rules and regulations in a police department and the preoccupation of supervisors is with corruption, drinking and sleeping on duty, marital infidelity, the destruction and abuse of city property, an officer's appearance, and the like. In fact, supervisors are more concerned with the enforcement of minor rules and regulations than with a man's conduct on the street—though most supervisors maintain that serious misconduct simply occurs less often than violations of trivial rules.

A similar emphasis on obedience is apparent in the formal training programs of the police. Police training programs are ostensibly designed to acquaint rookies with the criminal law and departmental rules, and to develop competence in certain basic, required skills such as shooting, self-defense, and driving; but more important than these is the attempt to adjust recruits to the discipline of the organization. Arthur Neiderhoffer, a policeman turned scholar, has argued that the defining characteristic of recruit training is that it is a total and inclusive process which seeks to strip away the recruit's previous identity and values and replace them with those appropriate to the police role. Other accounts of recruit training also note the preoccupation with discipline and obedience.[17]

The preoccupation with discipline is not completely the result of a penchant for obedience among police administrators. The emphasis on discipline—the concern for obedience to trivial rules and the punitive character of supervision—is partly due to the difficulties of closely supervising men who work alone and the inability of police administrators to specify, through policy guidelines, how a patrolman should behave in various kinds of circumstances. Discipline, in the tradition of the military, can be and is viewed as a substitute for the formulation of policy. Simply put, an officer who violates petty rules—who does not shine his shoes, does not keep his hair and sideburns cut to regulation length, writes unreadable reports, and is usually three or four minutes late to work—is presumed to be an officer who cannot wield his powers of discretion in a responsible fashion. Well-chosen, well-trained, and well-disciplined men obviate the need for explicit guidelines for the use of police power.

This is not to say that police administrators and field supervisors do not have ideas about what kinds of decisions patrolmen should make. They do. But these are typically vague admonitions to serve broader goals: an arrest is the best deterrent to future misbehavior; the laws should be enforced equally and impersonally; the use of profanity and insults is not a permissible means to convince a victim or suspect of the correctness of one's point; and so forth. Such exhortations are typically supplemented by impersonal measures of performance— arrest and citation rates, daily work records—but the import of these controls is less to regulate police discretion than to insure that patrolmen are working. Most of the formal administrative controls within a police department have very little to do with discretion. Hierarchical controls within police departments are largely negative, they limit rather than direct the action of patrolmen. Thus, hierarchical controls set only the outer limits to the use of police power, while the day-to-day process of decision making is played out free of restraint. The question is, Why?

The limited impact of hierarchical controls and even the sheer punitiveness cannot be fully explained by the difficulty administrators face in attempting to frame rules and policies to structure discretion. The important fact is that police administrators are really capable of controlling only the more trivial and mundane aspects of a patrolman's behavior. The reason lies in the systemic limits to hierarchical controls in a professional police department.

The systemic limits to hierarchical controls derive from two sources. First, the demand for loyalty and solidarity leads to the formation of a set of normative limitations on hierarchical controls. The pressures for loyalty and solidarity are refracted throughout the police bureaucracy; the same norms which serve to limit public scrutiny of the police are turned inward toward police administrators. One of the strongest norms in a police department is the norm which precludes "second-guessing" another officer's decision. The belief is that the officer on the scene alone knows the complexity of the situation and is in the best position to make the decision.[18] The animosity that some patrolmen display toward a supervisor who attempts to monitor closely their actions and the reluctance of many supervisors to interfere with patrolmen stem largely from the force of this norm. A good supervisor, many patrolmen believe, is one who keeps his distance. (When asked what he would do if a supervisor told him to handle a particular situation differently, one patrolman said that he would listen patiently and agree, but when he was alone he would do things his own way.)

Second, patrolmen are able to acquire considerable power within a police department, and this reinforces the normative limits to hierarchical controls while further limiting the ability of administrators to control the decisions of patrolmen. Power within an organization is related to the predictability of behavior. It accrues to those individuals and groups whose behavior cannot be predicted; whose behavior, by virtue of their function or expertise, cannot be completely stabilized through rules or a rationalized technological process. Power is thus intimately related to the routinization of activities within an organization. If an activity or process in an organization cannot be routinized and therefore brought under the purview of administrative controls, and if it is important to the continued success of the organization, those groups or individuals who control the outcome of that process can obtain power.[19]

Given the intrinsic uncertainties of police work, administrators are dependent on patrolmen to perform their job in a reasonably satisfactory way; to make arrests, control crime, and handle calls for service in a way that does not provoke the community (or specific groups) to hostility, thereby eroding the department's legitimacy. Such dependence provides the wherewithal for patrolmen to acquire and wield organizational power. The use of either excessive ticketing or a complete slowdown of police activity as a lever in wage negotiations with municipal governments in recent years amply testifies to the power patrolmen can wield if they so desire.

The relationship between patrolmen and administrators is characterized less by stringent control over discretion than by a continuous struggle over the prerogatives and autonomy of patrolmen. The acceptance of hierarchical authority and compliance to rules by patrolmen is contingent upon the belief that supervisors and administrators will defend them and grant them sufficient leeway to do their job as they see fit. A supervisor who attempts to directly control discretion in ways that counter deeply held beliefs and values is subject to the charge of not "backing up the men." On the other hand, administrators are sensitive to the vicissitudes of public opinion, especially where nonprofessional behavior, such as rudeness, is concerned. Yet because of demands for group solidarity and loyalty (demands which are magnified under intensive public criticism), and their dependence on the actions of patrolmen, the ability of administrators and supervisors to control an officer's behavior is sharply curtailed.

Police administrators and supervisors are caught between demands for loyalty to the men on the street and demands from the public that police power be used in a specific way or even curtailed. This dilemma is at the heart of a supervisor's relationship to the men under him. After reciting the usual litany of recently committed crimes and descriptions of "hot cars," a sergeant rose during the daily briefing to discuss the matter of personnel complaints in the department. He began by noting that the number of personnel complaints was on the rise, and that the previous night all five sergeants were busy investigating complaints filed by citizens. Warming up to his audience, the sergeant momentarily digressed to suggest that perhaps the rise in personnel complaints was part of a radical conspiracy to harass the police. He went on to point out that in any event 99 percent of all personnel complaints are false. But, if charges of brutality, hitting, and kicking were always false, charges of "bad-mouthing" citizens were often true. Verbal harassment of citizens, the sergeant declared, was a major problem in the department and it had to stop. This provoked chuckles from some patrolmen and led one young policeman to exclaim, "But sergeant, what constitutes bad mouthing an asshole?" With a reddened face, the sergeant weakly replied that it was against department rules to bad mouth an asshole. He then turned to a discussion of the possibilities of suing people who abuse policemen; it was, needless to add, much better received.

While conflict between patrolmen and field supervisors is always present, the authority of field supervisors is subtly corrupted. Field supervisors may be part of management and thus obligated to assert organizational authority, but their working relationships with patrolmen strengthen their identification with the difficulties cops on the street face and their sensitivity to the pervasive demand for loyalty and protection. Professional departments have tried to cope with the difficulties of internal control by circumventing them; they have resorted to the creation of special units (internal affairs) devoted to investigating and prosecuting misconduct. Although these units are more isolated from patrolmen and hence less susceptible to the pressures of the police culture, they are not entirely immune from the conflict between the police culture and police professionalism. Patrolmen may derisively refer to the men in internal affairs as "headhunters," but the fact remains that such units are typically more successful in ferreting out corruption and dispensing punishments for violations of minor rules than in controlling egregious offenses such as brutality. Complaints originating within a department, usually for intoxication, insubordination, and like offenses, are far more likely to be sustained than complaints originating with citizens. And the punishment for a trivial offense is often severe, while that for misconduct on the street is less so.[20] Internal affairs, then, operates within the context of the pressures and conflicts characteristic of administrative control within police departments, not apart from them.

A professional police department is thus an admixture of two distinct systems of internal control. One, reflecting the uncertainties of police work and the consequent police culture, is based on the regulation of behavior through adherence to group norms, and idealizes individualism, the "good pinch," and the shared loyalty among men performing a dangerous task. The other, reflecting the impact of police reform, is bureaucratic, and demands conformity to trivial rules while asking policemen to serve contradictory objectives. The structural combination of these two systems of control represents a compromise between police professionalism and the police culture, and leads to a bifurcated system of internal control. If these two systems of internal control can (and do) come into conflict with one another, they coexist because they are directed at different aspects of police behavior. Hierarchical controls are directed toward the extrinsic requirements of police work, those indulgent behaviors believed to detract from the professionalism and image of the department, and from the more mundane aspects of job-related behavior. The group controls, on the other hand, are directed at those behaviors of immediate concern to the performance of the police task—those pertaining to the exercise of discretion. The compromise between police professionalism and the police culture substitutes spit and polish for effective control of police discretion.

The Structural Contradictions of Police Bureaucracies

The ever present conflict between the values of the police culture and the need to maintain strict hierarchical control demanded by the values of police professionalism is the root of significant tensions and conflicts within police bureaucracies. Even though the police culture acts to minimize the impact of administrative controls, counter pressures exist that maintain the need to impose such controls. The excessively rigid and punitive system of hierarchical controls that develops in police departments flows from the combined effects of police professionalism and public pressure. Police professionalism, as I have said, has heightened the conflict between means and ends that is intrinsic to police work. Administrators cope with the dilemma between the demand to live up to the normative requirements of professionalism and the demand for loyalty by emphasizing discipline and obedience to organizational rules. This preoccupation with discipline is augmented by external pressure. Hierarchical controls are viewed as an alternative to external, that is public, controls over police behavior. As long as the police are not subjected to extreme criticism and public demands to control patrolmen, the bureaucratic and group controls can coexist without detrimental consequences. But, given the coercive role of the police, this is not always possible, and these two systems of control will come into conflict—as in the case of a charge of police brutality or harassment, or in a shooting.

The operation of control systems within a professional police department reflects a deeply rooted structural contradiction. Public pressure to control misconduct increases the proclivity of administrators and supervisors to use hierarchical controls to maintain discipline—to "tighten down the screws" internally. Though it is possible for supervisors to influence the way patrolmen use their discretion, the compromise between hierarchical and group controls is not casually breached. Rather, they turn their attention, often with a vengeance, to those matters they can control, such as violations of organizational rules, and they raise the cost of aggressive police work. The presumption of many supervisors is that such action will effectively curtail misbehavior by patrolmen. How far a supervisor will go depends not only on his own view of his relationship to patrolmen—the extent to which he identifies with management or patrolmen—but whether he is willing to tolerate the decrease in aggressiveness that the emphasis on discipline brings.

Since the hierarchical controls employed to instill discipline are directed by and large at the extrinsic aspects of police behavior, they do not really control the way patrolmen exercise their powers of discretion. Rather, they serve only to increase the uncertainty and tension with which a patrolman must cope. The consequence of this is to increase group solidarity and loyalty among patrolmen and the dependence of a patrolman upon his immediate peer group, while exacerbating the ongoing conflict between patrolmen and administrators. In a curious way, the conflict which animates the relationship between the police and the public is reproduced between patrolmen and administrators.

An individual patrolman is confronted, then, by a system of punitive controls more likely to punish him than reward him. This encourages a stay-low-protect-your-ass ethos among patrolmen, and discourages the inclination to work hard and take risks. It leads, in other words, to a pattern of avoidance. What is often construed as laziness among patrolmen is a rational adaptation to a punitive bureaucracy. After having worked hard to make an arrest of a heroin pusher, two patrolmen said that although the arrest was a "good pinch" it was primarily a morale booster for them. The arrest would make them feel good for a few days, but the department would not give them any commendations and it was just as likely that somebody would find something wrong with it. Most patrolmen thus learn that the way to survive in a police bureaucracy is to stay low and avoid trouble.[21] Or they learn that one has to be, as a street-wise patrolman calmly put it, just "a little bit slicker."

Reform has led to the bureaucratization of police departments and the apparent centralization of administrative control. But this centralization is illusory: hierarchical controls merely constrain a patrolman's decisions without really controlling them. At the same time, centralization may lead to a cautious style of action on the street or more subtle forms of resistance. This organizational system has enormous consequences for the exercise of discretion. It is an administrative system with substantial organizational autonomy, and it provides the illusion of strict control while granting virtual autonomy to patrolmen. Yet a patrolman cannot ignore the effect of these controls nor the wishes of his supervisors. He will attempt to tailor his actions to the whims of individual supervisors, if need be, and he will pursue a strategy of enforcement that is calculated to avoid trouble and validate where possible the central mission of the organization: crime fighting. But his chances of doing so are fraught with great uncertainty.

Chapter 5

The Dilemmas of Administrative Control

Discipline is a function of command. . . . The answer to the problem of police conduct and corruption is not the creation of an outside disciplinary agency. The answer is the creation of men who know and understand police work, to protect the innocent and punish the guilty.

O. W. Wilson

Management says inspections are good for morale. . . . It makes you feel like a third grader with no brains.

A disgruntled patrolman

THAT administrative controls within police departments affect the behavior and decisions of patrolmen cannot be denied. What is an open question, though, is the precise impact of the system of discipline, impersonal work controls, incentives, and the expectations of police administrators and supervisors on the choices of patrolmen. The ability of police administrators to influence and control police discretion may depend, as James Q. Wilson has suggested, on the type of incident a patrolman confronts.[1] When the choice is cut and dried, such as the choice of whether to issue a traffic citation for a palpable violation, a chief of police may be able to influence a patrolman's decision by insisting that most violations should be cited and by monitoring a patrolman's decisions through statistical controls. A family fight, on the other hand, may elicit only a prescription to "use your common sense."

96

Yet even if we grant that it is easier for police administrators to exert control over some types of incidents than others, this does not resolve the question. Take traffic, for instance. Police administrators typically expect other things of patrolmen than to simply issue citations and arrest drunk drivers. Such activity may be indicative of a hardworking patrolman, but as most administrators are aware, it does not measure effectiveness in containing crime or maintaining order. Most sergeants are inclined to be concerned if they discover that a patrolman is issuing traffic citations at 3:00 A.M. rather than carefully patrolling for commercial burglaries. In short, police administrators expect patrolmen to engage in a broad range of activities, and the expectations they convey are not necessarily consistent nor even coherent.

A further difficulty is that there is never complete conformity to procedures and objectives in any bureaucratic organization. To assume that police administrators shape police discretion is to assume that patrolmen not only understand what is wanted of them but that they willingly respond to organizational directives and the expectations of administrators. Yet this is precisely what is problematic. Once a police administrator has decided what it is he wants his men to do, he faces the difficulty of assuring that they, in fact, do it.

The ability of top-level police administrators to control the exercise of discretion by patrolmen and the overall impact of administrative controls also depends on the size of the department. Direct control over subordinates is more difficult in large organizations, and the impact of hierarchical controls may be more problematic.[2] In a small police department, by comparison, the proximity among administrators and patrolmen provides the access to an intimate knowledge of an officer's behavior that can replace or at least mediate formal controls. This proximity permits administrators to more directly and easily convey their expectations of the way events should be handled and to assure conformity.[3]

Yet any assessment of the impact of administrative controls on the behavior of patrolmen must be set within the context of the ongoing tension between hierarchical and peer group controls within police departments. Due to the conflict between these two systems of control, police administrators have only marginal control over the discretionary choices of patrolmen, while the possibility of patrolmen avoiding their responsibilities and the choices before them is greatly increased. Thus before we can assess to what extent the exercise of discretion by patrolmen is influenced by the expectations of administrators and administrative mechanisms, we must explore in some detail the implications of the structural bifurcation of internal control for the behavior of patrolmen. Does the internal bifurcation of control within police departments increase the uncertainty patrolmen face? Does it in fact limit the ability of field supervisors to directly influence the choices of patrolmen, and how do they cope with the tensions and conflicts that arise from the system of administrative controls? To what extent does the size of the department affect the impact of administrative controls? This chapter is devoted to answering these questions through an analysis of the attitudes and perceptions of patrolmen and field supervisors in Redondo Beach, Inglewood, and the LAPD toward the process of administrative control. This will require first establishing that there is a separation between control over administrative matters and discretionary choices within police departments, and then examining the implications from the point of view of field supervisors and patrolmen. This analysis will provide the necessary evidence for the argument I have advanced in regard to the structure of administrative controls in police departments, and will give some idea of the ways in which a patrolman's choices are or are not shaped and constrained by the department.

The Bifurcation of Internal Control

Outwardly at least, the LAPD comes closest to the bureaucratic model envisioned by police reformers. The two strongest chiefs of the postwar era—Parker and Davis—were stern disciplinarians who believed in the necessity of stringent internal control, though Parker was acutely aware of the difficulty of imposing it. In a revealing comment on the difficulties of rooting out corruption within the department, Parker once said, "One of the things we have done is to break down a false sense of fraternal obligation" among policemen.[4] Whether the sense of fraternal obligation has been broken down in the LAPD is debatable, but Parker's comment is a concise expression of the attitude of many administrators in that department toward discipline.

The attitude of the two top administrators in the small departments is more ambiguous. The chief in Redondo Beach, an ex-LAPD captain, is perhaps the most lax, and he takes great pains to point out that his policemen typically have more discretion than officers in the LAPD. Although he has the reputation among his men of running a somewhat loose department, in early 1973 he appointed a known disciplinarian as captain in command of the patrol bureau. The chief in Inglewood, on the other hand, views himself in the mold of Chief Parker. In the very small department he managed prior to coming to Inglewood in 1972, he had the reputation of strictly disciplining and controlling his men. The chief occasionally expressed a desire to implement similar controls in Inglewood, but by 1975 he claimed to have modified his views, and now thought that stringent control was neither necessary nor desirable. As he said at this time: "I believe in para-military organization to a point. . . . That's internally as far as rules, regulations, policies, procedures go. But . . . I think you have to leave a certain amount of flexibility or latitude to that policeman on the street."[5]

In a way, the chief in Inglewood could have been talking about all three of these departments, for all are characterized by a bifurcated system of internal control. Police administrators and field supervisors have enormous influence and control over administrative matters, the enforcement of rules, the allocation of organizational resources, training standards, assignments, promotion requirements, and so forth. They have little influence or actual control over the routine decisions made by patrolmen. In order to determine the extent to which internal controls are bifurcated, patrolmen and field supervisors were asked to estimate the amount of influence various levels of the administrative hierarchy (including themselves) had over administrative decisions and over the kinds of decisions made by patrolmen.[6] The results for patrolmen are portrayed in figure 5.1 (there are no significant differences in the estimates of field supervisors).

In regard to control over administrative matters, the top graph of Figure 5.1 shows that in all three departments the amount of influence attributed by patrolmen to an administrative level increases as one moves up the hierarchy. The chief of police and the command staff (which includes captains and the deputy chief in charge of Central Bureau in the LAPD) are accorded the most influence, though patrolmen in Redondo Beach rate the captain in charge of patrol as somewhat more influential than the chief.

The bottom graph of figure 5.1 portrays patrolmen's estimate of influence over their decisions, and reveals a very different pattern of influence and control. Patrolmen rate themselves as high or higher in influence than other hierarchical levels. In fact, in Redondo Beach

FIGURE 5.1
Perceptions of Influence by Patrolmen

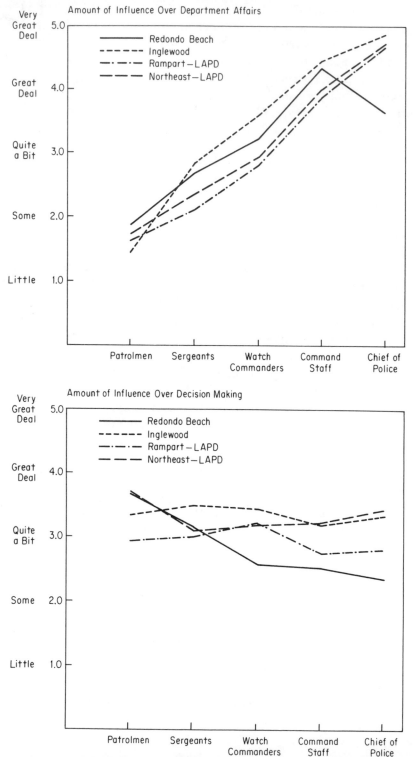

Amount of Influence Over Department Affairs

Redondo Beach
Inglewood
Rampart—LAPD
Northeast—LAPD

Patrolmen   Sergeants   Watch Commanders   Command Staff   Chief of Police

Amount of Influence Over Decision Making

Redondo Beach
Inglewood
Rampart—LAPD
Northeast—LAPD

Patrolmen   Sergeants   Watch Commanders   Command Staff   Chief of Police the pattern of influence reverses: the amount of influence *decreases* as one ascends the administrative hierarchy. Similarly, patrolmen in Northeast Division rate themselves higher than other levels of the hierarchy, though unlike Redondo Beach patrolmen they attribute slightly more influence over their decisions to the chief and the command staff than to watch commanders and field sergeants. In Inglewood and Rampart, by contrast, patrolmen accord themselves a high degree of influence over discretion but field supervisors (sergeants, watch commanders) are accorded slightly more.

What this figure reveals is not a pattern of influence and control in which patrolmen are completely autonomous, but one in which some control is exercised by all levels of the administrative hierarchy, with the edge given to patrolmen and field supervisors. Indeed, it is striking that the chiefs in the two small departments do not appear to be any more influential than the chief of the LAPD. Clearly, one should not overemphasize the importance of the chief's beliefs for the process of discretion and administrative control. If anything, the evidence points to the importance of the relationship between patrolmen and field supervisors. This is not surprising, for a chief of police is invariably preoccupied with the department's relationship to external institutions and groups, and unless he has reason to be concerned with internal matters (as some innovators are), the day-to-day chore of running the department is frequently in the hands of subordinates. The chief, through his actions, policies, and official pronouncements, may set the tone for the department, but the responsibility for enforcing rules, investigating citizen complaints, motivating patrolmen, and often deciding what constitutes an abuse of police power lies with field supervisors, the sergeants and watch commanders. It is their interpretation of departmental rules and the chief's policies that determines how stringent discipline will be, and whether and how departmental controls influence the choices of patrolmen.

The relationship between field supervisors and patrolmen turns on the contradictions embedded in the dichotomy between hierarchical and peer group controls, and on the dilemmas that both face as a result. Sergeants and watch commanders confront the dilemma of acting as both colleagues and supervisors. They tread a line between, on the one hand, the need to avoid second-guessing their men and backing them up in the street, and, on the other, attempting to adhere to the values of police professionalism and public demands to impose discipline. The central dilemma facing patrolmen is that of reconciling their autonomy on the street with the vague and uncertain expectations of administrators and the equally uncertain and often capricious reaction to any action they might take. The lot of a patrolman is to be free but not too free; and what makes his dilemma so painful is that frequently he does not know where the line between the two will be drawn. The question now is, How do patrolmen and field supervisors respond to these dilemmas and what are the consequences?

The View from the Middle: Field Supervisors and the Limits to Administrative Control

In sorting out their roles as bureaucrats and colleagues, field supervisors occupy a precarious position between top police executives, who desire strict and orderly supervision, and patrolmen, who are always ready to take offense at encroachments on their powers of discretion. There is no consensus among supervisors on how they should deal with the ambiguities and conflicts of their role; some become colleagues, others act as bureaucrats, and the rest tread the middle.

The very few supervisors who see themselves as colleagues completely identify with patrolmen rather than management, and define their responsibilities as a concern for the "welfare of the troops." For these sergeants, the most significant difficulty a supervisor faces is keeping track of what goes on in the street. One sergeant, who openly identified with the "troops," defined his role this way:

> [I must be in a] position to know what's going on with officers. I don't always follow the company line—my first loyalty is to officers. Some criticize this as a popularity contest, but I'm just trying to be effective in my own way. A lieutenant told me when I first became a supervisor that if there was another lawn mower caper, the officers would come to me and try to make a deal. I said at least they would come to me and I would know. I don't look at myself as a snitch, but an uninformed supervisor is worthless. I have prevented situations because of what I knew. I don't write guys up. . . . a guy can come to me and know that if he opens up he won't get fucked by me. If I got somebody it would be over.[7]

At the other extreme are those sergeants who see their role entirely as one of imposing the prerogatives of management on patrolmen. Their orientation derives from a belief that the chief responsibility of a field supervisor is to keep patrolmen working and out of trouble through strict and aggressive supervision. As one sergeant expressed it: "[You have] to get the job done. You have to guide those on the wrong path; if a policeman gets too far off line then he gets into trouble. A supervisor has to get him back on line. Thus, [the necessity] of using negative discipline." If those sergeants who identify with patrolmen could be accused of seeking popularity, these sergeants could be accused of isolating themselves from their men.

Most sergeants, though, avoid identifying with either management or patrolmen, and think of themselves as buffers or mediators between patrolmen and upper echelon administrators. This meant acting either as a more or less neutral communications belt by conveying and interpreting the orders of management to patrolmen and making the complaints of patrolmen known to administrators, or doing what some supervisors referred to as "training." The latter was described as, "keeping them from getting into trouble. I don't mean covering up, but give them the benefit of my experience so they don't have to learn the hard way." Whichever aspect of this role a supervisor stresses, the significant point is that these supervisors see themselves as both maintaining discipline *and* backing up patrolmen. As one sergeant put it:

> Supervision is like a double edged sword, primarily. The first edge is to make sure the men give the department its money's worth—a good eight hour's work. The second edge is to help men in any personal problems—on or off the job. For example, if they think they are getting screwed by the lieutenant, find out why. [You have] to be the buffer for the men.

These sergeants attempt, perhaps quixotically, to combine the roles of colleague and bureaucrat.

It is not surprising that most sergeants are inclined to view themselves as buffers, for regardless of the interpretation they bring to their job, field supervisors cannot avoid the pressures and conflicts that flow from the bifurcation of internal control.[8] The role of a field supervisor combines a great deal of formal authority with very real limits to their power. A field supervisor's right to command obedience to minor rules may be accepted by patrolmen, but the legitimacy of his authority does not depend on his position alone. He must also command the loyalty of the men working under him, he must demonstrate both his competence and his concern for their welfare.

The limits to the authority and power of field supervisors is most apparent when they attempt to directly influence how patrolmen behave. One obvious way a supervisor has of influencing discretion and maintaining some control over patrolmen is simply by being present at the scene of a call. Even if police executives and sergeants sometimes say that close supervision is necessary and desirable, sergeants are most conspicuous on the street for their absence. The norm of individualism and the overt hostility of patrolmen toward being second-guessed preclude close, intensive supervision. Most sergeants take care to avoid observing, much less intervening in, a situation being handled by a patrolman unless their assistance has been requested. One supervisor said that when he was first appointed sergeant, he attempted to go to every important call and monitor the actions of patrolmen. This caused so much resistance and hostility that he eventually withdrew, and now stays away from calls and intervenes only when requested to do so. Not every field supervisor is quite so reluctant to intervene; another sergeant insisted that he would always intervene if he thought the wrong decision had been made. But even this sergeant admitted that he did not closely supervise and he was more concerned with the way patrolmen filled out crime and arrest reports than anything else.

The alternative to close supervision in the field is to emphasize discipline, and this is precisely what many supervisors do. Practically all field supervisors in these three departments accept the need to enforce petty rules and regulations; 89 percent agreed that it was important to enforce departmental rules pertaining to dress, hair length, and tardiness (see table 5.1, statement a). Moreover, they are, by their own admission, preoccupied with violations of minor rules. The field supervisors were presented with a list of twelve potential problems of supervision they might confront and asked to choose the five most important and then rank them in order of priority. Six of the problems referred to the enforcement of petty rules and rather mundane work-related matters, for example, poor report writing, lack of hustle, sloppy dress, and bad driving. The other six referred to problems of discretion and misconduct such as making poor decisions, discourteousness, excessive force, and unequal enforcement of the law. The highest ranked item was assigned a value of five and the lowest a value of one, and the rankings for each category were then summed in order to obtain a measure of the perceived importance of either *work-related* or *discretionary* problems. The score of an individual supervisor for either type of supervision problem may range from a low of zero (which indicates that the supervisor chose

TABLE 5.1
Sergeants' and Watch Commanders' Attitudes Toward Supervision

ose Who Agreed th the Following Statement:	Small Departments		LAPD		All Departments (%)
	Redondo Beach (%)	Inglewood (%)	Northeast (%)	Rampart (%)	
It is important for field pervisors to enforce partmental rules regarding ess, hair length, tardiness, :.	90	92	94	82	89
The main job of a field pervisor is to enforce the es and regulations of the partment.	20	33	24	53	34
The main way for a pervisor to keep his men rking properly is that of nishment for what he siders ineffective formance.	10	18	12	0	9
Patrolmen are frequently nd guilty of violating artmental rules and cedures and are penalized erely.	10	0	29	12	14
The main job of a field ervisor is to assist rolmen in doing their job.	100	92	82	81	87
nber of Respondents	(10)	(12)	(17)	(17)	(56)

none of the problems for a particular category) to a high of fifteen (which means that a supervisor chose five problems for a particular category and ranked them accordingly).

The average scores for each department for work-related and discretionary problems are presented in table 5.2. A low average score means that many of the items for a particular category were not chosen, and those that were chosen were typically ranked low. In all three departments, the average scores for work-related supervision problems are substantially higher than for those pertaining to discretion—though the difference in Northeast Division is the smallest. Clearly, the field supervisors regard mundane work-related matters as the most important problems they face in supervising patrolmen.

Nevertheless, these supervisors neither consider themselves to be excessively preoccupied with enforcing rules nor regard rule enforcement as their primary responsibility. Only one-third of the field supervisors agreed that their main job was to enforce rules (though the proportion who agreed is higher in the two high-crime areas, Inglewood and Rampart Division). And very few seemed to think that the use of sanctions was an effective way to motivate patrolmen or that patrolmen were frequently found guilty of violating rules (table 5.1, statements b, c, and d). On the contrary, 87 percent of the

TABLE 5.2

Perceived Supervision Problems (Mean Scores)

	High-Crime Areas		Low-Crime Areas	
	Inglewood	Rampart	Redondo Beach	Northeast
Perceived Problems:[a]				
Disciplinary/Work-related Problems	7.75	8.28	7.40	6.00
Discretionary Problems	4.75	5.67	5.80	5.29

[a]The indexes of supervision problems measure both which problems supervisors regard as important and the relative significance of the problems they have chosen. If a problem was not chosen by a respondent it was scored as 0; otherwise each problem chosen was scored from 1 (the lowest rank) to 5 (the highest rank). Each index contains six problems, and the potential score for each respondent ranges from a low of 0 to a high of 15. The problems in each index are as follows:

1. *Disciplinary/Work-related*
   a. Poor report writing on the part of patrolmen.
   b. Lack of hustle while on patrol, officers are not active and are consistently "dogging it."
   c. Sloppy dress, shoes not shined and failure to conform to hair and uniform regulations of the department.
   d. Misuse of radio codes.
   e. Failure to take proper care of city equipment and property.
   f. Bad driving habits on the part of patrolmen.
2. *Discretionary*
   a. Making "bad" arrests—that is, arrests which are unjustified or illegal.
   b. Unequal enforcement of the laws in the community.
   c. Making poor decisions on the street.
   d. Failure to enforce laws at adequate level—that is, to make enough arrests and issue enough citations to deter crime and keep the peace.
   e. Discourteousness with the public.
   f. The use of excessive force while performing the job.

field supervisors believe that their primary responsibility is to assist patrolmen. What many sergeants mean by this is that they are there to back up patrolmen, to provide advice when needed (which is precisely the way they behave when their assistance is requested), and above all to keep patrolmen out of trouble.

These attitudes reflect a central difficulty that field supervisors confront: what power they possess can be used only in limited ways. The power that field supervisors possess is narrowly bureaucratic, and can only make life uncomfortable for patrolmen. They have no power to fire patrolmen; they cannot influence what a man is paid; and the rewards they can convey are usually limited to minor pats on the back in the form of commendations. What field supervisors can do is to harass and coerce patrolmen by strictly enforcing rules, writing up infractions and mistakes in their log, manipulating choice assignments, and affecting a patrolman's future through rating reports. But if they are to maintain control and sustain the legitimacy of their authority, they must limit the use of such controls.

Perhaps the chief problem a field supervisor faces in this regard is that strict enforcement of rules can cut him off from the sources of information he vitally needs. If a field supervisor is to maintain discipline and prevent complaints, he must acquire information about the actions of patrolmen. This is fairly difficult given the penchant for secrecy among patrolmen and their aversion to close supervision. Many field supervisors, not just those who view themselves as colleagues, attempt to cope with the barriers to obtaining information through the development of rapport. As one sergeant said: "I have to retain the loyalty of the men. I need information of what's going on in the field. . . . I have to know what's happening, how officers are relating to one another, and if they have family problems they might displace." But the development of such rapport is directly tied to the enforcement of departmental rules. A patrol car stopped to back up another unit that had stopped a carload of juveniles. As one of the patrolmen from the back-up unit stood aside watching the interrogation of the juveniles, a sergeant who happened to be driving by stopped, walked over to the patrolman, and criticized him for being out of his patrol car without his hat on, parking his car improperly, and turning off the red lights on his car. He was told he would be written up in the sergeant's log for these violations. Later, the patrolman said that the sergeant was widely known for being "swishy" and disliked by practically every patrolman, as he was the kind who was always on the lookout for violations of the rules. They made it clear that this particular sergeant would be the last to be told about a problem on the street.

Not every sergeant is oblivious to the connection between enforcing rules and gaining the confidence of patrolmen. As one young but shrewd sergeant, who tended to think of himself as a buffer between patrolmen and management, pointed out: "You must develop rapport and trust with the men, but you can't force them to it. You have to get it informally. I try to give in on little things to patrolmen. If I have to tell them I'm a sergeant I'm lost. . . . They don't like to do little things, for example, [the rule against] eating out of their beat. You have to be loose about this. . . . I let them eat out of their beat. . . ." The difficulty with this, of course, is that sergeants are under pressure from above to enforce rules strictly. The dilemma, as one sergeant put it, is that "a sergeant has to maintain discipline in the field and enforce rules, and at the same time do it with dignity so that you don't alienate patrolmen. . . ."

The ability of field supervisors to carry off their role in the middle is uncertain, for they are exposed to continual pressure from patrolmen to mitigate enforcement of detested rules, to allow them to pursue their task as they see fit, and in the event of trouble to back them up. Patrolmen employ a number of different strategies to get what they want from supervisors. First, they will openly manipulate a sergeant's ties and identification with patrolmen. Many supervisors retain a nostalgic identification with patrolmen, and believe the best feature of being a sergeant is that it combines status and authority with the opportunity to continue working the street. These field supervisors, many of whom think of themselves as colleagues, are especially susceptible to reminders that they were once patrolmen, and it is not uncommon for them to complain about the rules and regulations they have to enforce or to suggest that top-level administrators are largely unaware of the problems patrolmen routinely encounter in the street. But all supervisors are aware of the ties among working policemen and are open to more or less subtle appeals for understanding and support. The young patrolman who blithely asked the sergeant about the propriety of bad-mouthing "assholes" was subtly reminding him that there are two categories of people encountered on the street and that they should be treated differently.

Patrolmen may also use more direct methods in undermining a sergeant's authority and power. One strategy is what Jonathan Rubinstein has called "betrayal," providing information about a supervisor's mistakes or behavior to top-level administrators, a strategy one sergeant suggested was rather effective while a field supervisor's job status was still that of a probationer.[9] Another strategy is to bait sergeants or watch commanders, especially during roll call, in an attempt to make them look foolish. The most potent weapon patrolmen possess is their ability to deny sergeants their aid when they most need it. Discussing sergeants who continually harass patrolmen by strictly enforcing rules and the like, two street-wise cops said, "we'll just burn the guy." They explained what they meant with an anecdote: a sergeant, whom everybody hated, once put out an "officer needs assistance" call—a call that is normally taken very seriously by policemen—and only the beat car showed up. He got the message, they said, and straightened up.[10]

Though the limits to a supervisor's authority are very real, one should not exaggerate the power of patrolmen. If patrolmen can appeal to the bond of loyalty that working policemen share, field supervisors can invoke the legitimacy of command which, even if they may complain about it, most patrolmen accept. It is a rare patrolman who will refuse to obey a command; more commonly, patrolmen simply evade rules and commands when they can. Beyond this, the hand of field supervisors is strengthened for three reasons. First, field supervisors can influence patrolmen through the skillful use of evaluation reports and the enforcement of rules. Second, sergeants often have the initial responsibility for investigating personnel complaints. While they are constrained by departmental rules, they do have some discretion in investigating and processing complaints, and this latitude provides sergeants with the capacity to influence a patrolman's future conduct. This potential influence is augmented by the desire of most patrolmen to have field sergeants rather than the bureau of internal affairs investigate complaints, for the latter is not as inclined to be understanding. Third, and perhaps most important, field supervisors often have the edge in experience and knowledge. A seasoned sergeant can command enormous respect and can thus have influence over rookies and even over those patrolmen who have only two or three years on the street. The more problematic relationship field supervisors confront is with those veteran patrolmen who know what it is like to work the street and are not about to let a sergeant tell them what to do. Yet there is an irony here: a supervisor may have more influence over young patrolmen but these are often the most aggressive and hard-nosed street cops in the department, and thus the most difficult to control. A sergeant may be able to reach an accommodation with a veteran; it is not always possible with a young, aggressive patrolman.

Overt conflict between patrolmen and field supervisors is muted by the sheer need to get along and the subtle corruption of authority at the operational level. Both accept, to a greater or lesser degree, the primacy of crime control, and often there is no serious disagreement about the way incidents should be handled. And even when there is disagreement, most sergeants do not casually make a breach in the compromise between peer group and hierarchical controls. Actually, sergeants and watch commanders are frequently more concerned with a patrolman who is not aggressive enough or does not take action when he should than with a quasi-legal arrest. A sergeant understands the necessity of the attitude test and appreciates the satisfaction that accompanies a "good pinch." But field supervisors cannot escape the pressure for internal discipline, and all are inclined to bear down from time to time. In a curious way, field supervisors take the same cynical and mistrustful attitudes toward their men that patrolmen take toward citizens on the street. John McNamara observed that there is "a strong moralistic quality in the relationships between [police] supervisors and subordinates in which nonconformity is seen as stemming not from inability to conform nor errors of judgment but from willful disobedience or negligence."[11] The moralistic tone in supervisor-patrolman relationships is a mirror image of the moralistic attitudes patrolmen frequently display toward citizens. It is not uncommon for sergeants to apply the attitude test to the men working under them—to judge them by their deference to authority. The difference is that the moralism of supervisors is tempered by the shared experience of working the street. The outcome is a pattern of mutual accommodation in which field supervisors reassert the semblance of discipline and behave as bureaucrats in the station house, while confronting patrolmen as colleagues on the street.[12]

The View from the Bottom: The Uncertainties of the Police Bureaucracy

Patrolmen experience the conflict between their autonomy on the street and the impact of administrative controls in three ways: in trying to reconcile the conflicting goals of a professional police force;

in adapting to a disjuncture between rewards and performance; and in coping with the constraints imposed by a largely negative system of hierarchical controls. These three facets of administrative control make up the system of discipline as it confronts patrolmen. But if the disciplinary system has only a marginal effect on the routine discretionary choices of patrolmen, there is for many patrolmen, nonetheless, an illusory quality to the autonomy they possess. Even though supervisors do not closely watch them or are often unconcerned about the kinds of decisions they make, many patrolmen come to believe they are hemmed in by a capricious system of administrative controls. The reason for this is that the indirect effect of the disciplinary system is to increase the uncertainty with which a patrolman must cope.

THE AMBIGUITY OF DEPARTMENTAL GOALS: THE
ORGANIZATIONAL BASIS OF INDIVIDUAL CONFLICT

The expectations conveyed by police administrators to patrolmen are characterized, like the goals they reflect, by vagueness, ambiguity, and a contradiction between means and ends. A patrolmen is expected to pursue the *substantive* ends of police work, to prevent crime, enforce laws, keep the peace, and provide services. A patrolman is also expected to carry out a set of *instrumental* goals that will allow the responsibilities of the police to be carried out with a minimum of hostility and resentment from the community. Instrumental goals encompass the functions grouped under the rubric of community relations and the extrinsic elements of police professionalism. They rest on an awareness by the police of their inextricable dependence upon the public, a dependence which requires that the appearance if not the reality of trust and responsiveness be maintained at all times in order to preserve the legitimacy of their authority and thus the autonomy of the department. It is precisely because instrumental goals are linked to the legitimacy of police authority that they come into conflict with substantive goals. Administrators are more inclined to tolerate abuses of due process, which they often do, than actions such as discourtesy which, they believe, more directly endanger the legitimacy of the department.[13]

What do patrolmen believe administrators and field supervisors expect of them, and what is the relative importance placed on substantive and instrumental goals? Patrolmen were asked during the interviews to choose, from a list of ten possible departmental expectations, the five they believed were most important and then rank these in order of priority. Three of the expectations refer to instrumental goals: maintaining courteous relations with the public; maintaining a professional image; and staying out of trouble. Three refer to crime and law enforcement: patrolling for burglaries and robberies; being aggressive while on patrol; and issuing traffic citations and making felony arrests. And two refer to order-maintenance activities: keeping the peace and helping people when needed. Indexes of the rankings for the three kinds of departmental expectations were created by summing the individual expectations in the same manner as the question pertaining to supervisory problems (see page 000 for an account of the method). The scores range from zero to twelve for instrumental and crime and law enforcement expectations, and from zero to eight for order maintenance. The average scores for each department are displayed in table 5.3. A low average score means that many of the expectations for a particular category were not chosen, and those that were chosen were typically ranked low.[14]

TABLE 5.3
Departmental Expectations (Mean Scores)

	High-crime Areas		Low-crime Areas	
	Inglewood	Rampart	Redondo Beach	Northeast
Perceived Expectations:[a]				
Instrumental	7.00	6.75	8.27	7.47
Crime and Law Enforcement	5.71	4.45	3.44	3.75
Order Maintenance	2.16	3.57	2.15	3.06
Desired Expectations:				
Instrumental	5.37	5.73	5.32	5.35
Crime and Law Enforcement	7.60	5.92	6.29	5.80
Order Maintenance	1.95	2.82	2.91	2.94

[a]The indexes of departmental expectations measure both which expectations patrolmen regard as important and the relative significance of the expectations they have chosen. Perceived expectations refer to those expectations that patrolmen think administrators regard as important. Desired expectations refer to those expectations patrolmen think should be regarded as important. If an expectation was not chosen by a respondent it was scored as 0; otherwise each expectation chosen was scored from 1 (the lowest rank) to 5 (the highest rank). The Instrumental and Crime and Law Enforcement indexes contain three items each, and the potential score for each respondent ranges from a low of 0 to a high of 12. The index of Order Maintenance contains two items, and the potential score ranges from 0 to 8. The expectations in each index are as follows:
  1. Instrumental
    a. Maintain courteous and good relations with the public.
    b. Maintain a professional image.
    c. Stay out of trouble.
  2. Crime and Law Enforcement
    a. Patrol your beat for potential burglaries and robberies, that is, make business checks, patrol residential streets etcetera.
    b. Be active and aggressive on your beat: stop people, check them out, run warrant checks etcetera.
    c. Issue a substantial number of traffic citations; actively patrol your beat for drunk drivers; make a substantial number of good felony arrests.
  3. Order Maintenance
    a. Attempt to help people when needed.
    b. Work effectively with people in keeping the peace.

As the figures under perceived expectations in table 5.3 show, these patrolmen believe that administrators accord instrumental goals a much higher priority than either crime and law enforcement or order-maintenance activities. There are substantial differences, in particular, between the crime expectations and the instrumental expectations. The largest difference between instrumental and crime control expectations, however, is found in the two low-crime areas, Redondo Beach and Northeast Division. There is less difference in the two high-crime areas where patrolmen believe that administrators place a higher priority on crime control. This is hardly surprising given the steadily increasing crime rate in Inglewood and Rampart Division at this time. Even so, these patrolmen do not believe that administrators are totally preoccupied with instrumental goals, only excessively so. They believe they are required to honor both kinds of expectations.

One other pertinent observation can be culled from these data. The data show patrolmen believe those expectations pertaining to order maintenance and the execution of specific police functions such as issuing traffic citations, making felony arrests, and patrolling for drunk drivers are least important. Rather, these patrolmen think supervisors are more concerned with broad, general goals than with the specific actions they may take. More often, patrolmen felt that what was wanted was action, some tangible demonstration that one was working rather than goldbricking. One patrolman said that "the supervisors expect you to work, to be doing something for eight hours and not sliding by." Action is believed to be not only necessary but sufficient; what a patrolman does is much less important than his doing anything at all.

If they had their way, these patrolmen would de-emphasize instrumental expectations. When asked what they thought the most important objectives *should be* patrolmen overwhelmingly ranked crime and law enforcement objectives the highest. In particular, patrolling one's beat for potential burglaries and robberies and being active and aggressive on the street were the most frequently mentioned objectives. Some idea of the conflict between what patrolmen believe they are asked to do and what they would prefer to do can be gained by looking at the differences in the relative emphasis they place on instrumental and crime objectives. As the figures under *Desired Expectations* in table 5.3 indicate, patrolmen would simply reverse the priorities: in all three departments the average score of crime objectives increases and that for instrumental objectives decreases. The largest changes take place in the two low-crime areas, indicating there is somewhat more consistency between perceived and desired objectives in Inglewood and Rampart. Finally, note that there is far less difference in the average scores between instrumental and crime objectives in the ranking of desired objectives of patrolmen than in the ranking of perceived objectives. Instrumental objectives are not discarded by patrolmen; they merely have a lower priority.

It inevitably falls to patrolmen to fashion working solutions to the conflict between the instrumental and substantive goals of police work. Because administrators and supervisors expect patrolmen to do something about crime and at the same time avoid complaints, patrolmen find workable solutions are hard to come by. One especially frustrated patrolman suggested that if an officer was aggressive *and* received personnel complaints—which most patrolmen think likely if one is aggressive—he would create problems for the sergeants who have to investigate the complaints and have to take the heat from the administration.

What constitutes an acceptable level of aggressiveness is rather vague. Somewhat myopically, police administrators define the ideal cop as one who is aggressive and makes good arrests but otherwise keeps his nose clean. The fact of the matter is that police administrators do not usually own up to the conflict between instrumental and substantive goals, and if they do they assume it can be resolved. They are prone to view policemen as dynamic, resourceful men for whom anything is possible. Joseph Wambaugh has distilled the essence of this view: "Policemen thoroughly believe that no man-caused calamity happens by chance, that there is always a step that should have been taken, would have been taken, if the sufferer had been alert, cautious, brave, aggressive—in short, if he'd been like a prototype policeman. They saw themselves as the most dynamic of men, the ones who could take positive action in any of life's bizarre and paralyzing moments."[15] The resemblance between this view and Vollmer's preoccupation with finding the perfect men for police work is not coincidental. To the extent that police professionalism boils down to a search for the "perfect man," it boils down to hiring and training those men for whom even the most terrible moral dilemmas pose no difficulty. The concept of the dynamic man vindicates the search for the perfect policeman—whether he has been found or not.

Unlike administrators and field supervisors, patrolmen are more willing to accept the frailties of humans and to tolerate the consequences entailed by reconciling conflicting goals. For example, only one-third of the patrolmen agreed with the statement, "A patrolman who gets into a lot of beefs when making arrests or talking to people is *not* a good patrolman." Over half of the field supervisors, on the other hand, agreed with the statement. Faced with the conflict between means and ends and the belief of administrators that they could resolve it if they only tried hard enough, the incentive for patrolmen is to issue the requisite number of traffic citations and make a few arrests to demonstrate activity, but otherwise to maintain a low profile and keep from making waves. Not every sergeant would agree that this is what they want of their men, but they, like patrolmen, must attempt to resolve a conflict that is not entirely of their own making.

THE DISJUNCTURE BETWEEN REWARDS AND PERFORMANCE

One of the key mechanisms of control in any organization is the process by which promotions to higher positions are handed out. Both the formal process that leads to promotions and the criteria applied by supervisors in evaluating performance can structure incentives and thereby have a direct or indirect effect on behavior. Since promotions in all three departments are governed by civil service regulations, the kinds of decisions a patrolman makes may have little bearing on his chances for promotion. This also limits the ability of supervisors to influence the behavior of patrolmen, though it does not entirely preclude it. Promotions are based on a combination of written and oral examinations and subjective evaluations of an officer's work record. The latter include information on various aspects of an officer's performance such as the number of personnel complaints, commendations, and periodic evaluations conducted by field supervisors. Through criteria applied in the oral examination and in evaluating a patrolman's work record, supervisors are in a position to manipulate incentives and influence behavior.

The subjective evaluation of an officer's work record carried the least importance in Redondo Beach and a great deal in Inglewood where it accounted for 40 percent of an individual's total score. In the LAPD the likelihood of a subjective evaluation depends on the kind of promotion a patrolman desires. Aside from those patrolmen on probation, the LAPD distinguishes between Patrolman-II's (P-II), a status automatically attained when an officer completes probation, and Patrolman-III's (P-III), a position attained only by divisional promotion. The latter position is necessary if a patrolman wants to become an investigator or training officer (a patrolman need not be a P-III to apply for a promotion to sergeant, though it probably helps). A written and oral examination is required for promotion to P-III, but the decision is made by the captain in charge of a division, who has broad discretion in making these appointments, and, at the time of the study, relied heavily upon the recommendations of sergeants and lieutenants. Field supervisors are enormously influential in the decision to promote an officer to P-III. Thus, even though civil service regulations lead to a promotional system in which criteria for promotion are severed from actual performance, a promotion-minded patrolman in all of these departments cannot afford to ignore the impressions of their performance gained by field supervisors and incorporated in periodic evaluations.

What are the criteria patrolmen believe supervisors use to evaluate their performance? To what extent are these criteria related to their behavior in the street? In order to answer these questions, patrolmen were presented with a list of twelve criteria pertinent to promotion, asked to choose the five they believe the departments consider most important, and then to rank them in order of priority. These criteria may be classified into three categories. The first pertains to a patrolman's behavior in the street, his ability to work independently and to manage crime and disorder. The second refers to a patrolman's relationship to the community, his propensity to acquire personnel complaints, and his ability to maintain courteous relations with the public. The last category contains criteria relevant to a patrolman's relationship to the department and his attitude toward authority and departmental rules. Average scores for each department were calculated in the same manner as those for the question measuring the perceived expectations of the department and perceived supervisory problems. The score for each index may range from a low of zero (which means none of the criteria for a given category were chosen) to a high of fourteen (which means all four criteria were chosen). The average scores for each department are displayed in table 5.4. A low average score means that many of the promotional criteria for a particular category were not chosen, and that those chosen were typically ranked low.

By and large, these patrolmen believe that the criteria most salient for promotion are those peripheral to the way they handle themselves on the street and use their discretion. The average scores for departmental criteria and community relations are substantially

TABLE 5.4

Criteria for Promotion (Mean Scores)

	High-crime Areas		Low-crime Areas	
	Inglewood	Rampart	Redondo Beach	Northeast
Perceived Criteria:[a]				
Crime and Order Maintenance	3.53	3.37	2.97	3.47
Community Relations	4.15	4.86	3.74	4.71
Departmental	6.76	6.41	6.62	6.20
Desired Criteria:				
Crime and Order Maintenance	6.42	6.14	6.88	6.16
Community Relations	4.66	4.90	4.88	4.41
Departmental	3.90	3.51	3.21	3.90

[a]The indexes of criteria for promotion measure both which criteria patrolmen regard as important and the relative significance of the criteria they have chosen. Perceived criteria refer to those criteria patrolmen think administrators regard as important. Desired criteria refer to those criteria patrolmen think should be regarded as important. If a criterion was not chosen by a respondent it was scored as 0; otherwise each criterion chosen was scored from 1 (the lowest rank) to 5 (the highest rank). Each index contains four criteria, and each respondent's potential score can range from a low of 0 to a high of 14. The criteria in each index are as follows:

1. Crime and Order Maintenance:
    a. Be able to work independently, without supervisor—be able to initiate actions, make decisions etcetera.
    b. Make a substantial number of felony and misdemeanor arrests.
    c. Be active and aggressive on your beat: stop people, check them out, run warrant checks, patrol for burglaries and robberies.
    d. Be able to work effectively with people in keeping the peace.
2. Community Relations:
    a. Maintain good relations with the public; be known as an officer who can get along with people, and is always courteous and cool.
    b. Maintain an image of professionalism.
    c. Have very few or no personnel complaints in your file.
    d. Be active in community and civic affairs in the community in which you live.
3. Departmental:
    a. Complete your college education—go to college.
    b. Follow all rules and regulations of the department and orders of supervisors.
    c. Have good relations with supervisors in the department.
    d. Have no personal or financial problems—bad debts, etcetera.

higher than for criteria directly relevant to their task. The only task-related criterion considered important was the requirement that patrolmen be able to work independently, but almost one-third of the respondents did not choose this criterion. Missing are those things that patrolmen actually do on the street, namely, attempt to control crime, make arrests, and keep the peace. This is not to imply that these are the best measures of a patrolman's performance; only that in the minds of patrolmen they are irrelevant to their prospects for promotion. Finally, these patrolmen believe that supervisors place more importance on their ability to follow rules and accept the authority of sergeants than on the character of their relationship with the public.

While the average score for departmental criteria is approximately the same in all three departments, these data conceal a significant difference between the LAPD and the two small departments. In the

LAPD, patrolmen believe that administrators place the greatest value on obtaining a college education; in the small departments patrolmen believe that following the rules and cultivating supervisors is what counts. Table 5.5 presents the mean rank and percentage missing for each of these three criteria. The data show that patrolmen in the LAPD are more likely to choose education and to rank it higher than their counterparts in the small departments, while in Redondo Beach and Inglewood patrolmen rank both following the

TABLE 5.5
Mean Rankings for Departmental Criteria for Promotion

Perceived Departmental Criteria	Small Departments		LAPD	
	Redondo Beach	Inglewood	Northeast	Rampart
a. Complete your college education: Mean rank[a]	2.80	3.44	3.60	4.00
Percentage who did not choose this criterion	71%	42%	22%	16%
b. Follow all rules and regulations of the department and orders of supervisors: Mean rank	3.88	3.31	2.67	2.68
Percentage who did not choose this criterion	27%	32%	29%	28%
c. Have good relations with supervisors in the department: Mean rank	3.63	3.26	3.04	2.42
Percentage who did not choose this criterion	29%	26%	55%	63%

[a]Mean rank refers to the rank for each separate criterion in a department, and may range from a low of 1 to a high of 5.

rules and cultivating supervisors higher (in fact they are almost twice as likely to choose the latter criterion as patrolmen in the LAPD). The salience of education in the LAPD may reflect the importance of the written score on civil service examinations and the emphasis that the department places on a college degree for promotions to higher ranks. In the small departments, on the other hand, there is greater pressure to conform to the whims of individual supervisors.

Further evidence that patrolmen experience a conflict between the demands of the task they perform and what administrators expect of them can be found when one compares the average scores for those promotional criteria patrolmen believe administrators employ with scores for the criteria they think should be employed (see under *"Desired Criteria"* in table 5.4). There is very little change in the average scores for community relations criteria, while those for crime and order maintenance increase and those for departmental criteria decrease. Most patrolmen think that administrators do not place enough emphasis on an officer's ability to work independently, as almost all of the change in the crime and order-maintenance index can be accounted for by a change in this criterion. Finally, note that patrolmen believe their relationship to the public ought to be of more concern than their dealings with the department. What patrolmen mean by this is that maintaining courteous relations with the public and preserving a professional image, *but not personnel complaints,* should be of concern to administrators.

The implications of these data are twofold. First, there is a radical disjuncture between a patrolman's performance on the street and the criteria used to evaluate it.[16] Though field supervisors have some leverage over patrolmen through periodic evaluations that could be used to influence discretion, the way a patrolman exercises his discretion does not, in the minds of patrolmen, figure in their calculations. On the contrary, field supervisors rely upon those criteria that are the most tangible and obvious—those encompassed under the rubric of discipline—to determine whether or not an officer's performance is adequate. In a sense, they are both unable and unwilling to evaluate the exercise of discretion. In the absence of policies which designate how different incidents should be handled, supervisors have to fall back on more peripheral criteria. But they are also unwilling to directly evaluate a patrolman's decisions, for to do so would be tantamount to "second-guessing" an officer. Civil service regulations may separate rewards and performance but they do not preclude the use of direct evaluations of an officer's decisions. What does preclude

TABLE 5.6

Perceptions of Supervisors' Behavior

| Perceived Behavior | Small Departments | | LAPD | | All Departments (%) |
	Redondo Beach (%)	Inglewood (%)	Northeast (%)	Rampart (%)	
Frequency of Supervisors' Observations[a]					
Often/Very Often	36	58	20	26	36
Sometimes	18	32	37	39	33
Not Often/Hardly	46	10	43	35	31
Frequency of Supervisors' Interventions[b]					
Often/Very Often	9	23	6	2	11
Sometimes	6	20	14	18	15
Not Often/Hardly	85	57	80	80	74
Mean Scale Score:	53.21	44.15	52.25	53.14	
Number of Respondents	(34)	(62)	(51)	(51)	(198)

[a]How often do the field supervisors in this department drive by and observe you while you are on a call?
[b]How often do the field supervisors in this department intervene and take charge of a call?

it are the systemic limits to hierarchical controls within a professional police department.

The second implication is that field supervisors cannot help a patrolman with their evaluations so much as they can hurt him. The impact of evaluation procedures and practices is decidedly negative. Whether it is a matter of following rules or of minimizing personnel complaints, it is negligence and mistakes that count. Patrolmen were frequently heard to complain that anytime they made a mistake, violated a rule, or got a complaint, however trivial, it was held against them. Patrolmen may exaggerate the oppressiveness of administrative controls, and most will admit that not every supervisor is out to "burn" them for minor infractions and mistakes. At the same time, the disjuncture between rewards and performance augments the uncertainty that impinges on patrolmen, and they are faced with discerning what rules will be enforced and who will enforce them.

THE NEXUS BETWEEN AUTONOMY AND DISCIPLINE

Just as patrolmen believe that the procedures for evaluating their actions and handing out promotions have little to do with their behavior on the street, so they believe that the routine actions of field supervisors have but a marginal impact on the way they use their discretion. In this their perceptions mirror the reported behavior of field supervisors. Consider first the issue of how closely patrolmen are supervised. The admitted reluctance of field supervisors to closely watch the behavior of patrolmen is corroborated by the perceptions of patrolmen. They believe that their activities are not observed very often, that field supervisors rarely intervene to take charge of an incident or—more significantly—talk to them about the way they handled a particular incident (see table 5.6).

Yet there are some differences worth noting between the LAPD and the small departments. Patrolmen in the two small departments, but especially in Inglewood, indicate that field supervisors are more inclined to observe them. Fifty-eight percent of the patrolmen in Inglewood said that field supervisors observed them often or very often compared to 36 percent in Redondo Beach, 20 percent in Northeast Division, and 26 percent in Rampart Division. The data also show that Inglewood patrolmen believe their supervisors are far less reluctant to intervene actively in an incident than their counterparts in the other two departments. These two statements were combined into a scale, and the lower the scale score the greater the perception of aggressive monitoring by field supervisors.[17] The mean scores for each department (see table 5.6) show that patrolmen in Inglewood, in contrast to patrolmen in the other two departments, are far more likely to believe that supervisors are actively engaged in observing them and intervening in incidents. These data are confirmed by the field observations in Inglewood. There, sergeants were observed to be present at a number of incidents, and they made a point of initiating a fair amount of contact with patrolmen, if only to check crime reports and such. The supervisors in Redondo Beach and in the LAPD were rarely seen at the scene of a call. (It is worth noting that the high mean score for Redondo Beach is somewhat misleading since, unlike the two divisions of the LAPD, there is greater disagreement in the perceptions of patrolmen. A fair number of patrolmen in Redondo Beach did feel that supervisors were not reluctant to monitor their actions.)

Similarly, patrolmen in all three departments think that supervisors are less concerned with enforcing rules which limit their discretion than punishing violations of minor rules and to a lesser extent misconduct. When asked which rules were most frequently enforced, 57 percent of patrolmen mentioned rules pertaining to minor problems of discipline such as personal appearance, tardiness, too much time at a coffee stop, and so forth. Twenty-three percent thought that minor rules relating to their job such as bad driving habits, misuse of radio codes, poor report writing, and the like were matters that preoccupied supervisors. Only 20 percent mentioned misconduct (excessive force, insulting behavior toward citizens) or discretion as matters that concerned field supervisors.

Some patrolmen suggested that supervisors are less concerned with misconduct because it occurs infrequently. There is an element of truth in this; excessive force and insults do occur less often than tardiness or poor report writing. But what constitutes an insult or excessive force is a matter of interpretation, and what excites a citizen may not excite a supervisor. And it is quite clear that instances of misconduct or even violations of due process do not come to the attention of a supervisor as often as infractions of minor rules because they are concealed by patrolmen.

The perceptions of patrolmen are thus in agreement on one fact: field supervisors do very little overtly to influence police discretion. Yet patrolmen attribute to field supervisors a moderate amount of influence over their decisions. Is it possible that sergeants and watch commanders influence the choices of patrolmen in less direct ways? If so, how and with what effect? Do field supervisors directly influence the priorities of patrolmen? It was often said by patrolmen that they took their cues from sergeants and watch commanders, and they would enforce those violations that appeal to supervisors. The only difficulty is that supervisors are as variable as patrolmen in their choice of priorities and pet peeves; the norm of individualism holds sway here as elsewhere. Some sergeants want patrolmen to be concerned with felonies, others with traffic violations, and still others merely exhort patrolmen to enforce all the laws. A few patrolmen said they would attempt to follow the priorities of supervisors they were working for; but most exhibited a predilection to go their own way. There was no indication in any of the departments that patrolmen went out of their way to enforce those laws supervisors considered important. The one instance where a supervisor attempted, vainly, to persuade patrolmen to enforce the law in a particular way occured when a sergeant in one of the small departments made a fetish over writing parking tickets. He regularly held forth on why they should be written—obtaining revenue for the city seemed to be his primary justification—and he would occasionally order patrolmen to write tickets, usually in a specific section of the city. Patrolmen, for their part, would write parking tickets when ordered, but otherwise ignored him.

Administrators, however, may influence a patrolman's choices through the use of statistical controls. Ostensibly directed toward monitoring an individual patrolman's production, these controls do not direct patrolmen toward one kind of violation rather than another so much as they make all violations important in some sense. The impact of statistical controls is to move patrolmen from a concentration on felony violations to a concern for all violations.

Statistical controls were used in both divisions of the LAPD and in Redondo Beach, but not in Inglewood. The effect of these controls, however, depends on the attitudes of both patrolmen and supervisors toward them. Many patrolmen disliked the use of statistical controls, frequently complaining that they simply measured production, and took no account of a patrolmen's effort to prevent crime. What underlies this complaint is a conflict between the use of statistical controls and the pragmatic approach most patrolmen take toward their job, their bias toward problem-based, selective enforcement. A patrolman should be worried, as one patrolman argued, about the "people that are capering (committing crimes) in his area."

Another patrolman offered a slightly different interpretation of the effect of statistical controls. He suggested that what sergeants look for is a hustler, and what they want is diversity. A patrolman who does nothing but arrest drunk drivers and issue traffic citations for running stop signs will be appropriately admonished by the sergeants. Even so, patrolmen displayed varying degrees of concern over the "numbers game." Some indicated they could not care less how their statistics looked at the end of the month, while others demonstrated an acute preoccupation with their standing in the division.

Nor are all sergeants inclined to take the controls very seriously. Some assiduously monitor the monthly tabulations while others ignore them. Many sergeants, not unaware of the conflict between the use of statistical controls and selective enforcement and mindful of the limits of their powers, simply push for a minimum level of work and do not attempt to systematically control the choices of their men.

The pressure of statistical controls, such as they are, is really rather mild. Low production may lead to some negative comments, but for an experienced patrolman whose longevity is assured by his civil service status this is rather meaningless. Statistical controls will usually be more important to an officer on probation or one who strongly desires a promotion. And the impact may be more significant in a large department such as the LAPD where it is impossible for a supervisor to have a close and detailed appreciation of a patrolman's capabilities and performance—though there was considerable disagreement in the LAPD over the utility of statistical controls, and the department was trying, at the time of the study, to move away from them.

All of the available evidence indicates that patrolmen have considerable freedom to use their powers of discretion as they see fit. And in fact patrolmen in all three departments believe they are allowed sufficient autonomy to perform their task. Seventy-four percent believe the department allows them more than enough discretion in making arrests and tactical decisions and only 22 percent think most supervisors will *not* let them make their own decisions (see table 5.7, statements a and b). But despite this freedom, patrolmen believe they confront an overly harsh and punitive disciplinary system. When asked how frequently they were reprimanded for violations of rules, 48 percent of patrolmen responded often or very often—though 57 percent in LAPD felt this way compared to 39 percent in the small departments.[18] Moreover, 61 percent of patrolmen think supervisors are overly preoccupied with enforcing trivial rules and 47 percent think they act as if enforcing rules were their only responsibility (see table 5.7, statements c and d).

TABLE 5.7
Perceived Limits on the Exercise of Discretion

hose Who Agreed ith the Following Statement	Small Departments		LAPD		All Departments (%)
	Redondo Beach (%)	Inglewood (%)	Rampart (%)	Northeast (%)	
The department allows trolmen more than enough scretion in making arrests, uing citations, or making ctical decisions.	91	58	80	73	74
In general, in this partment there are very w field supervisors who lieve in letting patrolmen ake their own decisions.	21	34	14	16	22
The field supervisors act as their only job is to enforce e rules and regulations of s department.	44	55	45	41	47
In general, field supervisors this department are more erested in enforcing petty es about dress, hair length, d whether or not you wear ur hat when you get out of car or whether you are a minutes late to work than sort of job patrolmen do.	76	57	55	61	61
Patrolmen often fail to take cessary police action due to eling that supervisors will approve of their actions.	56	60	16	18	37
atrolmen who are always looking for situations uiring police attention are ones who usually get into ible with their supervisors.	44	27	18	18	25
A patrolman will usually along better on the job h his supervisors if he sn't go looking for ations requiring police ntion, but handles them ituations arise.	59	29	33	31	36
an Scale Score:[a]	46.44	47.33	53.18	52.39	
nber of Respondents	(34)	(62)	(51)	(51)	(198)

he difference in means between LAPD and the small departments is significant @ $P \leq .001$.

The autonomy of patrolmen and the harshness of discipline, of course, are not unrelated, since field supervisors resort to enforcing rules in the absence of more effective ways of controlling the actions of patrolmen. The issue, though, is the impact of this disciplinary system on patrolmen. It is quite possible that these data merely reflect the dissatisfaction of men who are forced to obey petty rules and cope with the vindictiveness of some supervisors. Alternatively, I have argued that it increases the costs of action and leads to a pattern of avoidance among patrolmen. Is there any reason to believe that the overall impact of administrative controls within police departments increases the uncertainty that patrolmen face, thereby resulting in a reluctance to act? Looking at the responses to those statements in table 5.7 (statements e, f, and g) which closely measure the relationship between discretion and administrative control, we find that anywhere from one-fourth to almost two-fifths of all patrolmen are reluctant to exercise the discretion they have; or at least they believe there is considerable risk in doing so. Thus, one key effect of administrative controls is to increase the uncertainty confronting patrolmen and hence the likelihood of a pattern of avoidance.

This effect, however, appears to be more pronounced in the small departments than in the LAPD. Not only are patrolmen in the small departments slightly less likely than those in the LAPD to believe that supervisors will leave them alone (table 5.7, statement d), they are far more inclined to believe that aggressive police work leads to trouble with supervisors. For instance, 56 percent of patrolmen in Redondo Beach and 60 percent in Inglewood compared to 16 percent in LAPD believe that "patrolmen often fail to take necessary police action due to a feeling that supervisors will disapprove of their actions." The difference in perceptions between the LAPD and the small departments is not attributable to chance. The questions in table 5.7 form a coherent attitudinal scale, and the higher an individual patrolman's score, the greater the perception of autonomy.[19] The average score for the two divisions of LAPD is considerably higher than that for Redondo Beach and Inglewood, and, more important, the difference is statistically significant. Department size, then, is an important factor in affecting the amount of uncertainty generated by administrative controls. This of course is not inconsistent with some of our other findings, namely, the greater pressure for conformity in small departments indicated by the criteria used to evaluate performance and the perceptions among patrolmen of closer supervision.

The Administrative Consequences of Professionalism

One significant effect of administrative controls in professional police departments is to increase the uncertainty patrolmen face. In a way, patrolmen are confronted with an extension of the idea of the dynamic policeman in the disciplinary system, the presumption that they can reconcile the contradictions of their task, live up to the rules, and still perform their job. Their lot is made all the more difficult because of the independence of field supervisors—the tendency of some to go "headhunting" periodically, while others seek to become "father confessors"—for patrolmen must adapt to the whims of each supervisor if they are to cope. Some patrolmen may think it is possible to surmount the contradictions of their task, but for many the effect is only to increase their frustration and their sense of isolation from both the department and the public. These men are often inclined to follow a strategy calculated to demonstrate they are working and to minimize their involvement in potentially risky situations.

Yet there are counterpressures to the impact of this system. Field supervisors are susceptible to the demands of patrolmen for autonomy, and because they are frequently as dedicated as patrolmen to hard-nosed, aggressive police work, they can understand if not always tolerate the minor abuses of power that are characteristic of routine police work. For their part, patrolmen are often willing to take the risks that aggressive police work entails because of the value they place on crime fighting and their own penchant for action. Beyond this, police unions (or even the patrolmen's benevolent association) may provide the basis for institutional limits to the pressures generated by departmental controls—although the existing patrolmen associations in Redondo Beach, Inglewood, and the LAPD were not important in this regard at the time of the study.[20]

The tension between the realities of police work and the demands for discipline can be managed so long as the police are not subject to stress. But external pressure in the form of a rising crime rate combined with a demand that the police do something about it, and worsening relations with those groups that bear the brunt of aggressive enforcement, exacerbate the conflict between the values of the police culture and those of police professionalism. To be sure, under the force of external stress the tendency of the police is to band together, and police administrators may be tempted to abandon—and may in fact do so—any attempt to secure internal discipline. But because internal discipline is viewed as an alternative to external control and is closely tied to the legitimacy of police authority, and hence to the autonomy of the department, in a highly professional police force the more likely consequence is to step up the pressure for internal control. Indeed, the intense criticism leveled at the police during the late 1960s did lead in some instances to a greater emphasis on internal discipline.[21] The effect of this, though, may be merely to increase the costs of action for patrolmen without necessarily controlling discretion. And this outcome is, as a rule, more likely in small, professional police departments. The question is, Why?

Part of the answer, I would argue, has to do with the relationship between organizational size and administrative control. In a small department there are more constraints on a patrolman's discretion. These constraints derive from the decrease in scale—principally fewer levels in the administrative hierarchy and the smaller geographical area to be policed—which permit administrators to develop a more intimate knowledge of a patrolman's activities. In a small department, there are fewer links in the chain of communications, and not only can the chief of police more easily communicate his desires, but rumors of mistakes and indiscretions work their way up the hierarchy. Errors of judgment are less easily concealed in a small department. Moreover, if there are fewer incidents to be evaluated, a more thorough check of what has happened is possible; and the small geographical area allows supervisors, if they so desire, to monitor more closely the actions of patrolmen. Finally, a man in a small department will develop, for good or ill, a reputation as a particular kind of officer, and this reputation will stick with him. A poor decision is something that everyone will know about sooner or later, and from which a patrolman can only infrequently escape. The elements of an officer's reputation—coolness under fire, a series of bad arrests, a propensity to get into altercations—are indelibly imprinted on a man, and he will be watched and judged accordingly. There exists in small police departments, therefore, in addition to the typical hierarchical controls, a system of highly developed informal controls (this of course leaves aside the question of whether or not administrators choose to act on the basis of the information they obtain). The existence of these informal controls leads to more personalized judgments of an officer's performance and explains the proclivity of patrolmen in small departments to say that administrators stress conformity to organizational norms in evaluating them.

Compare a large department such as the LAPD. Size imposes limitations on the process of formal control and communications. Information which flows from the bottom of the hierarchy is more easily distorted, and administrators have neither the time nor inclination to closely examine every incident that occurs. Mistakes and indiscretions do not surface as easily, and they are not as costly to the department. Combined with the surfeit of resources in a large department (that is, the sheer number of men available to respond to calls at any one time), these limitations on formal controls create more latitude for a patrolman to move around and get involved in the kind of incidents he likes, and make it more difficult for supervisors to closely monitor his actions. Because the department is larger, relationships among individuals must be more impersonal. Judgments of a man's competence are based less on his informal reputation than on his formal record: the number of personnel complaints, test scores, rating reports by supervisors, and number of arrests. In the absence of the personalized judgments available to supervisors in small departments, it is reasonable to suppose that the preoccupation with *formal* discipline—for example, obedience to rules—increases. This probably explains the somewhat more stringent enforcement of rules in the LAPD. Yet such controls offer few real constraints on a patrolman's actions, and more importantly, he can escape his reputation in a large department. A transfer to another division offers the possibility of starting anew; a man's reputation and especially his mistakes do not always follow him. In short, in a large department there are few informal controls over patrolmen and the effects of hierarchical controls are sharply limited. A patrolman has more latitude and autonomy in a large department, and hence he is more inclined to act.

If the impact of administrative controls is so much stronger in small than in large police departments, why should the effect be that of a reluctance to act? The answer, in brief, is that a decrease in scale enhances public pressure on the police, and complaints about the provision of police services will have more of an impact. A small department's legitimacy is more precarious, and there is a sense of propriety that is not always present in a large professional department like the LAPD. On the other hand, the vaunted autonomy of the LAPD, its predilection to intervene and enforce the law as it sees fit, is partly dependent on organizational size. A large, professional department with a high degree of autonomy will act as a buffer between a patrolman and community opinion. And this provides precisely the kind of environment that facilitates the emergence of the aggressive and strict brand of law enforcement mandated by police professionalism. As one patrolman, who had moved from a small department to the LAPD, put it, "It's easier to be impersonal and strict" in a large department. Ironically, then, the consequence of a decrease in scale may not be greater responsiveness to community demands, but, on the contrary, a disincentive to act.[22]

Whether there is in fact a greater reluctance to act among patrolmen in small departments, and how the uncertainty generated by the bifurcation of internal controls affects the routine decisions patrolmen make, are questions that will be considered at length in subsequent chapters. But does the analysis in this chapter mean that the department as such is relatively unimportant in influencing the choices of patrolmen, and that most of the variation in the exercise of discretion could be explained by the beliefs and attitudes—or operational style—of individual patrolmen? Not necessarily. For one thing, patrolmen differ in the extent to which they will conform to what they believe are the desires and wishes of administrators and supervisors. Second, what I have demonstrated is only that hierarchical controls and the actions of field supervisors do not overtly shape the choices of patrolmen. What has not been considered to this point is whether administrators convey to patrolmen a relatively coherent set of expectations of the way they should behave and whether patrolmen conform to these.

Authority systems in formal organizations are underpinned by a set of normative beliefs that serve to regulate action. As a result of specific attempts at indoctrination and a broader process of organizational socialization, the members of an organization may come to share expectations of the appropriateness or inappropriateness of various actions in differing contexts. To the extent that such norms are shared and accepted as legitimate and binding, they can be characterized as social sanctions.[23]

There is some justification for assuming that the exercise of police discretion is extensively influenced by shared norms. Given the limits to hierarchical controls in police departments, there is correspond-ingly a greater emphasis upon normative controls, the inculcation of a shared outlook about the propriety of various actions. This is re-flected in both the extraordinary homogeneity of outlook in police departments and the attempt, through professionalization, to incul-cate among working policemen a new set of values. On the other hand, patrolmen are fiercely individualistic and inclined to go their own way. There is no reason to assume that patrolmen share all of the expectations of administrators, or even if they do that they will always act on them. Whether patrolmen and field supervisors share a common outlook and the extent to which this explains discretion is an empirical question, and one that will be explored in detail in the following chapters.

Police discretion turns on the pattern of choices made by patrol-men. Police professionalism and the relative autonomy of the depart-ment that results provide patrolmen with the freedom to make un-fettered choices. Whether they do so and with what consequences is the matter to which we now turn.

PART THREE

Working the Street

The policeman fundamentally has a ringside seat on the greatest show on earth. One of the beautiful things about being a policeman is that you're at the center of action all the time. You are seeing people . . . under the most incredible circumstances. You're in on every secret of society in a sense. And that's very exciting. The public doesn't understand everything you see. You can't even explain it. Most policemen have a tighter relationship with their partners than they do with their wives, which is a whole different situation. So the insularity grows, the secretiveness grows, the parochialism grows. Society doesn't understand. The policeman is shocked that society doesn't appreciate him sufficiently. And that really creates a kind of ineluctable drift that I don't know how to combat. . . .

Anthony V. Bouza
Bronx Borough Commander
NYPD

Chapter 6

Crime Fighting

ALL TOO OFTEN the behavior of patrolmen is understood only in terms of their responsibilities for maintaining order and providing services. The presumption is that since these activities—settling family disputes, handling drunks, chasing noisy juveniles, looking for lost children—are what patrolmen most often do, and since very little of their time is spent on crime-related activities, the responsibility and difficulty of performing these tasks define the role of patrolmen.[1] This view may be a necessary corrective to the popular image of the police but it is insufficient as a statement of the patrolman's role. Quite simply, it omits a patrolman's interpretation of his role and functions. Most patrolmen define their task largely as the responsibility for controlling crime, and include almost nothing else.

Crime fighting in professional police departments—and hence the use of discretion in this capacity—rests on two ideas: initiative and deterrence. As elsewhere, the late Chief Parker succinctly summed up the point of view of a professional police in this regard: "The function of the police insofar as [crime] prevention is concerned lies in two general fields: (1) the prevention of criminal acts by actual or potential physical intervention, and (2) performance so effective that the fear of apprehension, conviction and punishment tends to prevent criminal actions; in other words, crime repression."[2] Initiative has become the mainspring of police work, for as professionals patrolmen are expected to, and believe they should, seek out and repress crime. Crime is to be treated as any other social problem; it is to be attacked with a variety of techniques and ultimately subdued. Underlying this belief is an optimism that presumes that a more professional and highly rationalized police can eventually stem the rising tide of crime and violence.

The second idea that underpins crime fighting—deterrence—rests on the hope of preventing crime through vigorous and aggressive police work. Deterrence means more than the acknowledged presence of the police in an area. Ultimately it is the threat and the fear of apprehension that the police rely upon to control crime—hence their concern that the courts often undermine their efforts. Patrolmen often engage in activities on the street that yield rather meager results (random stop and frisk activities) solely because of the presumed deterrent effect.

The acceptance of these two premises has led to the widespread use of aggressive or preventative patrol by professional police departments. Tactically, aggressive patrol requires the widespread use of field interrogations ("stop and frisk" activities, moving loitering juveniles off the street) to both detect and deter crime. Whatever the effectiveness of aggressive patrol—and its efficacy is in doubt—all of the crucial decisions necessitated by the strategy are made by patrolmen. Every patrolman must come to terms with the constraints and opportunities in his role as a professional crime fighter.

Legally, patrolmen have broad powers in fighting crime and engaging in aggressive tactics. A felony arrest or a field interrogation is subject only to the stricture of "reasonable cause," a belief that the individual in question has in fact committed a crime. But what constitutes reasonable cause in any particular set of circumstances is rather vague and subject to varying interpretations—by the courts, the residents of a neighborhood, and the police themselves. The courts have not confronted the basic legal issues raised by field interrogations, and most departments have no policies to guide patrolmen. Further legal issues arise in connection with due process, especially the constitutional guarantee against illegal search and seizure. When and under what circumstances a patrolman may legally engage in a search on the street is often unclear and subject to considerable abuse.[3]

Closely connected to the legal issues is the problematic nature of the information patrolmen use to detect crime and apprehend felons. Patrolmen depend upon citizens to report crime, but their dependence may be ill-founded: citizens do not always report crimes, and if they do, they may do so too late for the police to do anything about it. Patrolmen fall back on a host of vague indicators to detect crime, and one of the important stages of a patrolman's development is learning how to separate the innocuous from the deviant. Much of what a patrolman does in crime fighting is judging different kinds of information.

Another difficulty facing patrolmen is the question of priorities. Patrolmen must learn to balance conflicting responsibilities and to assign priorities to various kinds of violations. A patrolman has to learn how to manage one of his more precious resources, time, and decide which out of the welter of violations he encounters deserve his attention. The question of priorities comes up in another, more subtle way also: what specific charges best fit the behavior in question? Police professionalism has sought to make the law the standard, but the law is not always clear and patrolmen are frequently in the position of deciding what charges are in the interest of what they perceive to be justice. The attitude many patrolmen take toward the law in crime fighting is pragmatic and instrumental rather than legalistic—the law is merely one tool among many to control crime.

Finally, as crime fighters patrolmen must face the possibility that their tactics will deepen the already existing rift between the police and the communities they serve. Aggressive patrol is a widely cited reason for the current disaffection between the police and minority communities, and one of the reasons it is now subject to increasing scrutiny. It juxtaposes for the police the ever present question of means and ends, of repressing crime but maintaining a modicum of community support. To be sure, maintaining the confidence of the public in minority communities has not always been an important concern of the police, but the dilemma cannot be avoided. Inevitably, it falls to patrolmen to decide how far they can go in suppressing crime.

Each patrolman must develop a capacity for judgment, a capacity for handling the legal requirements, the uncertainty of information, the necessity of establishing priorities, and the always problematic relationship with the community that aggressive crime fighting entails. The development of this capacity for judgment is *the* crucial step in the elaboration of a patrolman's operational style. Yet a patrolman finds little guidance in the law, scant help from departmental administrators or supervisors, and only ambiguous directives from the community in meeting the dilemmas and pitfalls involved in the role of aggressive crime fighter. Consequently, patrolmen have considerable freedom to respond as they choose, and their response has significant implications for the way they manage their other responsibilities and adapt to the impact of administrative controls. Patrol-men may vary a great deal in the extent to which they live up to the role of crime fighter, but regardless of their initial motivation, living up to that role entails a specific set of rewards and risks. The way in which patrolmen handle these is the subject of this chapter.

Hitting the Street: The Initial Choices

Whether or not he cares to reflect on the matter, a patrolman makes a series of initial choices that influence his subsequent actions. These choices stem from intrinsic dilemmas of police work that must be successfully managed if a patrolman is to become a competent practitioner of his craft. Initially, a patrolman must be able to reconcile the conflicting demands made upon him. The rationale for having policemen patrol the street on a twenty-four-hour basis can be summed up by two words: availability and deterrence. Though these define the purposes of patrol and are thus complementary, they may also conflict.

A patrolman is expected to be available to respond to people in distress, and most incidents that patrolmen become involved in originate as a call for service. Table 6.1 shows that 57 percent of the incidents observed in all three departments are calls for service. These represent three kinds of incidents: disturbances such as family disputes, fights, or noisy parties; hot calls such as "robbery in progress"; and minor service calls such as crime reports, dead bodies (non-homicide), and the like. There are few differences in the kinds of calls for service handled by each department, and supervisors in all departments expect patrolmen to handle their calls quickly and completely.

Most patrolmen think their presence on the street is a deterrent to crime, indeed perhaps the major deterrent. The visibility of patrol cars prowling about is thought to be a warning to would-be felons, and the more police cars there are—and by implication the more active they are—the lower the crime rate is likely to be. There is some question of whether the visible presence of the police affects the crime rate in any way; and even if it does it is not clear which crimes are affected and how. There are numerous crimes which patrolmen do not consider "repressible," such as crimes of violence that take place within the confines of someone's home, and petty crimes like drunkenness or shoplifting. Crimes that involve some forethought and take place in public—robbery, auto theft, burglary, street muggings—can, most policemen believe, be prevented. Yet the effect of vigorous patrol, if it has any at all, may be more that of displacing crime than deterring it.[4] In any event, patrolmen think they are on the street to do more than just respond to calls for service.

Patrolmen in these departments are involved in crime-related incidents slightly less than a third of the time: 31 percent of all incidents observed involved either the apprehension of felons or the investigation and suppression of crime (see table 6.1, Felony Violations and Field Interrogations). These figures include incidents where a felony has been committed as well as those where a serious crime has potentially been committed—hot calls such as "man with a gun" or "burglary in progress." Not all of these incidents ultimately involve an actual crime. What often counts in the exercise of discretion, though, is not the outcome of these incidents, but rather what a patrolman anticipates and the kind of decision he makes on the basis of the information he has at hand. A "man with a gun" or a "burglary in progress" call, even if it turns out to be unfounded, is handled in a much different way than a routine "disturbing the peace" call. But even if we eliminate burglar alarms and activities such as bar checks, 21 percent of all observed incidents still involve crime control. The majority of crime-related activities that patrolmen engage in are field interrogations—56 percent altogether. Based on these data one would conclude that these patrolmen are more involved in crime-related activities and more aggressive than those observed in previous studies.[5]

The need to provide services and the desire to control crime conflict to the extent that a patrolman views his role as largely one or the other. The values of the police culture—the desire for a "good pinch" —and the centrality of crime fighting to a professional police assure that service activities will be viewed with less than complete acceptance by patrolmen. But regardless of what a patrolman thinks, the expectation of administrators that he ought to give priority to calls for service means there will always be some conflict. Patrolmen respond to this conflict in quite different ways: some simply accept the duality with more or less equanimity and take things as they come; others actively resist and devote their time to the pursuit of felons. The way this conflict is resolved is an important stage in the development of a patrolman's operational style.

TABLE 6.1
Observed Field Incidents by Department

Observed Incidents	High-crime Areas		Low-crime Areas		All Departments
	Inglewood	Rampart	Redondo Beach	Northeast	
Mode of Intervention	(%)	(%)	(%)	(%)	(%)
On-view	39	45	40	45	43
Call for Service	61	55	60	55	57
Number of Incidents Observed	(108)	(174)	(98)	(131)	(512)
Type of Incident					
Minor Violations[a]	32	32	46	24	34
Disturbances[b]	28	22	24	24	24
Felony Violations[c]	15	12	11	17	14
Field Interrogations[d]	11	20	8	26	17
Miscellaneous Service[e]	14	12	11	8	11
Number of Incidents Observed	(108)	(174)	(98)	(131)	(512)

SOURCE: Field Observations, 1972–73.
[a] All calls or stops involving miscemeanors, such as, traffic stops, petty theft, "drunk in public," parking violations.
[b] All calls or stops involving order-maintenance problems, such as, fights, family disputes, noisy parties.
[c] All calls or stops involving the commission or *potential* commission of a "Part I crime," such as, major assaults, robbery, burglary, "man with a gun."
[d] All calls or stops to investigate suspicious circumstances and/or a suspicious individual, and selective enforcement of laws.
[e] All service calls—crime reports, traffic accidents, missing children, recovery of stolen property, dead bodies, suicides, and community meetings (team policing in the LAPD).

CRIME FIGHTING

In balancing the demands of these two roles a patrolman confronts the limits on his time and has to make decisions about relevant priorities. Time can be a precious resource for a patrolman, especially if he takes his role as crime fighter seriously. It should be apparent that if a patrolman must respond to calls, his freedom of action is greatly limited; not only does he lose time but the situation and available legal alternatives may preclude much in the way of independent action. A patrolman's free time may be spent in any way he chooses, and the more free time he has at his disposal, the more he is able to exercise his powers of discretion in a way that fits his own interpretation of his task. The management of the conflict between crime fighting and service responsibilities manifests itself in a choice of whether and how to create and use free time from calls. A patrolman's choices here have implications for the way he handles the crime fighting function and other responsibilities. The decision of how to use free time is a direct expression of an officer's priorities and thus his operational style.[6]

One indication of the importance of free time is the proportion of independently initiated (on-view) actions undertaken by patrolman. Table 6.1 shows that 43 percent of all observed incidents were the result of decisions by patrolmen to take independent action. And these stops were overwhelmingly devoted to crime fighting and law enforcement; 95 percent of all on-view actions were undertaken either to enforce minor violations or to conduct field interrogations.

How much free time do patrolmen actually have? Reiss estimates that in the typical tour of duty 70 percent of the time is spent simply patrolling an assigned area. While this is somewhat higher than observed in this study, the average amount of free time available to a patrolman is higher than he would lead you to believe. Nevertheless, if free time is not given to a patrolman, it can be and often is taken. Many patrolmen, well aware of the limitations imposed by the radio, seek to manipulate their activities so as to create more free time for independent action. This process, sometimes called "engineering", often amounts to a refusal to clear with the dispatcher once an assignment has been completed. By refusing to clear immediately after a call has been completed, a patrolman gains some uninterrupted time in which he can pursue his favorite violation.

Another variation of engineering is to actively look for another violation in order to get out of an assigned call. Two crime-minded patrolmen received a call to respond to a routine family dispute. They acknowledged the call, but in order to get out of it, they stopped five different individuals looking for a "hype" (heroin addict) they could arrest. These stops included a heroin addict they had previously arrested and saw driving down the street; a man making a phone call in front of a market; and two juveniles driving slowly down a street. They arrived at the call about an hour after they received it. Finally, though it must be used judiciously, patrolmen may go "code six" (out for investigation) at a particular location in order to avoid radio calls.

As a rule, engineering is more prevalent in a large department like the LAPD because of the surfeit of resources, the sheer number of patrol cars available to respond to calls for service, and the larger geographical area which facilitates mobility. These conditions allow patrolmen to move about and get involved in the kind of incidents they prefer. Practically every observed instance of engineering occurred in the LAPD.

A second choice a patrolman confronts prior to leaving the station turns on his *mood,* the tacit decision of how he will work. What one does, patrolmen liked to point out, depends on how one feels. As one patrolman said: "Some days you feel like getting everybody and you go out and really scratch; other days you take it easy, make a few stops and write a few F.I.'s (Field Interrogation reports) to make your log look good and let it go at that. You just hang loose and have tunnel vision." Mood may also influence decisions: the same situation might result in an arrest one night and a warning the next. Decisions, many patrolmen insist, depend on "small" things, how one feels and even what just seems interesting.

Mood is not something to be dismissed. There is often an arbitrary quality about the act of discretion, a whimsical attitude that may result in one man's arrest and another man's release. This is partly because making an arrest is a rather routine affair to a patrolman. Yet there is more stability in their behavior than most patrolmen would have one believe; the fluctuations in their behavior are neither as radical nor as totally arbitrary as the idea of mood might suggest. Stability in the act of discretion stems from limitations imposed on a patrolman's freedom, his personal objectives and interests, and the kind of operational style he develops. Mood may dictate deviations from this style but it does not fundamentally alter it. Rather mood is an intrinsic characteristic of police work which modulates a patrolman's style. Mood as it affects discretion is highly unstable. To see why, we must inquire a bit further.

In the most trivial sense, mood simply means that an officer may not want to work very hard. Yet, more fundamentally, mood as a factor in discretion involves the resolution of two problems facing all patrolmen. Mood first of all denotes the continual temptation and opportunity facing a policeman to displace private frustrations, anxieties, and hostilities on the public. This will necessarily influence the kinds of decisions he may make. For instance, an officer may have had an especially nasty fight with his wife, and act as if every woman he meets in the context of a family dispute deserves the same as his wife. Hostilities toward racial groups or juveniles may be vented through the process of discretion. These actions, however, are less a reflection of an officer's momentary mood than of the displacement of private anger. Much of what the police designate as mood is a result of this phenomenon.

The other problem stems from an intrinsic characteristic of police work, *boredom*. The daily routine of burglary reports, barking-dog calls, kids shooting off fire crackers and bothering the old couple up the street, stumbling and vomit-splattered drunks, daydreaming people running stop signs, missing children, and just plain driving around deadens even the dullest of men. The threat of the unexpected is always present, but occasionally one is required to create the unexpected in order to relieve the boredom. In the absence of numerous calls for service or an especially interesting situation that patrolmen just happen upon, one's mood may dictate looking for a particular violation, going to the park and looking for some juveniles smoking marijuana or drinking, bothering parked lovers, or even "buying" a call from other patrolmen. Mood in this context is a euphemism for problems or violations that seem interesting and may provide an outlet to the need for action.

Coping with the boredom of the job is especially difficult for the patrolman who takes the role of crime fighter seriously. Crime fighting requires that one dig and scramble to "come up with something," but what an officer comes up with is not always as good as he would like, and sometimes what happens is a frenzied search for activity of any kind. In such situations a patrolman's sense of propriety and his interpretation of the law is perhaps looser than normal. Violations that might normally entail only a warning or some other informal action will be subject to arrest or citation. It may also lead to the abuse of authority in minor, but to the people involved, important ways.

Two highly aggressive young officers were having trouble coping with a rather uneventful evening, and decided to go to the park to "check out the lovers." This game, which was rationalized as looking for would-be rapists or muggers, involved pulling along side a parked car in which a couple was necking or otherwise engaged, jumping out of the patrol car and getting both occupants out in order to check their identification. The patrolmen checked four parked cars and broke up four couples. More than the possibility of a crime, it seemed that the officers were concerned with catching a couple of lovers engaged in sexual intercourse. To their obvious delight, they were successful in one instance on this night. Much of the reprehensible behavior of policemen is due less to a predisposition to be authoritarian than to boredom.

A patrolman's mood, then, as it affects discretion turns on the problem of controlling private anger and attempting to cope with boredom. Both factors give many decisions a whimsical, even an arbitrary quality, but from the patrolman's point of view it simply allows him to adjust to personal frustration and the demands of his task. For this reason mood is a factor that modulates an officer's operational style without substantially altering it. Not every patrolman copes with boredom by harassing lovers.

The Felony Pinch: Limitations and Opportunities

In an occupation in which the rewards are few, one of the great satisfactions for its practitioners is the making of a felony pinch (arrest). Much police lore is taken up with the problems and prospects of making such a pinch; and while the goal of crime fighting may not be everything, for all but a very few policemen a good felony arrest provides the personal satisfaction that comes with the competent practice of any craft. The anecdotes of good arrests passed back and forth in the locker room and in the watch commander's office inevitably become war stories, the recounting of past exploits and the possibilities of future ones.

The popular image of the detective as crime fighter notwithstanding, most felony arrests are made by patrolmen. Patrol, as the department sages put it, is where the action is; the detective bureau is for "paper pushers." Most of the arrests for major felonies (homicide, robbery, and burglary) in these departments are made by patrolmen. Yet patrolmen in both divisions of the LAPD are more likely to become involved in crime-related incidents than their counterparts in the small departments. Of the observed crime-related incidents in the LAPD, 75 percent concerned field interrogations or felony incidents where a crime had been committed. The comparable figure for the small departments is 60 percent. Most of this difference is attributable to the greater propensity of patrolmen in the LAPD to stop and interrogate individuals on the street. Indeed, they are twice as likely to do so: 23 percent of all observed incidents in the LAPD were field interrogations compared to 10 percent in the small departments (see table 6.1). A further indication of the greater preoccupation with crime in the LAPD is the arrest rates for narcotics violations and illegal possession of weapons. Arrest rates for these two offenses are a good indication of the overall aggressiveness of patrolmen, and the rates are considerably higher for both divisions of the LAPD. All three of these departments have specialized narcotics units, but some of the difference in narcotics arrests is attributable to the greater inclination of patrolmen in the LAPD to seek out and make narcotics arrests—including possession of marijuana or heroin, and on one occasion, dealing. The higher arrest rate for weapons offenses is another indication of the seriousness with which crime fighting is viewed by patrolmen since many of these arrests take place in the context of a field interrogation.

CHOOSING PRIORITIES

Patrolmen are confronted with an enormous variety of violations which they can enforce if they so choose. All patrolmen must decide how serious they regard different violations and where they will apply their energies. One of the more clear-cut choices facing a patrolman is whether to concentrate on serious felony violations or to emphasize the enforcement of a wide range of violations. Most of the patrolmen in these three departments are more oriented toward a wide range of violations than to crime fighting per se. That is, they do not believe that a patrolman, as a rule, should ignore misdemeanor violations and concentrate only upon felonies. Only 24 percent believed that an effective patrolman was one who patrolled only for felony violations; and only a slightly higher percentage (29 percent) thought that patrolmen should not make arrests for minor violations (table 6.2, statements a and b). A felony pinch may be one of the supreme rewards but among these officers it is a rare policeman that will turn down a good traffic citation or other misdemeanor. This tendency is doubtless reinforced by the expectations of field

TABLE 6.2

Patrolmen's and Supervisors' Attitudes Toward Priorities of Law Enforcement

Those Who Agreed with the Following Statement	High-crime Areas				Low-crime Areas				All Departments	
	Inglewood		Rampart		Redondo Beach		Northeast			
	Patrolmen (%)	Supervisors (%)	Patrolmen (%)	Supervisors (%)	Patrolmen (%)	Supervisors (%)	Patrolmen (%)	Supervisors (%)	Patrolmen (%)	Supervisors (%)
a. A really effective patrolman is one who patrols for serious felony violations rather than stopping people for minor traffic violations and other misdemeanors.	27	8	22	6	18	10	26	12	24	9
b. A patrolman should not make a lot of arrests for minor violations (such as drunks) or issue a lot of citations for minor violations.	34	36	22	31	29	30	31	35	29	33
c. It's a waste of time and takes time away from more important things to arrest someone for possession of 2 or 3 marijuana cigarettes.	24	17	20	12	21	20	22	18	22	16
Mean Scale Score[a]	48.59		51.31		49.06		51.14			
Number of Respondents	(62)	(12)	(51)	(17)	(34)	(10)	(51)	(17)	(198)	(56)

supervisors, all of whom are even less inclined than patrolmen to single out felonies as the chief priority. There are, moreover, *no significant differences among the departments* in this regard. In short, most of the patrolmen in these departments are concerned not just with crime fighting but with law enforcement. Yet at least one-fourth, by no means an insignificant portion, take what might be called a strict crime fighter stance toward their task; that is, they are selective in the enforcement of misdemeanors and emphasize felony violations.

Even though a patrolman may take the point of view that all of the laws are important, and that a policeman should pay as much attention to minor violations as to serious ones, no patrolman entirely escapes the necessity of choosing priorities. The decision to make an arrest has consequences other than those affecting the person arrested. It means one less car is available to answer calls or act as a deterrent. In fact, some patrolmen argue that the enforcement of minor violations dilutes the deterrent effect. A patrolman faces a choice, one said, "between making a lot of stops and being taken out of the field for a minor or even trivial reason or staying in the field in order to be available if something really big goes down." The decision to arrest a drunk may mean a lost opportunity to catch an armed robber, and the latter is conceded to have more importance than the former. Even though the decision of whether to enforce a minor violation is not always consciously evaluated at this level, these concerns are nonetheless present.

Regardless of the law enforcement stance of most of these patrolmen, the autonomy legitimized by the norm of individualism facilitates the emergence of an informal pattern of specialization among patrolmen, a tendency to concentrate on specific kinds of violations. This is most apparent for avowed crime fighters, but other patrolmen indulge themselves as well.[7] Often specialization amounts to working those violations deemed important or interesting. But skill is also relevant. One patrolman admitted that burglary was a more serious crime than drunk driving and that he would rather catch a burglar than a drunk driver; but since he seemed to be unable to catch burglars and had a knack for catching drunk drivers, he concentrated on the latter. The most prominent specialists observed were those cops who worked narcotics, who focused their time and skills on the apprehension of heroin addicts. Other patrolmen were observed concentrating on traffic violations.

Field supervisors may complain about the informal pattern of specialization which exists among patrolmen from time to time, but there is little they can do about it since it is sustained by the disjuncture between performance and rewards, specifically promotions. In the assessment of an officer's performance for a promotion, as we have seen, his actual performance on the street—the kinds of decisions he makes—has only marginal significance. But if an officer wants to get out of patrol and is not interested in becoming a sergeant, specialization helps. For instance, a patrolman who wants to get into "motors," the specialized motorcycle traffic enforcement unit, may spend most of his time enforcing traffic laws in order to demonstrate his proficiency in this area. Two promotion-minded patrolmen were observed to select obscure sections of the vehicle code for enforcement during a tour of duty. They believed this was a good way to learn the vehicle code and that it would look good on their records. Yet it is among avowed crime fighters that the link between specialization and promotional opportunities is most apparent. These men are motivated not only by the desire to contain crime but also by their own ambitions—typically the desire to move up the ladder or into an investigative unit. Crime fighting is not the only way up the ladder, but it can be an important one.

Clear-cut choices of priorities, a single-minded concentration on felonies, and the link between specialization and promotions is most apparent among those patrolmen specializing in narcotics. Some of these men are resourceful and aggressive patrolmen, and their activities cover the gamut of investigative techniques, including the development of narcotics informants or staking out a known narcotics drop. But actions such as those undertaken by the patrolmen in Case Histories 1 and 2 are the exception; for most patrolmen, rousting suspected addicts on the street is the preferred tactic. In cultivating informants or even staking out a suspected drop-off point, patrolmen must maneuver their way out of calls for service, and they run some risks since, at least in the LAPD, there is a rather restrictive policy governing the recruitment of informants by patrolmen. For these reasons it is typically the common addict that bears the brunt of the specialist's forays.

Case History 1

A patrolman, who avidly worked narcotics, drove to one of the seedier areas of his beat to "check out" his snitch. His snitch was a 26-year-old prostitute who was addicted to heroin. She typically provided information about small-time dealers, usually holding very small quantities of marijuana or heroin. The patrolman then went to the location on a pretext and tried to gain permission to search the house, a strategy which had—rather surprisingly—been successful more than once, and resulted in several arrests. On this night, she provided information about a man named Xavier who had a large stash of marijuana and had provided her with "two spoons" of very good heroin that afternoon. The patrolman attempted to get her to make some buys so that the man could be arrested for dealing rather than possession. The patrolman was off the air approximately thirty-five minutes talking to his informant.

Case History 2

Two patrolmen went "code six" and staked out a well-known drop-off point (a bar) for narcotics. They observed a man walking in and out of the bar as if he were looking for someone, and making a phone call from a booth in front of the bar. When he eventually left the bar, the patrolmen followed him, stopped him, and arrested him for possession of heroin after they discovered heroin in his car.

In order to apprehend heroin addicts, the narcotics specialists proceed by checking areas where they are known to hang out, and then stopping and investigating suspected addicts to see if they are under the influence of heroin. If the suspect had, in the patrolman's judgment, used heroin within the previous ten hours, he was "under the influence," and could be (at the time of the study) legally arrested for possession of heroin. Inevitably, this loose standard was subject to abuse: two patrolmen brazenly arrested a man for being in withdrawal, that is, for having used heroin two days previously. While the narcotics specialists all asserted that it took some acquired skill to ferret out addicts, most of the stops were rather random and often made on the flimsiest of criteria (decision rules used in stopping suspects on the street are discussed later). There were other patrolmen who regarded these arrests as "shaky" and a waste of time. But as long as these patrolmen were making felony arrests, they were usually left alone by supervisors (most of them said they were rarely under pressure to enforce traffic laws or any other minor violation).

Notwithstanding the one arrest of a dealer I observed (Case History 2), these patrolmen are not really interested in choking off the supply of narcotics as much as in curbing a narcotics-related crime such as burglary. Narcotics addicts, these patrolmen believe, resort to burglary to support their habit, and the arrest of a heroin addict means one less burglar on the street. Whether the tactics of these officers are successful in curbing burglaries is debatable. What is not debatable is that reducing the crime rate is the only incentive for these officers. By specializing in narcotics, these patrolmen believe they can demonstrate their proficiency in arresting "hypes," developing informants, and making buys to narcotics investigators. The enterprising patrolman may even be in a position occasionally to share information with them and provide leads to narcotics activity in his area. Through these informal relationships with narcotics investigators a patrolman enhances his chances, or so he believes, of being promoted to an investigative position. All of the patrolmen observed specializing in narcotics expressed, at one time or another, the desire to "get out of the bag" and into a narcotics unit. Given the ease with which many of these patrolmen picked up personnel complaints, the only way many of them would ever "get out of the bag" was by getting into a specialized investigative unit.

There is little difference in regard to obvious background characteristics between patrolmen who concentrate on felonies and specialize in narcotics and other patrolmen. What does distinguish them is that many of them either trained with a patrolman who displayed the same keen interest in narcotics or felonies or they learned to work the street in one of the city's high crime areas. Beyond this it is their burning ambition and their willingness to take risks that set them apart. Happenstance is clearly a factor in police work, and many felony arrests are made as the result of encountering a fortuitous set of circumstances. But the crime fighters remind one of capitalist entrepreneurs: they have the time and resources to create their opportunities, they calculate their risks, and then they take their chances.

The emergence of single-minded crime fighters and the tendency to specialize is present in all three departments, but it is most prominent in the LAPD. The dearth of resources and the limitations on a patrolman's time and freedom in the small departments preclude extensive specialization and make crime fighting somewhat more difficult. And there is less incentive to specialize in one of the small departments since there are fewer opportunities for promotion and only small specialized enforcement units. In LAPD, where there are fewer constraints on a patrolman's freedom, those who are singularly devoted to crime fighting have more maneuverability, and specialization is one solution to the problem of promotions.

DECISION RULES IN THE FELONY PINCH

While felonies offer patrolmen less latitude than minor violations or disturbances, discretion is not eliminated. Patrolmen must interpret behavior, and in doing so they are guided less by the law than by pragmatic judgments of what a situation requires. The law becomes a tool to be manipulated in the interest of what they conceive to be justice, and while this may lead to a more desirable outcome than a literal application of the law, it often leads to minor, and not so minor, abuses of power.

The police believe that their ability to deter crime and apprehend felons depends on their capacity to respond quickly to the scene of an occurring crime. The hot call is a central event for the men in a patrol car even though many are false. The radio is monitored continuously for such calls, and any patrol car in the immediate vicinity will respond to a hot call, even if it is assigned to another car. Not all hot calls are treated with the same degree of concern. Burglar alarms are often treated perfunctorily, since so many are false; an armed robbery call or alarm, on the other hand, is treated seriously, both because of the serious nature of the crime and the likelihood that it is genuine. Yet many hot calls cannot be so easily judged on the basis of the radio communication, and thus must be treated as real until proven otherwise.

Hot calls pose two different issues for the exercise of discretion. If a patrolman arrives soon enough at the scene of a hot call, there is a very real possibility that he will catch the culprit in the act or, more importantly, in the immediate area. Hot calls thus create situations that result in other police activities, namely, the stopping and questioning of persons in the area. This process is an important aspect of probable cause, and will be discussed in greater detail later.

More important, hot calls necessitate decisions about tactics, especially the use of lethal force. These decisions are predicated on the potentially "real" nature of the call, the possibility that violence will be encountered; but in the event the call is false a decision to shoot can result in the death of an innocent person. Many patrolmen believe that lethal force is justified only as a matter of self-protection, but the definition of what constitutes a threat to a patrolman's life is ambiguous. An individual need not be armed and threatening the life of a patrolman or innocent bystander for an officer to shoot; he need only make a "furtive movement," a vague indication that he might use a weapon. Matters are complicated by the uncertain quality of information patrolmen possess when they arrive at the scene of a hot call.

Two patrolmen responded, one morning, to what appeared to be a good breaking and entering call in a residential area. When they arrived it was apparent that some persons were in the house and the officer with the shotgun leveled it on them and ordered them out. Any indication of potential violence and he would have pulled the trigger. As it turned out the individuals in the house were thinking of purchasing the house and had come to inspect it; finding it locked they entered through a window which caused a neighbor to call the police. The police had no way of knowing this and treated the situation as a burglary until proven otherwise. Here as elsewhere, though there are decided differences of opinion and approach among patrolmen, some will resort to the use of their gun on the basis of very little information while others rarely if ever feel compelled to do so.

In one sense, felonies are the least interesting of discretionary incidents, for these violations are usually enforced. Refusal to arrest a person who has committed a felony not only counters the police code, but many policemen believe they have no discretion where a felony is concerned. This does not mean that every person who commits a felony will be arrested, since the determination of whether or not a felony has been committed is often a matter of interpretation. This is particularly true of assaults. Circumstances may also minimize the latitude of the officer. The matter may be very clear-cut when a man is caught walking out of a liquor store with money and gun in hand; but this kind of situation occurs rather infrequently. More commonly, the decision turns on a strict determination of the facts. In the following burglary what mattered to the patrolmen was the ability of the suspect to verify his story in some acceptable manner.

Case History 3

A patrolman responded to a "459 in Progress" (burglary) call. Motorcycle officers were present when he arrived and they described the situation as follows: neighbors observed two men loading a stereo set into a Volkswagan van, and thinking that a burglary was taking place called the police. The men claimed that one of them had purchased the stereo from the owner of the house, and that he (the owner) had given them permission to enter the house through the rear door and remove the stereo. The back door was opened through a broken window pane, which the men claimed was broken before they arrived. Moreover, they left a note for the owner which the police found inside. The two men had very little identification on them, and had no clear idea of where to find the owner in order to verify their story. The police said that the story must be verified by the owner before they would be released. The dispatcher was unable to locate the owner at the phone number provided by the men, and the people at the man's presumed place of work knew nothing about a stereo. Consequently, the two men were booked on suspicion of burglary.

The physical evidence could be interpreted as requiring either an arrest or release in this case. The officers believed that they had good circumstantial evidence that a burglary had been committed. The lack of adequate identification was interpreted as something that any intelligent burglar would do, and the note inside the house, they concluded, could be a ploy. Thus, they were reluctant to let the men go until their story could be verified, reasoning that if they did not insist on verification they would risk releasing two burglars.

Discretion entered into this situation insofar as the officers decided not to take the men's story at face value. With the exception of this decision, the case turned on a determination of the facts, and to this extent precluded independent action. As a rule, the police are reluctant to give the benefit of the doubt to the suspect, and in an ambiguous situation they will resort to some other method of determining the facts. Thus, in this regard, the police adopt a rather conservative rule of thumb, one which posits that most, if not all, suspects are lying and that most stories cannot be taken at face value. This is not so much cynicism as it is the inclination to expect the worst.

But the question raised by this incident is, What makes a story believable to the police? Both of the suspects in this case were black. Did their race influence the officers' inclination not to believe their story? This is possible, and the fact that blacks are more likely than whites to be arrested for felonies may be indicative of this. On the other hand, I did observe an incident in which two black youths convinced two patrolmen that they had nothing to do with a street robbery (see Case History 8). The only reason the youths were not released was that the victim arrived at the scene before the officers released them, and she was able to identify one of them. The question of whether race influences an officer's inclination to believe a suspect's story is important since the social consequences of being arrested are rather severe, even if the person is innocent. I believe it is a plausible hypothesis that race is an influential factor in a decision of this sort, but there is little evidence bearing on it one way or the other.[8]

Another fact about felony arrests is that a surprising number of them come about through happenstance. It is a rare occasion when a patrolman catches a burglar or armed robber in the act; more frequently, patrolmen stumble on a crime or a suspect. Again these situations preclude much in the way of independent action since they are normally clear-cut—though there may be decisions in regard to due process, such as whether or not to search a person or a vehicle. The following two incidents illustrate the happenstance nature of some arrests.

Case History 4

A patrolman was issuing parking citations in the parking lot of a local bar known among policemen in the department as a trouble-spot. While doing so he discovered a stolen car (the car had been mentioned during briefing) and arrested the occupant for auto theft.

Case History 5

A man driving down a residential street crashed into a parked car. He appeared to be drunk or under the influence of narcotics, but since nobody had witnessed the accident or had seen him driving the vehicle he could not be arrested for drunk driving. The traffic officers called to the scene two patrolmen known to specialize in narcotics violations. They checked his arms for needle marks and his pupils for the amount of dilation. They said he was under the influence of heroin, and he was booked for possession of heroin.

In both of these cases, patrolmen stumbled onto a felony violation which was more or less clear-cut. Yet, despite what seems to be rather immutable limitations on a patrolman's discretion in these situations, patrolmen are not completely hemmed in by circumstances. From one point of view, the problem of discretion is largely that of finding some correspondence between *behavior* and *legal rules.* Often, as in the case of the stolen vehicle, the meaning of an individual's behavior and the applicable laws are not in question. Yet not all felony situations afford such a clear-cut choice; there is often room for interpretation of the meaning and intent of behavior and, consequently, some latitude in the preference of charges. And the choice of charges often depends on what patrolmen think should be done in a particular case. The man in Case History 5 could just as easily have been booked for "plain drunk," but since the police were intent on holding him accountable for the wreck and a drunk driving charge was precluded (drunk driving is a misdemeanor and therefore subject to the "in presence" requirement), they attempted, successfully, to arrest the man on a felony. The question of what charges to prefer is of enormous significance in assault cases since there is more at stake than the enforcement of a minor violation. This is clearly shown in the following incident.

Case History 6

Two white youths (eighteen to twenty years of age) armed with knives, broke into an apartment occupied by the ex-wife of one of them. They broke down the door but as they entered they were confronted by another man (a boy friend) armed with a gun. He ordered them to leave. They left, and ran into the arms of the police, who had been called by the ex-wife. The two youths were armed with hunting knives sharpened on both sides, and they had been accompanied by two friends who had remained behind in their car. Investigation revealed that earlier in the day the husband had threatened to kill his ex-wife. The police had initially decided to arrest the two youths for carrying concealed weapons and to release the other two. However, after discussing the matter, they decided to arrest the two who broke into the apartment for attempted murder and the other two on charges of conspiracy, that is as accessories. Superficially, the police had the elements of attempted murder and conspiracy: the threat to the ex-wife, the break-in, and fact that the youths were armed. Yet the officers also knew that the prosecutor would not file charges on attempted murder and conspiracy; he would be more likely to reduce the attempted murder to disturbing the peace and drop the conspiracy charges. They decided, partly on the advice of a sergeant, to charge the youths with the more serious violations in order to keep them off the street for a few days and to "throw a scare into them."

There was no question that the men in this case would be arrested, but the police did have some latitude in choosing the charges. The choice of charges was important because they would have some bearing on the outcome of the case if it went to court and they could be instrumental in accomplishing objectives of concern to the police. The police in this instance were motivated to prefer charges for more serious offenses for two reasons. They were first concerned with preventing another assault, for they had reason to believe that if the men were booked on a misdemeanor they would be out on bail immediately and in a position to come back to the apartment. Second, they were aware that if the charge were carrying a concealed weapon, it would be reduced to disturbing the peace, a very minor violation which usually results in nothing more than a small fine. By preferring the higher charge, the police sought to limit the alternatives of the prosecutor and hopefully assure a conviction for a more serious (and in their opinion deserved) charge such as assault and battery.

Both of these reasons are extra-legal considerations that can have a decisive impact on the exercise of discretion. Although most policemen will not take responsibility for the solution of interpersonal problems which may lead to a crime, they are concerned to prevent violence in the immediate circumstances. The law, however, does not admit of such considerations; immediate, practical, albeit short-range solutions such as that described in the attempted assault Case History are usually precluded by the law, and patrolmen may be required to bend the law in order to solve what they see as a serious problem. The belief that circumstances may require an extra-legal action is relevant to a wide range of discretionary decisions, but it is most important in the context of disturbances (this is discussed at length in the next chapter).

There are two other kinds of incidents where extra-legal considerations come into play in the determination of charges and the decision to arrest. These are situations in which the police want to detain a person for purposes of investigation or where an arrest is used as a means of harassment—often under the guise of selective enforcement. In a number of cases, individuals were arrested for the possession of very small quantities of marijuana, one or two grams at most. (At the time of the study, I should note, possession of marijuana was a felony in California; possession of small quantities of marijuana has since been changed to a misdemeanor.) These arrests were made even though the arresting officers were well aware that the prosecutor would not file charges (the Los Angeles County D.A. files only if 30 grams or more are found). In one instance, a man originally arrested for a traffic warrant was arrested for possession of marijuana —the remains of a marijuana cigarette were found in the ashtray of his car. After transporting him to the station a credit card was found behind the back seat of the patrol car. The credit card, the patrolmen discovered, had been stolen from a woman in a neighboring city about six months previously. The man could have been arrested on a traffic warrant, but he was charged with possession of marijuana in order to detain him in jail long enough to investigate the credit card. (It is worth pointing out that the patrolman who made this arrest did search under the rear seat of the patrol car prior to leaving the station that night, so there was little question that this man had dropped the credit card. On the other hand, the search they conducted that turned up the marijuana was, at the time, illegal.)

The pragmatic cast of police decision making and the conscious manipulation of the law is even more apparent in selective enforcement. Selective enforcement, as the police use the term, denotes the conscious and systematic use of the law to control a particular crime problem. Suppose that a substantial portion of traffic accidents are due to motorists running a stop light at a particular intersection. A strategy of selective enforcement would dictate that patrolmen "work" that intersection for all traffic violations but primarily those believed to cause the accidents. (Some administrators argue that simply bringing pressure to bear on a problem makes the difference and it does not matter what laws are enforced so long as the police make their presence known.) Selective enforcement thus concentrates police power on a problem believed to be especially noxious and which the police feel is not amenable to another kind of solution. The problem that arises is when the police use their powers of enforcement as a tool of harassment. Consider the following example:

Case History 7

Just prior to closing time for bars (2:00 A.M.) two patrolmen stationed themselves, out of sight, near a bar frequented by members of two motorcycle gangs. As different gang members left the bar they were stopped and given traffic citations for illegal U-turns in a commercial district, noisy mufflers, and equipment violations. The officers said later that they were intentionally harassing the bikers, hoping to provoke one of them to a more serious violation or to get him to leave the area. For the past two weeks there had been a lot of assaults committed by members of the two gangs against one another, the most recent involving a gun. The police had been unable to make an arrest since no one would reveal what had happened or prefer charges. They believed they had to handle the problem in another way, and they decided to continue issuing traffic citations to the bikers until they left town or settled down.

While a strategy of selective enforcement can be based on an administrative decision or policy, most such decisions are made by patrolmen on the basis of their knowledge of a particular problem and their desire to do something about it. The patrolmen in the example were simply fed up with the bikers and decided to act. In another, similar, situation patrolmen periodically dropped by a local service station suspected of being a drop spot for stolen Volkswagons. In one instance, two patrolmen saw a car parked on the sidewalk at the station, and two Mexican-American youths working on a small motorcycle next to it. After they ascertained that the motorcycle was not stolen, they gave one of the youths a citation for parking on the sidewalk. They did this, they said, in order to let them know the police were around and watching.

Selective enforcement and the propensity to specialize in narcotics are simply extensions, though more sophisticated, of the use of police power to cope with the problem of crime. While the ultimate goal is always that of apprehension, the proximate goal—and the one that animates the decisions of patrolmen—is that of prevention, of utilizing police powers in legal, quasi-legal, and illegal ways to demonstrate the presence of the police and to deter crime. Selective enforcement often involves enforcing violations not ordinarily enforced in order to control groups suspected of crimes or causing a problem that the police are otherwise unable to solve. These decisions are not always illegal (the parking citation issued to the youths in the service station was perfectly legal) as much as they sometimes involve the dubious application of enforcement powers.

Nevertheless, patrolmen do engage in outright harassment, often as a way of asserting their authority over individuals and ensuring that their vision of justice is implemented. Two patrolmen, who were piqued after almost becoming embroiled in an altercation with a Mexican-American, decided to stop a Mexican-American youth and check him out, that is, interrogate him. They turned on the red light, but the youth did not stop; rather he drove slowly down the street, and as he did so, he hung his arm out the side of the car and seemed to be dropping something from his hand. The patrolmen concluded it was marijuana, and after stopping him they were able to find a few leaves on the floor board. He was charged with drunk driving and for possession of two-tenths of a gram of marijuana, even though the patrolmen were well aware that the marijuana charge would be dropped by the prosecutor. They pointed out that what was involved was the "principle of the thing," and even if the prosecutor would not act, the suspect would spend a few days in jail and have a marijuana arrest on his record. Their justification for their action was somewhat disingenuous though; the youth's fate was sealed the minute he decided not to come to an immediate stop. Having been brought to the boiling point by a near altercation with another Mexican-American, these patrolmen were not about to tolerate any defiance of their authority.

In sum, although a patrolman's discretion is circumscribed in the case of a felony, it is not eliminated. Patrolmen have some choice in the interpretation of circumstances and in deciding what charges to prefer. The law is often used pragmatically and instrumentally by patrolmen to accomplish objectives they deem important, and extralegal considerations are introduced into many decisions. The decision of what charges to prefer is based on the need for further investigation, on the desire for harassment, and on the belief that a crime-related problem can be solved only by preferring higher charges than justified. Patrolmen may also be influenced by the practices of the prosecutor—though they clearly ignore the policies of the prosecutor if it suits them—and their inclination is to prefer the highest possible charges in anticipation of a decision by the prosecutor to reduce charges. These decision rules were common to all three police departments, though the propensity of patrolmen to engage in harassment varied.

Unlike misdemeanor arrests, a felony arrest may be subject to a number of formal departmental controls. Sergeants are required to be at the scene of a hot call or a major disturbance, and if they arrive in time, they are in a position to direct patrolmen and make the decisions themselves. There were incidents in which supervisors did take over, but the typical response was to wait and see if the patrolmen needed any assistance or if their help was requested.[9] In the attempted murder situation (Case History 6), a sergeant was present, his advice was requested by the patrolmen handling the call, and he was instrumental in persuading them to charge the youths with attempted murder. Yet this was less an instance of administrative control over discretion than of the mutual collaboration of colleagues.

Of the three departments, only the LAPD has a formal pre-booking approval procedure. The procedure presumably applies to all arrests, but it is really mandatory only for felonies, for only in the case of a felony is a booking-approval slip, which must be signed by the watch commander or station sergeant, required at the jail. This is clearly a formal control over discretion, but my observations of the process suggest that supervisors are almost always quite willing to defer to patrolmen; approval ordinarily seemed to be a formality. Yet the existence of this procedure does put supervisors in a position to influence and on occasion dictate the decision. Two officers arrested a man for burglary, though all they had was some circumstantial evidence that he intended to commit a burglary. As a field sergeant advised them to book the man for burglary, they detained him and requested the watch commander's advice. He pointed out that all they had was some very weak evidence that the man might be intending to commit a crime, and that they could not arrest him. The man was released. This example is instructive for two reasons. First, there are situations where patrolmen will seek to pass the decision to a supervisor, either because they really do not know what to do or in order to protect themselves. Second, it illustrates the collegiality characteristic of the relationship between patrolmen and supervisors. Most supervisors take the position that their responsibility is to assist patrolmen in the accomplishment of a task which is of mutual concern. Their actions in approving a booking are less a matter of bureaucratic control than of providing the support and assistance deemed necessary. Many supervisors, when asked about the efficacy of this procedure, said that they rarely had to overturn a decision, simply because patrolmen did not make many mistakes. Some supervisors were rather protective of patrolmen in this regard. As one sergeant in the LAPD vehemently explained:

> "Look you take a high school graduate, give him a twelve-week crash course in the law, a badge, a gun, and a uniform and put him on the street and tell him to crush crime. He says "great." Then he is expected to go out and make decisions in a split second that a judge and jury has a month to deliberate on. The officer is put on trial in the courtroom, he is made to justify himself to an unreasonable extent. There's too much concern with civil rights, the stuff about always being innocent until proven guilty —ninety percent of the time the man is guilty. We don't make that many mistakes.

Whatever else one might say about this it does not appear that this sergeant is unwilling to approve felony arrests very often. As a colleague he appreciates the ambiguity of probable cause and shares the preoccupation with crime control.

The goal of crime control and the values of the police culture take precedence over the requirement of bureaucratic efficiency and control. The effect of the formal booking procedure is diluted not only because a supervisor may agree with a patrolman's decision, but also because he must be concerned about the norms that govern the relationships among working policemen, especially the stricture against second-guessing another man's decisions. Another compelling reason this procedure is weakened is that the release of a suspect because he was falsely arrested entails the risk of a civil suit. The prudent course of action may be to let the prosecutor and the courts make the decision. Yet the knowledge that their decisions will be scrutinized may have an effect on the kinds of decisions patrolmen will make in a felony situation. A patrolman always has to be on the lookout for the aggressive and upwardly mobile supervisor who will make things tough.

Stopping and Questioning: Playing the Slot Machine

The most important use of the broad powers of arrest the police possess are in police-initiated actions, usually field interrogations. Field interrogations are stops undertaken to determine if a crime has been committed, and they are to be distinguished from field actions which are preventative, for example, the dispersal of a group of juveniles standing on a street corner. Police-initiated field stops may have either goal or both; it is common for a patrolman to first interrogate a person on the street and then perhaps order him home. The purpose of aggressive patrol, the frequent use of field interrogations, is to keep would-be felons off balance, and to establish a reputation for tough, decisive action. This belief in the deterrent effect of aggressive patrol often takes precedence over other objectives.

A police-initiated field interrogation or action is defined here as any police-citizen contact undertaken for purposes other than enforcement of a specific law. Crimes which are discovered after the officer has made a stop for another reason—the enforcement of a traffic violation, for example—are defined as happenstance. This distinction rests on a patrolman's reason for making the stop and not his ultimate justification. Seventeen percent of all observed incidents may be classified as field interrogations (see table 6.1), and these make up 40 percent of all on-view police actions. They are not an unimportant aspect of discretion.

Both the courts and police administrators are notoriously vague

about what constitutes probable cause to stop and interrogate someone or to disperse individuals. Such discussions are patently aca-
demic to patrolmen; probable cause is important, in their view, only
if you catch somebody doing something and have the opportunity to
make an arrest. Patrolmen distinguish between two kinds of criteria
in making these decisions. First there are those criteria that arouse
an officer's suspicion that something is amiss. Second, there are legal
criteria that may be used to justify any action taken. An arrest and
the initial stop that led to it may be eventually justified on the basis
of a violation of the traffic laws, but this is not usually the reason the
officer stopped the person in the first place. Rather, the person was
stopped because he "fit" a set of expectations as to his probable
future or past behavior. The person's appearance, for example, may
lead the patrolman to believe that a crime has been committed or
will be committed. The inferences drawn from a person's appearance are not inherently ambiguous or even meaningless, and there
are a few instances in which such nonlegal criteria meet the test of
reasonable cause. If a robbery had just taken place, and the suspects
were described as driving a yellow Ford Falcon, patrolmen would be
justified in stopping most yellow Ford Falcons in the immediate area,
and perhaps Mercury Comets as well.

The vehicle code is the most ubiquitous source of probable cause
for patrolmen. Minor violations of the vehicle code such as broken
taillights, the absence of a light over the rear license plate, bald tires,
or the absence of a current registration sticker can and are used as
justifications for field interrogations. Depending on the circumstances, these violations are used to justify the stop either before or
after the fact. The manipulation of the vehicle code as a source of
probable cause raises serious legal problems, but for most street-wise
patrolmen it is a way of pragmatically adapting the law to the requirements of their task.[10] After interrogating and releasing a young
black man whose car had no current registration sticker, a patrolman
was asked why he had not given the man a citation. He answered:
"I'm saving probable cause; if I give him a ticket he will have to
correct it, this way if I see him again and think he's dirty, I can stop
him."

After stopping an individual, the first step will be to check his
identification and perhaps his vehicle registration. Next the individual may be checked for wants or warrants through the Automated
Wants and Warrants System (AWWS). Patrolmen are linked through
the dispatcher to a data bank, which, given appropriate information

on a person, can determine if there are any outstanding wants or warrants on the individual. In addition, this information system keeps track of stolen property. An officer usually also has the opportunity to conduct a cursory flashlight search of the car, and if necessary a more thorough search may be conducted. A few basic questions will be asked—Where you are going? What have you been doing? Is this your car?—and a patrolman's subsequent steps depend on the kind of answer he gets to his inquiries and whether or not his suspicions are allayed. A normal field interrogation to investigate for a burglary or stolen car may take only five minutes; a quick check of a person's identification and registration takes even less time. It is thus rather quick and easy for a patrolman to determine if some kind of crime has been committed, and if he is clever he can normally accomplish this without bruising too many feelings. A person who is told that he has been stopped because his rear tire is bald is mollified when the patrolman tells him that he is not going to get a citation, only a warning.

THE INCLINATION TO BE AGGRESSIVE

The majority of the patrolmen in Redondo Beach, Inglewood, and the two divisions of the LAPD are aggressive. Just over three-fifths define a good patrolman as an aggressive patrolman. And contrariwise, merely two-fifths think patrolmen should spend their free time simply patrolling for robberies and burglaries (table 6.3, statements a and b). Many of these patrolmen believe that the best way to catch a burglar or armed robber is by working traffic, by stopping "suspicious" vehicles and individuals. As one patrolman said, "You can look for twenty years and never catch a burglar. . . ." A felony pinch, in his view, is something a patrolman happens upon; one doesn't catch burglars as they come out of the bedroom window, they are caught as they drive away. Patrol, in the opinion of these officers, is preventative to the extent that it is aggressive. The assumption is that there is a relationship between crime and how well a beat is patrolled. This is often reflected in traffic and other minor violations: if there are lots of minor violations (for example, people parking every which way) the area will not be orderly, and there will be a crime problem. To maintain order and prevent crime, then, a patrolman must aggressively and vigorously enforce the law. Not every patrolman so explicitly links strict law enforcement with aggressiveness on the beat. Some believe that a more selective approach accomplishes just as much.

TABLE 6.3

Patrolmen's and Supervisors' Attitudes Toward Aggressiveness and Crime Fighting

| Those Who Agreed with the Following Statement | High Crime | | | | Low Crime | | | | All Departments | |
| | Inglewood | | Rampart | | Redondo Beach | | Northeast | | | |
	Patrolmen (%)	Supervisors (%)	Patrolmen (%)	Supervisors (%)	Patrolmen (%)	Supervisors (%)	Patrolmen (%)	Supervisors (%)	Patrolmen (%)	Supervisors (%)
a. A good patrolman is one who aggressively patrols his beat, stopping lots of cars, checking on vehicles that look suspicious and so forth.	77	83	51	75	43	70	63	53	61	70
b. All of a patrolman's free time from calls should be spent patrolling for burglaries and robberies.	52	18	41	35	24	20	39	41	41	31
c. In some neighborhoods, one must rigorously enforce all laws just to maintain order and prevent crimes.	98	75	80	82	74	80	78	53	84	71
d. In some neighborhoods, the prevention of crime requires that patrolmen stop people walking down the street, especially juveniles, and ask them where they are going and	89	83	80	69	71	80	80	82	81	78

regarding a Black and/or Mexican-American juvenile as a person who needs to be watched more than others.										
f. In order to prevent crimes and apprehend felons, the police are sometimes required to violate search and seizure laws and other procedural safeguards.	73	50	47	47	56	90	43	71	56	63
g. Preservation of the peace requires that the police use their authority to order people to "move along" or "break it up" even though no law is being violated.	60	50	54	71	35	40	51	71	52	61
h. In some neighborhoods, physical combat skills and an aggressive bearing will be more useful to a patrolman on the beat than a courteous manner.	80	67	84	63	62	60	67	47	75	58
Mean Scale Scores[a]	45.57		51.08		54.44		51.47			
Number of Respondents	(62)	(12)	(51)	(17)	(34)	(10)	(51)	(17)	(198)	(56)

[a] Difference in mean scores significant $\theta \leq .01$.

But however aggressive patrolmen may be, their aggressiveness is tempered to what they believe are the crime problems of an area. Over 80 percent of the patrolmen believe that rigorous enforcement and stop and question tactics are justified in "some neighborhoods" (table 6.3, statement c). The field observations and comments from patrolmen indicate that the phrase "in some neighborhoods" refers to high-crime, lower-class and/or minority neighborhoods. One patrolman said he would be more aggressive in the high-crime area of the community because "the kids down there are more likely to have weapons or other kinds of things in the car, they're more likely to be dirty, and you have gang activity. . . ." The almost unaminous agreement of Inglewood patrolmen with these questions buttresses this interpretation. The one anomaly in these responses is that with the exception of patrolmen in Inglewood, only a small proportion agreed that black or Mexican-American juveniles should be singled out for special attention. This may accurately reflect the attitudes of these patrolmen, though I doubt it. Race, the field observations reveal, is one of the most salient criteria to patrolmen in deciding whether or not to stop someone.

Aggressiveness also denotes a predisposition to take extra-legal or illegal actions when deemed necessary. Fifty-six percent of the patrolmen agreed that due process may occasionally have to be sacrificed in order to prevent crime, and 52 percent believed that preservation of the peace required that police break up groups and order people to move along even though no law is being violated (table 6.3, statements f and g).

Thus, aggressiveness for a patrolman means taking decisive action in a high-crime area, and when necessary, extra-legal actions. The questions in table 6.3 form a coherent attitudinal scale, and the lower the scale score, the more aggressive the patrolman. Based on the mean scores for each department, patrolmen in Inglewood appear to be the most aggressive and those in Redondo Beach the least.[11]

The field supervisors are just as inclined as patrolmen to be aggressive, and in some instances are more aggressive. Overall, the field supervisors are more likely to agree in three of the eight statements (a, f, and g), though the differences between the two are not large. This difference is perhaps sharpest in Redondo Beach where the supervisors are far more aggressive than patrolmen, especially in regard to making numerous stops, the necessity of sometimes violating due process, and the belief in strict, rigorous enforcement. In the LAPD there is no general pattern, though the differences between supervisors and patrolmen tend to be less pronounced. Inglewood presents an interesting exception to the overall picture. Here it is the patrolmen who are most aggressive. This is true for all statements but the first, and even there the difference is a mere 5 percent.

The question on which patrolmen and supervisors register the sharpest disagreement is whether a brusque, discourteous manner is a useful tactic in some neighborhoods (statement h). Seventy-five percent of patrolmen think that it is, compared to 58 percent of the supervisors. If supervisors are more concerned about misconduct than patrolmen, a majority are still willing to tolerate less than a professional demeanor. More striking is the greater willingness of field supervisors to accept abuses of due process (statement f). Judging from these data, the uncertainty some patrolmen may entertain over a supervisor's inclination to scrutinize their decisions for violations of probable cause or search and seizure is generally unfounded. If anything, field supervisors are willing accomplices.

Are the aggressive attitudes of these patrolmen translated into action on the street? The data in table 6.4, which contains a breakdown for all important police-initiated stops, provides an answer. The breakdown includes on-view stops for crime and disturbances (felonies, field interrogations, fights) and minor violations (traffic laws and drunkenness). I have calculated the ratio of crime control on-view stops to those undertaken to enforce a minor violation. The lower the ratio, the fewer stops for crime control in relation to those for minor violations. Not surprisingly, the ratio is substantially higher for the LAPD than for the small departments. Patrolmen in the two divisions of the LAPD made on-view stops in a ratio of 1.17 compared to .41 for Redondo Beach and Inglewood. Perhaps the most striking piece of information is that the highest percentage of on-view stops for crime control observed were in Northeast Division, a low-crime area. The observations for Northeast Division could be biased to some extent, but I am more inclined to think these figures reflect the actions of the rather high number of avowed crime fighters who patrol Northeast Division, many of whom had transferred from other high-crime divisions in the city.

The field observations are generally consistent with the survey responses in the LAPD, since a majority in both divisions felt that a good officer needed to be aggressive. And the lack of aggressiveness in Redondo Beach is also consistent with the survey responses there. The surprise is Inglewood. Here patrolmen believed that they should be aggressive but apparently they did not act on this belief. Why?

TABLE 6.4

Breakdown of On-view Incidents by Department

On-view Incidents[a]	High-crime Areas		Low-crime Areas		All
	Inglewood	Rampart	Redondo Beach	Northeast	Departments
Minor Violations	66%	53%	74%	38%	56%
Crimes and Disturbances	33%	47%	26%	62%	44%
Ratio of On-view Crime Stops to On-view Minor Violation Stops	.50	.90	.34	1.63	.80
Number of Incidents Observed	(42)	(77)	(39)	(58)	(216)

[a]These figures include all on-view stops except those for miscellaneous service calls. Crimes and Disturbances include on-view stops for felony violations, field interrogations, and fights. Minor violations include all stops to enforce traffic laws, drunk in public, and other misdemeanors.

One explanation might be that patrolmen in Inglewood deliberately modified their behavior in light of my presence. This is entirely possible, and there is some evidence that this might be the case (I base this on a conversation with one police officer in Inglewood). On the other hand, it is possible that this difference between attitude and behavior is a manifestation of the impact of administrative controls in Inglewood. A great many patrolmen in Inglewood are deeply frustrated over the rising crime rate; they do not really know what to do about it, and feel hemmed in by the department. Two rather aggressive officers went to some length to argue that many patrolmen in Inglewood feel constrained in their actions because, as they put it, "the department is overly P. R. conscious." They pointed out that patrolmen would often hesitate before getting involved in a situation because of a fear of getting a "personnel beef" and perhaps a suspension by the department. Their feelings are entirely consistent with the survey data in chapter 5 which revealed that Inglewood patrolmen feel constrained from using the discretion they have. Because supervision is more strict in Inglewood and officers have less opportunity to move around and get involved in things, they may be somewhat more reluctant to intervene. Or to put the matter another way, if they do get involved the risks are somewhat greater than they would be for a patrolman in the LAPD. The responses of field supervisors in Inglewood to the questions on aggressiveness indicate that the reluctance of patrolmen there to initiate on-view stops is not entirely unfounded.

THE AMBIGUITY OF THE STREET: SEPARATING THE INNOCUOUS FROM THE DEVIANT

Patrolmen are confronted with the problem of determining on the basis of vague and ambiguous information what is normal and thus innocuous behavior and what is abnormal and potentially deviant behavior. To do this, they must rely on a set of indicators which have, as David Matza has pointed out, "a specific but by no means perfect probability of leading them either to the discovery or prevention of a crime."[12] These indicators will be drawn from a patrolman's knowledge of the society in which he lives, especially from the groups of people he is most familar with from his day-to-day working experience on the street. Most policemen believe that working the street heightens their sensitivity to deviant behavior and suspicious circumstances, and facilitates the development of the "expertise" needed to discriminate between the innocuous and the deviant. Patrolmen do not believe their actions are arbitrary, for if their decision to stop someone is based on a "hunch," it is not an indiscriminate hunch. These "hunches" are filtered through a set of beliefs derived from working the street and dominated by an officer's operational style.

There are three types of indicators used by patrolmen in deciding whether or not to stop someone. These are *incongruity, prior information,* and *appearance.* Incongruity becomes an indicator of deviant behavior to the extent that something is perceived to be out of place. A young boy driving a new car is considered to be an adequate indicator of a potential car thief. The proverbial black man in the all-white neighborhood late at night needs no comment. Less well-known examples include dirty license plates on a clean car, or an older man parked in front of an elementary school. Prior information refers to specific information obtained about a crime that has been committed, for example, a description of the suspects or even knowledge of the people and "trouble spots" in an area. In a more general fashion, prior information refers to rules of thumb based on previous experience that lead a patrolman to believe that something is amiss. The lack of a current registration sticker indicates to many patrolmen that the driver may have warrants and cannot get his or her registration renewed or that the car is stolen.

Appearance is the vaguest of the three indicators and the one that is based on widespread social stereotypes and beliefs. Race, age, sex, and social class are the criteria typically considered. A young black male dressed in Levi's and a white T-shirt is more likely to be stopped and questioned than a middle-aged white man in coat and tie. Most policemen feel that such practices do not constitute "racism" or discrimination, but rather the application of relevant knowledge of who is likely to commit a crime. A patrolman ran a warrant check on a car with a broken rear taillight and four young blacks in it. He found the car had a warrant, and stopped the car and checked the driver for warrants. The driver was not wanted, and the patrolman did not cite him for the rear taillight because, as he put it, the man had the "right attitude." Later the patrolman said he investigated the car in the first place because there were blacks in it, and with blacks "there is always a greater chance of something wrong." If he admitted that he always checks blacks closer, he attempted to justify it by saying, "that's not prejudice, I can't turn my back on the truth."

Regardless of the criteria used, all of a patrolman's judgments in deciding to stop someone are characterized by a high degree of *uncertainty.* Any stop that a patrolman makes is a calculated risk: if the person has committed a serious crime, the likelihood of violence is present; if the person is innocent, feelings may be bruised. Obviously, some of the information the police use is better than other kinds, but all of the indicators patrolmen employ are extremely crude. The accuracy of these indicators will depend on the officer's experience, especially the extent of his exposure to street crime, and his understanding of the values and behavior of the people in his beat. Where there is a vast difference between the values and beliefs of the patrolmen and the people they are policing, behavior is easily and often misinterpreted.[13] The alternative to reliable information about suspicious persons may simply be random checks on whoever appears to be suspicious. Even an experienced officer will have difficulty getting around this problem, and the present organization of the police with its emphasis on aggressive street patrol allows no other alternative (whether innovations such as team policing can alleviate this problem remains to be seen).

Each of the three types of indicators—prior information, incongruity, and appearance—varies in terms of its uncertainty. A patrolman's information, as the following examples illustrate, is likely to be most certain in those instances where a crime has occurred and the police have a description of the suspect and his vehicle.

Case History 8

The dispatcher broadcast that an armed robbery had taken place minutes ago. Two black youths in hats pointed a gun, described as a .22 caliber pistol, at a woman and her daughter as they were walking home from the grocery store and demanded their money. Two patrolmen immediately began searching the area for suspects. While stopped at a traffic light they noticed two black youths in a 1964 Chevrolet drive in front of them. On a hunch, they stopped the vehicle and questioned both occupants: the youths said that they were returning from a visit to a girl friend's house. Neither had any warrants. A patrolman arrived with the victim, and she identified one of the youths but was unsure of the other. A search failed to turn up either the gun or the money, but the police believed that the youths had had time to hide them, and they were arrested for armed robbery.

Case History 9

An armed robbery occurred at a fast food take-out stand. The suspects were described as young, Japanese, and driving a yellow Mustang. Minutes after the robbery a patrolman picked up one of the suspects three blocks away in the yellow Mustang.

In each of these incidents a serious crime had been committed and the patrolmen had definite information about the suspects. In only one of these, however, was the information reliable enough so that the stop was made with more than a reasonable assurance that the person stopped had in fact committed the crime. The officer in Case History 9 knew he had his man (he also had a very good description). In the other case the stop was made on the basis of a calculated hunch. Both patrolmen admitted prior to stopping the two youths that they were taking a chance and that they were probably not the suspects. Yet the description "fit" just enough so that they thought it was worthwhile making the stop. It was clearly an action taken "just to be sure" that no stone had been left unturned. Thus even in those situations where patrolmen have some information to go on, such as a description of the suspects, the decision to stop and interrogate is still characterized by ambiguity and uncertainty. Paradoxically, the occurrence of a serious crime and the broadcasting of any information at all on the suspects can lead to two different and contradictory types of behavior. Patrolmen may make stops based as concretely as possible on the information they have at hand. But they may also resort to widespread stops of anybody that even remotely resembles the suspect. It often depends on the seriousness of the crime. Most patrolmen also know that the descriptions given by victims immediately after the commission of a serious crime are likely to be misleading; prudence requires, in their opinion, that they stop even people who only remotely fit the description.

A patrolman often relies on other kinds of prior information, which are much less accurate than those obtained after the commission of a crime.

Case History 10

"Funny Freddy," a known acid freak and burglar, was seen walking down a busy street with a friend in the early afternoon. One of the officers had not seen "Funny Freddy" in a while, and they stopped him. Both men were patted down and field interrogation (F.I.) cards made out. "Funny Freddy" said that he had just gotten out of jail and was clean. There were no warrants on either man and they were released.

Case History 11

While cruising his beat, a patrolman recognized the brother of a man he had arrested earlier in the year for murder driving down the street. The time was about 2:00 A.M. The patrolman decided to stop him to see what he was doing. He was a Mexican-American youth and a young white girl was in the car with him. He had no identification nor any proof that the car was his. The officer informed the youth that he could be arrested for no identification (sec. 40302A C.V.C.) and Grand Theft Auto, but since he (the patrolman) knew him, he would not be arrested. The youth was released after being given a stern warning. Later the patrolman said that "the kid's problem was that he was just plain dumb," and that one had to, "get on him once in a while in order to keep him in line."

In addition to knowledge about a crime, the police often rely, as these illustrations make clear, upon their knowledge of the individuals. Those with arrest records or even a reputation for being in trouble will be stopped, as "Funny Freddy" was. And there is a tendency to presume that association with a "local bad guy," even if he is related, is indicative of guilt of some kind. Yet the reason for stopping these people is only partly based on the expectation that a crime will be discovered; in both of these examples, the intention of the patrolmen was as much prevention of a crime as detection. Stopping and questioning is a way of letting individuals know that the police are around and that they had better watch their step.

More ambiguous and uncertain yet are those stops made in the context of suspicious circumstances. The indicators of incongruity and appearance taken singly or together are the criteria by which a patrolman decides whether to stop and interrogate in the following situations.

Case History 12

Driving down a residential street an officer noticed some people, Mexican-Americans, moving some belongings from a house to a truck parked adjacent to the curb. It was about 9 o'clock in the evening. The patrolman asked what was going on and was told that the people were moving. The patrolman frisked several of them and then checked one of them for warrants. The man had no warrants and the officer decided to stop. Before leaving he told the people that burglars often tell the police they are moving and this was why they were questioned.

Case History 13

A car with a discontinued out-of-state license plate was stopped (there was also a minor equipment violation). All three occupants in the car were ordered out, patted down for weapons, and questioned separately. The driver had no identification and said the car belonged to a girl friend; they were driving home. There was no registration in the car, but the officers did find an insurance slip with the girl's name on it. Each occupant gave the same story, and the officers believed them. They were released with a warning.

Case History 14

Two officers patrolling a residential area observed a young black standing on a balcony at the end of a hallway on the second floor of an apartment building. Thinking he might be a burglar they called him to the car to question him. He did not know the address of the apartment building and said his name was John Smith. The patrolmen seriously considered arresting him until he showed identification proving that his name was John Smith and convinced them that he had only moved into the apartment building one week earlier.

Case History 15

As two officers drove by a cut-rate gas station, they noticed a black man, bent over, standing in front of the front door. A Cadillac with a woman and several children in it was parked next to the gas pumps. Suspecting a burglary, they stopped and questioned him. He said he worked at the station, but when he gave the wrong address of the station, they checked his identification and ran him on AWWS for warrants. The man said that he misunderstood the question and the officers believed him. He was released.

Case History 16

A young Mexican-American man walking down the street was stopped and questioned. He was checked for warrants but none were found. The officer said later that the man was stopped because he "looked suspicious."

Case History 17

Late at night a black youth was observed standing near an automobile on a residential street. As the patrol car drove by, he turned and walked away. The patrolmen went back and stopped and questioned him. The youth explained that he was waiting for a friend to pick him up. One officer examined the car and found no evidence of any attempt to break into it. The youth had poor identification, but he said that he had been with friends in a nearby apartment building. The people in the apartment verified the story and the youth was released.

174

Case History 18

A young black man walking down the street with a large portable radio to his ear was stopped and asked where he had got the radio. He replied that it belonged to his sister, and when he demanded to know why he had been stopped, he was spread-eagled on the hood of the car and frisked. He had some identification and said he was on his way to work at a local elementary school where he was a janitor. One officer examined the radio and discovered that the serial number had been removed. The officers were about to book him when the man's supervisor at the school, who happened to be driving by, stopped and certified that the man worked at the school and that the radio belonged to him. The man was released into the custody of his supervisor.

It ought to be apparent that the kind and quality of information that patrolmen use to make judgments of the intention of individuals is much different than in the previous cases. Seemingly innocuous behavior is imbued with an aura of criminality, and the commonplace becomes suspicious. The seven incidents described here illustrate three rules of thumb that patrolmen use in evaluating behavior. The first is a straightforward application of the idea of incongruity. Time and circumstance can often make a great deal of difference to a patrolmen. What was important to the officer who stopped and questioned the Mexican-American men moving furniture into the van was the time of day—9:00 P.M.—and the fact that he was in a high-crime area. Similarly, an out-of-state license plate that the officers knew was no longer in use was taken as an indication that something was amiss. The second rule hinges on the vague criterion of appearance. A young black standing on the balcony of an apartment building, a black man who appeared to be trying to get in the front door of a service station (he was actually trying to lock up), or a Mexican-American walking down a residential street were all presumed to be suspicious. The third rule is based on a person's reaction to the police. Flight from an approaching patrol car implies guilt; an innocent person, patrolmen reason, would have nothing to fear from the police and would not walk away as the juvenile did in Case History 17.

The reaction of the person to police authority will have a bearing on the inclination of patrolmen to *believe* the individuals they are questioning. The police rely upon the wants and warrants system, a search (when they can carry it out), and some pointed questions to determine if in fact something is amiss. A real burglar, they reason, is not likely to know the address of the place he is burglarizing; and a man who says he lives in an apartment building should know the address of that building. But if patrolmen adopt rather loose standards for deciding when to stop and question people, their standards for taking further action are usually somewhat stiffer. In most of the incidents described they were rather easily convinced that nothing was wrong. The exception to this is when the person challenges their authority, their right to stop and ask them questions. The question, "what right do you have to question me" is not construed as rightful indignation but as implicit guilt. Patrolmen may believe that people have a right to an explanation after an interrogation, but they will rarely tolerate interference until they are satisfied that nothing is amiss. The reaction of the black youth in Case History 18 to questions about his radio was the basis for the excessive reaction of the two patrolmen.

THE EFFICACY OF "PLAYING THE SLOT MACHINE"

It is perhaps less important to know that the police do not always find what they are looking for than to understand the process by which they reach decisions. In making judgments of whether a person is acting suspiciously, a patrolman must draw inferences from the observed behaviors and the character of the people involved, and decide, on the basis of his knowledge and experience if a crime has been or will be committed. A parked car, people moving furniture from a house, a young black man walking down the street with a radio to his ear are rather commonplace events that, in and of themselves, are not suspicious. In labeling the innocuous clandestine, the patrolman relies upon concrete but biased indicators which presuppose that he knows something about the character of the persons involved. In other words, the patrolman must interpret actions by imposing upon the situation pragmatically derived categories which make the behavior meaningful to him, that is, suspicious. A group of Mexican-Americans moving furniture from a house in the evening becomes suspicious only in terms of the *meaning* that a patrolman assigns to this event.

The pragmatically derived indicators that policemen use are biased according to more general social stereotypes of American culture. Yet from a patrolman's point of view, the adequacy of a particular indicator is measured according to its usefulness. Behavior is judged in light of the goals of preventing and discovering crime, and these judgments, to the extent that they are reinforced by an officer's personal experience and the experiences of his fellow patrol-men, become part and parcel of the police lore that is handed down to each successive generation of rookies. Indicators that prove to be inadequate will eventually be modified.

Yet many of these beliefs as a whole are remarkably consistent and ultimately self-reinforcing: concentrating on the activities of a partic-ular subgroup may lead to biased estimates of the propensity of that group to commit crimes. This is the case with both Mexican-Ameri-cans and blacks, but especially with the latter. Most studies consis-tently show that blacks are arrested at a higher rate for more serious offenses (major felonies) than whites, and the differences appear in all types of departments.[14] The departments studied here are no exception. The ratio of minority (black and Mexican-American), juve-nile, and adult arrests per 10,000 population for major felony offenses to white arrests is 10.35 in Inglewood; 3.48 in Rampart; 2.04 in Redondo Beach; and 2.53 in Northeast. These figures actually un-derestimate the differences for blacks and whites since Mexican-Americans are less likely to be arrested for major offenses than blacks. For misdemeanors, on the other hand, the ratios are closer, and in a few instances whites are arrested more often than minorities (for example, whites are arrested more often than minorities for drunk driving in Inglewood and Redondo Beach).

These figures are less a reflection of the presumed propensity of blacks to commit crimes than of the widespread use of highly selec-tive indicators in deciding to stop and interrogate an individual on the street. Perhaps the best indications of this are the numerous warrant checks patrolmen run on vehicles occupied by blacks. Not only were whites rarely observed to be the subject of a warrant check, but blacks in all three departments are substantially more likely to be arrested for traffic offenses, most of which come about as the result of a warrant check or a decision to stop and interrogate. Indeed, in Rampart and Inglewood blacks are *fourteen times* as likely to be arrested for traffic offenses as whites. If there is a gross measure of truth in the set of beliefs about social behavior and its connection to crime upon which decisions to stop and interrogate are based— stopping a carload of black teenagers is more likely to produce mari-juana than stopping a white insurance salesman—this hardly ex-plains, much less justifies, the inordinate preoccupation with the behavior of blacks and other minorities displayed by patrolmen. Blacks are singled out by patrolmen, and such a strategy inevitably exposes innocent people to the intrusion of police authority.[15]

The selectivity of a patrolman's beliefs about what constitutes suspicious behavior must be understood in light of another characteristic of these decisions. In using a set of indicators to separate the innocuous from the deviant, a patrolman operates less on the basis of carefully derived probabilities than on the inclination to be experimental and find out what is happening in a particular set of circumstances. While the propensity to engage in aggressive patrol work varies among patrolmen, it does not, as a rule, take much to arouse an officer's suspicion, and this leads aggressive patrolmen to investigate just to see if they "can come up with something." Ordinarily, then, there is a very low threshold for action. The benefits of this strategy are thought to be quite high; enough stops will eventually turn up something, if only a traffic warrant, and the costs can usually be minimized. Yet some of these patrolmen remind one of the little old lady standing in front of four slot machines in Las Vegas with a purse full of nickels—if she plays enough machines, enough times, she will win.

The low threshold for action is partly an attempt to find a respite from the boredom of routine patrol; but it also flows from the logic of aggressive patrol. The doctrine of aggressive patrol, as the principal instrument in the war on crime, leads patrolmen, motivated by the desire to come up with something and justified on the basis of deterrence, to take what are selective but essentially spontaneous actions. What counts is not effect but action.

Decisions to stop and interrogate are rarely subject to administrative controls of any kind. They are some of the least visible decisions that a patrolman will make, and unless an arrest is made the only record is a short notation in the patrolman's log. Legally, they raise serious questions about the use of probable cause, and, for the reasons presented earlier, the scrutiny of probable cause by field supervisors is usually less than satisfactory. There is, however, one important constraint on the probable cause used by policemen, and that is the possibility that some criteria will be challenged in court and overturned. Most patrolmen are aware of the possibility of making "bad case law" as they call it. Many patrolmen refuse to arrest for a little known section of the California Vehicle Code (40302a) which allows them to take into custody anyone who is driving an automobile without proper identification. By using this statute only when they think it is clearly necessary the police preserve an important option.[16] Whether or not vague criteria for probable cause will meet standards of due process in even the most serious of offenses is moot; the relevant point is that the possibility of a court challenge does place a damper on some police actions.

From the point of view of police administrators and patrolmen, the real dilemma of aggressive patrol is that it inevitably leads to resentment from the community. One officer, who was skeptical of the results of aggressive patrol, suggested that the consequences of bringing the tactical squad (Metropolitan Division in the LAPD) into an area to work a crime problem were a lot of arrests for traffic warrants and increased public hostility toward the police. If the administrator risks public pressures, the patrolman risks an increased number of personnel complaints, though the risk of personnel complaints has not always been a strong one. (Several patrolmen in the LAPD said that personnel complaints were often taken as a sign of aggressiveness and therefore evaluated positively, but they indicated that this practice seemed to be changing.)

Crime Fighting and a Professional Police

August Vollmer believed that the only worthwhile function that the police could serve was that of suppressing crime. He argued, vainly, for turning many of the minor enforcement functions of the police —traffic, for example—over to other agencies, and all of his proposed reforms were predicated on making the police efficient enough and autonomous enough to control crime. Any attempt to understand how a patrolman uses his discretion must begin with an understanding of the centrality of the crime-fighting role for patrolmen, and the way they adapt to the dilemmas and ambiguities of this role.

Crime fighting is one way patrolmen can validate their competence in the eyes of their colleagues and the public, and it is a respite from the tediousness of the job. It is also in some instances a way of resolving the problem of promotions, especially in specialized units such as narcotics or traffic. But even though there are very real personal rewards in crime fighting, and sometimes even rewards in the department, this course of action entails risks. An aggressive style of patrol brings a patrolman into conflict with the instrumental goals of the department, especially those that bear on the legitimacy of police authority. Most field supervisors want their men to be concerned with a wide range of violations and they want aggressive police work. They are quite willing to tolerate the abuses of probable cause and due process that accompany crime fighting, but they are more restrained than patrolmen when it comes to that vague category of abuses labeled "misconduct." The conflict between crime fighting and the demand to sustain the legitimacy of the department can be and is a source of tension within the police bureaucracy. The administrator, to the extent that he is concerned, is caught between pressures to control his men and to support them in the pursuit of an objective he takes as deadly serious. Patrolmen who bear the brunt of these pressures may back off or become more devious, but they do become increasingly frustrated.

The effect of this conflict hinges on the autonomy of the department from community pressures and the autonomy of patrolmen within the department. As the autonomy of either increases, the conflict between the substantive and instrumental goals of police work is mitigated. And this autonomy, I believe, is more likely in a highly professional, large department such as the LAPD than in a small department. It is in the LAPD where one finds the highly aggressive but relatively autonomous patrolman working. Inglewood is a decided counterpoint where patrolmen face enormous pressures both to control crime and to avoid shaking up the community.

Police professionalism has not resulted in greater administrative control over some of the most important decisions patrolmen make. There is also reason to be dubious about the effectiveness of aggressive patrol as a strategy of crime control. In the early 1970s the Kansas City Police Department conducted an experiment to determine what, if any, effects varying levels of patrol had on crime, arrests, and the community's sense of well-being. The findings showed that variation in the level of patrol—from minimal to highly aggressive—made very little difference in the rate of reported crimes or victimization, in arrest rates, or in a community's feeling of protection. This is not entirely surprising. While there are a number of patrolmen who rely upon the rather methodical application of the skills of their craft, much of the activity in the street is random and spontaneous, guided more by a sense of adventure and the fond hope of coming up with something than by anything else. The findings of the Kansas City experiment and others strike at the heart of the role and organization of a professional police.[17] It has led in recent years to widespread experimentation with alternative approaches, the most fashionable of which is team policing. What this augurs for police work is debatable. Innovations such as team policing, underpinned by the continuing evaluation and criticism of the extant model of police work, may presage the emergence of a new wave of reform. Or they may simply continue the rationalization of police work that is the thrust of police professionalism.

Chapter 7

Nonenforcement: Minor Violations and Disturbances

THE ENFORCEMENT of misdemeanor laws presents difficulties for the police that laws pertaining to more serious crimes do not. If a misdemeanor is, by definition, a less serious violation than a felony, the irony is that many misdemeanors cover rather serious offenses. Drunk driving, a rather commonplace offense and the cause of an undue amount of traffic fatalities, is a prominent example. The problem for the police is that many misdemeanors are not taken very seriously by the public. Traffic offenses are considered by most people as a mere hazard of driving; petty theft offends more basic values but it is directed at large chain stores which, many rationalize, can afford it; drunkenness most people agree is a social, not a legal problem, even though political leaders seem unwilling or unable to develop alternative methods of coping with it. And although most people caught speeding or driving "under the influence" accept with some equanimity the right of the officer to make an arrest, it is still not an occasion for grave soul-searching. The public, then, is apt to believe that some behaviors should not be against the law (and even if the law cannot be changed they are likely to persevere in the notion that the police should not take them so seriously), or they regard these violations as the result of error and carelessness rather than malicious intention, and thus think they should be taken less seriously than other violations. The problem of law and order has never been one of the violation of misdemeanor laws.

Moreover, the enforcement of misdemeanor laws brings the police into contact with a different type of person, not the so-called "hardened criminal" but the solid middle-class person who has a sense of his own status and power within the political system, and who more likely than not will ask, "Why aren't you out chasing crooks rather than stopping me for a petty traffic violation?" Most policemen are well aware of this aspect of police work. Indeed, much of the hostility toward the police that William Westley noted so long ago stems from the rancor that attends enforcement of these laws.

Another difficulty with misdemeanor violations is that a patrolman is given, at the same time, both more and less discretion than he has with a felony. Misdemeanors are subject to the "in-presence" requirement, and in order for an officer to legally arrest, the violation *must be committed in the officer's presence.*[1] The police can get around this limitation through a citizen's arrest. In a citizen's arrest the burden of arrest and the consequences are shifted to the victim; the police merely act as the instrument of enforcement. The citizen's arrest is applicable to any violation, but by convention its use is restricted to a few select crimes, notably those arising out of disturbances. Yet the citizen's arrest procedure is double-edged: if it can be used to enforce the law where the policeman, because of the in-presence requirement, is unable to take any action, it can also be used to shift responsibility and therefore the burden of action to the citizen. It is not uncommon for patrolmen to use the citizen's arrest procedure as a way of shifting the decision from them to the victim, often with the knowledge that the citizen will not act. This is especially true in disturbances.

If the officer's opportunity to make an arrest is more restricted with a misdemeanor, his ability to refuse to enforce the law is significantly enhanced. With misdemeanors, more so than felonies, policemen have the right, though it is not acknowledged by the courts, to handle a situation without making an arrest. Much of the power that a patrolman possesses derives from his ability not to enforce the law if he so chooses. It is well known that the police underenforce the law; what is less well understood is why some laws are not enforced rather than others. Central to the ensuing analysis is the question of under what conditions and for what reasons a patrolman decides

TABLE 7.1

Patrolmen's and Supervisors' Attitudes Toward Enforcement of Minor Violations

| | High-crime Areas | | | | Low-crime Areas | | | | All Departments | |
| | Inglewood | | Rampart | | Redondo Beach | | Northeast | | | |
Those Who Agreed with the Following Statements	Patrolmen (%)	Supervisors (%)	Patrolmen (%)	Supervisors (%)	Patrolmen (%)	Supervisors (%)	Patrolmen (%)	Supervisors (%)	Patrolmen (%)	Supervisors (%)
a. If the crime is not very serious and if it is inconvenient or too difficult to enforce the law, it's okay for a patrolman to let it go.	21	17	18	38	27	20	28	29	23	27
b. A person who has broken the law should be arrested or cited since there are very few reasons for not enforcing the law.	32	33	40	35	15	60	35	35	32	39
c. Everybody's behavior should be judged only according to the law; one should not take their background, appearance, culture or age into account when making a decision.	34	17	47	29	35	40	51	65	42	39
Number of Respondents	(62)	(12)	(51)	(17)	(34)	(10)	(51)	(17)	(198)	(56)

nonenforcement is an acceptable solution in a given incident. This will enable us to explore in some detail the relationship between police professionalism and nonenforcement, and the consequences for those individuals affected by nonenforcement.

The Nonenforcement of Minor Violations

The nonenforcement of minor violations may consist either of a willful decision by a patrolman to *ignore* a violation or a decision to take an *informal* action (issue a warning) rather than a *formal* action (issue a citation). Due to the modernization of American society and the triumph of reform the systematic nonenforcement of the law is much less widespread than thirty or forty years ago. Aside from trivial exceptions such as spitting on the sidewalk (a municipal violation systematically ignored by most policemen), the presumption in a professional police department is that the law will be enforced. The professional values of impersonality and equality demand that a person's behavior be judged only by the standards of the law and nothing else. Despite their freedom to ignore violations, only 23 percent of the patrolmen interviewed said they would ignore a minor violation for a casual reason (see table 7.1, statement a).

Ignoring a violation removes a patrolman from the process of enforcement altogether; the decision not to take a formal action is made within the context of a confrontation between the policeman and suspect, and it requires that the policeman do something to resolve the problem at hand. In a strict sense, labeling the decision not to arrest as nonenforcement is something of a misnomer, for this does not at all reflect a patrolman's view of his action. An informal action such as a warning to a traffic violator does not mean letting a violation go by; on the contrary, it is nothing more nor less than an alternative means of coping with deviant behavior. A patrolman regards a warning as enforcing the law, and the only argument among policemen is whether it is effective. Nor is the choice between an informal and a formal action mutually exclusive: a warning may be employed as a first step in controlling a situation; but if this strategy is unsuccessful, or at least if the officer believes it is, he may resort to an arrest (a citation, I should point out, is technically an arrest). Once an officer decides to stop someone on the street or when answering a call for service, he is bound to play out the dynamics of the interaction between himself and the citizen; simply walking away is not always a viable course of action. An officer can do nothing, but he must come up with a way out of the situation, something that is easiest in an order-maintenance situation and most difficult where a straightforward violation has occurred.

If the majority of patrolmen believe that an officer should not ignore a violation for a casual reason, they do not believe that the law must be enforced in all cases. Only a minority of patrolmen (32 percent) agree with the proposition that an arrest is always the best course of action when the law has been broken (table 7.1, statement b). Patrolmen in Redondo Beach and Inglewood are somewhat less likely to agree with this proposition: 15 percent in Redondo Beach and 32 percent in Inglewood agreed compared to 35 percent in Northeast Division and 40 percent in Rampart. Nor are these patrolmen especially legalistic, as only 42 percent believe that an individual's behavior should be judged by the single standard of the law (table 7.1, statement c). Again there is a sharp difference between the LAPD and the small departments; patrolmen in the latter are less inclined to agree.

Overall the field supervisors are slightly less legalistic than patrolmen, though the differences are small (table 7.1, statements a and c). But there are some sharp differences of opinion between patrolmen and field supervisors in each of the departments. Redondo Beach field supervisors are far more legalistic than patrolmen, while Rampart patrolmen are inclined to be more legalistic than field supervisors. Even so, if both patrolmen and field supervisors believe that some action should be taken in most circumstances, the majority do not tailor enforcement to a strict legalistic standard; they temper it with a consideration of factors extraneous to the law.

In the enforcement of minor violations, patrolmen are presumed to act less as professionals with wide powers of discretion than as bureaucrats. Yet a patrolman, no matter how strict he might think he ought to be, is faced on a day-to-day basis with the necessity of making choices, of confronting people and weighing the intangibles as well as a person's overt acts. Since most patrolmen do not entirely accept a legalistic standard, but, like other decision makers, do not have the opportunity to evaluate thoroughly every situation, rules of thumb must suffice in lieu of more definitive criteria. These rules are not spelled out in any policy manual, but they are common to all of the departments observed in this study. Before we can pursue the question of what explains differences in the exercise of discretion among departments or patrolmen we need to understand what kind of decision rules are used in deciding whether to ignore a violation or treat it informally.

THE DECISION TO IGNORE A VIOLATION

On the whole, decisions to ignore a violation are spontaneous, even arbitrary, rather than deliberate and reasonable. Most are governed not by policy or even painful reflection about priorities, but by personal inclination and the ubiquitous and salient factor of mood. Many patrolmen, for example, ignore violations for personal, albeit work-related, reasons. Tunnel vision, as it is euphemistically called, afflicts patrolmen prior to the end of watch, and violations that could result in overtime will be ignored. In two separate incidents, patrolmen were observed to ignore drunk drivers. The common element in both incidents was that the drunk drivers were observed close to quitting time. A drunk driving arrest takes from one to two hours to process, and in neither case were the patrolmen willing to make an arrest that would result in a ten-hour day. In this regard policemen are not very different from their counterparts behind a desk or on an assembly line.

Patrolmen do on occasion resort to a more rational calculus in deciding to ignore violations: they sometimes evaluate the difficulties of enforcement and the consequences of a decision to enforce the law. A traffic violation, for example, which necessitates that patrolmen make a U-turn in heavy traffic, may be passed up because it is not worth disrupting the flow of traffic. The pertinence of a logical but crude assessment of the costs and benefits of enforcement depends greatly on the patrolman's judgment of the seriousness of the violation. It is more applicable to minor traffic violations and drunks, incidents that can be conveniently overlooked; more serious violations will not be ignored regardless of the difficulties or consequences of enforcement. Pursuits, which usually begin with a minor traffic violation and in which the suspect is, as often as not, guilty of nothing more than the initial traffic violation or a traffic warrant at worst, are an obvious example. Patrolmen believe that these individuals have to be stopped regardless of the consequences, which are often high. For many patrolmen, the logic of weighing action against consequence pales before the opportunity to make a good pinch.

A more important reason for ignoring a violation has to do with the seriousness of the *behavior* rather than the violation itself. There exists for some minor violations a threshold below which the behavior is not considered serious enough to warrant enforcement.

Case History 19

A patrolman using radar to enforce speeding laws set the radar at 45 miles per hour in a 25-mile an hour speed zone. The street was in a residential neighborhood, but it was a major thoroughfare and wide enough to handle faster speeds. Only those individuals going faster than 45 miles per hour were stopped.

Circumstances clearly have a lot to do with whether or not a violation is judged serious enough to be enforced. The patrolman in the incident above said that forty-five miles per hour was a reasonable norm for that street even though it was higher than the posted speed limit. In part, he was simply adapting himself to the reality that most people drove rather fast on that stretch of road; but he was also establishing a norm for what he believed to be a safe speed. More hazardous circumstances, he argued, might require setting a norm lower than the prevailing speed limit.

In evaluating the seriousness of the behavior rather than the violation in reaching a judgment of what constitutes safe driving in a particular set of circumstances, patrolmen are interpreting the intention of the law. This applies to other violations, especially drunkenness, but with somewhat less force. The criterion which patrolmen say they avail themselves of in deciding whether to stop or even arrest a drunk is that he be able to care for himself. This criterion is justified on the basis of preventing the drunk from being mugged or facing some equally horrible fate, but it may and often does cover other, perhaps less acceptable, reasons for arresting or not. Finally, the evaluation of the seriousness of an individual's behavior is a crucial element in a patrolman's assessment of disturbances.

Another way patrolmen go about setting priorities and deciding whether to ignore a violation is through a ranking of the violations themselves. This may consist of an emphasis on felony violations as opposed to misdemeanors, as we have seen, or a decision to ignore certain classes of violations. Traffic enforcement provides a particularly striking example of the latter. Some patrolmen regard traffic violations as unimportant and assiduously avoid enforcing them (the variance in the number of traffic citations per officer in Redondo

Beach ranged from a low of 15 to a high of 300 for one year). Yet such a strategy of leniency entails some risks for a patrolman; it is not possible, even if he is not ambitious, to systematically ignore a class of violations and avoid incurring, sooner or later, the wrath of the sergeant. Most police administrators have an ambivalent view of the issue of priorities in traffic enforcement. It is not regarded as the primary responsibility of patrolmen, even in a department like Redondo Beach which has no specialized traffic enforcement unit, but the need to determine priorities competes with the need to be watchful for goldbricking. Many field supervisors feel that no patrolman can work the streets for eight hours without seeing at least one or two traffic violations, and these are not to be ignored. Yet if a patrolman were making a substantial number of felony arrests, the tendency of most field supervisors would be to ignore a low rate of traffic citations.

For an officer to establish a set of priorities does not mean that low-priority violations are always ignored. Rather he merely takes a passive attitude toward these violations and they are not actively sought out. In all three of these departments, patrolmen are biased toward action; the tendency is to at least stop someone if a violation has occurred. There is always the possibility, patrolmen believe, of uncovering a crime. Decisions to ignore violations, even where patrolmen were observed to think about it, were often rash, made unhesitantly and without a great deal of reflection. For most patrolmen the decision to ignore is idiosyncratic and arbitrary. This is less so in decisions not to arrest.

THE DECISION NOT TO ARREST OR CITE

Decisions not to arrest or cite are rarely made on the basis of legal considerations. Here as elsewhere the law shapes alternatives but does not dictate action. In making these decisions, patrolmen confront a contradiction between a professional code that insists upon interpreting events in light of the law, and the knowledge, derived from the brutal reality of the street, that most incidents do not and cannot turn upon a strict evaluation of the law. Most recognize there are a wide range of intangibles that must be weighed in any decision to enforce the law. The question is, What are those factors and how are they weighed?[2]

One reason frequently offered by patrolmen for refusing to enforce a law is the belief that the incident can be solved in some other way than enforcement. As the following two incidents show, an alternative to arrest may be considered a more effective way of dealing with the problem at hand.

Case History 20

A juvenile was apprehended shortly after he had hit a parked vehicle with his car and left the scene. The owners of the damaged auto could not identify the youth as the driver, but he admitted to the hit and run. He could have been arrested, but the officers elected to take only an accident report. Their decision was based on the knowledge that the victims only wanted the damage paid for and the parents of the youth were present. Later the officers said that if the parents had not been present to take custody they would have made an arrest.

Case History 21

Two patrolmen, on a rainy night, saw a car with the window on the driver's side open parked near the side of the road. They stopped to find out if anything was wrong and found a man sleeping inside the car on the front seat. He was very drunk. They had the dispatcher call his home and ask his wife to get in a cab and come get her husband. They said the man deserved a break because he had had sense enough to pull off the road rather than drive home. Moreover, one of them remarked, "He looks like me a couple of weeks ago." They left only when they received another call.

In the first incident, if the police were aware that they had a crime and a confession, it quickly became clear that all the owner was concerned about was obtaining restitution. The crucial fact, however, was that the boy's parents were present, and they assured the police that he would get his due. In the second incident, all that really mattered to the patrolmen was that the man not drive home under his own power.

Yet if it is clear that patrolmen will not enforce the law as long as an acceptable alternative is available, the converse is also true. The fear that a person may do something if he is not arrested will result in an arrest that would not have otherwise been made. Consider the following cases:

Case History 22

Two officers received a call of a drunk down in an apartment building. They found the man passed out in the front seat of his car which was parked in the subterranean garage of the building. Some questioning revealed that he lived upstairs, and at this point they were ready to take him up to his apartment. It was then discovered that the car the man was in belonged to his brother-in-law, and his car was parked outside. The man mumbled something about moving the cars, and at this point one of the officers changed his mind and decided to book the man for "plain drunk." The reason for arresting him, according to the officer, was to prevent him from getting in his car and driving away.

Case History 23

An officer was told by the employees of a Taco Bell stand where he stopped for coffee that a man was sleeping in a car in the parking lot. The officer investigated and decided that the man was drunk enough to arrest. He explained that the man was too drunk to drive, and if left in his car he would eventually attempt to drive home. Thus, an arrest was mandatory.

In Case History 22, the man would not have been arrested had he not indicated that he might leave his apartment some time later and move the cars. The patrolman's action was based to a certain degree on the need for self-protection; as he said later, if the man got into his car and drove off there was no telling what might happen. Whether this was a realistic assumption was beside the point. If the man did get into an accident and it was discovered that two officers had failed to arrest him earlier they would be subject to disciplinary proceedings and would possibly be liable.

The other incident is far more interesting. The circumstances in this incident were exactly the same as in Case History 21, and in neither case were the officers under any pressure to handle other calls or perform other tasks. Yet they were handled in opposite ways. This is not unusual. In another instance two patrolmen encountered two separate drunks in approximately the same circumstances—one was found lying in an alley and the other lying on the sidewalk in front of a bar—but the first was driven home and the other arrested. Why do patrolmen feel so compelled to arrest in one instance but not in another? From the police point of view the end result is much the same. A potential drunk driver is off the street and cannot kill someone; a drunk is off the street and cannot be mugged. From the suspect's perspective, however, the decision obviously makes a big difference, both financially and socially.

There is an arbitrary quality to these decisions, and the temptation is to explain them, as those to ignore a violation are explained, by the

idea that patrolmen often act on the basis of the unfathomable quality of mood. There is a certain element of truth in this. After extensive questioning, the reasoning of the two patrolmen in arresting one
drunk but not the other seemed ultimately to reduce to, "sometimes
you just feel like it." But even if we grant that some decisions are
spontaneous, reflecting the whims and petty concerns of the officer,
this explanation is not entirely convincing, for the appeal to mood by
patrolmen as a rationale for their decisions often covers other, more
fundamental, reasons. No decision made by a patrolman is ever entirely capricious. The decision may be unreasonable, it may defeat
the intent of the law and it may abrogate any reasonable standard of
justice, but it reflects pressures arising from the nature of police work
and the officer's beliefs and values about justice and the law, the
people he confronts, and ultimately his own sense of what is right.

More important than the individual and spontaneous decisions
made by patrolmen are the patterns of decisions. Beyond mood there
are three kinds of decision rules that shape the decision not to enforce the law in situations concerning minor violations. They are all
in some way intrinsic to the task of police work, though the degree
to which they are taken seriously varies among patrolmen. There are
first decisions that are based on the attempt to achieve objectives
unrelated to law enforcement; second, those that stem from personal
pressures arising from the task; and third, those based on the need
to maintain respect for police authority.[3]

Nonenforcement is frequently used to attain objectives that have
nothing to do with the intent of the law, and when this happens, the
relationship between patrolman and violator is governed by a process of exchange. Both corruption and the development of informants are based upon the same quid pro quo, nonenforcement in
exchange for money or information. Other objectives for which patrolmen will trade enforcement include the need to husband legal
resources, and the need to maintain public support and the legitimacy of police authority. Decisions not to enforce the law in exchange for a desired good may be extended to either individuals or
groups.

The use of enforcement powers to develop informants is a widely
accepted practice in the criminal justice system, and deemed absolutely necessary in areas such as narcotics enforcement. What is
perhaps not as well known is the degree to which patrolmen engage
in these practices. This is not confined to those patrolmen who spe-

cialize in narcotics; even an officer, such as the one in Case History 24, who does not go out of his way to work narcotics will attempt, when he has the opportunity, to parlay a violation into an obligation.

Case History 24

An officer stopped what appeared to be a drunk driver. The man was given a field sobriety test, and while he had been drinking, he was, at the most, a borderline drunk. More important, the man was identified as a local ex-convict who was suspected of pulling a number of armed robberies, though the department could not pin anything on him. He was told by the patrolman that he could be arrested, but the officer went on to say, "I'm going to come to you sometime and I'll expect a favor." The man replied, "take me in, I don't care"; the officer then said that he did not expect the man to snitch on a friend but he did expect some information. The man continued to balk at this suggestion and he was finally released.

Case History 25

A yellow Corvette passed a patrol car on the freeway going 80 mph. The car was stopped, and when the patrolmen asked for identification, the driver flashed the badge of another police department. They made small talk with him for a few minutes and then left. The patrolmen said that the reason they didn't give the man a ticket was "reciprocity; we give them a break and they give us a break."

Less well known, also, is that nonenforcement may be systematically extended to groups. This is partly a matter of courtesy. Many patrolmen indicated that they would never issue a traffic citation to a doctor or a member of the clergy. There is also the matter of reciprocity among law enforcement personnel themselves as Case History 25 indicates. These decisions normally obtain only for minor violations, though attempts are occasionally made to cover up more serious offenses.[4]

A further reason for nonenforcement is to "husband resources." Some laws may be only sparingly enforced in order to use them for other purposes or to preclude a court challenge of a useful tool. As LaFave points out, vagrancy and even disorderly conduct statutes have been interpreted as aides to investigation, and unless there is an investigative reason for an arrest it will not be made.[5] Many equipment violations are not enforced by patrolmen as a way of "saving" probable cause. In a sense, one consequence of the value of impersonal law enforcement in professionalism is to create a conflict with the goal of crime fighting. Nonenforcement is often based, as these incidents point out, on the need to apprehend a felon or otherwise fight crime. Once again, this indicates how the ideals of professionalism will be tempered to the realities of the street.

Since minor violations arouse the most hostility between patrolmen and citizens, patrolmen may occasionally circumvent the law and trade leniency for desired public support. There is no way of knowing how successful the police are in trading nonenforcement for support, but given the wide range of minor violations that the police come across, the possibility is always present. Moreover, a situation does not always turn on only one factor; in Case History 26 the patrolmen believed that the triviality of the violation and the "attitude" of the juveniles were equally important.

Case History 26

Two officers responded to a prowler call and discovered four juveniles drinking malt liquor behind the back fence of the "victim's" house. They ordered the juveniles to clean up the empty cans and leave, while ribbing them with comments such as "I used to take my girl to a better place to drink." One of them said that they did nothing because it was not serious, the kids passed the attitude test, and the police need all the friends they can get: "If we let them go they'll think we are nice guys."

Nonenforcement may also stem from the personal pressures that arise from police work. Jerome Skolnick has pointed out that the police have the same status as clergymen, and it is presumed that they are law-abiding and morally upright in all that they do. Yet it is a rare policeman who does not break the law now and then—speed on the way to work, drive home after drinking five or six highballs, or, among some younger policemen, try marijuana now and then. The public may feel that this kind of behavior represents less than the ideal of professionalism but for most policemen the difficulty is less one of living up to socially accepted ideals than resolving personal conflict over enforcement of laws. How does one justify enforcing laws that one violates? The simplest answer is that one does not enforce these laws, or at least not very strictly. This implies a certain tolerance for the normal human weaknesses, but as a rule such tolerance applies only to very minor violations like that in the following incident.

Case History 27

As two patrolmen left the station after a short stop, they followed a car that seemed to be trying to get away from them. They stopped the car and found three juveniles: the driver had been drinking a little and one of his passengers had a bottle of beer in his hands. They talked to the youths for awhile, sternly warning them of the evils of alcohol, and then left. They said they didn't enforce the law in a situation like this because it would be a waste of time and everyone has done it at one time or another. Both went on to say that as kids they used to drink all the time.

There are substantial obstacles to nonenforcement for the purpose of easing one's own conscience, and the pressures for enforcement in a professional police department produce a mild hypocrisy among policemen. These pressures also contribute to the dilemma every patrolman faces between the demand for compassion and strictness. The adage here is that "everyone has their story," and many a patrolman will look with a jaundiced eye at pleas for mercy or the consideration of extenuating circumstances. Even so, some situations bring forth leniency rather than enforcement. Whether or not a patrolman is lenient often turns on his perception of the intent of the person. Carelessness, particularly among the young or aged, often dictates leniency.

In deciding to refuse to enforce the law a patrolman is acting, more explicitly than usual, as a judge, something that flatly contradicts some of the most dearly held tenets of professionalism. If police professionalism demands that only one standard be applied in judging behavior, the officer's own sense of what is right may dictate that other standards be brought to bear. These other standards may of course reflect personal values of the officer, but they may also derive from traditional ideals of police work, from the notion that police work requires compassion as well as coercion. Professionalism changes the calculus in a decision of this sort. Leniency not only means acting as judge rather than bureaucrat, it contradicts the notion of deterrence. What this means is that leniency will be extended only in the case of very minor violations, and in order to extend it, a patrolman must believe that such a decision meets the tacit approval of his peers.

One of the most frequently used, though rarely acknowledged, criteria that a patrolman uses in making decisions is what has been euphemistically called the "attitude test." A rough but accurate definition of the attitude test is that the person confronted by police authority must exhibit acceptance of that authority and deference to the officer and his admonishments. It is rooted in two requirements of police work: the necessity of maintaining control on the street and the necessity of assessing an individual's willingness to mend his ways. These two requirements are not mutually exclusive and they are often combined; but circumstances may enhance the emphasis on one rather than the other.

Outright defiance of police authority will usually, but not always, result in an arrest, and if not arrest some other action that demonstrates to the "erring" person the authority of the police. For example, a man who questions what the police are doing while they are interrogating someone may not be arrested for interfering, but he would be checked for wants and warrants and given a stiff warning. The attitude test is a way of maintaining police authority and punishing those who would defy it. It amounts, as policemen like to put it, to "talking yourself into jail."

This is the most common understanding of the attitude test, but it is not the only one. A person's "attitude" toward the law and, in particular, his feelings about the violation he may have committed become rough criteria for deciding whether a citation should be written or a warning given. In this sense, the attitude test is an indirect way of determining whether an informal action will sufficiently deter future behavior rather than a formal action. The use of the attitude test, then, may lead to an arrest where none was intended (or even thought necessary), or a warning where an arrest or citation was first thought necessary.

Case History 28

Two officers observed a youth turn a "wheelie" on his motorcycle in heavy traffic (i.e. go up on the rear wheel). They stopped him and gave him a warning. He was not cited, according to one officer, because he had a good attitude, he was going to a local trade school, and he took the warning seriously and seemed to listen to the officer's admonishments.

NONENFORCEMENT: MINOR VIOLATIONS

Case History 29

A drunk man in an area with an abundance of small stores and restaurants was stopped by a patrolman and told to go home. Though he was rather drunk and making a lot of noise, he agreed to go home without arguing and he had a friend to escort him who was somewhat more sober.

In Case Histories 28 and 29 the attitude of the person was the determining factor in the decision not to arrest or issue a citation. What each patrolman wanted, and got, was some indication that the person took the warning seriously; that is, an admission that he was wrong and a willingness to repent. But as the following examples make clear, belligerence quickly changes the stakes in the game; the stakes for both officer and citizen are higher, and the police believe something must be done.

Case History 30

Driving down the street an officer noticed a pickup truck, ahead and in the lane next to him, weaving a bit. At first he thought that someone was playing a joke, but the truck pulled into the parking lot of a doughnut shop, and as the driver got out of the truck it was clear that he was drunk. The officer followed and asked the man to stop; the man turned and said that all he wanted was a cup of coffee and proceeded toward the shop. The patrolman ordered the man to stop again, but he kept walking toward the door of the shop. The patrolman then went up and arrested him for drunk driving.

Case History 31

As a late model, expensive automobile passed through an intersection in front of them, two patrolmen observed a man drinking in the car. They followed and stopped the vehicle. The driver quickly got out of the car, strode up to the patrolmen as they were getting out of their car, and said, "all right what's wrong here, what's the problem?" The driver went on boldly and aggressively to question the patrolmen as they asked him for his identification. He said he was a lawyer and worked for one of the biggest firms in Los Angeles. The patrolmen reacted quickly and aggressively to this: the driver was given a field sobriety test; the passenger was pulled from the front seat and checked for wants and warrants. At one point, the driver stepped off the curb to close the door of his car, and his action was met with a loud "get back over here." To put it mildly, he was surprised. The driver was not drunk enough to be arrested for drunk driving, so the officers decided to give them both a ticket for "having an open container in the car." Both men pressured the patrolmen for some indication of what the ticket would cost, but they said they had no idea. After some haggling, the officers finally got the ticket signed and left. Later, they said it was an $80 ticket.

The officer in Case History 30 said that he was only going to give the drunk driver a warning until the man refused to stop. As the patrolman was in the process of going to get coffee, he would have preferred that the drunk driver bloat himself with coffee and drive home. But the man's attempts to avoid the officer and his nonchalant attitude toward the whole matter changed the situation for the officer, and he believed that an arrest had to be made, even if, by his own admission, it was quasi-legal.

Case History 31 provides an even more graphic example of this process. The two patrolmen in this incident had earlier made a felony arrest of a narcotics dealer, and they were rather pleased about it. They had no intention of writing a citation; indeed, one of them remarked prior to stopping the car that they would just warn the occupants. The driver's belligerence radically changed the outcome of this situation. Patrolmen believe that if someone is stopped, he is stopped for a good reason (this is almost always true insofar as minor violations are concerned; much less so in the context of a stop for purposes of interrogation). To question their authority under these conditions is to question the authority of the state. Consequently, they will do what they feel is necessary to put the person in his or her place. The most interesting aspect of this incident is not that the driver got a ticket, for that was decided the minute he got out of the car and challenged their right to stop him; rather, that these two staunch upper-middle-class citizens were checked for wants and warrants and ordered about in a way not at all typical for the middle class. What might have happened if they had not been middle-class was made clear in a rather revealing comment by one of the patrolmen as they left: "If that had been a Mexican that had walked off the curb, I would have choked him out."

The attitude test lends itself to frequent abuse. Patrolmen do not view this as abuse or even harrassment, but as a matter of people getting their just deserts, of being treated the way they should be treated. This rationale is somewhat disingenuous for the implicit assumption is that a person should *never* question the authority of the police or what they are doing. An officer is judged by his peers and his supervisors for his ability to get things done and keep control on the street. This means that he must, at all costs, maintain respect for the authority of the police. This belief leads a patrolman to take a very narrow view of a situation: extraneous questions, no matter how important to the individuals, are not to be entertained; people should stay out of the way and let events take their course. This is reinforced, of course, by belief that the action is legitimate. A person who has violated the law is wrong, and failure to pass the attitude test is just one more demonstration of his weaknesses. The police do have to keep order at the scene of an accident or a melee, or during the course of routine field interrogation. Yet if we grant that the police should not let people walk all over them and that patrolmen often have good reasons for refusing to entertain questions, we also have to understand that the belief and assumptions that lie behind the attitude test erect an arbitrarily high standard of desired conduct on the street, one that screens out legitimate as well as illegitimate inquiries. What is often desired is not respect but deference.[6] Take the following incident.

Case History 32

A man was stopped for throwing a lighted cigarette out of the window of his car. The patrolmen berated him for throwing his cigarette out the window, ran him for wants and warrants, and ordered him to replace the dog-eared driver's license he was carrying. He was released without a ticket. One of the patrolmen commented that this was an "attitude test ticket: if he complains it's an automatic ticket."

The patrolmen seemed concerned less about the trivial violation for which the man was stopped than about extracting a certain amount of deference to police authority. They were not vicious or blunt about it, but neither was the point lost on the man.

The attitude test seems like a holdover from an earlier era of police work, more typical of the burly and gruff beat cop than of an occupation imbued with a singular fascination with professionalism. The legalistic assumptions behind the doctrine of professionalism preclude the injection of an extra-legal citerion such as the attitude test; but the need to maintain control on the street and the beliefs of the police culture mandate it. Patrolmen are not unanimous in their opinions about the attitude test. Evidence drawn from the

TABLE 7.2
Patrolmen's and Supervisors' Evaluations of the Attitude Test

Those Who Agreed with the Following Statement	High-crime Areas				Low-crime Areas				All Departments	
	Inglewood		Rampart		Redondo Beach		Northeast			
	Patrolmen (%)	Supervisors (%)	Patrolmen (%)	Supervisors (%)	Patrolmen (%)	Supervisors (%)	Patrolmen (%)	Supervisors (%)	Patrolmen (%)	Supervisors (%)
a. It is important and right for an officer to take a person's attitude into account in deciding whether or not to enforce the law.	66	36	59	44	62	60	63	59	63	50
b. A patrolman who makes an arrest or issues a citation because of a person's attitude is making a "bad" arrest.	40	67	43	59	53	90	39	82	43	73
c. A person who verbally abuses a police officer when he has been stopped for a violation of the law, who calls him names and challenges his authority, should be arrested.	24	17	32	35	24	20	29	24	27	25
Number of Respondents	(62)	(12)	(51)	(17)	(34)	(10)	(51)	(17)	(198)	(56)

survey indicates that the attitude test is most acceptable when used in an instrumental fashion, as an indirect way of assessing character; it is less acceptable when used as a way of coping with disrespect and challenges to police authority. The data in table 7.2 show first that 63 percent of all patrolmen agreed that a person's attitude should be taken into account when making a decision (statement a). On the other hand, two-fifths (43 percent) of patrolmen agreed with the proposition that an arrest or citation made on the basis of the attitude test is a "bad" arrest (statement b). Only a minority of these patrolmen—just 27 percent—think that someone who challenges the authority of the police after he has been stopped should be arrested (statement c). This may underestimate the degree to which the attitude test is an acceptable means to exact deference, both because of biased responses and the way the statement was worded.[7] Still, for one-quarter of the patrolmen to agree says something in and of itself.

The field supervisors in all three departments represent a decided contrast: they are less likely than patrolmen to believe a person's attitude should be taken into account; almost three-quarters of them believe that an arrest made on the basis of the attitude test is a "bad" arrest; and they are slightly less inclined to view the attitude test as a legitimate measure of the acceptance of police authority—though the difference on this last question is really quite small (table 7.2). Some field supervisors may see the need for the attitude test but most are loath to accept it. The difference between patrolmen and field supervisors on this score again illustrates the tension between the values of the police culture and those of professionalism.

In some measure, legalism is characteristic of the decisions of patrolmen in all three departments. But the goal of impersonal enforcement may be unreachable, for discretion can never be entirely eliminated, and to admit discretion is to admit considerations peripheral to the law. The departures from the standard of impersonal enforcement derive from the multiple objectives the police seek to attain, the judgment of character and intention that patrolmen make on a day-to-day basis, and the intrinsic difficulty of managing a complex task in a diverse society. Yet insofar as minor violations are concerned, reform has narrowed the legitimate grounds for nonenforcement, and, to this extent, greater control over police action is achieved. But it may be that it is only in the case of minor violations that such control obtains. Nonenforcement in disturbances is a far different matter.

Disturbances: The Decision Not to Arrest or Take Action

The problem of nonenforcement is most apparent in the way the police handle disturbances. Twenty-four percent of all activities observed in the three departments involved disturbances—family fights, noisy parties, business disputes, and the like—and the bulk of these (97 percent) originated through calls for service. Disturbances accounted for 41 percent of all calls for service observed, and if miscellaneous service calls (crime reports, traffic accidents, dead bodies by natural causes, missing children, and the like) are included this figure rises to 59 percent. In terms of sheer numbers alone, then, order-maintenance and service calls make up a large proportion of a patrolman's daily routine. (These figures may slightly understate the actual number of order-maintenance calls patrolmen deal with since some calls classified as felony incidents involved felony assaults, and these ordinarily take place in the context of an interpersonal dispute.)

From a patrolman's point of view, order-maintenance and service calls are *not* the most important part of his job; rather they are an aspect of his work to which he must adapt. Many of these situations are considered peripheral to the main functions of the police. Unlike minor violations, where the impetus is toward enforcement, in disturbances the impetus is toward nonenforcement. It is in disturbances that the political implications of nonenforcement become most apparent, for it is in these situations that the police can and do systematically deny the protection of legality, and even assistance, to individuals who need it. Patrolmen are not at the mercy of citizens in these incidents, and here, as in crime fighting, they do not respond to events so much as they manipulate them. How they do so and why are the crucial questions.

THE DILEMMAS OF ORDER MAINTENANCE

Order-maintenance situations present a different range of problems for the patrolman than law enforcement or crime fighting. A disturbance may vary from the trivial—being called to ask a neighbor to turn down a radio—to the deadly serious, a dispute between husband and wife that has erupted into violence. And these incidents are always ambiguous. A patrolman must decide whether a violation has actually occurred, and even if he believes some law has been broken, he must decide what charge to prefer—felony assault, misdemeanor assault, disturbing the peace, or drunk in public to name only a few possibilities.

The adequacy of a patrolman's response turns partly on the seriousness of the situation. Any disturbance has the potential for violence, but in most it is not really probable. Here the police perform a service function, they act as "philosopher, guide, and friend." This often requires nothing more than acting as a sympathetic listener and providing the kind of advice and counsel most people need at one time or another. Given that the bulk of these calls come from the poor, the elderly, and the lonely, the police—at their best—render a needed and useful service. Far more serious are those incidents that have erupted into violence or are on the verge of it. Judging the potential for violence is a highly subjective matter, but it is an element of any disturbance that a patrolman must consider. Though many of the service functions the police perform could be handled by other agencies, these incidents cannot, for they require that the police attempt to prevent violence and disorder, and often necessitate the use of coercion, legal or otherwise. In the analysis of discretion, it is these serious order-maintenance incidents that are of concern.

Many disturbances involve the police in a dispute between two or more people who are acquainted with one another, often a husband and wife, and the decisive characteristic of these situations is that their presence has been requested by a citizen to resolve what is essentially a personal problem. This may enhance the legitimacy of the patrolman's authority, as Albert Reiss, Jr., suggests, but it also involves the police with citizens in a way that is not true of law enforcement or crime fighting. For one thing, their involvement is far more *intimate* than is true in other circumstances. It is one thing to confront a patrolman over a traffic violation where the roles of enforcer and violator are well-defined; it is another when the intimacy of one's personal life is rawly exposed to public view, when the bitterness, the fear, and the failures of a lifetime spill out.

Because these disputes turn on personal problems, because they involve, most deeply, the matter of people simply living together, the police ordinarily draw a fundamental distinction between these incidents and crime: order-maintenance problems cannot be resolved or settled in any permanent way. Except in a very immediate sense, the idea of deterrence does not apply. Assault, murder, and even rape, it is believed, are not crimes that can be prevented by any sort of effective police strategy. Consequently, an arrest is ordinarily deemed to be the last resort. An arrest in a family squabble does not resolve the underlying problems, and it may simply aggravate matters, especially if a husband is arrested. He will eventually get out of jail, and he may return home, angrier than before, to pick up where he left off.

In most order-maintenance incidents, but particularly in interpersonal disputes, the burden of enforcement is reversed: it rests with the citizen rather than the police. The typical disturbance will be resolved only through an arrest when the person who called the police, or the victim, agrees to make a citizen's arrest. Since many disturbances occur prior to the arrival of patrolmen, and technically they cannot arrest for any misdemeanor violation they have not witnessed, this is partly a matter of meeting necessary legal requirements. Of course, the "in-presence" requirement is applicable only if the officer believes a misdemeanor rather than a felony has been committed—a distinction that is not always unambiguous in these incidents. More important perhaps, if a patrolman decides to arrest on his own, he may be acting counter to the wishes of the victim. To this extent he decreases the legitimacy of his authority.

Interpersonal disputes typically occur in private and ought to be distinguished from disturbances that occur in public places, in a bar or bowling alley for example. These latter disturbances pose more clearly the problem of public disorder for the police. These are not personal problems which the police are asked to resolve so much as they are issues of the relationship between groups of citizens, such as a group of juveniles and the other patrons at a bowling alley. The absence of any personal relationship between the antagonists and the ever present potential for a larger disturbance put a public disturbance in a different light from a private one. The police have more incentive to act, and legally they have greater leeway since any violations that have occurred have occurred in public. Moreover, they do not confront the norm of privacy. It is one thing to arrest a man for being drunk and disorderly in a bar; it is quite another to arrest him in his home. In a public disturbance, while the burden of enforcement still rests with the citizen, the police may be more likely to act without waiting for someone to agree to make a citizen's arrest.

Patrolmen approach order-maintenance situations with the attitude that all that can be done is to handle the immediate problem, almost always by some means other than arrest. It is the belief that most, if not all, order-maintenance situations are not amenable to legal solutions—a belief that is reinforced by the oft-quoted dislike patrolmen display toward these incidents—that underlies a basic presupposition about the law as it is applied by patrolmen in these incidents: the law is to be applied narrowly, and an arrest is an appropriate course of action, as a rule, only if it will result in a prosecution.[8] In other words, enforcement is meaningful only if it results in a sanction of some kind. The reluctance of citizens to prosecute reinforces the predisposition to interpret the law in this manner. The attitude of many patrolmen is, "If they [the victim] won't take it seriously why should we?" An arrest without prosecution is not only futile but wasteful; it takes time away from more "serious" problems, and the courts and prosecutors will not take them seriously anyway. Needless to say, this attitude toward the law stands in stark contrast to that in criminal and law enforcement incidents where patrolmen often ignore the views of prosecutors. The complaint that prosecutors and judges are undermining enforcement is not often heard in regard to an order-maintenance problem.

What is at issue in serious order-maintenance disputes is the kind of protection extended to citizens by the police. Widespread nonenforcement in these situations has meant de facto acceptance of violence among some groups of individuals, and has denied the protection of legality to those so affected. This is an issue despite the serious questions that may be raised as to the adequacy of a legal remedy and the necessity of coping with an overloaded judicial system.[9] Protection presumably means more than the protection of property; it means freedom from violence. At the very minimum the problem is that of preventing violence and making more than a cursory attempt to resolve matters. Nevertheless, the bias of the police (and prosecutors) has traditionally been toward ignoring or minimizing the potential seriousness of these problems. And this bias is most often directed at specific groups in American society, notably blacks and women.[10] The analysis of discretion should not be interpreted narrowly in these situations. In a broad sense the problem turns on the adequacy of the action taken by a patrolman. There are often a variety of ways to deal with these incidents, and legal action is not always required, though that might be necessary. What really matters is how a patrolman interprets the incident and how seriously he views it. The reluctance of citizens to prosecute and of prosecutors to take action is often used as a pretext to avoid taking any action at all.

Professionalism, ironically, has added to the dilemmas a patrolman must cope with in trying to handle order-maintenance problems.

Professionalism requires responsiveness in answering calls and meeting the requests of citizens. Much to the chagrin of some patrolmen very few calls are screened out, and supervisors expect their men to handle their calls to completion. What this means to a patrolman is often vague; what it does not mean is clear. A patrolman is ordinarily expected to take some kind of action, even in the most trivial of calls; he is not supposed to "kiss it off." He is also expected to treat calls equally and give every citizen his or her due, though this does not require strict enforcement. In fact, administrators expect that arrests in these incidents will generally be made on the basis of a citizen's arrest. Yet these expectations for responsiveness and thoroughness conflict with the priority of crime fighting. The reliance on a citizen's arrest is partly used as a way of resolving this conflict; it allows the police to appear to be responsive to citizen demands while freeing them for more important tasks. Most policemen are well aware that the use of this procedure decreases the amount of enforcement that takes place in these incidents. For many disputes this is entirely satisfactory, but the conflict is never completely resolved; the question of responsiveness is always begged. Offering the victim a choice between a citizen's arrest and no action may not be a choice at all. In any event, it is up to the patrolman to resolve this conflict.

A further dilemma stems from the requirement of impersonality. Patrolmen are expected to act impersonally in what is a highly personal set of circumstances. Unless he is extraordinarily detached, a patrolman, whether he likes it or not, will be drawn into the situation. This may mean outright sympathy for one of the participants, but more often it engenders disdain, disgust, and resentment at the pathos of people's lives and their personal weaknesses. Attitudes toward cleanliness, drinking, and work, and prejudices based on race and sex enter into and shape the response. A patrolman's personal values and his attitude toward the people may draw him toward some action. This is especially true where children are involved and the officer believes action is required to protect their interests. Most often, though, what is reinforced is the inclination not to act or at least to take only the minimal action necessary to more or less resolve the situation. The feeling is that these are personal problems which are the result of personal weaknesses and hence of no real concern to the police. Here as elsewhere, though, there are profound differences among patrolmen: some display openly hostile attitudes toward these calls, while others become skilled and effective mediators.

ALTERNATIVE RESPONSES TO DISTURBANCES

How do patrolmen generally handle order-maintenance situations? What kinds of alternatives are available and what are the criteria that patrolmen employ in making a decision? What determines how seriously they will take an incident? To consider the first question, patrolmen will often attempt to handle the problem in a way that will satisfy both parties. This often requires some manipulation.

Case History 33

Two patrolmen were called to a dispute between the owner of a donut shop and two female customers. The owner became irritated when the baby of one of the customers began playing with the straws in a dispenser. When he asked the women to make the baby stop, they used profanity and became hostile toward him. He asked them to leave, they refused, and he called the police. One of the officers, a rookie, first attempted to find out from the women what had happened, and then to explain the rights of the owner and why they should leave. They would have none of it. Believing that the rookie had lost control of the situation, the other patrolman jumped in and asked for identification from both women. He then said that if they did not leave immediately he would arrest them. They refused and he turned to the owner and secured his consent for a citizen's arrest. At this point he put his hand on his handcuffs as if he were getting them out and said they better leave or they were going to jail. The women, aware that they had lost the game, slowly moved out of the restaurant.

Case History 34

Two officers responded to a "415" family-dispute call involving an argument between a couple who had just separated over custody of their children. The wife had left her husband who was taking care of the children, and she returned to take custody. The husband refused to give them up. The officers immediately separated the two of them, taking the woman outside the house. What they did was to convince the woman to leave and to resolve the matter in the courts. She was reluctant, but after considerable discussion she agreed to leave.

The dispute in the doughnut shop is most interesting as an illustration of the strategies employed by the police. The rookie lost control, and as his mentor explained to him afterwards: "The object is to solve the problem but keep both parties satisfied. The solution in this case would have been to threaten and order the girls out of the restaurant quickly, and then to soothe their feelings by telling them that the owner was a son-of-a-bitch." He went on to say that the story could be embellished by telling them that the owner was known to act that way all the time and the best thing was just to avoid him. Then, he counseled, one should go back into the restaurant and tell the owner that if he has any more problems he should give them a call. He explained that this way the problem would be solved and everyone would be more or less satisfied with the results.

The other incident illustrated the way in which many family disputes are handled. The strategy is to separate the people, attempt to calm everybody down, and if necessary convince one of them to leave for the night. Unless an extremely serious injury has occurred or a weapon of some kind is involved, the police will attempt to solve the dispute through informal mediation. While patrolmen in this family dispute worked to resolve the problem, some patrolmen will treat the same situation perfunctorily.

Almost 60 percent of these patrolmen think that a crime involving a dispute is better handled by warning than by arrest (table 7.3, statement a). Patrolmen in Inglewood are the most likely to agree with this proposition and those in Redondo Beach the least. At the same time, about one-third eschewed an impersonal assessment of these incidents in favor of more particularistic criteria, and agreed that since assaults and the like were common among some social groups—blacks, Mexican-Americans, Okies—an informal action was preferable to arrest (table 7.3, statement b). In contrast, the field supervisors are less inclined to tolerate either ignoring a minor dispute or nonenforcement because of the presumed characteristics and social behavior of different groups.

If an attempt at mediation is unsuccessful in resolving a dispute, a patrolman may first attempt to persuade the victim to make a citizen's arrest. As a rule this is most common when the victim is the owner or manager of a business or when there have been repeated calls back to the same place. (In fact it is not uncommon in a business dispute for a patrolman to refuse to take any action at all unless the manager agrees to make an arrest if all else fails.) Overall, the attitudes of patrolmen toward urging the victim to file a complaint are sharply divided. Forty-eight percent agree that persuasion is not acceptable, though patrolmen in the small departments are somewhat more likely to agree (table 7.3, statement c). On this question there is little disagreement between field supervisors and patrolmen.

In the event that the victim will not act and the disturbance is serious, the patrolman is left with the choice of ignoring it or making an arrest for an offense that may not stand up in court, that is, resorting to a pretext arrest. Two-thirds of patrolmen say they will make arrests to keep order even if they know the charges won't stick (table 7.3, statement d). There are no appreciable differences among the departments, and, with the exception of Inglewood, most field supervisors accept the necessity of a pretext arrest. The attitude of field supervisors in Inglewood is further evidence of their somewhat more restrictive attitudes insofar as aggressiveness is concerned.

If patrolmen make a pretext arrest in a serious order-maintenance disturbance, how much leeway do they actually have and what are the likely charges? First, patrolmen have more legal authority in dealing with juveniles, and they are often more concerned with taking action. Juveniles can be arrested under a variety of catchall charges, for example, "incorrigible" or "runaway." With adults, weak but justifiable grounds often exist for making an arrest for felony assault, but the more common strategy is to use a catchall offense such as drunkenness. If the disturbance takes place in public, the patrolmen can simply go ahead and make the arrest; otherwise, as most patrolmen will admit, the suspect must be lured out of his or her home and then arrested.

An examination of a random sample of arrest reports in Inglewood and Redondo Beach showed that about one-fourth of arrests for drunkenness were made in the context of a disturbance of some kind. Many of these arrests originated in "415 disturbance" calls and were clearly pretext arrests. In Inglewood, for instance, two patrolmen responded to a fight between a Mexican-American couple, and as the officers attempted to help the woman leave the house her husband followed them into the street yelling obscenities. When he reached the street and showed no intention of desisting he was arrested for drunkenness. In both departments, arrests for drunkenness for reasons of "drunk and disturbing" were significantly more likely to take place on the basis of a call for service and in the context of a disturbance of some kind.[11]

There are, then, different responses to an order-maintenance situation that may be taken by a patrolman. The disturbance may be ignored or only perfunctorily handled; various actions aimed at mediating or breaking it up may be undertaken. And there are two alternative ways of making an arrest: either by persuading the victim to make a citizen's arrest or by making a pretext arrest of some kind.

TABLE 7.3
Patrolmen's and Supervisors' Attitudes Toward Order-maintenance Incidents

Those Who Agreed with the Following Statement	High-crime Areas				Low-crime Areas				All Departments	
	Inglewood		Rampart		Redondo Beach		Northeast			
	Patrolmen (%)	Supervisors (%)	Patrolmen (%)	Supervisors (%)	Patrolmen (%)	Supervisors (%)	Patrolmen (%)	Supervisors (%)	Patrolmen (%)	Supervisors (%)
a. If a crime involves a dispute between two people, a fight or a petty theft, it is better to handle it informally by a warning rather than an arrest.	71	50	55	47	44	40	59	35	59	43
b. There are some groups of people (Hippies, Blacks, Mexican-Americans, Oakies, etc.) for whom some types of conduct (for example, assaults, family arguments, carrying knives) are normal even though they may involve crimes, and it is just as well to handle these violations by talking to the people involved, disarming them, etc. rather than making an arrest.	37	33	39	12	38	40	18	12	33	21

c. In 415 disturbances, malicious mischief calls or petty thefts, a patrolman should never urge the victim to file a complaint.	57	67	43	41	50	50	42	41	48	48
d. A good policeman will sometimes make an arrest to keep order even if he knows the charges won't stick.	66	42	67	77	68	90	67	71	67	70
e. A "victim" who is party to a crime or disturbance should probably be ignored by the police and no action need be taken (for example, in the case of a man involved in a fight which he may have helped start who wishes to press charges).	45	8	29	12	41	40	22	18	34	18
Number of Respondents	(62)	(12)	(51)	(17)	(34)	(10)	(51)	(17)	(198)	(56)

Of course, an officer may make an arrest because he believes that a legitimate violation has taken place, though his standards for arrest may be considerably looser than those of the prosecutor. But on what basis does a patrolman choose any of these alternatives? What is central to an order-maintenance incident and the choice that a patrolman makes is the seriousness with which the patrolman views the situation and the belief that action, especially an arrest, is necessary and will be worthwhile. Patrolmen are more dependent on citizens in handling these problems than in other situations, and whatever choice is eventually made will be partly contingent on an evaluation of the victim's claims and desires. But if the interaction between policeman and victim shapes the outcome of these situations, it is not a one-sided relationship: patrolmen do not simply acquiesce to a victim's wishes. They evaluate them, and the decision hinges on this evaluation. A patrolman makes choices by the very options he presents to a citizen, and these options can be and are manipulated to obtain the outcome that a patrolman wants. Thus, if there is a very real dependence of the patrolman upon the actions of the citizen, it is not complete.[12]

EVALUATING DISTURBANCES

Patrolmen are most sensitive to the demands of citizens when the request is *not* to take an action such as an arrest. The tendency of most patrolmen is to refuse to act unless the citizen agrees to take the burden of arrest. If the citizen desires no other action than dispersal the patrolman may go along with this, though he may demand that the citizen agree to make an arrest if all else fails in order to make his threats credible.

Case History 35

As two patrolmen arrived at a disturbance call, they saw a man throwing a large rock against the door of a house. He was immediately apprehended. The house was owned by the mother of the man's ex-wife. Angry at his ex-wife, the man had evidently broken into the house through a rear window, but he was met by a boy friend who hit him and threw him out. He then went around to the front and threw the rock against the door. Legally the police could have arrested on a misdemeanor, malicious mischief, but the mother said that she did not want to press charges if the damage was paid for. The suspect's mother, who had been called, arrived at the scene and agreed to pay for damages. The suspect was then released.

Case History 36

Two patrol cars responded to an assault call. A black woman had been knifed but refused to reveal the identity of her assailant. By talking to people in the apartment building the police became aware that there was a possible suspect in the building, another woman named Alice. They had good reason to believe that she had committed the assault, but no one would identify her or make a complaint. After discussing the matter, a sergeant, who had arrived on the scene, said, "If they don't want to do anything about it, we won't do anything about it."

The patrolmen in Case History 35 could have legally made an arrest for malicious mischief since they witnessed the violation. Yet they were reluctant to act, not only because the woman simply wanted restitution, but because, as they said, "It would be too much of a hassle with no results. . . ." They did not believe that the case would be filed by the prosecutor, and since the man would be back on the street within an hour there was no reason to detain him for preventative purposes. The issue for these two officers was clearly a matter of priorities; both considered themselves to be crime fighters, concerned with felony violations. A malicious mischief violation was simply not worth the time or effort.

The other incident is more complicated. The police could have arrested the woman, Alice, on probable cause, but it would never go to court since no one was willing to press charges or testify. But beyond these considerations the policemen involved did not consider the matter to be serious. They were convinced that the incident was over and there was no potential for further violence; hence, there was no need to make an arrest for preventative purposes. Since this was clearly a borderline situation, one could argue that a more thorough investigation was required and that the potential for retribution did exist. In some ways this is a difficult problem for the police since the victims prefer to keep such matters out of the hands of the police. On the other hand, the patrolmen were clearly happy to let the matter go. One patrolman commented that the sergeant was a "good man": some sergeants, he observed, would have demanded a more thorough investigation and a report. In both of these incidents there was some congruence between the wishes of the victims and of the police, and thus the patrolmen acted as much in deference to the desires of the citizens as on the basis of their own subjective evaluations of the disturbance.

Where the situation is such that the victim wants the police to act, or where the victim is unwilling to take the burden of arrest but some kind of decisive action is still required, the responses of patrolmen will turn on other factors. The decisive matter is the patrolman's evaluation of the victim's legitimacy. And this turns on two considerations: the culpability and perceived social characteristics of the victim. Policemen are sensitive to the question of culpability because they are often used by the public. Calls for police assistance may be based less on an actual need than on a desire to use the police to obtain vengeance against a neighbor or spouse. Patrolmen were asked in the interviews if they believed that a crime or disturbance should be ignored when the "victim" is a party to the incident, that is, in some way culpable. One-third of all patrolmen agreed with this statement, and over two-fifths of the patrolmen in the small departments agreed (table 7.3, statement e). Since this statement is rather strongly worded it probably underestimates the actual amount of agreement with this criterion. Agreement requires that the patrolman ignore the problem altogether when his more likely response will be to take an informal action of some kind.

The kind of choice a patrolman makes when there is some conflict between his aims and those of the victim depends not only on the kind of evidence the patrolman has that the "victim" did indeed precipitate the incident, but also on a more subjective evaluation of the social and personal characteristics of the victim. This latter evaluation takes into account race, sex, personality characteristics, and whether or not the victim has been drinking (or using drugs). Contrary to the survey responses, most patrolmen are acutely sensitive to individual characteristics in evaluating disturbances. All of these factors come into play in the following incidents.

Case History 37

Two patrolmen responded to an "Assault with a Deadly Weapon (ADW) Ambulance" call. When they arrived they found the victim, a woman in her fifties, in the ambulance. She had a bandage over her eye and her pants were spattered with blood. The attendants said that she had a cut over her eye but was not otherwise injured, and they were taking her to the hospital. The woman told the police that she had been sweeping her back porch when her neighbor had hit her with an iron rod of some kind for no apparent reason. She lived in a small bungalow in which the rear door and porch faced the rear door and porch of an adjacent bungalow; the distance between the porches was approximately five to seven feet. The officers went to question the neighbor. He was a somewhat "hip"-looking man in his late twenties with modishly long hair. He came out to meet the officers, and immediately admitted hitting the woman, but his version of the events was rather different. He claimed that he had been cooking steaks on his hibachi on the porch when the woman came outside and began sweeping dirt (cat litter as it turned out) on his steaks. Using rather hostile language he told her to quit, and she started swearing at him and beating him on the back with a broom. At this point he lost his temper and hit her with a plate he had in his hands. He went on to say that they had been having problems for a long time: she called him a queer quite regularly and referred to him and his wife as the "faggot" and "maggot." He appeared to the patrolmen to be contrite and rather sorry about the whole incident. The patrolmen told him that they would have to take a report, but they didn't know if they would arrest him as they wanted to talk to the woman some more (privately, they agreed at this point that it looked like a case of self-defense rather than an ADW). The man was given a stern warning and the patrolmen went off to the hospital. The woman reiterated her story, but did admit after some hemming and hawing that she was having a dispute with her neighbor. Neither officer entirely believed her version of the events; they thought that she precipitated the assault, and they decided to take a simple battery report incorporating both versions. Both of them believed that nothing should be done.

Case History 38

An officer responded to a fight at a bar. As he pulled up, he saw a number of people and a man with a bloody face standing in a parking lot. There was a parking problem involving some of the customers: a Cadillac had been parked so close to an Oldsmobile that the driver of the latter car could not get out. The driver, looking for the owner of the Cadillac, was rather upset. The man with the bloody face said that he had been making a phone call in a phone booth nearby when the driver of the Oldsmobile dragged him out and beat him. He believed that his assailant thought he was the owner of the Cadillac. The man had been drinking, but was not excessively drunk. The owner of the Oldsmobile denied the story and asserted that he had found the man lying on the ground behind the Cadillac when he and his wife came out of the bar. He said that the man had fallen down and hurt himself. At this point the victim told the patrolman that he wanted to file a complaint for assault and battery against the owner of the Oldsmobile. The officer simply ignored him, and when the parking problem was solved he left.

Case History 39

Two patrolmen responded to a "415 fight" at a large apartment building. When they arrived they were met by a man who said that his common-law wife was raising hell in their apartment. She was always drunk, he said, and he thought that she was "psycho." He claimed that he had been kicked out of twelve apartment buildings because of her behavior. He requested that the officers commit her for psychiatric observation. The patrolmen went up to the apartment and found the woman, sprawled on a couch, totally drunk. They immediately recognized her as a "local wino." Despite evidence that she had been beaten earlier in the day by her common-law husband, they told her that there was nothing they could do and the best thing was for her to "sober up." They went back downstairs and told the man that they would not commit her and they could not arrest her. They advised him to leave her, and then left.

Case History 40

Two patrolmen responded to a 415 disturbance at a local grocery store. The owner of the store was well-known to the police and generally well thought of. His problem concerned a "twenty-six-year-old wino" who had been in the store bothering customers. He had left but the owner thought the police should be alerted. The officers went looking for "Bob," and vowed that if they found him he was going to jail. As they were cruising the area they were hailed by a man who said that there was a man lying on the ground behind his store, apparently hurt. The patrolmen thought it might be Bob. It was, and he had been beaten severely around the head. When questioned, Bob, a Mexican-American, first said that he had been beaten by "two niggers with a baseball bat," then it was "five niggers with a tire iron"; and finally, "some Mexican" had beaten him. They sent Bob off in an ambulance and made out a report. They were rather unconcerned with Bob's beating and made no attempt to really investigate the matter. They did talk to a "friend" who said he had no idea who had done the beating but observed that Bob deserved it, that it was too bad that he had not been killed. Both officers said that the friend was lying and that Bob knew who beat him but wouldn't say. As far as the patrolmen were concerned the matter was closed.

In all of these incidents patrolmen took only the minimal action necessary or simply ignored the problem. The decisions in each case were based on an evaluation of the victim's culpability and characteristics. Though more explicit in the last incident, the attitude in all was that the victims got what they deserved. The first is perhaps the most straightforward. The officers did have good reason to believe that the woman precipitated the fight and that she had been struck in "self-defense." In making this evaluation, though, they relied upon the young man's attitude, his contriteness, as much as anything else. Their solution was not to ignore the matter so much as to pass the buck. By making a battery report incorporating both versions they merely shifted any decision about a criminal action to the detectives.

But this was done with the knowledge that an action of any kind would probably not be forthcoming. In addition to their evaluation of the victim, they justified their decision on the belief that the prosecutor would not take the matter very seriously. How much this was a rationalization for not taking any action is impossible to tell, but it is clear that these two justifications reinforce one another.

In the other three incidents it was not only the legitimacy of the victim that was at stake, which was not as doubtful as in the first, but the officer's attitudes and feelings toward the victims. The use of alcohol or drugs tends to be an important factor in a patrolman's evaluation. In Case History 38 the officer first justified his decision to ignore the man's request for a complaint on the grounds that he probably had fallen and hurt himself. He reasoned that the owner of the Oldsmobile did not look as if he had been in a fight and that it was unlikely he would fight with his wife present. He also commented that the man looked like a reasonable, solid citizen. The "victim," on the other hand, had been drinking, and besides being bloody was rather disheveled. The patrolman said that since the man had been drinking his case would not stand a chance in court. Yet it was not clear why the man would have chosen to make a complaint if he had in fact fallen down nor why somebody called about a fight. This officer was a teetotaler and had an abhorrence of drinking. While he did not say so, it is possible that his attitude toward drinking colored his attitude toward the victim. The patrolman, I should make clear, made no attempt to investigate the substance of the man's charges. Indeed the ease with which he ignored the whole matter is one of the most striking aspects of the incident.

The next incident brings sex, in addition to drinking, into the equation. The officers in this incident were singularly unsympathetic to the complaints of the woman. The officers in Case History 39 did in fact have only tenuous legal grounds on which to act, but because of the woman's reputation and her obvious inebriation they saw no point in acting. Indeed, even though they had some evidence that she had been beaten (the manager told them that he was sure she had been beaten earlier in the day) it was *her* behavior that was in question and not her husband's. The decision was again justified on grounds that the prosecutor would not act, but perhaps more important was one patrolman's observation that "these situations are a pain in the ass."

The attitude that the victim got what was deserved is most apparent in the last incident. Just before these officers found Bob in back of the store they had agreed that Bob "probably should get his butt kicked." What they meant, if I need to point it out, was that a beating would straighten Bob out. Apparently other people in the neighborhood felt the same way. Consequently, the officers believed there was no real reason to attempt to apprehend Bob's assailants.

The chief characteristic of the exercise of discretion among patrolmen in order-maintenance situations is a reluctance to act, even in the face of reasonable cause for action. A patrolman is most sensitive to the demands of citizens when their requests are congruent with aims of the police. A patrolman will normally make a citizen's arrest when requested, though adherence to a citizen's wishes is not guaranteed. My impression is that patrolmen are somewhat more likely to honor such requests from the owner of a small business or a security guard of a department store since the legitimacy of the victim, in their view, is not usually in question. Independent police action occurs only when a patrolman has no other way out of the situation or when his authority is at stake. This is usually in the context of either excessive violence or the strong likelihood of further violence or disorder and belligerence toward the police. Depending on the circumstances, independent action by patrolmen is more likely in a disturbance that occurs in a public rather than a private place. Both the concern to prevent a larger problem and the need to maintain respect for the authority of the police are present.

Professionalism and Nonenforcement of the Law

Widespread nonenforcement of minor violations is simply not characteristic of a professional police department. Strict enforcement is not in and of itself required by the values of professionalism, so why should reform result in a brand of enforcement that is more strict? It cannot be entirely explained by the value of impersonality—the ideal of equality before the law—that attaches to professionalism, nor by the attempt to minimize the discretion of policemen. The value placed upon strict enforcement cannot be detached from the preoccupation with crime fighting, for at bottom, the preference for strict enforcement is rooted in a preoccupation with order. There is a close relationship between the enforcement of minor violations and crime control, and strict enforcement is, in many ways, part of a larger strategy of crime control which rests on the ideas of deterrence and initiative.

Yet patrolmen do not entirely accept the imperatives of police professionalism, and they are willing both to admit considerations other than the law into their deliberations and to accept the continued utility of the attitude test. Devotion to professional values varies among patrolmen, but on the whole such values appear to be more firmly entrenched in the LAPD than in the small departments —at least as measured by the attitudinal questions. There is somewhat more consistency in the attitudes of field supervisors, and they tend to be far less tolerant of deviations from the values of professionalism. More important though, in all three departments, but especially Redondo Beach and Inglewood, there are significant differences in the attitudes of patrolmen and field supervisors. In Redondo Beach, for example, field supervisors are more legalistic than patrolmen and in Inglewood they are less tolerant of pretext arrests or the attitude test than patrolmen. In the LAPD the differences, though less sharp, tend to cut in different ways. We may reasonably conclude from these data that field supervisors, assuming they act on their beliefs, do not convey to patrolmen a wholly consistent set of expectations, and if they do, their admonitions are not always accepted by patrolmen.

Finally, in contrast to the pattern of aggressive patrol and strict enforcement which prevails with crime fighting and minor violations, the pattern with order-maintenance problems, especially those that stem from personal disputes, is not to act and not to enforce the law. Let me sharpen the contrast. A patrolman will never refuse to arrest a drunk driver because the city attorney will reduce the charge to reckless driving or because judges do not take drunk driving seriously. Yet patrolmen consistently refuse to take action in disputes with a potential for violence because the "prosecutor won't act on it." Burglars and armed robbers are actively sought; family disputes are avoided or perfunctorily handled. In one sense we have come the full circle: nonenforcement in order maintenance is simply the reverse side of aggressiveness in crime fighting and law enforcement. These are not so much different roles which the police may or may not adopt as they are a conscious choice of priorities. If professionalism has minimized discretion in the case of minor violations, the policeman as judge is most clearly seen in the way disputes are handled. To be sure, there are valid reasons for supposing that legal action will never entirely suffice in these problems, and the present trend toward diversion should certainly be pursued.[13] And the prosecutors and courts surely bear some of the responsibility for nonenforcement. Yet it is not as if these matters could not be handled better than they presently are. Why should a woman suffering at the hands of her husband be considered less important than a two-bit car thief?

Chapter 8

Police Discretion
and Operational Style

THOUGH there are important commonalities in the experiences of patrolmen, though they confront the same dilemmas and choices while working the street, there are profound differences in the way they respond. The occupational pressures that impinge on patrolmen do not lead to a distinctive "police mentality." Rather, these occupational pressures facilitate the formation of a bond of solidarity among policemen, one that provides the emotional support and trust necessary to perform an arduous task in the face of a deep-seated sense of isolation from the community. This bond also, in conjunction with the ethos of individualism and the limits to formal administrative controls, contributes to a tendency among patrolmen to fashion highly individualized approaches to police work.

Police discretion is above all a behavioral process in which the interpretation of events and the choice of alternatives is strongly influenced by the values and beliefs of the actor. The dynamics of the encounter between patrolman and citizen and the law may constrain a patrolman's choices but they do not dictate them. Despite the ability of citizens to limit a patrolman's options through their own decisions of whether to prosecute or through their capacity to resist, patrolmen still have the power and opportunity to manipulate citizens and get what they want. And the law is used pragmatically by patrolmen to accomplish ends that are important to them.

Nor can police discretion be understood entirely as a matter of the development and application of "routines" or decision rules in response to the contingencies and pressures of their work environment. It is true that the choice of what charges to prefer in a felony incident, the kind of information used to separate the innocuous from the deviant, the use of nonenforcement to obtain information or community support, the salience of the attitude test, and the criteria applied in disturbances all constitute decision rules, more or less held in common by patrolmen, which serve to make their task more manageable.[1] These routines are buttressed by shared beliefs about, among other things, the propensity of various individuals and groups to engage in crime and the role of the courts in sustaining or limiting police decisions. Although these beliefs and decision rules reflect the common difficulties patrolmen face in working the street, the significant fact is that knowledge of the street will be interpreted differently and the decision rules applied differently. Despite commonly shared decision rules and despite the penchant for aggressive patrol and the emphasis on strict enforcement that is characteristic of police work in professional departments, patrolmen were observed to respond differently to similar situations on the street. Equally important, our somewhat crude measures of attitudes revealed differences of opinion among an otherwise homogeneous group of men about what constitutes good police work and how patrolmen should handle themselves on the street. This suggests that we need to go beyond an analysis of decision rules to an understanding of the values and beliefs patrolmen acquire while working the street. What counts, in short, is a patrolman's operational style.

If our analysis of police discretion thus far is highly suggestive of the salience of a patrolman's values and beliefs, numerous questions remain. What kinds of operational styles do patrolmen develop, and what are the elements of these? To what extent do these beliefs lead to different responses on the street? What is the genesis of an operational style? Does it reflect the subtle effect of background characteristics and deeply rooted psychological factors? Or is it a product of organizational socialization, and do the training practices and policies of different departments result in a single operational style unique to the department, as James Q. Wilson's argument would suggest? And finally, do patrolmen with different operational styles react differently to the pressures and constraints of the police bureaucracy, and if so, how?

I intend in this chapter to explore the characteristics of four different operational styles actually observed on the street. The analysis will be restricted to an elaboration of the distinctive beliefs and practices associated with each of these four operational styles, and to the development of operational style. I shall ignore, for the moment, the impact of administrative controls on a patrolman's decisions.

A Typology of Operational Styles

A patrolman's operational style is based on his responses to the central problem of a professional police force, the difficulties and dilemmas he encounters in attempting to control crime. Yet an operational style is more than a mere set of strategies to cope with crime, for it encompasses not only a patrolman's considered reflections on the difficulties of crime fighting but also the ways in which he accommodates himself to the pressures and demands of the police bureaucracy. An operational style thus defines both how a patrolman will go about working the street and how he adapts to the contradictory requirements of behaving as a professional performing an uncertain task and as a bureaucrat subject to the stringent but uncertain discipline of the police bureaucracy.

An operational style initially derives from the choices a patrolman must make about how to work the street. Our observations of crime fighting revealed that patrolmen could be differentiated in terms of two characteristics: how *aggressive* they were in pursuit of the goal of crime control, and how *selective* they were in the enforcement of the law. Beliefs toward aggressiveness and selectivity are the core elements of a patrolman's operational style.

The ideal of many patrolmen is that of the inner-directed, aggressive policeman. Aggressiveness is both a matter of taking the initiative on the street to control crime and a preoccupation with order that legitimizes the use of illegal tactics. A patrolman must also make some decision in regard to priorities, and the most common basis for such a choice is a distinction between enforcement of felonies and misdemeanors. Selectivity thus distinguishes between patrolmen who believe that all the laws should be enforced insofar as possible, and those who consciously assign felonies a higher priority.

An operational style structures a patrolman's responses to three kinds of incidents in addition to crime fighting: the enforcement of minor violations; serious order-maintenance incidents in which the police are required to contain violence and disorder; and service order-maintenance calls which merely require that the police provide minor services of one kind or another. Crime fighting, of course, refers not to the reaction of a patrolman to a single, concrete event, as in the other sorts of incidents, but how he patrols the street in light of the objective of crime control. All of these types of incidents pose different legal requirements, imply different kinds of organizational goals, and often involve different kinds of people. The use of discretion in two of them—crime fighting and the enforcement of minor violations—initially turns on the decision of a patrolman to intervene; discretion in the other two, in which a patrolman normally becomes involved through a call for service, turns on the character of a patrolman's response.[2]

By combining the attitudinal dimensions of aggressiveness and selectivity it is possible to derive a four-fold typology of operational styles (see table 8.1). There are two types of patrolmen who are highly aggressive, dedicated crime fighters: the *Old Style Crime Fighter* who is selective, and the *Clean Beat Crime Fighter* who is not. The other two styles are much less aggressive; the *Professional Style,* like the Clean Beat Crime Fighter, is not selective, while the *Service Style* is. This typology was developed inductively, largely on the basis of the field observations. Individual patrolmen who "fit" any one of these styles were observed in all three departments, but only a few patrolmen perfectly exemplify any of these styles. These operational styles are analytical types that highlight the distinctive characteristics of a particular approach to police work.

The differences between these styles may be clarified by describing in greater detail the characteristics of each, the typical responses to different kinds of incidents, and related attitudes associated with each style. The discussion that follows is based upon data derived

TABLE 8.1

Typology of Operational Styles

Selectivity of Enforcement	Aggressiveness on the Street	
	High Aggressiveness	Low Aggressiveness
Selective	Old Style Crime Fighter	Service Style
Non-selective	Clean Beat Crime Fighter	Professional Style

from the field observations. I have classified all patrolmen for which sufficient information about beliefs and behavior on the street is available into one of the four categories. It was possible to classify 82 of the 95 patrolmen observed.[3]

OLD STYLE CRIME FIGHTERS

This patrolman is very aggressive but selective: felonies are believed to be the only violation worth pursuing; minor violations and service activities are not "real" police work, and if possible they are avoided. "Real" police work is not the fortuitous arrest of a burglary suspect, but rather the *skillful* application to crime problems of techniques learned on the street: the assiduous cultivation of informants; the uncanny ability to spot a narcotics suspect walking down the street; a rough but effective method of interrogation; and above all a wealth of knowledge about people and their foibles, and the area in which they work. These officers have "street sense," the ability to judge people and situations quickly and deftly. If the Old Style Crime Fighter attempts to practice the art of police work in its highest form, he does not hesitate to solve problems on the street by whatever means are necessary, legal or otherwise. From his point of view, society must decide whether or not it wants to protect its members from predators; legal restrictions sometimes do more harm than good, and it is often the case that curbstone justice does more to deter an offender than the courts.

What strikes the observer about these patrolmen is the depth of their preoccupation with crime and the assiduous application of the tools and skills of their craft to the task at hand. They are never unprepared. One Old Style Crime Fighter, upon entering the patrol car, produced a pair of high-power binoculars, black leather gloves, and a fat notebook containing the names, crimes, and dates last encountered of resident heroin addicts, burglars, and thieves. The stress placed upon the meticulous use of sheer skill is most apparent in the way these cops go about accumulating information about suspects and crimes. Any stop is worked for information about the area and activities of various individuals. For instance, after investigating a call about some juveniles disturbing the peace, one Old Style Crime Fighter stopped to talk to some juveniles sitting in front of a house, and proceeded to make small talk about a football team the police were organizing. Under the guise of recruiting one juvenile for the football team as a tackle, the patrolman obtained a very good description of him, his name, his address, and what he was doing. The

225

patrolman's interest derived from his suspicion that the juvenile was a potential suspect in some strong-arm purse snatches that had recently occurred. Often the use of skill amounts to nothing more than the straightforward application of "textbook" principles to situations on the street. Patrolmen are notorious for the perfunctory way they handle burglar alarms, yet two avowed Old Style Crime Fighters always took plenty of time to check a building with a ringing burglar alarm. They made more than their share of burglary arrests as a result.

Beyond the skill these men display, what stands out is their ruthless and aggressive demeanor on the street. Most of their free time is spent prowling down darkened streets, often with the car lights out, and stopping any vehicle or individual that looks even remotely suspicious. While these patrolmen pride themselves on their ability to separate the innocuous from the deviant—an acquired skill in their estimation—their aggressiveness often gets the better of them and diminishes the salience of skill. Some of their stops, especially those made for narcotics, are outright sloppy, based on the flimsiest of criteria or the ever present inclination to play the slot machine. On the other hand, there is a measure of truth in their frequent assertion that they are stopping people on the basis of justifiable suspicions. They are frequently right when they pick a man out of a crowd on a street corner as a possible "hype," and there is less randomness in their stops than with the Clean Beat Crime Fighters.

The aggressiveness of these patrolmen does not extend to minor violations, which most of them regard with disdain. One said he would never waste his time on trivial violations such as misdemeanors or arrests that involve juveniles; only felonies are important, and of these, burglaries and narcotics are the preferred offenses. He was observed to act on his beliefs. In one instance, this patrolman saw three juveniles looking under the hood of a stalled car at 3:30 A.M. He stopped, the juveniles were interrogated, the car searched, and then they were released. None of the juveniles had any identification, there was no conclusive evidence the car was theirs (though the patrolman believed it was), and there were several different charges that could have been used to make an arrest had the patrolman wanted to. But he took no action because, in his opinion, juveniles take too much time to process and nothing ever comes of it.

Traffic violations are also regularly ignored by Old Style Crime Fighters. It was rare to observe them stopping a car for any kind of traffic violation, and one of them admitted that he usually wrote no more than five tickets a month. Similar attitudes prevail in regard to drunks and drunk drivers. On the whole, these patrolmen are far more likely than any of the other styles to believe that violations they regard as trivial can safely be ignored. Yet it is safe to say that if nothing else turned up after a long night on the street, a "good" drunk driver would be arrested.

Data drawn from the field observations bear out these impressions. Seventy-two percent of the on-view stops made by those patrolmen who could be justifiably classified as Old Style Crime Fighters were for field interrogations; only 28 percent were for minor violations. Of those individuals they stopped for a minor violation, only one-third were cited or arrested.

The aggressiveness of Old Style Crime Fighters in the street is complemented by a taste for controlled violence: Violence and the use of coercive tactics are accepted as a necessary element of routine police work, not an indulgence. The objective on the street is to maintain control, but tactics are proportional to the end. Here again the accent is on skill. If these patrolmen were frequently involved in altercations on the street, they insist that when they use force it is necessary. One Old Style Crime Fighter claimed to have been involved in a lot of fights on the street but said he had never had a brutality complaint since he only "decks" people when they deserve it—and they know, he insists, they deserve it. Despite the bravado, this patrolman characterizes both the acceptance and skill that is attached to violence by the Old Style Crime Fighter. What they regard as necessary, however, and what the department regards as necessary often differ, and these patrolmen invariably come into conflict with supervisors. But their attitude toward the department on the question of tactics is openly disdainful, for they believe that most supervisors and administrators are hopelessly out of touch with the realities of the street.

Driven by a preoccupation with crime, the Old Style Crime Fighter regards most order-maintenance calls as trivial matters to be avoided if at all possible. In handling order-maintenance incidents, the Old Style Crime Fighters are far more predisposed than other patrolmen to resolve matters informally, to rely on a warning rather than an arrest. The standards these patrolmen bring to bear derive from their assessment of the character and intentions of the individuals involved rather than an assessment of the intent and requirements of the law. The victim's culpability is always at issue and a justification for ignoring the dispute. And there is a propensity to apply particularistic standards: people are often treated by the Old Style Crime Fighter according to his interpretation of the differing moral standards that might prevail among different groups of individuals.

The Old Style Crime Fighters usually attempt to avoid these calls through engineering, indeed they appear to engage in engineering more frequently and with more skill than other patrolmen. If they cannot avoid a trivial order-maintenance call—and much of the time they cannot—these patrolmen handle them in as perfunctory a manner as possible. What they are often unwilling to do is to act as "philosopher, guide, and friend." Sometimes incidents are handled with a brutal callousness. In one instance, two avowed Old Style Crime Fighters answered a family dispute call between an elderly couple in an old dilapidated apartment building. The woman who answered the door immediately began talking in a rambling, desultory manner. She explained that her husband, who was lying on a dirty bed across the room, was extremely sick and needed help. She then switched tracks and said her husband always beat her and she couldn't take it any more. The response of these two patrolmen was to advise her in a jocular manner to get a divorce, and then to leave as quickly as possible. Clearly, there was no police "problem" involved; all the woman really wanted was a few moments of compassion which they were unwilling to extend. It was as much the way they dismissed her as anything else that signified their attitude toward these incidents. The woman's plight was not ignored because of other pressing demands or the tough choices between compassion and responsibility that any professional concerned with human affairs must often make; she was literally dismissed, her plight treated as insignificant.

Yet there are exceptions. Order-maintenance calls in which there is or has been violence will bring forth a more skillful and thorough response. The aggressiveness and the acceptance of violence characteristic of these officers often result in a willingness to resolve a serious order-maintenance incident. If they chose to rise to the occasion, some of these patrolmen could be awesomely effective in coping with the ambiguities of family disputes and the like. Perhaps the decisive fact about the Old Style Crime Fighter's stance toward order-maintenance incidents is that he draws distinctions, and those incidents regarded as trivial are ignored while more serious incidents are treated with all the skill and street sense he can muster.

The Old Style Crime Fighter is frequently found in a large department like the LAPD, where his emergence is facilitated by the surfeit of resources which permit independent action, and by a departmental tradition which legitimizes sleuthing. Yet both his style of action and his attitudes bring the Old Style Crime Fighter into conflict with the department and the values of professionalism. He manages this conflict partly through the respect he has acquired by virtue of his skill, by his ability to do the job. In a way, the Old Style Crime Fighters earn the right to flout rules to which other policemen are subject.[4] Failing this, they survive by dint of sheer skill in outmaneuvering supervisors. But this kind of police work comes at a high price; Joseph Wambaugh is correct when he suggests, as he did in his sentimental recreation of a crime fighter in the *Blue Knight,* that this style represents both the best and the worst that the police have to offer. These men dominated law enforcement when there were fewer constraints on police action than now; and despite their skill, they were (and are) brutal and often given to the worst abuses of police power.

CLEAN BEAT CRIME FIGHTER

These patrolmen are as aggressive and preoccupied with controlling crime as the Old Style Crime Fighters, and like them, exhibit the same dislike of order-maintenance and service calls. What is different is a legalistic frame of mind, and a different view of crime control. The Clean Beat patrolman believes in the rigid and unrelenting enforcement of the law. If he believes, like the Old Style Crime Fighter, that the primary function of street patrol is to prevent and control crime, he thinks this can be done only through aggressive enforcement of minor violations and through stopping and interrogating suspicious individuals. An effective patrolmen, in his opinion, looks for all kinds of violations on his beat, from jaywalking to homicide, and makes as many stops as he can. In a sense, Clean Beat patrolmen are more consciously preventative than Old Style Crime Fighters. Their justification for aggressive enforcement of all laws is not that the law should be enforced impartially; it is the presumption that crime can be deterred only through aggressive enforcement. Crime is really controlled, they think, by keeping a clean beat, by establishing a reputation for consistent, hard-nosed enforcement.

Like the Old Style Crime Fighter, the Clean Beat patrolman is quite willing to violate procedural rules or to bend the law to serve his immediate purposes, and is prone to complain about the limitations placed on a policeman's activity by the courts and police administrators. What distinguishes the two is that the Clean Beat patrolman fails to bring the skill and subtlety to encounters on the street that is characteristic of the Old Style Crime Fighter. The Clean Beat patrolman acts like a rampaging Don Quixote in his efforts to suppress crime. He is something of a rogue elephant in a police department, the kind of officer who will make a lot of felony arrests but will be consistently in trouble. The Clean Beat patrolman thus lives in a continual state of tension: his proclivity for aggressive action conflicts with the demands imposed by an increasingly watchful department and a hostile public. He is, in a word, frustrated.

The most striking thing about the Clean Beat patrolman is the pace of his activity; he is continually on the move, stopping cars, interrogating people, always trying "to dig something up." Consider the activities of a patrolman I shall call Appleby (the name is fictitious), who is representative of this style of police work. On the tour of duty that I observed, Appleby's frustration at being unable to turn up anything reached a crescendo, and culminated in an ever more frenzied search for a crime. The first four hours had been taken up with service calls, and as the night wore on Appleby and his partner became increasingly aggressive. Driving down a major thoroughfare, Appleby saw a man jaywalking; he stopped the man, who had been drinking but was not especially drunk. Deciding he needed an arrest, Appleby booked him. After more frenetic driving, Appleby stopped to investigate a parked car in a vacant lot. Finding a young Mexican-American and his girl friend in the front seat, Appleby rousted them out, and proceeded to thoroughly interrogate them and search the car from top to bottom. All this effort produced only a meager packet of Zig Zag cigarette papers. Angry that once again his efforts were to no avail, Appleby let the young man go only after impressing upon him that the police meant business. The aggressive search for crime continued, and the final incident of the evening was, in many ways, the most instructive. Driving down a major street Appleby observed a young man with long hair walk across the street, in the crosswalk but against the "Don't Walk" sign. The time was just after 2:00 A.M. Appleby told his partner to pull over to the curb, and as they stopped, he leaned out of the window and yelled at the top of his lungs, "You sir, have committed a violation of the law, stop!" The man, who revealed that he had just arrived in Los Angeles from Hawaii, was utterly perplexed by the whole incident. For his carelessness he received a citation for jaywalking and a warning that he had better watch his step because "this is how things are done in Los Angeles."

Not all patrolmen who adopt the Clean Beat style are as aggressive and frustrated as Appleby, but their pace is just as furious. To take another example, two Clean Beat patrolmen in the course of an evening cited one jaywalker; made three traffic stops, two of which resulted in citations; arrested six drunks, although two were the result of backing up a vice unit in a bar; stopped and interrogated one suspected heroin addict; and made two other investigative stops in "suspicious" circumstances. This was in addition to handling a moderate number of calls for service. Clean Beat patrolmen make as many, if not more, stops for field interrogations than the Old Style Crime Fighters, but they make far more stops to enforce minor violations. A fairly equal mix between stops for field interrogations and for minor violations is characteristic of this style. Calculations based on the field observations reveal that just over half the stops Clean Beat patrolmen make are to enforce minor violations (55 percent), and two-thirds of these result in citations or an arrest.

Clean Beat patrolmen evidence a distinct distaste for order-maintenance calls, though they are less prone to avoid them through engineering than the Old Style Crime Fighters, preferring to simply handle a call as quickly as possible. Unlike the Old Style Crime Fighters, the rigid legalism of the Clean Beat patrolmen precludes the use of particularistic standards. They do, however, treat a victim's claims with suspicion, and the plight of a victim they think is somehow culpable will be treated with complete indifference much of the time. What does distinguish the Clean Beat Crime Fighters is that they often go to extremes in handling disputes. Minor disputes are often handled abruptly and crudely. Two Clean Beat patrolmen answered a disturbing-the-peace call in which a lady in an apartment complained that her neighbor was making so much noise she could not sleep. The patrolmen went to the door of the neighbor's apartment, banged loudly, and when the occupant, a young black woman, answered, she was told they had a complaint she was making noise and she had better stop. The woman denied making any noise, and the patrolmen replied that she and the "male object" (her boyfriend) in her room had better "shape up" since they did not want to come back. Clearly, in some sense, the problem was solved, but with what consequences? In a more serious situation, the tendency of the Clean Beat patrolmen is to resort to an arrest rather than mediation. The aggressiveness and the frenzy that is characteristic of these patrolmen on the street carries over into their handling of order-maintenance problems.

The core of the Clean Beat approach, the dedication to crime suppression and the penchant for aggressive, strict law enforcement, is not regarded as harassment, or as an extreme policing style, but as sound law enforcement. Clean Beat patrolmen are slaves to the values of police professionalism, and it often seems as if they have taken the rhetoric of police professionalism too literally. They have no proportion, and some are inevitably consumed by the means they employ. This is vividly illustrated by their attitude toward tactics on the street. Unlike the Crime Fighters, they often appear to have no comprehension of the limits to violence, and their choice of tactics often reveals no understanding of the necessity for measured responses. Their aggressiveness simply outstrips any sense of proportion. Clean Beat patrolmen thus tend to apply coercion spontaneously and very often indiscriminately.

These officers are unable to reconcile the dilemma between the instrumental and substantive goals of police work and the numerous moral choices patrolmen routinely confront. Often it is not the sacrifice of someone's civil rights that gets them into trouble, but their single-minded, rigid approach to law enforcement. Innocuous incidents have a way of blowing up in their hands. Yet because they wholeheartedly accept the canons of professionalism and display an undue sense of obedience and deference toward supervisors, these men come to feel a deep sense of betrayal when supervisors fail to support their decisions and their tactics. Unable to reconcile their aggressive style of patrol with the external limits imposed upon them, these men are reduced to frustration. Appleby, whose frustration stands out from that of others only in its virulence, is an extreme instance of this. As he put it toward the end of the evening:

> You come on the job with balls, you want to act like a man, you want to burn the world up, you want to put guys in jail, you want to solve problems and do something for people. But you find out that you can't act like a man, that you can't be the man you once were until after twenty years on the job [that is, after retirement].

PROFESSIONAL STYLE

If the Clean Beat style denotes extreme aggressiveness and the frequent use of illegal tactics, the Professional Style denotes an active but not overly aggressive patrolman. There is no reluctance to stop people for purposes of a field interrogation, but it is done less often and usually with somewhat more justification. These patrolmen are legalistic without being rigid. Perhaps flexibility is the adjective that best describes their attitude. If they believe that control of crime is the major function of the police, they also accept—some with more, some with less equanimity—the legitimacy of competing goals. Family disputes may often be trivial and petty (adults behaving like children), but people have a right to assistance and courteous treatment from the police. According to the Professional Style, although the law should be enforced and a patrolman does not have the right to presume innocence or guilt, the act of enforcement should be tempered with a judicious understanding of the foibles of human nature. Yet flexibility does not mean that a patrolman should let things go by; even if a citation is not issued, a person who breaks the law should be stopped and warned. These patrolmen are often tough and firm, but they are not obsessively preoccupied with order.

The attitudes and views of the Professional Style are vividly illustrated by a young patrolman with four years experience whom I shall call Joe Fisher. Unlike Appleby, he is not overpowered by the compulsion to control crime; indeed Fisher is overtly hostile to Appleby's style of police work. He has a strong aversion to what he calls "415 police officers," men whom he describes as "badge heavy": they rush to every hot call, they drive at excessive rates of speed, they throw their weight around, and they are usually sarcastic and abrupt with people. Fisher's training officer was like this, and as he reflected on his experiences he observed, "I hated him; I thought the job was to help people."

Yet the law is there to be enforced; there are criminals on the street, and they have to be apprehended. The difference between the Professional Style and the two types of Crime Fighters is the steadfast belief that law enforcement is tantamount to serving people, provided it is done in the proper way. Two incidents involving Fisher and his rookie partner illustrate this belief. In the first, Fisher and his partner stopped in front of a house where they observed a car raised on jacks parked in the street. They contacted the owner and told him that the car was illegally parked and dangerous; it could fall and injure someone, especially a child. They ordered the owner to move the car by the next day or they would issue a citation. The second incident concerned a young man stopped for speeding who talked Fisher out of a ticket. In not issuing the ticket, Fisher said he was being "compassionate," even though giving the man a warning might not have been in his best interests. A ticket, Fisher suggested, may have been more effective in suggesting to him the errors of his ways. While Fisher would let people off with a warning, he was not averse to hard-nosed law enforcement when he thought it necessary and justified.

Nonetheless, field interrogations and like tactics are the exception rather than the rule with these patrolmen. If anything, they are preoccupied with traffic offenses. Where the Old Style Crime Fighter virtually ignores traffic and the Clean Beat Crime Fighter uses traffic enforcement as an instrument to maintain order, the Professional enforces traffic laws in order to prevent accidents and because, after all, it is the law and ought to be enforced as often as necessary and as impartially as possible. Some of these patrolmen were observed to spend a large proportion of their free time patrolling for traffic violations and, what is most unusual, issuing parking citations on their own initiative. At the same time, they are less likely to "play the slot machine," to stop someone just to find out if something is amiss. This is partly because these patrolmen are not inclined to make a stop except in light of fairly compelling evidence that it is justified. Whether this results from an unwillingness to disregard probable cause or a reluctance to take the risks that an aggressive style of patrol entails is not clear. In any event, the legalism and the lack of aggressiveness that is characteristic of the Professional Style are readily apparent among these patrolmen. Judging from the field observations, these patrolmen make far more stops for minor violations than either type of Crime Fighter. Seventy-nine percent of the on-view stops made by the Professionals were made to enforce minor violations; the other 21 percent were for field interrogations. Like the Clean Beat style, however, these patrolmen cite about two-thirds of those individuals stopped for minor violations.

The Professional's perspective on disturbances and service calls is that every call should be treated as unique, and even the trivial ones should be thoroughly handled. These patrolmen rarely engaged in engineering, did not display the disdain for these affairs so characteristic of the Crime Fighters, and were not reluctant to spend as much time as necessary to resolve a dispute. Upon arriving at a routine dispute between two neighbors, two Professionals were told by the complainant that the man living next door had torn down a fence in the backyard near a garden he was cultivating with the permission of the landlord. He wanted action. He was told by the patrolmen that they would have to learn to live together, but they said they would talk to the man next door. The other man's version of the dispute was much different: he said that the complainant was a hostile man, always fighting and arguing with him and his wife. He admitted tearing down the fence in the garden but said that had to do with an argument over the boundaries of their gardens. The dispute was not serious, and there was good reason to doubt both stories. But both patrolmen took quite a bit of time to talk to both parties and made a concerted effort to resolve the dispute. They later explained that if they are often reluctant to make arrests in disturbances, neither are they willing to ignore them. Not every Professional patrolman is willing to be quite so patient, but the inclination to do so if possible is what distinguishes this patrolman from both Crime Fighters.

Like the Clean Beat approach, the Professional Style incorporates many of the essential beliefs and values of police professionalism. The differences between the two turn on the emphases they give to the elements of police professionalism, and the ways they accommodate themselves to organizational and community pressures. The Professionals adhere as much as possible to departmental rules and policies. They are preoccupied with doing a good job as that is defined by their supervisors. As one of them said in the midst of issuing parking tickets, "I'm out here for eight hours and I might as well give the city its money's worth." They firmly enforce the law, but they believe they are flexible enough to know when not to; they vigorously pursue felons, but they are less likely to indulge themselves in the frequent and wanton use of illegal tactics; in short, they believe that a policeman can enforce the law and cope with crime while maintaining rapport with the people in the community. For these officers the conflicts inherent in police work are either sublimated or do not exist.

SERVICE STYLE

There are two distinct groups of patrolmen who exhibit the two basic characteristics of this style, which are selectivity in enforcement of the law and a lack of aggressiveness. The attitude of one group was concisely summed up by a patrolman who said, "I don't want to chase every asshole on the street, I'm just as happy if things don't come up." These patrolmen neither worked very hard to enforce the law nor paid much attention to people's problems; their actions were calculated to keep the sergeant happy and do the minimal amount of work necessary to get by. They were notorious for ignoring violations and treating disturbances in as perfunctory a manner as possible. Some of these individuals were merely using police work as a means to another occupation, as they either went to school or worked at another job. Others were "burnt out" patrolmen; at one time in their career they may have been "hustlers," now they were coasting and hoping to make twenty years and retirement in one piece. Their code was to take problems as they occur and above all stay out of trouble.[5]

The second group, those few individuals who advocate the Service Style as a positive method, are quite different, for they advocate a qualitatively unique approach to police work. What distinguishes them from the other three styles is their belief that crime suppression is *not* the most important goal of a police department. They argue that the police should take a positive role in assisting people to solve their problems. Consequently, impersonal and legalistic law enforcement is deemphasized, and one of the defining characteristics of this approach is the belief that the exercise of discretion ought to be based on a sensitivity to community values and needs. In one sense this style attempts to return to the concept of the beat cop; but if it stresses the beat cop's sensitivity to community values and his selectivity, it is modern in its emphasis upon legality, especially in regard to due process, and a code of professional conduct. It seeks to combine the best of the beat cop and the professional policeman.

The implications of this style are manifold. It prescribes a definite set of priorities: vice laws are de-emphasized and crimes of violence become the fundamental concern. Enforcement is selective in that it is based on the presence of an identifiable problem. The utility of an arrest or citation is often questioned on the grounds that perhaps other techniques would be more effective. To this extent these officers find themselves pushing for diversionary approaches in handling family disputes, and while they stress strict enforcement in regard to serious crimes the strategy of crime control advocated is quite different. The approach moves away from aggressive patrol to more traditional police techniques, business checks and the like, and to more modern but indirect methods, for example, neighborhood watch programs.

Yet as a whole this style is ill-defined; the bits and pieces of the beliefs described here have been taken from comments and observations of a number of patrolmen. Rather than a coherent approach, what unites these patrolmen is a skepticism of present approaches to police work and a good deal of criticism of many of their fellow officers. Consider a patrolman whom I shall call Ralph Williams. Williams is severly critical of the kind of law enforcement practiced by the men in his department, and he caustically refers to other patrolmen as "order-freaks." He frequently challenges their conduct on the street, especially the propriety of strictly enforcing some minor violations such as drunk in public, and the way some members of a minority group were being treated. At this point, however, Williams can only articulate his criticism of professional police work, for he has not yet defined a working alternative.

The Service Style, more than anything else, reflects submerged ideological conflicts which presently animate the practitioners of the police craft. This is partly a matter of the changing values among young policemen, but it is also indicative of the responses of policemen to the social and political turmoil of the late sixties. Be that as it may, what unites the few individuals who, to a greater or lesser degree, practice this style is a singular distaste for the doctrines of police professionalism and many of the practices endemic to contemporary police. But whether this portends far-reaching changes in American police work is unclear.

In sum, there is strong empirical justification for concluding not only that patrolmen have the latitude to fashion diverse approaches to police work but also that they actually do so. There are first clear differences in the propensity to conduct field interrogations and to intervene to enforce minor violations. Calculations based on the field observations show that the ratio of stops for field interrogations to stops for minor violations (the higher the ratio the more stops for field interrogations in relation to minor violations) is 2.55 for Old Style Crime Fighters, .83 for the Clean Beat Crime Fighters, .27 for the Professional Style, and .38 for the Service Style. Clean Beat patrolmen are by far the most active, and make the most stops for either kind of incident, while the Service Style is the least active. Both the Clean Beat and Professional patrolmen cite 67 percent of the individuals they stop for minor violations; in contrast the Old Style Crime Fighters cite only 33 percent and the Service Style only 25 percent. Differences in the way order-maintenance and service calls are handled are more difficult to discern, but both types of Crime fighters exhibited less tolerance for these calls than either Professional or Service patrolmen.

The Development of Operational Style

If it is clear that patrolmen manifest distinctive operational styles, two important questions remain. First, to what extent is operational style influenced by the expectations of police administrators, and do patrolmen who adopt different operational styles react in distinctive ways to the conflicts and pressures of the police bureaucracy—to the conflict between the values of police professionalism and those of the police culture? And, second, how are we to explain the origins of a patrolman's beliefs?

In order to provide some tentative answers to these questions, I have used the survey data to construct a serviceable but crude measure of operational style based on two attitudinal scales that measure aggressiveness and selectivity. The aggressiveness scale combines questions that measure a patrolman's inclination to take the initiative on the street and to take extra-legal factors into account in making a decision. A patrolman who is high on this scale is one who has presumably adopted an aggressive style of patrol. The selectivity scale measures whether a patrolman emphasizes felony violations over misdemeanors. A patrolman who is high on this scale is one who believes that traffic laws, drunkenness and the like are not as important as felonies. Each scale has been dichotomized at the mean and then recombined into the four different types. For example, all those patrolmen with a score *higher* than the mean on the aggressiveness and selectivity scales were classified as Old Style Crime Fighters. On the other hand, those patrolmen with a score *lower* than the mean on the aggressiveness and selectivity scales were classified as Professionals.[6]

A patrolman develops an operational style in response to the exigencies of controlling crime and coping with the ambiguities and conflicts inherent in working the street. The development of operational style is partly dependent on the kind of community in which a patrolman first learns his craft. Patrolmen who first learn what it means to be a cop in the harsh environment of a crime-ridden, lower-class community are probably more preoccupied with crime fighting than those who begin in a more affluent community. But an operational style also grows out of the way a patrolman interprets and reacts to his experiences within the department. This raises the question of whether the traditions, training practices, and administrative policies of a police department lead to a single operational style unique to that department. James Q. Wilson argues that the beliefs (operational style) and hence decisions of patrolmen are shaped by the administrative style of the chief of police.[7] In general, then, a single, unique operational style will be associated with different police departments.

Neither the field observations nor the survey evidence show that any of the three departments are characterized by a single distinctive style (see table 8.2). Yet there are some differences worth noting. Almost three-fifths of the patrolmen in the two divisions of the LAPD can be classified as either Clean Beat or Professional patrolmen, a slightly higher proportion than in either of the small departments. Inglewood, in contrast, has the highest concentration of Old Style Crime Fighters, almost twice as many as the other departments, and a slightly higher proportion of Clean Beat patrolmen. At the other extreme, Redondo Beach is dominated by the Professional and Service styles. The traditions and policies of a department are not irrelevant to the formation of operational style, but the beliefs of patrolmen cannot be explained simply in terms of the expectations of the chief of police. The rising crime rate in Inglewood and the placid environs of Redondo Beach may have more to do with the concentration of Crime Fighters in the former and of less aggressive patrolmen in the latter than with the expectations of administrators. The matter is clearly more complex than Wilson's argument would suggest.

Regardless of the expectations of administrators, every patrolman must still come to terms with the pressures of the police bureaucracy —the disjuncture between rewards and performance, the punitive style of supervision and control, and the pressure to reconcile the substantive and instrumental goals of police work. Our discussion of the four styles suggests that each handles these conflicts in a different way. Yet it is also clear that the impact of departmental controls is

TABLE 8.2
Operational Style by Department

Operational Style:[a]	Small Departments		LAPD	
	Inglewood (%)	Redondo Beach (%)	Rampart (%)	Northeast (%)
Old Style Crime Fighters	42	24	20	24
Clean Beat Crime Fighters	32	12	26	28
Professional Style	8	38	29	28
Service Style	18	27	26	22
Number of Respondents	(62)	(34)	(51)	(51)

[a]Significant @ P ≤ .01

related to the size of the department, and the pressures generated by the system of administrative controls are more intense in Inglewood and Redondo Beach than in LAPD. The immediate empirical question is whether all patrolmen experience these pressures in much the same way, notwithstanding the differences in operational style, or if operational style makes a difference in the way a patrolman reacts to the police bureaucracy. Table 8.3, which displays the relationship between operational style and attitudes toward the process of administrative control, offers some evidence on this score.

The perceptions of patrolmen toward administrative control are measured by three attitudinal scales, and table 8.3 presents the mean score on each scale for each operational style. The first scale measures the degree to which patrolmen believe that supervision in the department is strict and punitive (the lower the score the more the patrolman believes supervision is puntitive). Patrolmen in the LAPD are slightly more likely to believe that supervision is punitive, though the difference is not large. The other two scales measure the extent to which patrolmen believe their discretion is constrained by departmental controls (the lower the score the greater the perception that discretion is constrained). The "Perception of Supervisor's Behavior" scale measures the frequency with which patrolmen believe supervisors observe and actually intervene in incidents they are handling. The "Perceived Limits on Discretion" scale is an overall measure of the degree to which patrolmen believe their actions are limited by departmental controls.[8] On this latter scale patrolmen in the small departments perceive greater constraints on their actions than patrolmen in the LAPD. On the "Perception of Supervisor's Behavior" scale patrolmen in Inglewood sense the greatest monitoring of their actions by supervisors.

There are clear-cut differences in the perceptions of the four operational styles of the process of administrative control. Old Style Crime Fighters in all three departments are the most likely to believe that supervision is punitive (their mean score on this scale is 47.21), and the most likely to believe that administrative controls are severely confining (their mean score on the "Perceived Limits on Discretion" scale is 46.00). They are also highly inclined to believe that supervisors aggressively observe their behavior on the street. If the Old Style Crime Fighters have the darkest view of supervision, the Professionals are the best integrated. They stand at the other extreme from the Crime Fighters, as they have the highest mean scores on all three scales. The Clean Beat and Service styles stand in between, though the Clean Beat patrolmen, largely those in the small departments, are the most likely to believe that supervisors frequently observe their behavior. The Service Style, mostly because it is more selective, is more likely to perceive departmental limits on choices than either the Clean Beat or Professional Style.

This pattern, as table 8.3 clearly indicates, holds up in both the small departments and the LAPD, although there are some exceptions and in some cases the differences are not large (for example, there is little difference among patrolmen in the LAPD in their perception of supervisors' behavior). Moreover, length of experience makes little difference. In other words, despite differences in experience and the differing impact of administrative controls in the small departments and the LAPD, the four types of patrolmen—especially the Old Style Crime Fighters and the Professionals—have radically different perceptions of the impact of administrative controls. Thus, operational style entails consequences not only for a patrolman's decisions on the street but for his relationship to the department as well.

TABLE 8.3

Operational Style by Attitudes Toward Supervision

Attitudes Toward Supervision:	Old Style Crime Fighter	Clean Beat Crime Fighter	Professional Style	Service Style
Punitiveness of Supervision:				
Small Departments	49.29	51.79	51.78	52.45
LAPD*	44.00	46.96	53.17	50.63
Perception of Supervisor's Behavior:				
Small Departments*	46.47	43.30	53.94	47.45
LAPD	52.08	52.00	52.69	54.08
Perceived Limits on Discretion:				
Small Departments	44.62	48.38	49.17	47.55
LAPD**	48.14	54.00	54.38	53.75

*Difference in means significant @ $P \leq .02$
**Difference in means significant @ $P \leq .06$

In a way these findings are not at all surprising. Both the Clean Beat and Professional styles incorporate the essential beliefs and values of professionalism, and both are at root bureaucratic styles of action. Both, especially in their legalistic view of the world, are far more responsive to administrative controls than either of the other types of patrolmen. The Professional, in particular, is the consummate organization man. If any of these patrolmen have molded themselves in the image of the department it is the Professional. In his exaggerated legalism and his penchant for aggression, the Clean Beat patrolman is a caricature of a professional policeman. Administrators may not always like the results of this approach, but judging from their own attitudes they often believe that the risk entailed by tolerating a Clean Beat patrolman is worth it.

If administrators accept, and even encourage, aggressiveness they are reluctant to tolerate selectivity. This partly explains the perceptions of the Old Style Crime Fighters and the Service Style. But the reasons for the apparent estrangement of the Crime Fighters go deeper: these men are above all individuals, craftsmen in an increasingly rationalized world. Unlike either the Clean Beat Style or the Professional, the Crime Fighter is profoundly anti-bureaucratic. In a way they are anachronisms; their style of police work was far more pervasive in an earlier era of policing. Their inclination is to do police work the way it used to be done, and to have little truck with (as they see it) the petty concerns of departmental bureaucrats.

For slightly different reasons the Service Style is also in conflict with the department. For some of these men the reluctance to work hard and take risks incurs the enmity of supervisors, often for very good reason. Most supervisors hardly think they should tolerate a man who cannot measure up to the street or a man who has quit. Aside from these cases, those men who profess the Service Style, who are critical of contemporary police work, feel the hostility of supervisors for many of the same reasons as the Old Style Crime Fighters. Like them, they have rejected much of police professionalism.

Thus, one of the crucial attributes that distinguishes these styles is the way they react to the vision of police work expressed in the doctrines of police professionalism. In their own ways both the Clean Beat and Professional patrolmen have succumbed to the ideology of professionalism. The Crime Fighters seek to return to an older style of policing when there were fewer constraints on a patrolman's actions. And the Service Style, looking to the future, seeks to redefine the role of the police.

If the kind of community in which a patrolman first works and the pressures generated by administrative controls shape the caliber of a patrolman's experiences and thus influence the development of an operational style, why does a patrolman adopt one operational style rather than another? One possible explanation is that formal training and socialization within a police department do little to offset deeply ingrained attitudes learned while growing up in particular social environments, and these attitudes and the accompanying psychological attributes are the determinant forces in police behavior. In this view, the adoption of an operational style is to be explained in terms of background and psychological characteristics. Alas, with a couple of minor exceptions, none of the salient background characteristics for which I have measures (social class, ethnicity, education, religion, prior military service, region of birth) are related to the measure of operational style.[9] While it is possible, indeed probable, that deeply rooted psychological attributes contribute to the development of different operational styles—these cannot and should not be ruled out—the weight of the evidence here suggests that an alternative explanation, the role of occupational socialization, may be more significant and ought to be explored.[10]

If it is the process of occupational socialization into the department that is decisive for the development of an operational style, and if this process cannot be understood solely as a response to the expectations of the chief of police, how does a patrolman learn an operational style? What must be understood is that a patrolman doesn't grapple with his initial experiences alone; they are interpreted for him by his immediate peers. Patrolmen undergo an intensive rite of passage in which they acquire some general precepts of police work and learn the norms that govern the police culture.[11] Through this experience a patrolman not only comes to share the burden of performing an arduous task, but he also acquires a distinctive set of values and beliefs, and learns to be not just a policeman but a particular kind of policeman. A patrolman's initial experiences are mediated and interpreted by a significant elder officer, usually the field training officer, who assumes the role of father confessor and guide to the rookie. What happens, I suspect, is that rookie patrolmen model their style after that of an older officer, though they may sometimes react negatively to these initial experiences, as Fisher did, and adopt a style which is just the opposite. In any event, the field training officer passes on not just the "tricks of the trade" but a distinctive way of working the street.

The elder policeman who mediates a rookie's experiences need not always be a field training officer. A watch commander or sergeant can fulfill this role just as well, and there were sergeants in all three departments who had this kind of reputation among patrolmen. But not every supervisor can command this kind of respect and influence. Field supervisors are not ordinarily in a position to influence a patrolman's beliefs the way a field training officer can, and, more important, they must overcome the chasm between patrolmen and management. What often distinguished the more influential supervisors, aside from their personal qualities, was their overt identification with the plight of patrolmen. The limits to the influence of supervisors over the development of a patrolman's operational style is revealed by the fact that the attitudes of the large number of highly aggressive patrolmen in Inglewood and the equally significant number of selective patrolmen in Redondo Beach run counter to the desires and expectations of the field supervisors in those departments.[12]

By the time a patrolman finishes his second or third year on the street he will have more or less developed an operational style, though his behavior and perhaps some of his attitudes may be modified by further experiences on the street and with administrators. To what extent do patrolmen change their attitudes as they gain more experience? There is no appreciable difference between the lesser and more experienced patrolmen in their attitude toward selectivity, but their attitudes toward aggressiveness are modified. After five years on the street, aggressiveness drops off sharply: 43 percent of the patrolmen with two to four years experience are highly aggressive compared to just 18 percent of those with five years or more. By and large, it is the younger patrolmen who display a preference for the Clean Beat approach, while both the Professional and Service Style patrolmen have more experience. Though one cannot be absolutely sure in the absence of data that trace the development of patrolmen over time, it is a plausible hypothesis that the Clean Beat patrolmen (and the Old Style Crime Fighters to a lesser extent) shift toward a less aggressive style after five years. This is not really surprising, and it is probably the pervasive sense of frustration, especially among Clean Beat patrolmen, that accounts for this apparent shift in attitudes. After years of being asked to meet contradictory responsibilities and to take risks for meager rewards, some of these patrolmen lose their élan and retreat to a more subdued style.[13]

The Relevance of Operational Style for Police Discretion

An operational style represents a patrolman's initial response to the uncertainties of attempting to control crime and the demands of police administrators. A patrolman develops a predisposition toward aggressiveness and selectivity as he attempts to balance the conflict between crime fighting and providing services, as he confronts the contradictory impulses of police professionalism, and as he deals with unique citizens, hostile or otherwise, in a specific community. An operational style structures action, it leads a patrolman toward some alternatives and away from others, and it is frequently the decisive factor in determining his choices. But if a patrolman's operational style is influential in determining his choices, there are nevertheless limits on the ability of patrolmen to practice their craft in a way that is fully consistent with the dictates of their operational style. If patrolmen clearly have different ideas about how they should carry out their task, and if they vary in their motivation and sheer ambition, all of them must take account of the reactions of administrators and supervisors to their decisions. The question now is, What difference does the web of bureaucratic controls on patrolmen make for the exercise of discretion?

Chapter 9

Coping with
the Police Bureaucracy

A patrolman's discretionary choices turn partly on an evaluation of the organizational consequences of any action. Since an individual's position in an organization—the rewards he gains, his reputation, his status—often rides on the outcome of a discretionary decision, the choice of alternatives is influenced by a crude organizational calculus: how will this decision affect me personally? In general, individuals in administrative organizations exercise their powers of discretion to their own advantage, and seek to avoid those choices for which there are perceived to be disadvantages. The act of discretion thus involves an assessment of the risks and opportunities in any situation. Especially risky choices will be evaded either through simply avoiding a decision, taking the least risky course of action if there is no way out, or, if possible, by passing the buck. Opportunities will be cultivated for all they are worth.[1]

It is through their discretionary choices that patrolmen attempt to cope with the duality of their role, to adapt to the uncertainties of the street and the uncertainties of the police bureaucracy, while serving those objectives and purposes they deem important. The exercise of discretion by patrolmen is shaped and ultimately determined by the joint impact of the beliefs contained within an operational style and the assessment of risks and opportunities undertaken in any given situation. This raises a question we have dealt with only indirectly so far: how does the system of administrative controls within police departments affect the exercise of discretion? How far and under what conditions will patrolmen deviate from the dictates of their operational style and accommodate themselves to the expectations of field supervisors and administrators? The field supervisors may attempt to articulate a reasonably coherent set of expectations (though they do not always succeed), but the connection between these expectations and the decisions of patrolmen is clearly problematic. There is substantial disagreement between patrolmen and field supervisors on a number of issues, and the individualism and autonomy treasured by patrolmen mitigate against complete conformity. At the same time, field supervisors, motivated in part by the belief that the justification of police professionalism hinges on internal control, press on with the attempt to assert greater control over the actions of patrolmen. But since the structural limits to administrative controls within police departments preclude extensive, direct control over the routine decisions of patrolmen, the chief effect, ironically, is to increase the uncertainty patrolmen face and the possibility of avoidance. Does the bifurcation of internal control lead to a pattern of avoidance, and, if so, under what conditions? Is the resulting uncertainty greater in small than in large departments? The lack of aggressiveness on the street by patrolmen in Inglewood, despite their highly aggressive attitudes, and the contrasting aggressiveness in the LAPD, are suggestive of the impact of administrative controls in small versus large police departments. But are the choices of patrolmen in the LAPD and the small departments similarly affected in other kinds of incidents?

My intention in this chapter is to explore these questions through a comparative analysis of police discretion. What is required, in my judgment, is that one derive comparable measures of discretion, and compare these at the individual and departmental levels in order to assess the impact of departmental controls. The question is how to go about doing this. I have chosen to measure the discretionary choices of patrolmen by their responses to a series of hypothetical incidents in the survey. These hypothetical incidents might be described as "scenarios" or as vivid descriptions of patrolmen dealing with routine law enforcement or order-maintenance problems. These questions require that the respondent decide what kind of action he would take if he were the officer or to evaluate the decision of a hypothetical patrolman.

I have resorted to the use of hypothetical incidents as measures of discretion because the alternatives—more extensive field observations or the use of arrest rates—were either impractical or insufficient for my purpose. It was impossible for one observer to conduct the lengthy observations that would have been necessary to provide adequate measures of discretion in a wide variety of incidents. And I judged arrest rates unsatisfactory because they are not totally comparable and, more important, do not provide an adequate measure of nonenforcement or alternatives to arrest.[2] Using hypothetical incidents also has the advantage of permitting an exploration of a patrolman's reasons for a decision.

Although the hypothetical incidents serve a valid heuristic purpose, they do present problems of validity and interpretation. Some estimation of the validity of the responses can be obtained by comparing them with other measures of discretion such as arrest rates.[3] The question of interpretation is more troublesome. These responses do not represent the actual behavior of patrolmen, but they are, I would argue, indicative of a predisposition to take a specific kind of action in a particular set of circumstances. They can, therefore, be construed as a *proxy* for behavior. The assumption is that a response to a hypothetical incident is indicative of the way a patrolman would behave in the majority of cases when confronted by a similar situation on the street. Nevertheless, I should stress that I use these hypothetical incidents entirely in a heuristic vein. They are merely a useful device to provide information we would not otherwise have, and there is no pretense that the use of these measures enables one to "test" hypotheses about the exercise of discretion. Yet there is evidence for the validity of these measures, and if our conclusions are not definitive, they are certainly more than "suggestive."

A more important consideration the reader should bear in mind in evaluating these responses is that there is an inevitable tension between my observations of patrolmen on the street and their survey responses—a tension that is especially apparent as one compares the data in this chapter to that in the previous chapter. I have used both methods to cross-check the results of one with the other. This is a hazardous procedure, but at least it serves the purpose of preventing one from drawing rash conclusions. Taken singly, either method may skew the analysis in favor of one explanation rather than another. Taken together, they permit the development of more complex, and ultimately more adequate, explanations.

Departmental Variations in the Exercise of Police Discretion

A patrolman's discretion is constrained by the law and by the characteristics of the incident in which he is involved. Scenarios were constructed for three kinds of discretionary incidents: the enforcement of minor violations; a service order-maintenance call; and serious order-maintenance disputes. The latter includes two incidents, a private and a public dispute. The responses of patrolmen to each of these incidents are presented in table 9.1. There is a sharp and clear-cut difference between the LAPD and the two small departments across all four incidents: the patrolmen in both divisions of the LAPD are more likely to make an arrest or take some other kind of formal action (such as taking a report), while the patrolmen in Redondo Beach and Inglewood are inclined toward a pattern of nonenforcement and leniency. These findings are sufficiently intriguing to merit a more detailed examination of the responses.

LAW ENFORCEMENT INCIDENTS

Discretion in a law enforcement incident is based on the existence of a more or less clear-cut violation of the law. The hypothetical incident in this case involved a drunk driver:

Time: 2230 hrs.
Subject: white male adult, 30–35 yrs.

Situation:

Two officers are routinely patrolling their area when they observe a late model Ford ahead of them driving very slowly. They slow down and continue to observe the vehicle; as they watch it weaves somewhat, from one lane to another. They turn on their red light and stop the vehicle. The driver is asked to get out of his car and one of the officers proceeds to administer the field sobriety test. The man staggers as he gets out of his car, his eyes are red, and his speech is somewhat slurred. He doesn't pass all of the sobriety tests: he can walk part way putting one foot in front of the other; he can only stand on one foot for about thirty to forty seconds; and he cannot touch his nose with his fingertips when his head is tilted back. The man is in no condition to drive his car, yet he is not so drunk that he couldn't take care of himself.

Upon questioning the man, the officer learns that he is having financial and marital problems, and as a result, he has been drinking more than usual. The man said that he has never been arrested for drunk driving

TABLE 9.1

Patrolmen's Responses to Discretionary Incidents

Type of Incident:	Small Departments		LAPD		All
	Inglewood (%)	Redondo Beach (%)	Rampart (%)	Northeast (%)	Departments (%)
*Drunk Driving:**					
Would Arrest	22	35	67	73	49
Would Not Arrest	78	65	33	27	51
Number of Respondents	(59)	(34)	(51)	(51)	(195)
*Dispute Between Neighbors:**					
Patrolmen Solved Nothing	21	30	36	50	34
Patrolmen Handled Correctly	55	43	38	29	42
Cover Yourself, Prevent Complaint	3	20	6	13	9
Patrolmen Should Explain Reasons	21	7	20	8	15
Number of Respondents	(62)	(30)	(50)	(48)	(190)
*Family Dispute:**					
Arrest Husband	10	3	45	38	25
Get Someone to Leave	46	26	25	20	31
Ignore Dispute[a]	44	71	30	42	44
Number of Respondents	(61)	(34)	(51)	(50)	(196)
*Disorderly Juveniles:**					
Arrest Juveniles	30	47	51	70	49
Disperse Juveniles	39	24	33	18	29
Ignore Juveniles	31	29	16	12	22
Number of Respondents	(61)	(34)	(51)	(51)	(197)

*Significant @ P ≤ .01
[a]Includes both those who would handle incident in a perfunctory manner and those who would walk away.

before. According to the address on his driver's license he lives about 5 to 6 blocks from their present location. The man claims that he is on his way home.

The respondents were asked what decision they would make.

In the LAPD, two-thirds to three-quarters of the patrolmen said they would arrest the man; in contrast the same proportion in the two small departments said they would not make an arrest. If the patrolmen in the two small departments are less likely to make an arrest, they also evaluate the incident somewhat differently. The reasons patrolmen in Redondo Beach gave for refusing to make an arrest were a sympathetic attitude toward the man's personal problems or concern for the department's relationship to the community. As one Redondo Beach patrolman said, "I would explain the problems of drunk driving and tell him to park his car and walk home. . . . You could make a drunk driving arrest, but if he is aware and has emotional problems, give the guy a break." The public relations view was summed up by another patrolman: "Being a small city," he said, "and because we are public relations-wise, we would probably call a cab—being that he is close and lives in the city. . . . Or in other instances we have given a ride in the unit to the subject . . ." The concern of Inglewood patrolmen was whether the man was drunk enough to be arrested. The following rationale is typical of one-third of the patrolmen who refused to arrest: "A drunk driver is a mandatory arrest, but it appears he is a borderline . . . he can take care of himself. I lost a case like this once in court because it was a borderline, so I would not arrest him." In the LAPD, by comparison, most officers said they would make an arrest because the man had violated the law. As one said, ". . . you have all the elements. It's very clear-cut. No ambiguity at all. His condition, his personal problems, might be a factor in sentencing but that's for the courts to decide."

SERVICE ORDER-MAINTENANCE INCIDENTS

In these cases there is usually neither a violation of the law nor any serious potential for violence. Patrolmen are called upon to assist people in some capacity, to render a minor administrative service or to mediate a minor dispute. What is at issue here is not the degree of legal protection extended, but the quality of the service the police provide. Discretion is thus a question of whether a patrolman meets these obligations, whether he takes some action to resolve the immediate problem.

For this incident, respondents were presented with a minor but acrimonious dispute between two neighbors:

Time: 1810 hrs.
Subjects: Two white male adults, approximately 31 yrs.

Situation:

Two officers arrived at a residence in response to a "594" (malicious mischief) neighbor call and proceeded to talk to the informant. He said that earlier in the afternoon his neighbor had broken part of a fence that separated their yards and thrown garbage into his backyard. The officers took a look at the fence and found that several boards had been broken out and garbage was spread all over the man's backyard. The informant said that he wanted to file a complaint against his neighbor.

The neighbor, obviously having seen the police drive up, came out of his house at this time and walked toward the police. The officers approached the man and asked him what was going on. He admitted tearing the boards out of the fence and throwing garbage in the man's backyard; but he said that he was angry and had a good reason. The man (the informant), the neighbor said, continually let his dog run loose, especially in his (the neighbor's) yard. The dog had a habit of "crapping" in the man's backyard and getting into his garbage cans and throwing garbage all over. In addition, the neighbor claimed that the man played his record player loudly, and when he had been asked to turn it down and keep his dog in his own yard, the man got angry and told him to "get screwed." Things had come to a head this morning, the neighbor said, when the dog had spread garbage all over his yard. The neighbor said that he was just returning the garbage.

At this the informant said the man (the neighbor) was a "son of a bitch" and he still wanted to file charges. After further questioning the officers determined that this had been going on for quite a while and that both men had been guilty of instigating incidents.

At this time the officers told the informant that they were not going to do anything since he had been involved in provoking his neighbor. They told him that he was as guilty as his neighbor and that he was violating the city's leash law. They got in their car and drove off.

The respondents were asked if they agreed with the action of the hypothetical patrolmen and why or why not.

Patrolmen in the LAPD, especially Northeast Division, were more inclined to believe that the incident had not been handled in an appropriate manner, and to suggest that since nothing had been solved further action of some kind should be taken. As one patrolman in Northeast said, "You should get cross complaints from the people involved and go to the city attorney's office for action. It has been going on and it will take more of our time unless it is ended now. By not doing anything you are instigating further action by these parties. . . ." Fifty percent of the patrolmen in Northeast division and 36 percent in Rampart felt this way compared to 30 percent in Redondo Beach and a scant 21 percent in Inglewood.

The view in both small departments was that the incident had been handled in an appropriate manner. Most of the patrolmen who felt this way regarded the incident as trivial and a waste of time. As one said, ". . . they are both just as guilty. If the informant filed a complaint the other one would, just in retaliation, and it wouldn't accomplish anything. They are both acting like kids." In a slightly more cynical vein, another patrolman suggested, "There have been criminal violations, but these people want the police to act as the whipping post. It's a civil problem not police. . . ." This was the view of 55 percent of patrolman in Inglewood and 43 percent in Redondo Beach; in the LAPD, only 29 percent in Northeast division and 38 percent in Rampart felt this way.

If the percentage difference between patrolmen in Redondo Beach and Rampart who agreed with the hypothetical officers is quite small (43 compared to 38 percent), note that patrolmen in Redondo Beach were more likely to take some kind of action to protect themselves from a complaint (see table 9.1). One explained that,

> when they [the patrolmen] left they hadn't accomplished anything by going there, and chances are they're gonna get beefed by these guys. These people will call in and complain about these officers. I'd make a report and file it with the city prosecutor's office. He'd reject it but the citizen would feel we'd acted. Then they're happy when you leave. The other way they're both pissed off.

In other words, they agreed but thought that a prudent patrolman should act otherwise. Still the difference between the LAPD and the small departments is not as sharp as in the drunk driving incident. As we shall see, the reason lies in the importance of other factors, namely, operational style.

Serious Order-Maintenance Incidents.

These incidents involve disputes between two or more people that have the potential for erupting into violence. The stakes are clearly different from those in a less serious incident where all that may be at issue is the department's image as courteous and efficient. Here a patrolman must calculate, in highly ambiguous circumstances, both the potential for violence and the effect of any action he might take. His response determines the degree to which legal protection is extended to citizens.

The private dispute involves a family fight between a young black couple:

Time: 1910 hrs.
Subjects: black male adult and black female adult 25 yrs., and 2 children, black female 4 years and black male 1 year

Situation:

Two officers respond to a "415" (disturbing the peace) situation. They arrive and gain entrance to the subject's apartment. The woman is the informant, and it is immediately obvious that she has been beaten by her husband. Her cheeks are bruised, her lower lip is cut and bleeding, her dress is torn, and she is sobbing and barely able to talk. It is also evident that she has been drinking. They ask what's been going on and the husband says, "It's all over now." The woman says in response to a question from one of the officers that her husband hit her and beat her. The man says, "Shut up, woman."

The officers continue to talk to them and ask the woman what she wants to do. She says that she is afraid to sign a complaint out of fear of being beaten again by her husband. At this time the husband jumps up and says to the officers, "It's all over, goddamn it, I told you that, now get the fuck out of here." He continues to shout loudly and aggressively at the officers and demands that they leave at once.

Patrolmen responded to this incident in one of three ways. One group, about one-fourth of the respondents, decided that the husband should be arrested. For some it was a straightforward arrest for felony wife beating. As one patrolman explained, "It's wife beating, we don't need her to sign a complaint; I'd arrest him on 272 P.C. (wife beating). [What do you achieve by this?] I'd be fulfilling my responsibility as a policeman . . . you really have no choice." Yet some of these patrolmen thought the situation infinitely more complex, and while they would make an arrest, they would do so believing it to be illegal. One of these patrolmen said:

Try to find out if they are legally married, or if they aren't how long they have been living together. After these details ask if it's happened before. Here's where the variance comes in. Ninety-five percent it happens all the time, and my next question to the woman is, "Why are you still here?" If the husband is belligerent and the wife drunk, try to get the husband to come outside and book him for drunk in public. This usually works. You explain to him that his wife doesn't want him arrested, but we're doing it for drunkenness. This throws the blame off her. . . . Also, if he asks tell him that a neighbor called, not his wife. What this is doing is getting one of them out of the house. The woman must stay with the kids. This transfers his anger from her to us.

Not many patrolmen were inclined to make an arrest on the basis of a pretext in this incident; only 11 percent said they would do so.

A second group of patrolmen, 31 percent, thought that an arrest should not or legally could not be made, but believed the situation serious enough that they should get either the husband or wife to leave the premises for the night. What distinguishes these patrolmen is their determination to resolve the situation in an effective way without making an arrest. The following response is typical:

Don't leave just because the man says so. The main thing is to get one of them out of there. The man will calm down when you inform him that you won't leave. He might fight but if not get the woman to leave. I would like to take the man to jail, and it's possible to get the woman to sign a complaint—the big question is whether it happened before. [But you should] always handle by other means than arrest.

The third group of patrolmen more or less chose to ignore the matter. Practically all of these patrolmen believed that they could not act without a signed complaint from the woman, or rather they *would not* act without a complaint from the woman. As one patrolman said, "If she doesn't want to sign a complaint there's nothing you can do . . . we're not gonna arrest 'em . . . not a thing to do." Some of these patrolmen indicated they would take some steps to resolve the dispute, but these were often perfunctory, amounting only to advice for one of them to leave or to seek help elsewhere. Beyond seeking a complaint or proffering advice, these patrolmen were reluctant to do much of anything. One of them said, "I would ask the wife if she wanted to sign a complaint . . . unless she said yes there is nothing I could do. I would suggest to the husband he leave until they both cool down. . . . If neither wanted to do what I suggested, then we would leave." A minority of patrolmen, about 16 percent altogether, displayed a far more callous attitude and were unwilling to take even the more perfunctory steps to mediate the dispute: "I'd talk to the woman again," one of these patrolmen responded, "and if she still didn't want to sign a complaint I would leave, unless I determined that the children were in danger. If I thought the children were in danger I would arrest the man for felony wife beating. ... The woman is an adult and if she wants to get beat up or continue to get beat up that's none of my business. . . ."

Patrolmen in the LAPD are far more likely to make an arrest; 42 percent would arrest compared to just 7 percent in the small departments. Patrolmen in Inglewood may be reluctant to arrest but they do take the incident seriously; 45 percent opted for the middle course and said they would try to get either the husband or wife to leave for the night. In contrast, 71 percent of patrolmen in Redondo Beach treated the incident casually and more or less ignored it. This group consists of those who said they would offer a perfunctory solution (45 percent of all patrolmen in Redondo Beach) and those who would simply walk away from the dispute (26 percent).

Underlying these different responses between the LAPD and the small departments are decidedly different evaluations of the responsibility of the police and the scope of their authority in this incident. On the whole, patrolmen in the two small departments construed their legal authority far more narrowly: 60 percent insisted they could not act without a signed complaint from the woman compared to 33 percent in LAPD. Moreover, 24 percent of patrolmen in the LAPD believed there were legitimate grounds for making a felony arrest for wife beating; just a scant 2 percent in the small departments felt the same way.

In a public disturbance the police are ordinarily more predisposed to take decisive action because of the greater potential for the outbreak of a more serious disorder, and because they believe they have more legal authority. The hypothetical incident used to evaluate this kind of order-maintenance problem concerned a group of juveniles creating a disturbance at a bowling alley.

Time: 2030 hrs.
Subjects: 10 to 15 white and black males and females, 16 to 19 yrs.

Situation:

Two officers respond to a "415" (disturbing the peace) juveniles call at a local bowling alley. When they arrive 10 to 15 juveniles are milling in front of, and just inside of, the main door of the bowling alley. According to the security guard and the manager they had been there for some time, blocking the doorway, yelling and screaming and generally making nuisances of themselves. The officers know that this is not the first time this has happened and they are aware that some of the same juveniles are involved.

The officers ask them to leave and the youths begin to argue. They claim that they are not doing anything, that they have a right to come to the bowling alley, and that the manager gets "uptight over almost anything." The manager says that they are preventing customers from leaving and entering the bowling alley and offending some customers by their obscene language. In response to a question from one of the patrolmen, the manager says that he doesn't want to prosecute the juveniles, he just wants them off the premises.

The officers order the juveniles to leave and they begin to do so, but very slowly. Two or three break away from the main group and run back into the bowling alley, disappearing into the crowd. The rest mill around outside the front door and begin to yell obscenities at the manager and the police. One young girl with long blond hair walks up to the manager and calls him "a fucking prick." Other men, women, and children are having difficulty entering or leaving the bowling alley.

The officers order them to move along for the second time and they threaten to arrest the lot of them. The youths move a little further away, but they still keep milling about and yelling.

The responses to this incident parallel those in the family dispute. Almost one-half of the patrolmen believed they had a legitimate basis on which to act; the feeling was that things had gone far enough and the only solution was to make some arrests. A few patrolmen said they would arrest everybody they could catch, while others were more discriminating and directed their attention to the ringleaders or the young girl: "I'd arrest the main offenders like the blond. . . . I don't need the manager's complaint for a "415." They had plenty of time to leave. The girl used bad language in front of women and children." Another third of the patrolmen, who thought they lacked the necessary legal authority to arrest or believed an arrest was the wrong solution, said they would forcibly disperse the juveniles. This strategy amounted to demonstrating that the police meant business. As one creative patrolman said, ". . . I would take the loudest juvenile and frisk him, handcuff him, and put him in the back of the car. . . . This shows I mean business to the rest of the kids. Normally, they will then leave, and I would take the kid home. [Why?] Why should he carry the brunt of it, they are all guilty. He was just the one I happened to have caught." Finally there were those patrolmen who regarded the incident as trivial ("Kids will be kids" some of them responded), or who refused to act without a complaint. This was due partly to a rather adamant belief about the restricted scope of their legal authority in this incident; but it also reflected a judgment about the victims. One patrolman noted, "the eighteen- and nineteen-year-olds are classified as adults and if no one is willing to press charges, I'd let them stay around and do anything they want . . . you wouldn't want to do too much because the people around there don't want to prosecute. . . ."

Consistent with the responses in other incidents, the patrolmen in LAPD were more inclined to arrest all or some of the juveniles— though 47 percent of the patrolmen in Redondo Beach indicated they would make an arrest. Patrolmen in Inglewood were the most likely to attempt to forcibly disperse the juveniles, and patrolmen in Northeast division the least likely (see table 9.1). Yet patrolmen in both small departments were twice as likely to treat the incident perfunctorily or ignore it as patrolmen in the LAPD: 31 percent in the small departments compared to 14 percent in the LAPD. Like the responses to the family dispute these differences are under-pinned by differences in the way patrolmen construed their legal authority: patrolmen in the small departments were less likely to believe they had the legal authority to act.

A DIGRESSION ON THE QUESTION OF VALIDITY

As compelling as these responses might seem, is there any reason to believe that these differences in attitudes reflect differences in action? In particular, is the strategy of leniency characteristic of the small departments and the predilection toward enforcement among patrolmen in the LAPD apparent in arrest rates? Table 9.2 provides some convincing evidence that this is the case. The average adult arrest rate over a two-year period for both drunk driving and drunk in public is higher in both divisions of the LAPD than in either of the small departments. The average arrest rate for drunk driving in Redondo Beach was 65 compared to 101 in Northeast; Rampart was highest with an arrest rate of 141, which was almost three times as high as the Inglewood rate of 54. In fact, these data overstate the actual number of arrests for drunk driving made in Inglewood. Of the 436 arrests for drunk driving reported by the Inglewood police department in 1972, 207 were made by the California Highway Patrol and only 229 were made by Inglewood policemen. Thus the actual arrest rate is about 25 per 10,000 population. There is a similar difference in these departments for arrests for drunk in public. (The extraordinarily high number of drunk arrests in Rampart division stems from the activities of patrolmen working in and around the MacArthur Park area, a section that is rapidly acquiring the charac-

TABLE 9.2

Average Adult Arrest Rates for Selected Misdemeanors, 1972–73
(per 10,000 population)

Arrest Rates:	Small Departments		LAPD	
	Redondo Beach	Inglewood	Northeast	Rampart
Drunk Driving	65.00	54.00	101.00	141.00
Drunk in Public	51.00	51.00	67.00	342.00
Traffic Warrants[a]	77.00	168.00	121.00	197.00
Disturbing the Peace[b]	8.13	1.72	1.98	3.77
Disorderly Conduct[c]	1.96	3.06	2.84	7.20
Misdemeanor Assaults	10.80	8.66	8.40	11.81
Ratio of Felony to Misdemeanor Assaults	.46	1.48	1.63	2.36

[a]Based on 1972 figures.
[b]These are violations of Section 415 of the California Penal Code. The section reads: "Every person who maliciously and willfully disturbs the peace or quiet of any neighborhood or person, by loud or unusual noise, or by tumultuous or offensive conduct, or threatening, traducing, quarreling, challenging to fight, or fighting, or who, on the public streets of any unincorporated town, run any horse race, either for wage or amusement, or fire any gun or pistol in such unincorporated town, or use any vulgar, profane, or indecent language within the presence or hearing of women or children, in a loud and boisterous manner, is guilty of a misdemeanor. . . ." Most of these arrests are *citizen arrests.*
[c]Includes violations of Section 647 (c) (d) (e) of the California Penal Code. These refer to begging, loitering about public toilets, and loitering about the streets without reason and failure to reasonably account for one's presence.
SOURCE: Los Angeles Police Department, Statistical Digest, 1972 and 1973; Redondo Beach Police Department; Inglewood Police Department.

ter and population of a skid row. These officers are expected to and do make a large number of arrests for drunkenness.)

On the other hand, there are few significant differences in regard to order-maintenance offenses such as disorderly conduct, disturbing the peace, and misdemeanor assaults. The one noticeable exception is the substantially higher arrest rate for disturbing the peace in Redondo Beach. But this is a reflection of the propensity of citizens in Redondo Beach to prefer charges rather than a difference in the behavior of patrolmen: four-fifths of these arrests were citizen's arrests. Even so, these data do not necessarily invalidate the responses to the order-maintenance incidents. One of the things revealed by the data was a higher propensity among patrolmen in the LAPD to prefer a felony arrest in the family dispute, partly because they were willing to act without the woman's agreement to sign a complaint. Practically all arrests for misdemeanor assault are citizen's arrests, and a high number of felony assault arrests in relation to misdemeanor assault arrests would be indicative of a greater propensity to take independent action in incidents such as the family dispute. The ratio of felony to misdemeanor assault arrests is much higher for the LAPD than for either of the small departments, thus corroborating the tendency of patrolmen in the LAPD to make an arrest in the survey. The responses of patrolmen to the family dispute, then, are at least consistent with differences in the felony and misdemeanor arrest rates for assault.

The Ambiguity of Departmental Expectations

Can the sharp differences in the exercise of discretion between the LAPD and the two small departments be explained by the conformity of patrolmen to a coherent set of departmental expectations? The relevance of departmental expectations depends not only on the willingness of patrolmen to comply, but upon the degree of consensus among field supervisors about how patrolmen should handle different incidents. The absence of clearly formulated and agreed upon standards for the exercise of discretion increases the uncertainty confronting patrolmen, and means their decisions will turn upon factors other than the admonitions of supervisors. In order to determine the degree of consensus among field supervisors and whether patrolmen act in conformity to departmental expectations, I asked the field supervisors to respond to the same set of hypothetical incidents as patrolmen. The presumption underlying this approach is that, ordinarily, field supervisors will encourage patrolmen to respond as they would, and that congruence between the responses of the two is evidence of the influence of departmental expectations. The results are presented in table 9.3.

The lack of ambiguity in most minor violations enables administrators to formulate more or less clear-cut expectations as to the proper response. Not surprisingly, the closest fit between the responses of patrolmen and field supervisors occurs in the drunk driving incident. The field supervisors in the LAPD, like the patrolmen there, overwhelmingly opt for an arrest; in Inglewood they do not. The exception is Redondo Beach, where the majority of field supervisors prefer to see an arrest made, but where patrolmen do not. The disagreement over whether to arrest in Redondo Beach reflects the sharp differences in that department in the attitude of field supervisors and patrolmen toward minor violations (see chapter 7). Thus, if the expectations of field supervisors appear to be influential in the LAPD and Inglewood, they are not in Redondo Beach. Yet these data may overstate the degree of conformity in the LAPD and Inglewood, for in each a significant minority of patrolmen—anywhere from one-quarter to one-third—do not conform to the expectations of field supervisors.

Nor is there complete consensus among the field supervisors. Actually, it is only in the LAPD, where over 90 percent of the field supervisors think an arrest should be made, that we find a clear-cut consensus on the appropriate response. In both small departments there is more disagreement over how patrolmen should react. Underlying the disagreement among field supervisors in the small departments and the consensus in the LAPD are different views on the responsibilities of patrolmen in traffic enforcement. When asked if patrolmen should enforce traffic laws, at least a third and as many as two-fifths of the field supervisors in the small departments took the position that patrolmen should not work traffic. By comparison, none of the field supervisors in the LAPD took this position. The greater lack of consensus among field supervisors in the small departments can be attributed, I suspect, to disagreements over priorities. Given limited resources, the question of priorities is painfully obvious in most small departments, but especially in one like Inglewood which believes it confronts an escalating crime problem. In the LAPD administrators can afford to think that patrolmen should not have to choose between traffic enforcement and crime fighting.

Ambiguity and a lack of consensus over expectations is the rule rather than the exception in order-maintenance incidents. The lack of consensus appears to be greatest in the case of minor disputes like the argument between the two neighbors. Despite a superficial congruence between the responses of field supervisors and patrolmen in this incident—in the LAPD field supervisors believe that patrolmen should not simply walk away from the incident but should take some sort of action, while a significant proportion of supervisors in the small departments think the hypothetical patrolmen behaved correctly—there is sharp disagreement among the supervisors in all three departments. In Inglewood 42 percent of the supervisors believe that the hypothetical patrolmen solved nothing by leaving as abruptly as they did (twice the number of patrolmen who felt this way); but this is identical to the number of field supervisors who completely agreed with the patrolmen's actions (see table 9.3). Whom does a patrolman take his cues from in this case? The situation

TABLE 9.3

Supervisors' Response to Discretionary Incidents

Type of Incident:	Small Departments		LAPD		All Departments (%)
	Inglewood (%)	Redondo Beach (%)	Rampart (%)	Northeast (%)	
Drunk Driving:					
Would Arrest	33	60	89	94	74
Would Not Arrest	67	40	11	6	26
Number of Respondents	(10)	(12)	(18)	(17)	(57)
Dispute between Neighbors:					
Patrolmen Solved Nothing	42	30	61	41	46
Patrolmen Handled Correctly	42	30	11	12	21
Cover Yourself, Prevent Complaint	8	40	17	18	19
Patrolmen Should Explain Reasons	8	0	11	29	14
Number of Respondents	(10)	(12)	(18)	(17)	(57)
Family Dispute:					
Arrest husband	8	20	17	35	21
Get Someone to Leave	17	20	39	12	23
Ignore Dispute[a]	75	60	44	53	56
Number of Respondents	(10)	(12)	(18)	(17)	(57)
Disorderly Juveniles:					
Arrest Juveniles	42	90	50	59	58
Disperse Juveniles	25	0	33	12	19
Ignore Juveniles	33	10	17	29	23
Number of Respondents	(10)	(12)	(18)	(17)	(57)

[a]Includes both those who would handle incident in a perfunctory manner and those who would walk away.

in the other departments is not much different. Only in Rampart Division is there a clear majority for one response. The lack of consensus here is due, in part, to the choice of priorities posed by these incidents, the question of whether to spend time resolving a minor dispute or to fight crime. It is worth noting that the sharpest disagreement over this incident is in the small departments, where a significant proportion of supervisors thought either that the two patrolmen behaved correctly or that nothing was solved. The responses in the LAPD, on the other hand, can be construed to mean that supervisors thought patrolmen should at least take the time to give the men a courteous good-bye.

The most striking aspect of the responses to both serious order-maintenance incidents is the agreement among supervisors in all three departments compared to the sharp differences between patrolmen in the LAPD and those in the small departments. The field supervisors take the family dispute less seriously than patrolmen: 56 percent would ignore the family dispute compared to 44 percent of patrolmen. The field supervisors, however, do not advocate walking away from the incident; only 10 percent of all supervisors would advocate this course. What they want is perfunctory mediation, and nothing more. In contrast, the supervisors believe the incident with the disorderly juveniles should be treated more seriously, and altogether they are more inclined to arrest than patrolmen. Fifty-eight percent of the supervisors say they would arrest compared to 49 percent of patrolmen. There is, however, somewhat less consensus among the field supervisors in regard to the public dispute. Practically all the supervisors in Redondo Beach believe an arrest should be made, a clear majority in the LAPD take this view, but only 42 percent in Inglewood do so (see table 9.3).

While there is a tendency for patrolmen to conform to the broad expectations of supervisors to treat family disputes less seriously than public disorders, altogether there is less of a fit between the responses of patrolmen and supervisors in the order-maintenance incidents than in the law-enforcement incident. In the family dispute there is very little congruence between patrolmen and supervisors in particular departments (with the possible exception of Northeast Division). In the public disorder there is somewhat more congruence between patrolmen and supervisors in the LAPD, while in the small departments patrolmen are much less inclined to arrest than the field supervisors. The lack of congruence between supervisors and patrolmen can be explained, in part, by their different judgments of the legality of any police action. In the family dispute, supervisors, especially those in the LAPD, generally believe that a signed complaint from the woman is necessary to take action; patrolmen are less likely to believe this. But in regard to the disorderly juveniles, the supervisors are twice as likely as patrolmen to think that legitimate grounds exist for making an arrest: 39 percent of the supervisors believe an arrest can be made without a signed complaint compared to 16 percent of the patrolmen.

The evidence for the notion that patrolmen straightforwardly base their decisions on the perceived expectations of administrators is not persuasive. Only in the drunk driving incident do patrolmen appear to be acting on the basis of a widely shared expectation among field supervisors, and then only in two departments—the LAPD and, to a lesser extent, Inglewood. In Redondo Beach, patrolmen acted in a way contrary to the desires of most supervisors. In the other incidents there is a lack of consensus among supervisors and no clear parallel between the decisions of patrolmen and the expectations of supervisors. These data leave some important questions unanswered. What explains the propensity of patrolmen in the LAPD to arrest, especially in the family dispute, and the reluctance of patrolmen in small departments to do so? Why are the patrolmen in Redondo Beach and Inglewood reluctant to take more decisive action with the juveniles in the face of a departmental expectation that they should do so? All of this suggests the need to take a closer look at the responses of patrolmen to these incidents in light of the pressures and constraints of the police bureaucracy and operational style.

The Use of Police Discretion to Adapt to Organizational Uncertainty

A patrolman's discretionary choices, I have argued, depend on the joint influence of a patrolman's operational style and his assessment of the risks and opportunities in any given situation. The assessment of risks and opportunities turns on three factors: the actual risks and opportunities in a particular incident; the degree of uncertainty generated by departmental controls; and the factors that influence a patrolman's perception of the risks and opportunities.

Consider first the degree of risk and opportunity in the different kinds of incidents patrolmen routinely encounter. Crime fighting is obviously one of the riskiest endeavors a patrolman can engage in, but it is counterbalanced by the opportunities—the chance to demonstrate one's proficiency on the street and the sheer pleasure of it all. Serious order-maintenance incidents often are as risky as crime fighting, yet they rarely offer any of the compensating opportunities. An order-maintenance incident does not allow an ambitious patrolman to demonstrate his proficiency as a crime fighter, and if he decides to make an arrest, he not only uses time that could, from his point of view, have been more profitably spent working the street, he also takes a chance that the arrest may be legally dubious and might provoke violence. The incentives in a serious order-maintenance incident are not for aggressive, decisive action, although this may vary depending on whether the order-maintenance incident occurs in private or public.

Law enforcement and service order-maintenance incidents entail less risk but little or no opportunity. The risks in a service order-maintenance incident are not great, though they are not absent. Since the department's reputation for courteous service is all that is really at stake (and supervisors disagree about its importance anyway), at the very worst a patrolman risks only a minor reprimand. Because the opportunities are virtually nil, a patrolman preoccupied with crime fighting will often choose to ignore service calls.

Any stop on the street is a calculated risk, and a stop to enforce a minor violation can, depending on the reactions of the person stopped, lead to a complaint or worse. Reiss concluded that most arrests for interfering with an officer occur during the enforcement of minor violations.[4] If enforcing minor violations poses the risk of a complaint, not enforcing them increases the risk of being accused of "goldbricking." Every patrolman will do a bit of "stockpiling," make a few arrests for minor violations and issue a few traffic citations to keep the sergeant off his back. The opportunities with minor violations are a bit greater than with service calls. A patrolman can acquire a reputation as a hard working, energetic policeman. This is not to be dismissed, but neither is it the path to success.

The degree of risk or opportunity in any situation also depends on the level of organizational uncertainty. The most important factor here is the uncertainty generated by the bifurcation of internal controls, which is greater in small than in large departments. In addition, the degree of consensus among administrators and supervisors over the appropriate response affects the level of uncertainty that patrolmen face. In general, the greater the consensus among administrators and supervisors, the less the uncertainty.

Furthermore, a patrolman's subjective evaluation of the anticipated consequences of any decision will be influenced by three individual characteristics, all of which affect a patrolman's sense of *vulnerability* within the department, and hence the perceived level of uncertainty. The first is the extent to which a patrolman believes his actions are constrained by the actions of supervisors. On an individual level, this varies in terms of operational style, with the Old Style Crime Fighters sensing the greatest degree of constraint, the Professionals the least, and the Clean Beat and Service patrolmen ranging in between.

A patrolman's vulnerability also depends on the extent of his experience. Those patrolmen in the probationary stage of their career are, for obvious reasons, far more vulnerable than more experienced patrolmen. The least vulnerable are those patrolmen with more than five years experience. These men have not only cultivated the necessary skills of survival, but they have, by this time, usually resigned themselves to the reality that the duration of their career may be spent working the street, and feel, as a consequence, that they have little to lose in any situation. The vulnerability of patrolmen with two to four years experience is more problematic, and depends more on operational style or the desire for a promotion.

The last factor that affects a patrolman's sense of vulnerability is the desire for a promotion. Only if a patrolman is angling to get into an investigative unit is the desire for a promotion tied directly to his performance on the street. Otherwise, what an ambitious patrolman must cope with is the element of risk in the promotion process, the reality that his behavior on the street may not help and often can hurt his chances. A series of altercations, personnel complaints, and negative evaluations by supervisors can loom large when promotional decisions are made. The tendency in police departments to reward loyalty and deference to authority, a tendency that is especially pronounced in the small departments, injects an additional factor into a patrolman's calculus. It heightens his sensitivity to the risks in any incident and to the wishes of supervisors.[5]

Combined with a patrolman's beliefs about what he should do, the aforementioned factors shape a patrolman's response to the events he encounters. They determine whether he will make an arrest, adopt an informal solution of some kind, or evade his responsibilities altogether. The negative impact of administrative controls and the

266

disjuncture between rewards and performance mean that the risks in any situation are usually far more salient to patrolmen than anything else. It is often the case that a patrolman has more to lose by taking action than he has to gain. None of this is to arbitrarily exclude other factors, such as racial prejudice, that may influence a patrolman's response.[6] I only insist that operational style and a patrolman's assessment of the personal risks and opportunities are highly significant if not decisive in the exercise of discretion.

THE DRUNK DRIVING INCIDENT

Just as we would predict on the basis of our discussion of operational style, the most legalistic of patrolmen, the Professionals, prefer to make an arrest in this incident while the most selective, the Service Style, are the most reluctant to do so. In all three departments, 64 percent of the Professionals would make an arrest compared to 36 percent of the Service Style. There is far less difference altogether in the responses of the two types of crime fighters. More intriguing, perhaps, is that operational style is far more relevant in this incident for patrolmen in the LAPD than for those in the two small departments. There is a sharp difference between the Professional and Service styles in both divisions of the LAPD. In contrast operational style makes very little difference in the small departments (see table 9.4).

The greater relevance of operational style in the LAPD may be explained, I think, partly by the different pressures for conformity in small and large departments. In the LAPD there may be a widely shared expectation that the law will be enforced, but the cost of not adhering to this expectation is not especially high. One indication of this is that those patrolmen in the LAPD who desire a promotion to an administrative position are less inclined to make an arrest than those who aspire to an investigative position or those who do not want a promotion. Highly selective patrolmen of the Service Style, who, the data indicate, are more likely to want a promotion to an administrative position in the LAPD than the other patrolmen, may be more predisposed to enforce the law than their counterparts in the small departments, but some of them will act on the basis of their own ideas of when to enforce minor violations. The tendency of Old Style Crime Fighters to make an arrest in this incident is also connected to the desire for a promotion. Almost one-half of the Crime Fighters in Northeast Division who said they would make an arrest (by and large the Crime Fighters in Rampart were inclined not to

TABLE 9.4
The Drunk Driving Incident

	Small Departments		LAPD	
	Arrest (%)	No Arrest (%)	Arrest (%)	No Arrest (%)
Operational Style:				
Professional Style	33	67 (18)	83	17 (22)
Clean Beat Crime Fighter	25	75 (24)	70	30 (27)
Old Style Crime Fighter	26	74 (34)	73	27 (24)
Service Style	20	80 (20)	50	50 (29)
Number of Respondents		(96)		(102)
Desire for Promotion:				
Wants to Be Supervisor	20	80 (41)	*59	41 (51)
Wants to Be Investigator	25	75 (12)	76	24 (33)
Does Not Want Promotion	33	67 (43)	89	11 (18)
Number of Respondents		(96)		(102)
Perceived Limits on Discretion:				
High	24	76 (41)	82	18 (22)
Moderate	24	76 (33)	56	44 (39)
Low	32	68 (22)	76	24 (41)
Number of Respondents		(96)		(102)

*Significant $P \leq .04$

make an arrest) also said they wanted to get into an investigative unit. The desire for a promotion in this incident does not appear to increase the perceived risk, and it is believed by aspiring detectives to strengthen chances for promotion.

The situation is much different in the small departments. Confronted with a general expectation to ignore minor violations (Inglewood) or a conflicting set of expectations (Redondo Beach), the tendency of patrolmen will be to avoid an arrest or at least be more reluctant to make one. The more intense pressures for conformity in both these departments often preclude a patrolman from acting on the basis of his operational style. Again a key indication of this is the behavior of patrolmen who desire a promotion. Among those patrolmen in both small departments who want a promotion there is virtually no difference in their responses: they are all inclined not to arrest. Among those who do *not* want a promotion, however, the tendency is to act on the basis of their operational style. Hence, Professional and Clean Beat patrolmen who do not want a promotion are substantially more likely to make an arrest than those among the Old Style Crime Fighters or the Service Style who do not.

In Inglewood, at least, patrolmen who want a promotion adapt their behavior and decisions to the perceived expectations of supervisors; otherwise they act on the basis of their operational style. In Redondo Beach, though, it is not clear why patrolmen who are motivated to conform should refuse to make an arrest when 60 percent of the supervisors think an arrest should be made. There are two facts about Redondo Beach worth remembering. First, there is far more disagreement among the field supervisors over how minor violations should be handled than in either of the other two departments. Second, there is a greater sense of uncertainty among patrolmen in Redondo Beach (and Inglewood) over the impact of administrative controls. Does the differing impact of administrative controls in small versus large police departments have any bearing on the decision in this incident? In particular, does it facilitate avoidance and explain the predilection for leniency in the small departments? Overall, there is a strong relationship between the perceived limits on discretion scale and the decision in this incident: 60 percent of the patrolmen who do not feel their discretion is limited say they will make an arrest compared to 44 percent who do feel so constrained. Now if this factor is an intervening variable in the relationship between the departments and the choice in this incident, the relationship between the perception that one's discretion is limited and the decision to arrest the drunk driver should vanish when we look at it in each of the departments. As table 9.4 shows this is precisely what happens. I might add that this effect occurs independently of the effect of operational style.[7]

In Redondo Beach patrolmen confront both a conflicting set of expectations about how to handle minor violations and a more subtle set of cues which suggest the need to stay out of trouble. They were the most likely of all patrolmen to believe that administrators wanted them to avoid complaints and stay out of trouble.[8] Enforcing minor violations can lead to complaints, and confronted with the uncertain impact of administrative controls, patrolmen in Redondo Beach prefer to go easy. The same sort of pressures exist in Inglewood, but they are muted because the field supervisors do not emphasize enforcement of offenses like drunk driving to the degree that the field supervisors in Redondo Beach do. The reason why they do not, I suspect, comes down to a simple choice of priorities. When you believe you are faced with a crime wave, enforcing drunk driving laws can be considered a luxury. In any event, in both small departments it appears that one consequence of the impact of administrative controls is to foster a pattern of leniency in the enforcement of minor violations—regardless of the expectations of administrators.

THE DISPUTE BETWEEN NEIGHBORS

The more aggressive patrolmen, the Clean Beat and Old Style Crime Fighters, display an antipathy toward minor order-maintenance problems and service activities. How did the more aggressive patrolmen respond to the plight of the two neighbors? Not unexpectedly, they were prone to agree with the decision of the hypothetical officers to tell the men off and leave abruptly. The least aggressive patrolmen, on the other hand, treat the incident more seriously. Fifty-three percent of the Crime Fighters agree with the action of the hypothetical officers compared to 35 percent of the Professional and Service patrolmen. This difference is even sharper if one looks just at the dimension of aggressiveness: 60 percent of the highly aggressive patrolmen agree compared to 33 percent of the least aggressive.

The disdain of the aggressive patrolmen toward this incident is most apparent in the two small departments, and less so in the LAPD where Clean Beat patrolmen tailor their behavior to the presumed expectations of administrators (see table 9.5). Whether this is conformity or prudence is difficult to tell. The most extreme response to

TABLE 9.5
The Dispute Between Neighbors

	Small Departments		LAPD	
	Agree (%)	Disagree (%)	Agree (%)	Disagree (%)
Operational Style:				
Professional Style	*50	50 (18)	28	72 (29)
Clean Beat Crime Fighter	79	21 (24)	30	70 (27)
Old Style Crime Fighter	58	42 (33)	46	54 (22)
Service Style	30	70 (20)	38	62 (24)
Number of Respondents		(95)		(102)
Aggressiveness:				
High	*75	25 (36)	*44	56 (32)
Moderate	50	50 (34)	28	72 (32)
Low	36	64 (25)	32	68 (38)
Number of Respondents		(95)		(102)

*Significant @ $P \leq .02$

this incident occurred in Inglewood where a clear majority of patrolmen thought the incident should be ignored. In one regard, the responses in Inglewood may be explained in terms of the encroaching crime problem in the community and the greater aggressiveness, at least in their attitudes, of patrolmen in Inglewood. Preoccupied with crime, they may feel they have to make definite choices about priorities, and thus they must ignore complaints and problems they might otherwise take the time to handle. In contrast, patrolmen in the LAPD, largely because of the department's surfeit of resources, can take the time to make an incident report. There is undoubtedly some truth to this, but the fact remains that aggressive patrolmen in all three departments exhibit an extraordinary disdain toward this kind of incident.

The element of risk and opportunity in a service order-maintenance incident is minimal. Even those patrolmen who disagreed with the hypothetical patrolmen suggested taking only minimal steps at mediation. They often disagreed more with the way the patrolmen left than with the decision to leave. The desire for a promotion makes no difference in the response to this incident in the LAPD, and with two exceptions very little in the small departments. Thus, the decision appears to turn less on a response to departmental pressures than on the individual beliefs of patrolman.

THE FAMILY DISPUTE

If a service order-maintenance situation turns largely on a patrolman's operational style, in a serious order-maintenance incident such as a family dispute the risk element is all important. While there is a slight tendency for young aggressive patrolmen to avoid an arrest in this incident, it is the factors that affect a patrolman's vulnerability that loom large. Experience plays a significant role in the response to this incident. The younger, more aggressive patrolmen do not ignore this incident, but they are reluctant to make an arrest. The younger patrolmen typically prefer the middle course, that of getting one of the parties of the dispute to leave for the night. It is the most experienced patrolmen who exhibit the greatest propensity to make an arrest.

A similar relationship exists between the decision in this incident and the other two measures of vulnerability, the desire for a promotion and the perceived limits on discretion. In the small departments, given the tendency of patrolmen to adopt one of the two less risky alternatives, it is not surprising that neither the desire for a promotion nor the perception of stringent limits on the exercise of discretion makes much difference for a patrolman's decision—though the results for the latter measure do show that the younger, more aggressive patrolmen who believe their discretion is severely limited are more likely to opt for the middle course of action (see table 9.6). In the LAPD, on the other hand, the results are striking. It is primarily those patrolmen who do not desire a promotion or those who do not believe their discretion is greatly limited who are willing to make an arrest in this incident. In the LAPD, then, the findings for all three measures of vulnerability are clear and consistent: it is only the less vulnerable patrolmen who will accept the necessary risks of making an arrest in this incident.

The suspicion that a patrolman's vulnerability is the key factor underlying the decision in this incident is further corroborated by the relationship between vulnerability and the reasons patrolmen gave for taking the action they did in this incident. In all three departments, but particularly the LAPD, the most vulnerable patrolmen—those with less than five years experience, those who desire a promotion, and those who believe their discretion is severely limited by administrators—acted as they did because they said they could

TABLE 9.6
The Family Dispute

	Small Departments			LAPD		
	Arrest (%)	Disperse (%)	Ignore (%)	Arrest (%)	Disperse (%)	Ignore (%)
Years of Experience:						
Less than 1 year	13	57	30 (23)	25	50	25 (4)
2 to 4 Years	2	37	61 (41)	36	29	36 (45)
5 Years or More	10	29	61 (31)	48	15	37 (52)
Number of Respondents			(95)			(101)
Desire For Promotion:						
Wants to Be Supervisor	10	38	53 (40)	*30	38	32 (50)
Wants to Be Investigator	0	42	58 (12)	49	6	45 (33)
Does Not Want Promotion	7	40	54 (43)	61	11	28 (18)
Number of Respondents			(95)			(101)
Perceived Limits on Discretion:						
High	8	50	43 (40)	33	19	48 (21)
Moderate	9	30	61 (33)	39	26	36 (39)
Low	5	32	64 (22)	49	22	29 (41)
Number of Respondents			(95)			(101)

*Significant @ P ≤ .004

not do anything without a signed complaint from the woman. To mention only one instance: in the LAPD 36 percent of the patrolmen who wanted a promotion cited the absence of a complaint as the reason for their action, compared to 17 percent of those who did not want a promotion.[9] A similar but less pronounced relationship exists in the small departments. Thus, the decision in the family dispute is to be explained largely in terms of a patrolman's assessment of the anticipated risks of a particular course of action. Those patrolmen who are vulnerable and uncertain as to the reaction of administrators are the patrolmen who construe their legal authority as narrowly as possible and act accordingly. That patrolmen in the small departments are more likely to act this way is not surprising.

THE DISORDERLY JUVENILES

The risks and opportunities for a patrolman in a public disturbance are more mixed. There is less risk than in a private disturbance partly because the police have more legal authority, particularly where juveniles are concerned. There is also a greater incentive to take action in order to prevent a more serious conflagration from breaking out. Ironically, one of the key risks in this incident stems from the pressure to maintain control on the street. In failing to act decisively in this kind of situation a patrolman runs the risk of gaining a reputation among his peers of being indecisive, or worse, afraid. But if supervisors often want decisive, vigorous action they must also guard against actions by patrolmen that might incite the crowd. The opportunities are also more mixed in this incident. A patrolman does have the opportunity to demonstrate decisive, cool-headed action in the face of provocation, but little else. Arrests may sometimes be necessary, and they may even satisfy a taste for action, but it is not the kind of thing that will necessarily enhance a patrolman's reputation or chances for a promotion.

There is a slight tendency for the more aggressive patrolmen in both divisions of the LAPD to be more inclined to arrest in this incident (see table 9.7). Sixty-nine percent of the Old Style Crime Fighters and Clean Beat patrolmen would arrest compared to 53 percent of the Professional and Service patrolmen. Neither experience nor the perceived limits on discretion appear to make much difference to the response in this incident (the slight tendency for those patrolmen perceiving high or moderate limits to discretion to arrest partly reflects the responses of the more aggressive patrolmen). Nevertheless, vulnerability is still important, as the desire for

TABLE 9.7
The Disorderly Juveniles

	Small Departments			LAPD		
	Arrest (%)	Disperse (%)	Ignore (%)	Arrest (%)	Disperse (%)	Ignore (%)
Operational Style:						
Professional Style	45	22	23 (18)	55	21	24 (29)
Clean Beat Crime Fighter	33	42	25 (24)	70	26	4 (29)
Old Style Crime Fighter	30	37	33 (33)	68	23	9 (22)
Service Style	40	30	30 (18)	50	33	17 (24)
Number of Respondents			(95)			(102)
Years of Experience:						
1 year or less	35	44	22 (23)	50	50	0 (4)
2 to 4 years	43	33	25 (40)	57	24	20 (46)
5 years or more	28	28	44 (32)	65	25	10 (52)
Number of Respondents			(95)			(102)
Desire For Promotion:						
Wants Promotion	40	35	25 (52)	56	29	15 (84)
Does Not Want Promotion	30	33	37 (43)	83	11	6 (18)
Number of Respondents			(95)			(102)
Perceived Limits on Discretion:						
High	35	38	28 (40)	64	23	14 (24)
Moderate	27	30	43 (33)	69	13	18 (39)
Low	50	32	18 (22)	51	39	8 (41)
Number of Respondents			(95)			(101)

a promotion has an effect similar to that in the family dispute. Eighty-three percent of the patrolmen in the LAPD who do not want a promotion would make an arrest compared to 56 percent of those who do (there is scant difference between those who want to become managers and those who aspire to be investigators). Furthermore, the patrolmen who do not desire a promotion are more likely to believe that they have sufficient legal authority to act while promotion-minded patrolmen believe they need a complaint to act.

In Redondo Beach and Inglewood vulnerability would appear to be somewhat more important than in the LAPD. The more aggressive patrolmen in these departments have a tendency to opt for the middle course of action, that of dispersal, while the Professionals with two to four years of experience are more likely to elect to make an arrest in this incident. The desire for promotion does not have a significant effect, though those who want to become investigators are the most likely to arrest. But note that those patrolmen who perceive only low limits on their discretion are far more likely to make an arrest in this incident than those who do not. Not surprisingly, these patrolmen are more likely to believe they have sufficient legal authority to act in this incident. Finally, one other fact about the responses in the small departments is worth mentioning, namely, that it is the more experienced patrolmen who take the position that the incident should be ignored or handled with a minimum of fuss. They simply believe the incident is not very important.

If the results are not as clear-cut as they are for the family dispute, they nevertheless show that in the small departments, and in the LAPD to a lesser extent, the uncertainty underlying the anticipated reactions of supervisors to an arrest in this incident does influence the decisions of patrolmen. But since the element of risk is less severe there is a tendency for the aggressive patrolmen to get into the fray and make arrests. This is least true for Inglewood where the most aggressive patrolmen do not make an arrest. (The Crime Fighters and Clean Beat patrolmen in Redondo Beach are more inclined to arrest than their counterparts in Inglewood.) Why do the aggressive patrolmen in Inglewood behave so differently from those in the other two departments? I suspect that the reason again has to do with the necessity of making explicit choices about priorities. Believing they confront a "crime wave," the aggressive patrolmen in Inglewood may think they are better off concentrating their energies elsewhere. Thus, in the small departments both the greater sense of limits on the exercise of discretion by patrolmen and the need to make explicit choices about priorities appear to lead to the tendency to treat this incident without making an arrest.

Police Discretion and Organization

A police bureaucracy has a significant impact on the behavior of patrolmen. Judging from the survey data a patrolman's choices are more adequately predicted by his departmental affiliation than anything else. Patrolmen in the two divisions of the LAPD are formalistic and more willing to make an arrest in a variety of incidents than patrolmen in the small departments, who are consistently more lenient and less willing to invoke the force of the law in the same circumstances. A patrolman's operational style is of considerable importance in influencing his approach to crime fighting and the way he works the street (the frequency with which he stops individuals for field interrogations and minor violations and how often he issues a citation or makes an arrest); but clearly a patrolman's choices are modified by the impact of departmental controls. Otherwise legalistic patrolmen in Inglewood and Redondo Beach opted for leniency when confronted with a drunk driver, and the actual aggressiveness of Inglewood patrolmen on the street was more subdued than their attitudes alone would indicate. In the LAPD, on the other hand, there appears to be far more room for a patrolman to act on the basis of his operational style. The propensity for aggressiveness and, to a lesser degree, the decision to enforce minor violations in the LAPD depend on a patrolman's operational style. Simply put, the evidence indicates that operational style is more significant as an explanatory variable in large than in small police departments.

The other instance where operational style is decisive is in service order-maintenance incidents. Highly aggressive and somewhat younger patrolmen are more inclined to treat these incidents less seriously than other patrolmen. Departmental controls in all three departments are less important in these incidents both because supervisors do not accord these calls a high priority and because they disagree among themselves about the way they should be handled.

In the more serious order-maintenance incidents operational style is far less influential, and what is decisive is the negative impact of departmental controls. In a high-risk, low-opportunity situation, such as a family dispute, only those patrolmen with little sense of their vulnerability at the hands of administrators will risk an arrest. Otherwise, they resort to mediation or ignore the matter. In a public dispute, in contrast, the more aggressive patrolmen will resort to an arrest in the LAPD but not in the small departments. On the whole, in serious order-maintenance incidents most patrolmen are reluctant to take risks, and as often as not they take a low-key, "don't make waves" approach to their task. Given the disincentives for aggressive police work in most departments (notwithstanding the admonitions of supervisors), this is precisely what one would expect.

In sum, the survey data show that operational style counts, but only in some circumstances; otherwise, the exercise of discretion is to be explained by the impact of departmental controls. Yet this conclusion should be qualified in one very significant way. There is, as I have indicated, some tension between the field observations and the survey. If one relied solely upon the survey results, one might prematurely conclude that operational style counts for very little and the department is everything; but if one made a case solely on the basis of the field observations, one might place more weight upon operational style than it clearly deserves. Neither operational style nor the impact of departmental controls can be discounted, and nothing is to be gained at this point by rejecting one in favor of the other. Far more intriguing are those points on which both methods are in agreement. These results would appear to discount explanations of police discretion that reduce to a few background characteristics or psychological traits, an all-pervasive police mentality, or the outcome of the drama played out between policeman and citizen in unique encounters. Patrolmen clearly have well-defined views about how they should act on the street, these views are shaped through a process of occupational socialization, and their behavior is to be explained largely in terms of the resulting beliefs and the impact of departmental controls.

This leaves one critical question: What explains the difference in the exercise of discretion between the LAPD and the two small departments? The evidence suggests that these differences cannot be explained by differences in the expectations conveyed to patrolmen by field supervisors. One of the reasons why patrolmen do not base their decisions solely on the expectations of supervisors is that these ordinarily conflict. Patrolmen are told to control crime, enforce the law, respond thoroughly to service calls, be courteous, and avoid complaints; but when and how they do any of these things is left largely up to them. The expectations of supervisors are not irrelevant; they do define, if rather broadly and incoherently, alternative courses of action that serve to constrain a patrolman's actions. But because patrolmen confront a host of conflicting cues, the net effect is often to increase the uncertainty a patrolman faces rather than to guide discretion along a particular path.

The greater significance of operational style and the tendency toward enforcement in the LAPD in comparison to the reduced significance of operational style and the tendency toward leniency in the small departments can be explained by the differential impact of administrative controls in large versus small police departments. Three characteristics of the structure of administrative controls are related to these patterns. First, because there are fewer resources (less organizational slack) in small departments patrolmen have less room to maneuver on the street and administrators must make more conscious choices of priorities. Patrolmen in the small departments had less opportunity to move around and get involved in the kinds of incidents that interested them; and they had to make conscious choices of priorities, especially in Inglewood. The need to choose priorities also increases the possibility that administrators and supervisors will convey conflicting expectations to patrolmen, and this in turn increases the degree of uncertainty patrolmen face. This latter effect is especially pronounced under conditions of an escalating crime rate. These kinds of choices do not have to be made in a large department like the LAPD. There a patrolman has greater latitude to indulge himself, if you will, and enforce any law he so desires; and administrators can afford to think that patrolmen should not have to choose between crime fighting and other responsibilities.

Second, due to the greater limits on hierarchical controls in large organizations, there is a greater reliance upon impersonal controls in large compared to small departments. Since administrators must take these controls more seriously, there are stronger production norms. This was certainly true in the LAPD, despite feelings of some administrators that a man's "stats" should be de-emphasized. Given the pressure to produce and the awareness that he will be judged to some degree on this basis, the tendency of a patrolman in the LAPD is to act, to enforce the law more often than not. In the small departments, these pressures are less pronounced or are counterbalanced by other cues.

The third characteristic of the structure of administrative controls is the greater uncertainty patrolmen in small departments come to feel as a result of the negative impact of these controls. The combination of a need to make more conscious choices of priorities and the consequent conflicting expectations, on the one hand, and the greater pressures generated by the bifurcation of internal controls, on the other, all work to increase the uncertainty that patrolmen in small police departments face. If patrolmen in large departments like the LAPD face uncertainty, the effects are mitigated for two reasons. First, because size limits the impact of hierarchical controls in a large department, administrators must operate without the informal awareness of a patrolman's activities that prevails in a small department. Moreover, it is easier for patrolmen in a large department to conceal misbehavior or act contrary to the expectations of administrators. Second, because of the greater autonomy from community and political pressures that characterizes a department like the LAPD, there is less pressure upon administrators to bear down and thus less internal pressure and uncertainty confronting patrolmen. This is not to say that such pressure is absent; only that administrators can more easily ignore complaints and demands to enforce the law in a particular way.

These three factors converge to "produce" the patterns of police discretion we have observed: in a large professional department, the surfeit of resources, the greater reliance upon impersonal controls, and the greater ability of patrolmen to cope with the uncertain impact of departmental controls allow greater latitude for patrolmen to operate on the basis of their operational styles, and facilitate a tendency toward strict enforcement. Precisely the converse obtains in small departments. These effects exist independent of the expectations of field supervisors and administrators, though departmental expectations can and do reinforce tendencies that are a consequence of the structure of administrative controls. For example, in both the LAPD and Inglewood, the expectations of field supervisors for strict or lenient enforcement of minor violations reinforce the assessment of risks and opportunities conveyed by the system of administrative controls. In Redondo Beach, on the other hand, patrolmen are confronted with an inconsistent set of cues: a demand for strict enforcement *and* a host of cues that suggest they ought to take it easy. Redondo Beach patrolmen would probably agree that discretion really is the better part of valor.

The evidence strongly suggests that the greater uncertainty generated by administrative controls in small police departments leads to a pattern of leniency.[10] But why do these pressures result in leniency? It is important to bear in mind the broader implications of police reform. Isolation of the police from the communities they serve has been thought, from the time of the earliest arguments over the extension of police power until the present, to be fundamentally necessary to strict enforcement. Indeed, it has been presumed that effective enforcement and control of crime can come about only with substantial autonomy from community politics and pressure. But if the findings of this study are generally correct this may be possible only beyond a certain size of department (and city by implication). Because small police departments are less autonomous, they are constrained from enforcing the law as strictly as they might like. It really comes down to a question of the legitimacy of the authority of the police. To some degree, the police in small departments trade leniency for public support.

PART FOUR

The Politics of Police Discretion

The more that demands are made on a policeman's bravery and loyalty, on his understanding of vice and corruption, on his instincts for order and improvement, the more he can lead himself to believe that the police are the only truly moral force in society. The systematic attempt to dominate and lead the public separates the police from the public, and transfers the focus of police loyalties away from society at large to a new internal ethos. The police become forced into the closed conspiracy of a group apart from society, and a new and deformed esprit de corps emerges, increased by the police's new sense of public importance, fostered by public cringing, and a new delight in being the possessors of secret powers and secret knowledge. . . . The policeman who was a soldier becomes a hired assassin; he who was a priest becomes a clinical psychologist; and the one who was an artist becomes a predator.

Brian Chapman

In framing a government which is to be administered by men over men, the great difficulty lies in this: you must first enable the government to control the governed; and in the next place oblige it to control itself. A dependence on the people is, no doubt, the primary control on government; but experience has taught mankind the necessity of auxilliary precautions.

James Madison

Chapter 10

Political Control
of Police Discretion:
The Dilemmas of Reform

THE overt hostilities of the 1960s have subsided, but the contending political currents remain. Many of the issues raised during the latter part of that decade have not so much been resolved as postponed. This becomes apparent when we question the role, prerogatives, and behavior of the American police. If the fear of crime is still a very real concern to most Americans, the wanton brutality of Houston patrolmen, two recent shootings by the LAPD, and the death of a black businessman at the hands of the Miami police are grim reminders of what concerned so many people a decade ago.[1]

What is at stake now, as then, is political control over police discretion. It is a fundamental misunderstanding of what the police do to evaluate them as just another municipal agency delivering services. To be overly preoccupied with whether or not patrolmen respond as quickly as they should to calls for service, with the efficiency of the police in allocating resources, or with their effectiveness in dealing with crime—whether that is measured by crime rates, clearance rates, or victimization studies—is only to perpetuate, albeit in a far more sophisticated way, the flawed vision of the Progressive reformers. The important question is whom the police serve and how they serve them. Even the most obtuse patrolmen understand that they deal, day in and day out, with the primordial political issues—justice, equality, and liberty—that their decisions have momentous consequences for the fate of groups and individuals. The police may be nonpartisan in some sense, but they are not apolitical.

If we grant the necessity of obtaining some degree of political control over police discretion it is not at all clear what that control should be and, more disturbing, whether it will work. In one way, this book is concerned as much with the dilemmas and pitfalls of reform as with the police. The model of policing created by the Progressive reformers and developed and applied by Vollmer, Parker, and O. W. Wilson, among others, may have reduced the incidence of corruption, curbed the more egregious abuses of police power (though obviously not entirely), and made the police more efficient, but it is an open question whether it has made the police more responsive and more subject to restraint and external control. A variety of proposals and schemes have been advanced in recent years which address the question of police discretion and political control. Leaving aside for the moment the question of the political feasibility of any proposed reform, I intend in this concluding chapter to conduct an evaluation of some of the more prominent proposals for reform. But this presupposes that we absorb the lessons of the effort to professionalize the police, that we gain some understanding of what we have purchased with the extant model of police work.

Cops, Crime, and Disorder: Some Implications of Reform

What difference has police professionalism made? In particular, what difference has it made for the cop on the beat and the way he uses his powers of discretion? Do patrolmen in professional departments enforce the law equally and impartially? Are they sensitive to the legal restraints on their powers? To what extent have the values of the police culture, so vividly described by William Westley, been modified? And to what extent has professionalism made the police not only more proficient in what they do but also more responsive and accountable to the communities they serve? The burden of this analysis is that the answers to these questions are, on the whole, negative.

As a consequence of reform (and broader social trends toward the bureaucratization of American society) the values and beliefs that guide the exercise of discretion are based less on community norms and overt political pressures than on an ethos internal to the police. This ethos, and thus the priorities that inform the decisions of patrolmen and the standards routinely applied on the street, are rooted in the centrality of crime fighting. Under reform, crime fighting has become the primary purpose and justification of police work, and the ideas of initiative and deterrence the mainstays of a professional ideology. While the emphasis on crime control was a central element in the efforts of Vollmer and those reformers who followed in his footsteps to professionalize the police, one should not minimize its significance for working patrolmen. There is a sense in which patrolmen are modern day *condottiere* for whom adventure and risk are important rewards. Far from being captives of circumstances, or even plodding subprofessionals, the patrolmen I observed were calculating, manipulative men who thought that police work was action —crushing crime. One may lament this single-minded, narrow view of the police role, but it is a misunderstanding to fail to appreciate the extent to which crime fighting is one of the attractions of the job and a vital source of satisfaction for most working patrolmen. The result, though, is to sustain and reinforce some of the most significant and pernicious values and practices of the police culture. The pursuit of a good pinch continues to be a core occupational norm, and from all indications these patrolmen are not always worried about the legality of how they get it.

On the other hand, judging from these patrolmen, reform has made enforcement more impersonal and (formally) equal and less subject to whim. Minor violations are not casually ignored, and there is an emphasis on strict enforcement. This is partly due to the more legalistic cast of mind in professional departments and partly to the belief that strict enforcement has a deterrent effect just as vigorous stop and frisk actions do. Nevertheless, many of these patrolmen do not believe the law need be enforced in every instance, and despite the avowed legalism, they were frequently observed to employ extralegal and particularistic criteria in deciding whether or not to make an arrest—especially in disputes and disturbances. And the attitude test remains a significant criterion in the enforcement of the law.

If all of this is indicative of the limits to professionalism and the continuing significance of values and beliefs rooted in the uncertainties of police work, it is well to remember that the inclination to pursue crime aggressively, to enforce the law strictly and impartially, to ignore disturbances, and to violate due process varies greatly among individual patrolmen and between departments. More important, reform has had an impact beyond modifying some of the values policemen bring to bear on the street. By attempting to ground police work in a broader set of values, professionalism has sharpened the tension between means and ends that is at the heart of police work, and has led to a deeply rooted conflict within contemporary police departments. The reformers sought to institutionalize the new values by bureaucratizing police work. The autonomy to act as professionals toward the community presupposed internal control over the actions of policemen, which was to be accomplished through stringent discipline. Because the values of professionalism and the necessity of internal discipline are so closely tied to the legitimacy of police authority in professional departments, administrators are compelled to honor these values and to attempt to enforce discipline. Yet the uncertainties of police work and the consequent police culture serve to legitimize a distinctly different set of values than those of professionalism. The resulting conflict between the values of professionalism and the police culture is the root of the structural contradictions of police bureaucracies.

The most significant implication of this conflict is that it influences the structure (and ultimately the impact) of administrative controls in police departments. Far from being highly centralized, quasi-military bureaucracies, police departments are characterized by a bifurcated system of internal control. One system of control derives from professionalism and is based on the legitimacy of hierarchical authority; the other is rooted in the police culture and depends upon widely shared group norms for its legitimacy. The bifurcation of internal controls gives administrators and supervisors enormous control over administrative matters such as the allocation of resources and the enforcement of rules and regulations to maintain discipline, while preserving a wide degree of autonomy for working patrolmen.

These two systems of control overlap and come into conflict because of the uncertainties of police work and the ever present external pressure on the police. Much of the behavior of supervisors and patrolmen is based on coping with this conflict. For administrators the conflict is manifested in the dilemmas they confront in trying to control the behavior of patrolmen in the face of severe limitations on their ability to do so. Patrolmen face the necessity of resolving a conflict between acting as autonomous officials who perform an arduous, uncertain task and as bureaucrats subject to organizational discipline. The organizational pressures that impinge upon patrolmen are largely negative, and because they frequently have no idea of how the department will react, the uncertainty in any situation is increased and the risks of any course of action are often made more salient than anything else. It is no small irony that rather than creating smoothly functioning command bureaucracies, under reform the department has become a key source of uncertainty for patrolmen.

The discretionary choices of patrolmen as well as the salience of the moral dilemmas they confront turn on the way they resolve and adapt to the demands of an uncertain, ambiguous task on the one hand, and to the equally uncertain demand for organizational discipline on the other. Given the autonomy that patrolmen have, they come to grips with the conflicts and ambiguities of their role in profoundly different ways. Patrolmen fashion distinctive approaches to working the street—operational styles—and the values and beliefs of these styles explain some but not all of the variation in the exercise of discretion. The reason why operational style is not more significant is that patrolmen modify their actions to take account of the impact of administrative controls. Since the principal effect of hierarchical controls is to increase the uncertainty that a patrolman confronts without really controlling the exercise of discretion, patrolmen are often inclined to avoid taking any action at all or to take the safest way out of an incident. They may either behave in a way that is consistent with the perceived expectations of administrators (something that is more likely when there is a relatively coherent set of expectations), or they opt for a low-key approach which leads to a pattern of leniency.

In a broad sense, reform has not solved the question of democratic control. In some ways it has made democratic control more problematic. For one thing, it is not altogether clear that some of the changes precipitated by professionalism—notably the devotion to crime fighting—are entirely for the better. The implications of making crime fighting the fulcrum of police work are profound. The ideology of the inner-directed, aggressive policeman who views himself as the thin blue line between order and anarchy, greatly enhances the capacity of the police to act lawlessly. The policeman as crime fighter is, in many ways, a far more dangerous character than either of his predecessors, the nightwatchman and the nineteenth-century beat cop. Both the nightwatchman and the beat cop had a capacity for crudity and corruption, but they were not given to crusades. Besides the abuses of due process and the petty harassments that accompany crime fighting, the preoccupation with order fosters an instrumental, manipulative attitude toward the law. Empowered to use coercion to attain broad, ill-defined social objectives, the police come to regard the law as a doctor regards the instruments in his black bag: as a set of tools to be manipulated as circumstances require. That blacks, because of unique historical circumstances, should be thrust into the core of major cities to become the principal victims of this system of policing only makes the flaws more apparent. Without doubt professionalism has contributed to the trends in the twentieth century that Brian Chapman believes have warped policemen.

What makes these reservations all the more compelling is that the strategies thus far adopted by a professional police to control crime seem singularly ineffective. The burden of recent evaluations of preventative patrol is that it may be a notoriously ineffective way of controlling crime. In a recent review of the major empirical studies conducted over the past eight years, George Kelling and David Fogel concluded, "In almost every study, the impact of preventative patrol on reported crime is limited, negligible, or nonexistent."[2] While this study does not directly address this question, our findings certainly do not contradict, and perhaps even support, previous research. The haphazard methods of coping with crime employed by many patrolmen, what I have called "playing the slot machine," does not result in many felony arrests and may be a dubious way of deterring crime. While this issue is not closed, the weight of the evidence would seem to call sharply into question the theory of crime control embedded in police professionalism, and make salient its costs. There is no reason to tolerate abuses of civil liberties in the first place, but there is even less reason if the practices which lead to these abuses have little effect on the intended objectives.

Nor have serious inequalities in enforcement of the law been eliminated under professionalism. The flip side of the aggressive demeanor some patrolmen display in working the street to control crime is their neglect of domestic violence. Most patrolmen take the view that their primary responsibility is to control repressible crimes —burglary, armed robbery, auto theft. What they mean is that they presumably have a chance of preventing such crimes, whereas violence cannot be prevented. For too many patrolmen, though, this becomes a license to ignore interpersonal violence. The manipulation of the law that patrolmen use to snag a burglar or drug addict is used in instances of domestic violence to get out of doing anything at all. The police rationalize such practices by cultivating the fiction that since the victim will not file a complaint or prosecutors will not act there is nothing they can or should do. This is not to deny that these situations do not pose difficult problems for the police, nor is it to insist that an arrest is always the best solution. But when almost half of a sample of patrolmen respond to an incident portraying a woman who has been beaten by her husband by saying there is little they can do or that it can be ignored, one should realize more is involved than legal technicalities or the reluctance of the victim to prosecute. What is involved is a questionable choice of priorities that has the effect of denying a significant proportion of the population —women—the protection of legality.

In both the allocation of departmental resources and the enforcement of minor violations reform has achieved more equality. Patrolmen and other resources are deployed, to some degree, on the basis of need: high-crime areas get more than their share of patrolmen.[3] And when it comes to the enforcement of minor violations there is a tendency to act only on the basis of the law. The questions that can be raised about this development have to do with whether strict enforcement is always desirable. The rigid, unrelenting style of enforcement that typifies a Clean Beat patrolman like Appleby seems beyond the realm of common sense, whatever its presumed value as a deterrent. Many patrolmen are well aware of this difficulty and are often torn between the demand to behave like a bureaucrat and the necessity of acting like a judge. Indeed, the only reason to tolerate substantial discretion on the part of the police is that it permits them to temper the law to the ambiguities of the street. Finally, it is well-known that the high degree of formal equality obtained in this area weighs differentially on different social classes. There is no reason to believe that the poor drink any more or drive any worse than the well-to-do, but they pick up more than their share of tickets and arrests for such offenses. This is not a matter of discrimination. The poor drive older, more run-down vehicles with more equipment violations, and as a result they will be stopped more often and given more citations for such offenses.[4]

Strict enforcement may or may not be desirable, but to raise questions about it poses other issues. Under what circumstances should leniency be tolerated? One might agree that broken taillights and bald tires in the case of the poor might be safely ignored, but can more serious violations be treated as casually? Should drunk drivers be driven home rather than arrested? If a patrolman is to arrest some people for a minor violation but not others, what criteria should be employed?

As these remarks make clear none of these problems are to be remedied by simply obtaining greater adherence to relevant legal standards in police decisions. The fact that the police overenforce the law in some instances and underenforce it in others merely underscores what should by now be obvious: the issue is when the police use their discretion, for what ends, and with what consequences. The search for ways to bring police action in closer conformity with legal rules is largely misdirected and would only result, as Egon Bittner points out, in a specious kind of control.[5] I hardly intend to suggest that we ignore abuses of due process; but to presume that all that matters is the legality of police actions is to avoid rather than confront the reality of discretion.

The point I wish to emphasize here has to do with the matter of judgment. Police discretion turns on the judgment of patrolmen, on their ability to weigh competing ends, to assess the moral consequences of alternative courses of action, and to reach decisions which promote values society deems important. In both form and substance the decisions of patrolmen differ little from those of other politicians; both make decisions which can potentially augment or diminish liberty and sustain or mitigate inequalities. We should be less concerned with worrying about how much discretion patrolmen have and searching for ways to eliminate it (if that were even remotely possible), than with trying to enlarge their qualities of judgment and making them responsive to the people they serve.

This brings me to the key flaw in the reforms finally engineered by those who inherited the mantle of the Progressives, and to the crucial policy implication of this study. The failure of the reformers is an institutional failure. Professionalization has fostered the illusion of control over police discretion when in fact it has resulted in greater autonomy for the police. The enormous autonomy of professional departments coupled with internal limits to administrative control continues to permit extensive abuses of power on the part of patrolmen. But the failure goes deeper. The gaping oversight at the heart of police professionalism is not just that it avoids the matter of discretion, but that the maze of bureaucratic controls erected to control the behavior of patrolmen often inhibits if not warps their judgment. The ironic fact is that the bureaucratization of police work often compounds the very defects it seeks to remedy. Confronted with a host of negative controls which are largely irrelevant to the kinds of judgments they have to make but which increase the uncertainties of police work, patrolmen come to countenance manipulation, secrecy, and avoidance as a way of survival. Rather than assisting them to grapple with the moral dilemmas intrinsic to their work, the bureaucratic controls of police departments often compound them; rather than cultivating flexibility they often encourage rigidity; and rather than confronting the inevitability of nonenforcement and the choice of priorities, and providing reasonable standards for such decisions, they leave them to the whims and caprice of individual patrolmen. In short, in the attempt to rationalize police work, the reformers have done less to control discretion than to allow ample latitude for the full play of the most invidious prejudices, and less to nurture the requisite qualities of judgment than to inhibit them. That the police at times do some things rather well is less a tribute to the administrative system in which they operate than to the resilience of some patrolmen and to their sense of craftsmanship, which permits them to fashion working solutions to difficult problems. Police professionalism has performed an ideological function precisely to the extent that it has obscured these facts about the police.

In sum, the problem of political control over police discretion is a serious one, and it has not been solved by the reigning model of police work. The question now is, What can be done?

Four Models of Reform

At this juncture, what kinds of reforms make sense? And, more important, what, if any, are the limits to reform? To be effective any proposed reform must be geared not only to minimizing abuses of power by patrolmen but to enlarging rather than stunting their capacity for judgment. One of the important conclusions of this analysis is that the values and attitudes of patrolmen, and the institutional context within which these develop and take effect, do have significant consequences for their behavior. I would counsel against reforms which might marginally improve police work but which do not touch the institutional framework in which patrolmen operate.

Four broad kinds of reforms are offered today which would meet the criteria I have postulated. The first of these seeks to control discretion by treating the police as a policymaking agency. A second proposal, the professional model, argues that the police are not truly professional, and steps should be taken to make the police conform to the standards and practices of other professions. The other two models both argue for decentralization. One of these, team policing, seeks to delegate more authority and control for police operations in a specific neighborhood to an administrative team, and as such is a form of administrative decentralization. The other derives from the community control movement of the late 1960s, and argues for creating new administrative units based on more or less homogeneous neighborhoods and subject to the control of neighborhood governments or other small scale political jurisdictions. This last proposal is a form of political decentralization. An extended discussion of these models is beyond the scope of this analysis. What I can do is to indicate some of the possibilities and limitations of each in light of conclusions drawn from my empirical analysis of police discretion.

THE POLICYMAKING MODEL

This approach is a straightforward attempt to make police decisions, now made covertly through the exercise of discretion, overt and open to scrutiny. Discretion is to be controlled by structuring it through the proliferation of policies and rules. Rule making in police agencies would lead, in the opinion of one proponent, to "an improved system of regulating police conduct."[6] The reason is that the elaboration of rules which guide and therefore limit a patrolman's discretion would provide an improved basis for holding patrolmen accountable for their actions. Presently, Herman Goldstein points out, even if the actions of an officer appear improper there is usually no justifiable basis on which he can be disciplined since his actions may be neither in violation of the law nor any existing departmental rule. Thus, "the promulgation of policies to which police officers are required by regulation to adhere would provide a basis for disciplining those who violate such policies . . . [and] it would serve in a positive way to inform members of a force what is expected of them."[7]

What underlies this approach is a belief in the efficacy of hierarchical controls, the presumption that if the rules are made explicit and if they are enforced, the police can be made accountable. Jerry V. Wilson and Geoffrey M. Alprin, for example, argue that "police officers want to be told what to do. . . . Where clear-cut guidelines are laid down, and particularly when they are laid down and enforced by the police organization itself, policemen tend to comply with them."[8] The problem with rule making is not an intrinsic difficulty in either developing or enforcing such rules; it is rather that neither police departments nor prosecutors (and judges) have displayed any interest or willingness to devise such rules.

The approach has some obvious advantages. Doubtless, patrolmen would be better off if they had a clearer idea of what administrators expect of them in different situations. Clearly, one of the implications of this study is that patrolmen are all too often left hanging with a vague "just get the job done and use your common sense." More explicit policies would reduce some of the uncertainties patrolmen face. And the process of devising rules ought to facilitate a more thoroughgoing examination of the goals of police agencies and their relationship to the communities they serve. This may well be one of the prime benefits of more explicit policymaking by the police.

Yet one ought to have no illusions about the effectiveness of policymaking. Just as there are limits to specifying all contingencies when devising a law, so there are limits to the ability of police administrators to devise rules which will cover the wide variety of situations patrolmen encounter. Police administrators may be able to develop rules to guide discretion when there is an unambiguous problem; but it would be difficult to devise satisfactory rules that tell a patrolman when to stop someone on the street, how to proceed in a family dispute, or how much force should be used to quell a dispute. In fact, rules devised for these situations are likely to be vague and ambiguous at best and misleading at worst. Taken to an extreme, the proliferation of rules would only further rationalize police departments and lead to the attendant consequences. While there is a need for the police to more consciously make policy, devising a rule for every situation is no substitute for the development of judgment.[9]

The crucial deficiency with this approach, though, is the set of assumptions on which it is based. Wilson's and Alprin's belief in the effectiveness of hierarchical controls and the malleability of policemen is myopic and unrealistic. It ought to be clear by now that the mere formulation of rules does not guarantee they will be followed. It seems obvious that any proposal which fails to come to terms with the realities of police work and the police culture is bound to be ineffective. If I am right about the relationship between the uncertainties of police work and the consequent effects for organizational control, there seems to be no reason to believe that such rules could be adequately enforced. The blunt edge of enforcement, one ought to remember, rests with field supervisors, the men most exposed to the pressures exerted by patrolmen and the most cautious about breaching the compromise between hierarchical and group controls.

Even if I am wrong or if police administrators are able to break the power of the police culture, difficulties remain. There are obvious problems in supervising men who patrol the street alone, and patrolmen have not found it difficult in the past to evade rules or manipulate reports to meet external constraints. Nonenforcement poses a special problem here: how does an administrator tell when a law that should have been enforced was not enforced? Yet even if all these difficulties can be overcome (which is doubtful) there remains a final problem: it is still possible that administrators will refuse to act on information of misconduct for other reasons.[10]

Aside from naive assumptions about policemen and the effectiveness of hierarchical controls, the danger of the policymaking model is that it could result in illusory controls. Well-formulated policy statements may be used to satisfy the public that the police are under administrative control when in fact these policies are only imperfectly implemented. I do not mean to suggest that police administrators should not attempt to formulate rules and enforce them; clearly that would be desirable to some degree. My point is that reliance upon rule making alone will not solve the problem of political control.

THE PROFESSIONAL MODEL

This approach is based upon the idea of the "inner check." Members of a professional group are to be held accountable for their judgments to a set of ethical and technical principles by other members of the group. Since professionalism usually involves a high degree of technical competence, professional controls are thought to be a means of maintaining accountability without sacrificing such competence. The underlying supposition is that these standards are based upon scientific knowledge and are more or less "objective." If this is the case, then only professional colleagues are in a position to assess whether a decision is based upon appropriate criteria. Normally, these technical standards are coupled with moral principles and ideals.

The criticism lodged by those who advocate the professional model is that the police are not *truly* professional; rather they are command bureaucrats preoccupied with order and efficiency. The most sophisticated argument for making the police truly professional is that of Egon Bittner. Bittner's proposal is for the police to abandon the concept of professionalism based on managerial efficiency and the idea of the policeman as gendarme for a concept based, as in other professions, on scientific knowledge. He advocates the creation of professional schools for police work, the main purpose of which is to "make *specific education,* and the range of meaning associated with it, part of the concept of the occupation."[11] What Bittner wants is a policeman who is the "informed, deliberating, and technically efficient professional who knows that he must operate within the limits set by a moral and legal trust."[12]

Bittner's view has much to commend it, grounded as it is in a thorough knowledge of police work and patrolmen. His skepticism of the preoccupation with crime fighting and the bureaucratization of police work is borne out by the results of this study. And he usefully elaborates the kind of knowledge that a scientific concept of police work could be based on. Of all those advocating the professional model, he comes closest to setting forth the conditions necessary to meet Carl Friedrich's concept of "corporate objectivity."

Though there may be some value in putting police work on a more scientific basis, Bittner's proposal is subject to severe limitations. Bittner is guilty, I believe, of what Max Weber once debunked as "scientism." Unlike most contemporary social scientists, Weber had a keen sense of the limits of science, of the questions it could not resolve. Science might provide one with factual and even causal knowledge, but it could never answer fundamental questions, those pertaining to what should be done.[13] Yet it is precisely such moral issues that are at the core of the problem of discretion, and that a professional knowledge grounded in science cannot answer. Nor do we really want science to provide this kind of knowledge. The danger, as Weber feared, is that science and technology would encroach upon the realms of values and politics, and that political decisions would be made on the basis of scientific or pseudoscientific knowledge; or, perhaps worse, such knowledge would be used as a rationalization for decisions.

There are other limitations. Bittner usefully delineates some of the areas in which knowledge of police work can be rationalized, taken out of the realm of police lore and subjected to scrutiny. His suggestions are imaginative, but I am skeptical of how far this approach can be taken. The knowledge of the social sciences is so rudimentary that it is hardly a solid enough foundation on which to build a scientific knowledge of police work. Nor are all policemen as crude as either Bittner or public mythology believe (though Bittner seems aware of this in places); in many instances they have developed effective techniques for coping with difficult situations. Bittner is most persuasive when he suggests the real matter of concern is that police work is not recognized as the difficult craft it is, and that many continue to believe it is a refuge for those who cannot find work elsewhere. Police work ought to be taken seriously, and the knowledge that is the foundation of police work subjected to critical scrutiny. But we should frankly recognize that police work is a craft and much of it is not really subject to rationalization. Rather than attempting to ground police work in science, we should be concerned with developing among patrolmen a capacity for moral judgment. William Ker Muir, Jr.'s recent analysis of the police contains numerous provocative suggestions for enhancing the capacity for this kind of judgment, and offers a far better foundation for a professional police force.[14]

Yet there is no reason to suppose that a purer form of professionalism would make the police more accountable; in fact, the paradox is that it might make them less accountable. The only real restraint on autonomous professionals is the so-called "inner check," and this may be nothing more than a wishful hope judging from some of the research on this question.[15] More to the point, historically, professionalism has led to power and autonomy rather than restraint.[16] I find no reason to believe that this would not be the case with the professional police.

POLITICAL DECENTRALIZATION: THE COMMUNITY CONTROL MODEL

This approach is based on the idea of decentralizing urban government in order to make public agencies more responsive and to effect a redistribution of power within a city. It seeks to give local citizens, especially minority groups, greater control over the institutions that presumably serve them. Administrative decentralization is precluded since it is believed that this would not substantially alter the behavior of bureaucrats. Rather, the model proposes the delegation of power over a variety of municipal functions to residents of a particular neighborhood. Most proposals do not envision entirely autonomous neighborhood governments but advocate a kind of federalism wherein neighborhood residents have some control over administrative appointments, policymaking, and the responsibility to adjudicate complaints.[17] In its most radical form, community control of the police means control based on shared values between policemen and the residents of a community. More modestly, this model argues that there are benefits to be derived from a decrease in scale. Here community control is taken to be synonymous with suburban government.

Two claims are made for this model. First, it is argued that community control (or a decrease in scale) will increase the responsiveness of police departments to citizen needs and complaints. Citizens can more easily articulate demands, they will know more about the men who police them, and they will thus be able to obtain more effective control over the actions of policemen. Second, police administrators in a smaller jurisdiction and department will have more adequate knowledge of the community and of citizen demands and greater control over the actions of patrolmen. These conditions lead to a more responsive and effective department and higher satisfaction on the part of citizens.

There is a well-developed literature that supports the contention that citizen satisfaction is linked with the size of police departments: small departments are associated with greater citizen satisfaction.[18] We are in a position, on the basis of evidence developed here, to evaluate some of the other claims of the community control model. First, it is quite clear that there is a greater degree of administrative control over the actions of patrolmen in small compared to large departments. Patrolmen in the LAPD were *observed* to be more active and aggressive on the street, far more able to engineer their way out of calls for service and to maneuver about and get involved in the crimes that interested them, and to more easily conceal mistakes and misbehavior. This is not to suggest that these activities do not occur in small departments, for they do. But they are far less frequent due to the stronger administrative controls. This alone may argue for smaller administrative units.

Second, patrolmen in small departments are subject to greater administrative control and more sensitive to community pressures, but given the negative impact of administrative controls, the consequence is to facilitate a strategy of nonenforcement, or leniency. It is not clear that leniency is, in and of itself, an undesirable outcome. The conventional view holds that leniency leads, as often as not, to inequality. Strict enforcement entails a degree of formal equality, but it also leads to rigid, unrelenting enforcement. Is there, though, a trade-off, as James Q. Wilson puts it, between leniency and equality?[19] On the face of it this may not be the case. It would depend on the grounds for nonenforcement. For example, if the decision not to arrest a drunk driver were made on roughly similar grounds in a variety of cases, inequality would not necessarily be the result. As it stands, however, there probably is some inequality in decisions not to enforce the law in small departments, largely because neither administrators nor citizens display much concern with nonenforcement. In fact, there is clear evidence that in the absence of any coherent, formal standards, decisions are far more likely to be based on particularistic standards.[20] If small departments are characterized by a pattern of nonenforcement, it would appear that some inequality is bound to result.

There is an ironical twist to these findings. In small departments the actions of patrolmen are subject to greater scrutiny and there is greater responsiveness to community demands, but, depending on the reason for nonenforcement, the law may be enforced unequally. In a large department, on the other hand, the law may be enforced more strictly and to this extent more equally; but administrators will ultimately have less control over the actions of their men. In one sense, the real trade-off may be between controlling misbehavior and tolerating some degree of inequality. Whether or not this is the case depends on other factors. One of the difficulties here is that we really have no idea of which groups of individuals the police are responding to in a small community. Indeed, we lack a detailed analysis of the impact of community demands on the operations of the police in various kinds of communities. Even so, the particularistic values of some communities would probably work to the disadvantage of some groups as was the case in the South; and previous research on political participation would lead one to believe that it is largely middle- and upper-class individuals who would benefit from a decrease in scale.[21] But perhaps the most important implication of these findings is that simply decreasing the scale of police departments without both modifying the existing system of administrative controls and explicitly confronting the policy implications of police discretion would only lead to a specious kind of political control. A decrease in scale by itself is insufficient.

ADMINISTRATIVE DECENTRALIZATION: THE TEAM POLICING MODEL

Team policing has been adopted in a number of big-city departments in response to the demand for decentralization of police operations. It is regarded as a way of increasing the responsiveness of patrolmen to the residents of specific neighborhoods and as a more effective crime control strategy. The most interesting thing about team policing is that among the proposals I have considered so far, it is the only one which has the potential to modify radically the system of administrative controls within police departments. For that reason alone it ought to be taken seriously. Yet there are some difficulties. First, it is not entirely clear what decentralization means in this context. To the extent that decision making is already radically decentralized within a police department, one wonders how a strategy such as team policing would affect the behavior of patrolmen. Moreover, there is reason to question whether this strategy will actually increase the responsiveness of the police to the residents of a particular neighborhood.

What I shall contend is that team policing is potentially a strategy to *centralize* decision making to the level of the team leader (usually a sergeant or watch commander); and it may be successful as a strategy of decentralization only to the extent that it does so, that is, to the extent that it limits the autonomy of patrolmen. Team policing could increase citizen control over police operations, but as team policing is presently evolving, responsiveness to citizen demands is being sacrificed to the objective of crime control. Responsiveness to neighborhood residents is interpreted more as a matter of controlling crime than of changing priorities. In this sense, team policing is a manifestation of what Philip Selznick once termed "formal cooptation."

Team policing is designed to increase the responsiveness of the police to the needs and demands of neighborhood residents and to reduce the isolation between the police and community in two ways. First, it assigns patrolmen to a specific neighborhood for an extended period of time. This reverses a policy of rotating patrolmen among districts or precincts, which was common to many big-city departments in the 1960s. This is predicated on the assumption that stability in assignment will increase the identification of a patrolman with the residents of a specific neighborhood and their problems. Second, team policing typically requires contact with citizens through regular meetings. The rationale for such contact is often vague, but in most cases it is explicitly linked to crime prevention. For example, in the LAPD the adoption of the Basic Car Plan (BCP) and, later, Neighborhood Action Team Policing (NATP) was explicitly based on involving the community in crime prevention efforts.

Team policing requires that a department focus all of the necessary departmental resources on the problems of a particular neighborhood. A team of patrolmen, traffic specialists, and investigators, usually under the command of a sergeant or watch commander, is held responsible for the control of crime and disorder within a neighborhood. Contact and the exchange of information between patrolmen and neighborhood residents is enhanced by block meetings. The team is evaluated in terms of its success in controlling crime, and team members are expected to take some initiative in organizing citizens in the neighborhood.

What kind of authority is actually decentralized under team policing? For the most part, I would contend that it is control over administrative matters, decisions that once were the prerogative of middle management and to a lesser extent the chief of police. The team leader has greater authority to decide on appropriate dress, enforcement of minor rules and regulations, duty rosters, and the like. It also gives the team leader greater authority in the allocation of manpower to specific activities. Under team policing, a team leader would be able to allocate men selectively to concentrate on problems regarded as important by team members and presumably by neighborhood residents. What is important to understand is that team policing does not decentralize the key decision-making authority within the organization and the routine use of legitimate powers of coercion; and it could not because these are already controlled by patrolmen.

In order to effectively decentralize police operations and to increase responsiveness to a particular neighborhood, team policing must limit the autonomy of patrolmen. This could be accomplished in two ways. First, the team meetings, to the extent that specific strategies are developed and implemented, would serve to circumscribe the freedom patrolmen currently possess to decide which problems they shall attack and when. Team policing, in other words, is an attempt to substitute a group decision-making process for what is presently an individual decision-making process. Indeed, by giving the team leaders responsibility for the actions of patrolmen over a twenty-four-hour period and holding the group as a whole responsible for any action, team policing lends itself to precisely this kind of centralization. Second, team policing involves an expansion in the number and efforts of first-line supervisors to direct the actions of patrolmen. Greater control by supervisors would be facilitated by a more intense effort at supervision and by the concentration of police activity to a small geographical area. In this sense, administrative control under team policing is analogous to that of a small department. Where it differs is in attempting to develop a new system of management that requires the team to decide on strategy, and potentially on priorities, in consultation with neighborhood residents.

What are the effects of team policing for the behavior of patrolmen? At present, insufficient data are available for a complete analysis, and the conclusions advanced here must be regarded as tentative. Nevertheless, there are some suggestive findings in available evaluation studies. There is no explicit evidence one way or another on the extent to which the autonomy of patrolmen has been circumscribed. Most departments which have implemented team policing, usually on an experimental basis, have been unsuccessful in confining the activities of patrolmen to the team area. For example, in New York, Peter Bloch and David Specht report that over 50 percent of the calls assigned to team patrolmen were out of their area. Similar experiences are reported in other departments, including NATP in the Los Angeles Police Department.[22] Moreover, the available information suggests that the extent to which patrolmen tailor their actions to group decisions is dependent on the actions of the team leaders. In New York City, where team leaders held few meetings and appeared reluctant to take aggressive control of the teams, patrolmen went their own way. In the LAPD, on the other hand, there is some evidence that the patrolmen in the TEAM 28 experiment worked closely with supervisors and did tailor their actions to team decisions.

Yet team policing has not resulted in the less aggressive style of patrol that many of its advocates anticipated. In fact, in a number of cases it has resulted in a more aggressive style of patrol. Bloch and Specht's evaluation reveals that team policemen made more arrests than non-team policemen in New York City, and at least one team explicitly adopted a strategy of aggressive patrol.[23] An observer of team policing in Los Angeles has said that it has led to a more proactive style of policing.[24] Why? One hypothesis is that team policing has altered the traditional pattern of hierarchical controls: by decreasing the emphasis placed on discipline and by providing a group sanction for aggressive police work, it has minimized the disincentives that previously existed for this kind of police work. And to the extent that the team is evaluated in terms of its ability to control crime, the proclivity toward aggressive police work is probably increased.

The aggressiveness of policemen involved in team policing *may* also be a response to neighborhood residents. Team policing has evolved as a strategy for controlling crime, and in the LAPD, the only major department so far to try team policing on a department-wide basis, it is based on the assumption that the police could only control crime with the assistance of citizens. There is some evidence to suggest that, at least in the LAPD, residents are more involved in crime prevention efforts and are more willing to supply information to the police. But whether the aggressiveness of the teams is a response to neighborhood demands is impossible to tell.

Most observers believe that decentralization, to the extent it increases contacts between the police and citizens, will lead to greater openness on the part of the police and less conflict between the police and community. While there is evidence to suggest that some of the attitudes of both patrolmen and citizens have changed as a result of team policing, it appears that little else has changed. Most important, there is no indication that the contact between citizens and police has resulted in a significant shift in the priorities among patrolmen or an attempt to tailor enforcement to the demands of the neighborhood—that is, to adopt a decision not to enforce some laws.[25]

The principal result of team policing is to decentralize the authority over administrative decisions and to increase contacts between investigators and patrolmen. The relationship to the community is based on the preoccupation with crime control and thus may preclude the development of styles of policing which reflect other priorities. Team policing does not greatly increase citizen control over police discretion, and it is in this sense that team policing is more properly thought of as an attempt at formal cooptation—participation without control.

Finally, as a system of administrative control, team policing could limit the autonomy of patrolmen; but whether it will actually do so is an open question. In the absence of strong control by team leaders and extensive citizen pressure, team policing may only formalize the collusion between first-line supervisors and patrolmen that has always been characteristic of police departments.

The Limits to Reform

Each of the proposals for reform we have examined is limited, for each finally comes up against the contradictions of police work and the consequent police culture. This is hardly surprising. If there is a lesson to be learned from the experiences of the most recent generation of reformers, it is that simply enveloping policemen in a maze of institutional controls without grappling with the grimy realities of police work does not necessarily promote accountability and may only exacerbate matters.

If the limits to reform are to be found in the uncertainties of police work, part of the difficulty may rest with the interpretation the police have placed on their functions. Perhaps, as it is sometimes argued, change ought to begin with a reconstruction of police work. In particular, it is suggested that the crime fighting "law and order" stance of the police ought to be replaced with a conception of the police as providers of human services. There is no doubt that the infatuation with crime fighting has had pernicious consequences and, given current reservations of the effectiveness of the police in this regard, it would make sense to temper the obsession with crime fighting with a concern for other activities. But does this mean the police should not be concerned with crime? I think not. It is sheer illusion to believe that the police would not, or even should not, be concerned with crime some of the time. The real question here is a matter of priorities, the fact that the police have chosen to lavish their efforts on some crimes and not others: all too often a penny-ante burglar commands a higher price than a battered spouse. Beyond this, we ought to recognize that the contradictions of police work are rooted in the broader structural contradictions and conflicts of American society: the pervasive inequality among social classes, the intransigence of racism, and the deeply divided conceptions of morality. We ought to face the reality that the police are intentionally deployed to shore up the remaining vestiges of a crumbling morality and to sustain the privileges of the well-to-do, while our negligence permits the conditions that lead to violent crime to flourish. The problem of obtaining political control over the police is only minimally a problem for the upper class. To talk of the police as "social workers with guns" is not just a contradiction in terms, it is grossly misleading since it implicitly (or perhaps explicitly) obscures the coercive and political role of the police.[26] An emphasis upon service delivery in police work only cloaks the coercive function of the police in humanistic shib-

303

boleths; it does not eliminate the coercive powers of the police and it will not control them, particularly for those subject to abuses of police power.

What is needed is a system of institutions which will permit continued reflection on the ends of police work and encourage responsiveness, while forcing the policeman to reexamine continually the contradiction between the ends he serves and the means he uses to attain them. Decentralization, while not a panacea, is at least a step in this direction. The alternatives are singularly unpalatable. Neither continued rationalization of police departments through the proliferation of rules nor another form of professionalism will bring about a substantially greater degree of control over the police; and either would only perpetuate the technocratic and elitist bias at the core of Progressive ideology. Further, many of the arguments offered against decentralization are specious. They are elitist, presuming the incompetence of citizens to evaluate police work or reach reasonable decisions; they absurdly presume a return to something like the system of policing that existed under the political machines; and above all, these arguments assume that to allow politics to intrude into police work in any shape or form will be disastrous. In my judgment, a fourth-rate neighborhood politician is always preferable to a fifth-rate, pseudoprofessional command bureaucrat.

Nonetheless there are some very real problems with decentralization. To simply tout the virtues of small scale departments without engaging the difficulties of police work and the reality of discretion is to commit a dangerous oversight. Internal changes will be needed, perhaps some combination of increased policymaking and something like the team policing model; and the realities of citizen participation will have to be confronted. Aside from major changes, it would make a great deal of sense to think about ways to improve the caliber of field sergeants. The task of field sergeants is at least as difficult and significant as that of patrolmen, and both reformers and chiefs would do well to worry about them.

Yet no one should entertain any illusions about the outcome of any effort at reform. Police work inevitably entails the arbitrary use of power: brutality, corruption, the violation of individual rights, and the penchant to take the law into one's own hands, to use it as a tool to right wrongs and attain "justice." It is misleading and naive to think these abuses of power can ever be entirely eliminated, for they are the products of an occupation based on coercion. And as long as the police continue to wield broad coercive powers, the relationship between the police and the communities they serve will be characterized by a dialectical process in which the demand for external control by the public is contradicted by an effort of the police to limit such control. Whether we reach an accommodation with the police finally depends on our taking the police seriously, on recognizing that the police are intimately, excessively, and inevitably involved in politics. Police work may be a craft, but so is the work of ordinary politicians. Coercion is one of the roots of any political association, and its use is not something that either can be or should be rationalized. Police work comes down to questions of judgment, questions of value. Max Weber believed the vocation of politics required passion, a feeling of responsibility, and a sense of proportion. Yet Weber also believed the rationalization of Western societies narrowed the sphere of politics, substituting the judgment of the technocrat and bureaucrat for that of the politician. The irony of Weber's epitaph for politicians in the modern world is that it could have been written for policemen. That it was not and that we have not been able to see that it could have been is part of the problem.

Appendix

Scale Construction

THE attitudinal scales used in this analysis were created from Likert-type questions with key cluster analysis.[1] Key cluster analysis is a variation of factor analysis, but it offers some distinct advantages over the standard factor analysis programs. Factor analysis is a technique for simplifying a mass of data, for reducing different observations or measurements into "distinct patterns of occurrence."[2] It is obviously a useful tool in constructing attitudinal scales. One can take separate measures of attitudes, toward various aspects of police work for example, and use factor analysis to isolate the underlying patterns among these items. The output of a typical factor-analytic solution is based upon a correlation matrix of the observed variables. The factor loadings for these variables are a measure of the degree of "association" and the direction (positive or negative) for the variable and the (underlying) factor. Somewhat simplistically, we can say that the loading of a given variable is simply the (average) correlation of that variable with the variables which define the factor.[3] The number of factors obtained and the loadings for any set of variables depend on criteria selected by the analyst (which vary according to the species of factor analysis used), and can be rather arbitrary.[4]

Factor analysis is not magic and it does not obviate the need for conceptual judgments by the analyst about what items to include. Many of the misunderstandings about factor analysis stem from the naive belief that all one has to do is to factor-analyze a large pool of variables to come up with the "proper" solution. Yet there is a more difficult problem with factor analysis, and this, as Carl Hensler puts it, is that in most factor analyses there is a discrepancy between the analytical and operational factors. All of the variables included in a given factor analysis have non-zero loadings on the factors. As a result all of the obtained factors are "contaminated" with variables which the analyst might prefer to leave out in the final solution. In creating a scale from a pool of fifteen items, the analyst may select only those ten with the highest loadings and leave the others out. But by dropping these five variables from the analysis the factors are changed since the variation contributed by the low-loading variables is not included. This may create serious difficulties for the ensuing empirical analysis.[5]

Key cluster analysis gets around this problem by simply reversing the order of factor analysis: rather than defining the factor(s) by the loadings, key cluster analysis enables the analyst to first define the factor as a "subset (cluster) of observed variables" and then to determine the loadings of these variables on the (defined) factor. Thus in addition to the factor loadings this procedure provides the analyst with an additional criterion for initially including the variable in the analysis. Called a variable's *similarity,* this criterion is based on the pattern of relationships between the variable X and all other variables in the analysis. A variable's similarity is a measure of the extent to which it is correlated in the same way with other variables in the cluster. What is important is the pattern of correlation. For example, take a simple three-variable cluster, and assume that X and Y are positively correlated but that X is negatively correlated with Z, while Y is positively correlated with Z. In this case X and Y would have a low similarity because the pattern of correlation with Z is not similar. On the other hand, if both were positively correlated with Z they would have a high similarity. The similarity statistic ranges from zero if the variable's profile (the patterns of correlation) is unrelated to the profiles of other variables in the cluster to 1.00 where the profile between the variable and the cluster is exactly the same.

The use of key cluster analysis gives the analyst two measures of the relationships among a set of variables: first, the degree to which the variables are highly related to the underlying factor; and second, the extent to which they are related in the same way. For the analyst using attitudinal scales this procedure has definite advantages. Even though factor analysis can be used to determine the correlations among a subset of variables and an underlying dimension, one still does not have any idea of whether the variables are in fact measuring the same attitude. A high factor loading does not necessarily mean that a variable is tapping the same underlying attitude—for example, aggressiveness—as the other variables. By using the similarity matrix *and* the factor loadings, one can develop more precise and ultimately more reliable measures of attitudes.

A description of the items used in each scale with the factor loadings and similarity scores is provided in table A.1. In addition a measure of the reliability of the scale is reported. This measure is an estimate of the proportion of the scale's variance which can be attributed to the underlying dimension; the residual is the amount of variance due to random measurement error. The scale scores were produced by adding the values of each variable in the cluster, adding a score of 50 to each scale, and normalizing the score for a mean of 50.0 and a standard deviation of 10.0.

TABLE A.1

I. Aggressiveness Scale	Reliability = .72	
Item	Loading	Similarity
In some neighborhoods, one must rigorously enforce all laws just to maintain order and prevent crimes.	.54	66
The police are justified in regarding a Negro and/or Mexican-American juvenile as a person who needs to be watched more than others.	.48	66
In some neighborhoods, physical combat skills and an aggressive bearing will be more useful to a patrolman on the beat than a courteous manner.	.47	56
A good patrolman is one who aggressively patrols his beat, stopping a number of cars, checking out people, running warrant checks on vehicles that look suspicious, and so forth.	.46	63
In order to prevent crimes and apprehend felons, the police are sometimes required to violate search and seizure laws and other procedural safeguards.	.45	67
In some neighborhoods, the prevention of crime requires that patrolmen stop people walking down the street, especially juveniles, and ask them where they are going and what they are doing.	.44	68
A person who verbally abuses a police officer when he has been stopped for a violation of the law, who calls him names and challenges his authority, should be arrested.	.44	63
A patrolman who makes an arrest or issues a citation because of a person's attitude is making a "bad" arrest.	−.42	58
It is important and right for an officer to take a person's attitude into account in deciding whether or not to enforce the law.	.40	61
Preservation of the peace requires that the police use their authority to order people to "move along" or "break it up" even though no law is being violated.	.40	69

II. Selectiveness of Law Enforcement Scale	Reliability = .55	
Item	Loading	Similarity
A patrolman should not make a lot of arrests for minor violations (such as drunks) or issue a lot of citations for minor traffic violations.	.61	61

A really effective patrolman is one who patrols for serious felony violations rather than stopping people for minor traffic violations and other misdemeanors.	.52	62
It's a waste of time and takes away from more important things to arrest someone for possession of two or three marijuana cigarettes.	.49	63

III. Perceived Limits on Discretion Scale	Reliability = .77	
Item	Loading	Similarity
In general, in this department there are very few supervisors who believe in letting patrolmen make their own decisions.	.63	91
A patrolman will usually get along better on the job with his supervisors if he doesn't go looking for situations requiring police attention, but handles such situations as they arise.	.62	90
The field supervisors act as if their only job is to enforce the rules and regulations of this department.	.61	86
In general, field supervisors in this department are more interested in enforcing petty rules about dress, hair length, and whether or not you wear your hat when you get out of the car or whether you are a few minutes late to work, than the sort of job patrolmen do.	.59	86
Patrolmen who are always out looking for situations requiring police attention are the ones who usually get into trouble with their supervisors.	.54	83
Patrolmen often fail to take necessary police action due to a feeling that supervisors will disapprove of their actions.	.49	91
The department allows patrolmen more than enough discretion in making arrests, issuing citations, or making tactical decisions.	−.48	91

IV. Perception of Supervisors' Behavior Scale	Reliability = .65	
Item	Loading	Similarity
How often do the field supervisors in this department drive by and observe you while you are on a call?	.69	51
How often do the field supervisors actually intervene in a call or situation which you are handling?	.69	51

V. Punitiveness of Supervision Scale	Reliability = .51	
Item	Loading	Similarity
Patrolmen are *frequently* found guilty of violating departmental rules and procedures and are consequently penalized severely.	.54	79
The department expects supervisors to deal with their patrolmen in a very strict manner.	.49	83
The main method used by supervisors to keep their men working properly is that of punishment for what they consider ineffective performance.	.47	82

Notes

Introduction

1. Egon Bittner, *The Functions of the Police in Modern Society* (Rockville, Maryland: National Institute of Mental Health, Center for Studies of Crime and Delinquency, 1972), p. 41.

2. Arthur Woods, *Policeman and Public* (New Haven: Yale University Press, 1919), p. 27.

3. This and the following example is taken from Sanford Kadish, "Legal Norm and Discretion in the Police and Sentencing Process," *Harvard Law Review* 75 (March 1962): 910 ff.

4. For arguments that race plays little role in convictions and sentencing decisions see James Eisenstein and Herbert Jacob, *Felony Justice: An Organizational Analysis of the Courts* (Boston: Little, Brown & Co., 1977), especially p. 284; and John Hagen, "Extra Legal Attributes and Criminal Sentencing: An Assessment of a Sociological Viewpoint," *Law and Society Review* 8 (1974): 557–83.

5. See Albert Reiss, Jr., *The Police and the Public* (New Haven: Yale University Press, 1971), pp. 102–4.

6. Jerome Skolnick, *Justice Without Trial: Law Enforcement in the Democratic Society,* 2nd ed. (New York: John Wiley & Sons, 1977), chap. 3.

7. John H. McNamara, "Uncertainties in Police Work: The Relevance of Police Recruits' Backgrounds and Training," in *The Police: Six Sociological Essays,* ed. David Bordua (New York: John Wiley & Sons, 1967), pp. 163–252; see especially pp. 168–77, 199–203.

8. For a recent account which also emphasizes the diversity among patrolmen see William Ker Muir, Jr., *Police: Streetcorner Politicians* (Chicago: University of Chicago Press, 1977).

9. James Q. Wilson, *Varieties of Police Behavior: The Management of Law and Order in Eight Communities* (New York: Atheneum, 1970).

10. I believe that some of the differences Wilson reports among the eight departments he studied might be explained as artifacts of the data. The principal difficulty is that arrest rates are not always comparable. For example, a comparison between arrests for drunkenness or disorderly conduct may be misleading since patrolmen in different departments may invoke those charges for a wide variety of behaviors. In addition, Wilson studies police administrators, not patrolmen, and much of his argument hangs on suppositions about the behavior of patrolmen, which require further investigation. The extent of my disagreement with Wilson, as well as my debt, will be apparent in the course of the analysis.

11. The standard treatments of police reform include James F. Richardson, *The New York Police: Colonial Times to 1901* (New York: Oxford University Press, 1970); Roger Lane, *Policing the City: Boston, 1882–1885* (Cambridge, Mass.: Harvard University Press, 1967); and more recently, Robert M. Fogelson, *Big-City Police* (Cambridge, Mass.: Harvard University Press, 1977).

12. Appointed by President Herbert Hoover in 1929 to investigate the enforcement of prohibition, the Wickersham Commission produced, among other reports, a detailed study of police brutality and illegal arrests, which was later popularized by Ernest Hopkins in his *Our Lawless Police* (New York: The Viking Press, 1931). For recent accounts of police misconduct see your local newspaper and Albert Reiss Jr., *The Police and the Public,* chap. 3. Some of the most serious recent instances of police

misconduct have involved blacks and other minorities, who consistently view the police more unfavorably than do other social groups. A comparison of blacks' and whites' evaluations of the police can be found in Herbert Jacob, "Black and White Perceptions of Justice in the City," *Law and Society Review* 6 (August 1971): 69–90; and Harlan Hahn, "Ghetto Assessments of Police Protection and Authority," *Law and Society Review* 6 (September 1971): 183–94.

13. For a vivid account of this debate see Roger Lane's discussion of the argument between Thomas Coffin Amory and Charles M. Ellis of Boston over whether to create a Metropolitan Boston police force, *Policing the City*, pp. 129–33.

14. For critical views of police professionalism and urban reform see Paul Jacob, *Prelude to Riot: A View of Urban American from the Bottom* (New York: Random House, 1968), chap. 2; Marilyn Gittell, "Community Control of Education," in *Urban Riots and Social Change*, ed. Robert H. Connery (New York: Vintage Books, 1968) pp. 63–75; and Theodore Lowi, "Machine Politics—Old and New," *The Public Interest*, no. 9 (Fall 1967), pp. 83–92.

15. For representative discussions see Alan A. Altshuler, *Community Control: The Black Demand for Participation in Large American Cities* (New York: Pegasus Books, 1970); Elinor Ostrom and Gordon Whitaker, "Does Local Community Control of Police Make a Difference? Some Preliminary Findings," *American Journal of Political Science* 17 (February 1973): 48–76.

16. See, for example, Wilson, *Varieties of Police Behavior*, pp. 285–93; and Reiss, *The Police and the Public*, chap. 4 and especially pp. 207–12.

17. James Q. Wilson, "Dilemmas of Police Administration," *Public Administration Review* 28 (September/October 1968): 407–17.

18. For analysis of some of these developments see Lawrence W. Sherman, et al., *Team Policing: Seven Case Studies* (Washington, D.C.: The Police Foundation, 1973).

19. For a spirited argument in favor of this strategy see Eugene Webb, et al., *Unobtrusive Measures: Nonreactive Research in the Social Sciences* (Chicago: Rand McNally & Co., 1966), especially chap. 1.

Chapter 1

1. David Easton, *A Framework for Political Analysis* (Englewood Cliffs, N.J.: Prentice-Hall, 1965), p. 50.

2. Kenneth Culp Davis, *Discretionary Justice: A Preliminary Inquiry* (Urbana: University of Illinois Press, 1971), p. 3.

3. Davis, *Discretionary Justice*, p. 4.

4. Michael Lipsky, *Street-Level Bureaucracy: Dilemmas of the Individual in Public Services* (New York: Russell Sage Foundation, 1980), pp. 13–25, 81–83.

5. See, for example, William A. Niskanen, Jr., *Bureaucracy and Representative Government* (Chicago: Aldine, 1971), especially pp. 36–52; and Graham T. Allison and Morton H. Halperin, "Bureaucratic Politics: A Paradigm and Some Policy Implications," *World Politics* 24 (1972): 40–79.

6. See, for example, Bryan D. Jones et al., "Service Delivery Rules and the Distribution of Local Government Services: Three Detroit Bureaucracies," *Journal of Politics* 40 (May 1978): 332–68; and Frank Levy, Arnold J. Meltsner, and Aaron Wildavksy, *Urban Outcomes: Schools, Streets, and Libraries* (Berkeley: University of California Press, 1974).

7. Donald Schon, "The Blindness System," *The Public Interest* no. 19 (Winter 1970), pp. 25–32.

8. This conceptual scheme is partly drawn from Sir Geoffrey Vickers, *The Art of Judgment: A Study of Policy Making* (New York: Basic Books, Inc., 1965), especially chaps. 1 through 4.

9. James Q. Wilson, "The Police and the Delinquent in Two Cities," in *City Politics and Public Policy*, ed. James Q. Wilson (New York: John Wiley & Sons, 1968), pp. 173–96.

10. The concept of organizational domain is drawn from James D. Thompson, *Organizations in Action* (New York: McGraw-Hill, 1967), pp. 26–27.

11. In addition to Vickers, *The Art of Judgment,* see John Steinbrunner, *The Cybernetic Theory of Decision* (Princeton, N.J.: Princeton University Press, 1974) for a detailed discussion of the place of belief systems in structuring decision making.

12. The term *operational style* is based on Alexander George's notion of operational code; see his "The 'Operational Code': A Neglected Approach to the Study of Political Leaders and Decision Making," *International Studies Quarterly* 13 (1969): 190–222.

13. For a discussion of the structural characteristics of belief systems and the relevant evidence, see Steinbrunner, *The Cybernetic Theory of Decision,* pp. 91–103.

14. On the relationship between personality and operational style see George, "The 'Operational Code': A Neglected Approach," pp. 195–6.

15. This discussion draws upon J.D. Thompson's analysis of task environments; see *Organizations in Action,* pp. 27–29.

16. Michael Ban, "Local Compliance with Mapp v. Ohio: The Power of the Supreme Court, A Case Study" (Ph.D. dissertation, Harvard University, 1972).

17. Thompson, *Organizations in Action,* pp. 10–13, 66–73, 125–7.

18. See James G. March and Herbert Simon, *Organizations* (New York: John Wiley & Sons, 1958), chap. 6; Daniel Katz and Robert L. Kahn, *The Social Psychology of Organizations* (New York: John Wiley & Sons, 1966), chap. 7; and Charles Perrow, *Complex Organizations: A Critical Essay* (Glenview, Ill.: Scott, Foresman & Co., 1978), chap. 4.

19. This is the theme of much of the literature on municipal reform. For representative discussions see Robert Wiebe, *The Search for Order: 1877–1920* (New York: Hill and Wang, 1967); and Robert L. Lineberry and Edmund P. Fowler, "Reformism and Public Policies in American Cities," *American Political Science Review* 61 (September 1967): 701–16.

20. On the concept of organizational goals see Thompson, *Organizations in Action,* pp. 25–32, 132–43; Richard M. Cyert and James G. March, *A Behavioral Theory of the Firm* (Englewood Cliffs, N.J.: Prentice-Hall, 1964), pp. 26–43. For a more detailed discussion of the conflict over the goals of street-level bureaucracies see Michael Lipsky, *Street-Level Bureaucracy,* pp. 4–12.

21. These comments are partly based on Charles Perrow, "A Framework for the Comparative Analysis of Organization," *American Sociological Review* 32 (April 1967): 194–208; and James Q. Wilson, "Dilemmas of Police Administration," *Public Administration Review* 28 (September/October 1968): 407–17.

Chapter 2

1. Michael Banton, *The Policeman in the Community* (New York: Basic Books, Inc., 1964), p. 154; see also pp. 7–8, 87, and 150.

2. Allan Silver, "The Demand for Order in Civil Society: A Review of Some Themes in the History of Urban Crime, Police and Riot," in *The Police: Six Sociological Essays,* ed. David Bordua (New York: John Wiley & Sons, 1967), pp. 1–7, passim.

3. William F. Whyte first called attention to this dilemma; see *Street Corner Society* (Chicago: University of Chicago Press, 1955), p. 136.

4. Wilbur R. Miller, "Police Authority in London and New York City, 1830–1870," *Journal of Social History* 8 (1975): 84–85. The best overall account of this transition is Robert Fogelson, *Big-City Police* (Cambridge, Mass.: Harvard University Press, 1977).

5. Mark H. Haller, "Historical Roots of Police Behavior: Chicago 1890–1925," *Law and Society Review* 10 (Winter 1976): 303–24, provides a vivid description of how the Chicago police became increasingly oriented toward legal norms. But the evidence that professional police departments place greater emphasis on formal legal norms is by no means unequivocal. Michael Ban has found that a reform department (Cincinnati) was less likely to comply with the search and seizure ruling of the Supreme Court

in Mapp v. Ohio than a non-reform department (Boston). See "Local Compliance with Mapp v. Ohio" (Ph.D. dissertation, Harvard University, 1972), chaps. 3 and 4.

6. See Herman Goldstein, "Police Discretion: The Ideal Versus the Real," *Public Administration Review* 23 (September/October 1963): 143–45.

7. This discussion of professionalism is based upon Everett C. Hughes, "Professions," in *The Professions in America*, ed. Kenneth S. Lynn (Boston: Beacon Press, 1965), pp. 1–14; Peter Blau and W. Richard Scott, *Formal Organizations* (San Francisco: Chandler Publications, 1962), pp. 60–63; Ernest Greenwood, "Attributes of a Profession," *Social Work* 2 (July 1957): 44–45; and William J. Goode, "Community Within a Community: The Professions," *American Sociological Review* 22 (1957): 194–200.

8. Samuel Huntington, *The Soldier and the State* (Cambridge, Mass.: Harvard University Press, 1957), p. 9.

9. Amos Perlmutter, *The Military and Politics in Modern Times* (New Haven: Yale University Press, 1977), p. 4.

10. Robert Wiebe, *The Search for Order*, pp. 145–95; see also Samuel P. Hays, "The Politics of Reform in Municipal Government in the Progressive Era," *Pacific Northwest Quarterly* 55 (October 1964): 157–69.

11. Samuel Haber, *Efficiency and Uplift: Scientific Management in the Progressive Era* (Chicago: University of Chicago Press, 1964), pp. 56 ff.

12. Wiebe, *The Search for Order*, pp. 160–1; for a contemporary statement of this view see Herbert Kaufman, *Administrative Feedback: Monitoring Subordinates' Behavior* (Washington, D.C.: The Brookings Institution, 1973), p. 4.

13. Robert Fogelson distinguishes between two generations of reformers—the Progressives, drawn largely from civic and business groups; and law enforcement officials who were actually responsible for professionalizing the police from the 1930s on—and contends each adopted a different model of reform. The Progressive reformers based their recommendations on a "military analogy" while the law enforcement officials adopted a "professional model." This distinction obscures the continuities between the two approaches to reform, for the diagnosis of the ills of the police and the proffered reforms of both groups are remarkably similar. Each group may have placed a different emphasis on certain aspects of reform, but on the main outlines there was no disagreement, and, in fact, Fogelson suggests as much in his account of the legacy of the first generation of reformers. See *Big-City Police*, chaps. 2 and 6, and pp. 136–37. In my view, it is August Vollmer who provides the continuity between the first and second generation of reformers. The core of his approach is contained in his book, *The Police in Modern Society* (Berkeley: University of California Press, 1936). An illuminating account of Vollmer's role from the turn of the century to the 1930s is Gene E. Carte, and Elaine H. Carte, *Police Reform in the United States: The Era of August Vollmer, 1905–1932* (Berkeley: University of California Press, 1975). For more recent statements on police professionalism, see Bruce Smith, *Police Systems in the United States*, 2nd ed. rev. (New York: Harper & Row, 1960); O. W. Wilson, *Police Administration*, 3rd ed. (New York: McGraw-Hill, 1972); "Task Force Report: The Police," in *The President's Commission on Law Enforcement and Administration of Justice* (Washington, D.C.: U.S. Government Printing Office, 1967). Finally, see Gene Carte, "Technology Versus Personnel: Notes on the History of Police Professional Reform," *Journal of Police Science and Administration* 4 (September 1976): 285–97 for an account of the continuities between Vollmer and contemporary reformers.

14. Vollmer, *The Police in Modern Society*, p. 235. According to Nathan Douthit the impetus for police reform really came during an upsurge in crime during the 1920s and 1930s, and this was partly responsible for the emphasis on crime control. See his "Police Professionalism and the War Against Crime in the United States, 1920s–30s," in *Police Forces in History*, ed. George L. Mosse (Beverly Hills: Sage Publications, 1975), pp. 317–33.

15. Vollmer, *The Police in Modern Society*, pp. 146–47.

16. Carte, *Police Reform in the United States*, p. 84.

17. Banton, *The Policeman in the Community*, pp. 2–8.

18. Fogelson, *Big-City Police*, pp. 35–39.

19. Banton, *The Policeman in the Community*, p. 150.

20. Ira Katznelson, "The Crisis of the Capitalist City: Urban Politics and Social

Notes

Control," in *Theoretical Perspectives on Urban Politics,* ed. Willis D. Hawley and Michael Lipsky (Englewood Cliffs, N.J.: Prentice-Hall, 1976), pp. 218–26.

21. James Q. Wilson, "The Police and Their Problems: A Theory," *Public Policy* 12 (1963): 189–216.

22. Jerome Skolnick, *Justice Without Trial: Law Enforcement in the Democratic Society,* 2nd ed. (New York: John Wiley & Sons, 1977); Albert Reiss Jr., *The Police and the Public* (New Haven: Yale University Press, 1971); and Jonathan Rubinstein, *City Police* (New York: Farrar, Strauss & Giroux, 1973) all provide convincing evidence of the limits to professionalization.

23. William Westley, *Violence and the Police: A Sociological Study of Law, Custom, and Morality* (Cambridge, Mass.: The M.I.T. Press, 1970), chap. 4.

24. Ibid., p. 198.

25. Ibid., pp. xiv–xviii; Westley was the first to suggest that this would be one of the most significant consequences of police professionalism.

Chapter 3

1. For an account of the reform of the Los Angeles Police Department and Parker's role see Joseph G. Wood, "The Progressives and the Police in Los Angeles" (Ph.D. dissertation, University of California, Los Angeles, 1973).

2. Parker's general views on police work and professionalism can be found in William H. Parker, "The Police Challenge in Our Great Cities," *The Annals* 291 (January 1954): 5–13; O. W. Wilson, ed., *Parker on Police* (Charles C. Thomas Publishers, 1957); and Donald MacDonald, *The Police: An Interview with William H. Parker, Chief of Police of Los Angeles* (Santa Barbara: Center for the Study of Democratic Institutions, 1962). For an assessment of Parker's views see J. A. Gazell, "William H. Parker, Police Professionalization and the Public: An Assessment," *Journal of Police Science and Administration* 4 (1976): 28–37.

3. O. W. Wilson, *Parker on Police,* pp. 20–22; 28–29; the quote is from p. 21.

4. Jack McCurdy, "Campus Raids Opposed," *Los Angeles Times,* 22 June 1975, Part II.

5. Bill Hazlett, "Davis Hits Arena Manager as 'Crybaby' Over Festival," *Los Angeles Times,* 30 April 1975, Part II.

6. Jerry Belcher and David Rosenzweig, "Politics and the Police Department," in *The LAPD: How Good is It?* a special report in *The Los Angeles Times,* 18 December 1977, Section VIII, p. 13.

7. On the 1977 shooting see "Los Angeles County District Attorney to Probe Slaying of Nude Man," *Los Angeles Times,* 13 August 1977, Section I, p. 1; and Michael A. Levett and Dale Fetherling, "Police Bullets and Controversy," in *The LAPD: How Good is It?* pp. 18–19. On the more recent shooting and its aftermath see Carey McWilliams, "Second Thoughts," *The Nation,* 17 November 1979, p. 487; and *The Report of the Board of Police Commissioners Concerning the Shooting of Eulia Love and the Use of Deadly Force,* "Part I—The Shooting of Eulia Love," (Los Angeles Police Dept., October 1979).

8. Steven Erie, "The Los Angeles Police Department Budgetary Process: Politics, Power and the Public Interest," (Institute on Law and Urban Studies, 1972), p. 27. My account of the budgetary process draws on this essay and one other by Erie: "Trends in the Provision of Public Services: Los Angeles Police Expenditures and Manpower Allocations 1930–70," (Institute on Law and Urban Studies, 1972). See also Belcher and Rozenzweig, "Politics and the Police Department," pp. 13–14.

9. *Los Angeles Times,* 4 June 1971, Part II. In this instance, however, Davis's ploy did not work. See Erwin Baker, "Council Slashes Police Funds By $3.4 Million," *Los Angeles Times,* 9 June, 1971, Part II.

10. For a discussion of these and other tactics see "How 'Big Blue Machine' Deals with Pressure," in *The LAPD: How Good is It?* p. 15.

11. Bill Hazlett, "Police Rock Concerts: A Question of Priorities," *Los Angeles Times,* 12 May 1975, Section II, p. 6.

12. Interview with Jay Stroh, Chief of Police, Inglewood, California, 11 August 1975.

13. The term "communal" is drawn from James Q. Wilson, *Varieties of Police Behavior: The Management of Law and Order in Eight Communities* (New York: Atheneum, 1970), pp. 268–87.

14. In 1973 and 1974, the F.B.I.'s crime statistics revealed substantial increases in Part I crimes (homocide, rape, robbery, aggravated assault, burglary, grand theft, auto theft) in suburban areas. During the first nine months of 1974 the crime rate for Part I crimes was up 21 percent in the suburbs compared to 11 percent in the cities over 250,000 population. See the *Los Angeles Times*, 27 December 1974, p. 1. I suspect but have no hard evidence that many of the individuals arrested for felonies in Inglewood are not residents.

15. A caveat is in order: it is possible that the high robbery rate in Inglewood is due to differences between Inglewood and the LAPD in the criteria used to classify an offense such as robbery. The most ambiguous situation occurs with street robberies and purse snatches. A robbery is legally defined as a theft "accomplished by means of force or fear." I suspect, but do not know, that many purse snatches are classified as armed robbery in Inglewood but not so classified in the LAPD. However, there is no way of knowing how much this would reduce Inglewood's robbery rate. Differences in classification between Redondo Beach and the LAPD are not as important since the chief of police of Redondo Beach at the time of the study was an ex-LAPD captain. Finally, I would remind the reader that I am dealing with reported crimes only. For two astute discussions of the biases of crime rates see Donald J. Black, "The Production of Crime Rates," *American Sociological Review* 25 (August 1970): 733–45; and James E. Price, "A Test of the Accuracy of Crime Statistics," *Social Problems* 14 (Fall, 1966): 214–21.

16. Two kinds of criteria were relevant in selecting these communities: access to them and the extent to which they permitted a broad comparison of different types. These criteria can conflict. There were divisions in the LAPD that would have made better comparisons with the small departments (for example, Wilshire), but permission to conduct the study in the LAPD was partly contingent on my acquiescence to an administrative decision designed to minimize internal problems (and perhaps to preclude my studying some divisions). This decision required that I work with the Deputy Chief in charge of the Central Area, one of four administrative bureaus of the LAPD. Consequently, I had to choose two divisions from the Central Area.

Chapter 4

1. Some of these points are drawn from Egon Bittner, *The Functions of the Police in Modern Society*, (Rockville, Maryland: National Institute of Mental Health, Center for Studies of Crime and Delinquency, 1972), p. 41.

2. Orlando W. Wilson, *Police Administration*, 2nd ed. (New York: McGraw-Hill, 1963), pp. 39–40.

3. Albert Reiss, Jr. and David Bordua note that "given the lack of guidelines either from the public as client or from a specific victim or complainant as client, the police can become in effect their own clients." See "Environment and Organization: A Perspective on the Police," in *The Police: Six Sociological Essays*, ed. David Bordua (New York: John Wiley & Sons, 1967), p. 30.

4. David H. Bayley and Harold Mendelsohn, *Minorities and the Police* (New York: The Free Press, 1968), pp. 89–99; and Jerome Skolnick, *Justice Without Trial: Law Enforcement in the Democratic Society*, 2nd ed. (New York: John Wiley & Sons, 1977), chap. 3.

5. The difficulties patrolmen have in obtaining compliance is the theme of William Ker Muir, Jr.'s remarkable book, *Police: Streetcorner Politicians* (Chicago: University of Chicago Press, 1977).

6. The police are hardly unique in this respect. One observes a similar bond of solidarity among combat units during time of war and among coal miners. See Roger W. Little, "Buddy Relations and Combat Performance," in *The New Military*, ed.

Notes

Morris Janowitz (New York: W. W. Norton & Co., 1969), pp. 195–223; and Alvin Gouldner, *Patterns of Industrial Bureaucracy* (New York: The Free Press, 1954), pp. 105–56.

7. Hans Spier, "Honor and Social Structure," in *Social Order and the Risks of War* (Cambridge, Mass.: The M.I.T. Press, 1969), p. 37.

8. In a detailed study of the socialization of recruits in a police department, John Van Maanen concluded that the most important criterion used by experienced policemen in judging a rookie was the rookie's willingness to put himself in a risky position in order to back up his fellow officers. See "Pledging the Police: A Study of Selected Aspects of Recruit Socialization in a Large, Urban Police Department," (Ph.D. dissertation, University of California, Irvine, 1972), p. 272.

9. The statement they were asked to comment on was worded as follows: "When it comes to a problem related to work the only persons a patrolman can trust and depend on are his fellow patrolmen." Again there are no important differences between the three departments.

10. See Neal Milner, "Supreme Court Effectiveness and the Police Organization," *Law and Contemporary Problems* 36 (Autumn 1971): 467–87; and James R. Hudson, "Police Review Boards and Police Accountability," *Law and Contemporary Problems* 36 (Autumn 1971): 515–38.

11. For an offbeat analysis which, in my opinion, explains much of the attraction of twentieth-century police work, both to its practitioners and as a phenomenon of the mass media, see Hans Spier, "Risk, Security and Modern Hero Worship," in his *Social Order and the Risks of War*, pp. 112–28.

12. Joseph Wambaugh, *The Onion Field* (New York: Delacorte Press, 1973), pp. 3–4.

13. My own data on the prior occupations of patrolmen in these three departments show that 35 percent held jobs that could be classified as professional or managerial prior to becoming police officers.

14. The importance of crime fighting and the relative aggressiveness of patrolmen is discussed at length in chapter 6. I might note, though, that this contention is supported by other studies. See John Van Maanen, "Pledging the Police," pp. 191–95; and Jesse Rubin, "Police Identity and Police Role," in *The Police and the Community*, ed. Robert F. Steadman (Baltimore: The Johns Hopkins University Press, 1972), pp. 12–50.

15. While patrolmen do have freedom to exercise their discretion as they see fit, there is still strong pressure to conform to a wide range of political and social beliefs. It is important in this regard not to overstate the degree of freedom that patrolmen have. A man who challenged important beliefs would be suspect; but when it comes to deciding whether to stop someone on the street, or how to handle a family dispute, a patrolman has wide latitude. For a discussion of the homogeneity of political beliefs among policemen, see Bayley and Mendelsohn, *Minorities and the Police*, pp. 18–30.

16. Jonathan Rubinstein, *City Police* (New York: Farrar, Strauss & Giroux, 1973), chap. 1.

17. Arthur Neiderhoffer, *Behind the Shield* (Garden City, N.Y.: Anchor Books, 1969), pp. 51–57; see also Richard N. Harris, *The Police Academy: An Inside View* (New York: John Wiley & Sons, 1973), chaps. 4 and 5.

18. For a fascinating discussion of this norm and some of the implications for police administration see Wambaugh, *The Onion Field*, pp. 223–33. The question raised by Wambaugh is whether police administrators have the right to ask policemen to resist at all costs when they are cornered by gunmen as Karl Hettinger and Ian Campbell, the policemen of Wambaugh's book, are cornered. Wambaugh, and most policemen, believe that decisions like this one should be made by the officer at the scene and no one else, and if an officer chooses to put down his weapon, so be it.

19. Michael Crozier, *The Bureaucratic Phenomenon* (Chicago: University of Chicago Press, 1964), pp. 145–74.

20. Dale Fetherling and Michael A. Levett report that in 1976 the internal affairs division in the LAPD sustained 87 percent of complaints originating in the department compared to 17 percent of citizen complaints; see "The Paradox of Policemen Policing Policemen," in *The LAPD: How Good is It?*, *Los Angeles Times*, 18 December 1977, p. 9. Linda Wallen in a detailed study of internal affairs found this to be a consistent pattern over a twenty-year period. During this time period, only 6 percent

of complaints for excessive force were sustained. See her "Professional and Bureau-cratic Processes of Organizational Control: Internal Discipline in the Los Angeles Police Department" (Ph.D. dissertation, University of California, Los Angeles, 1976) chap. 4. For comparable findings in an Eastern department, see James R. Hudson, "Organizational Aspects of Internal and External Review of the Police," *Journal of Criminal Law, Criminology, and Police Science* 63, no. 3 (1972): 427–33.

21. Learning to cope with a punitive bureaucracy is one of the central experiences for a rookie patrolman. John Van Maanen found there was a steady decrease in the motivation to act (in the belief that action will lead to various outcomes) from the time rookie patrolmen were in the police academy to the end of their first year on the street. The most pervasive feeling among the patrolmen Van Maanen studied was frustration, and while much of it was directed at the courts and the public, a great deal was caused by the practices of supervisors and administrators. See John Van Maanen, "Police Socialization: A Longitudinal Examination of Job Attitudes in an Urban Police Department," *Administrative Science Quarterly* 20 (1975): 207–28.

Chapter 5

1. James Q. Wilson, *Varieties of Police Behavior: The Management of Law and Order in Eight Communities* (New York: Atheneum, 1970), pp. 83–139.

2. There is evidence to support the contention that an increase in organizational size makes internal control more problematic. John Child, "Predicting and Understanding Organization Structure," *Administrative Science Quarterly* 18 (June 1973): 168–85, shows that increased size is associated with greater decentralization. See also Gordon Tullock, *The Politics of Bureaucracy* (Washington D.C.: The Public Affairs Press, 1965). But for a different view see Herbert Kaufman, *Administrative Feedback: Monitoring Subordinates' Behavior* (Washington, D.C.: The Brookings Institution, 1973).

3. For a similar argument that administrators in small police departments will have greater control, see Elinor Ostrom and Gordon Whitaker, "Does Local Community Control of the Police Make A Difference? Some Preliminary Findings," *American Journal of Political Science* 17 (February 1973): 48–76, especially p. 50.

4. Donald McDonald, *The Police: An Interview with William H. Parker, Chief of Police of Los Angeles* (Santa Barbara: Center for the Study of Democratic Institutions, 1962), p. 10.

5. Interview with Jay Stroh, Chief of Police, Inglewood, California, 11 August 1975.

6. For this analysis I have used the control graph originally developed by Arnold Tannenbaum. A full discussion of the method and its application can be found in Arnold S. Tannenbaum, *Control in Organizations* (New York: McGraw-Hill, 1968).

7. The "lawnmower caper" mentioned in the quote refers to an investigation of two patrolmen who were accused of receiving stolen property.

8. I asked field supervisors what they thought were the most important aspects of their job as a supervisor. Responses indicated that 67 percent classified themselves as "buffers." Twenty-two percent responded like "bureaucrats," and 11 percent like "colleagues." There were no differences between the departments.

9. Jonathan Rubinstein, *City Police* (New York: Farrar, Strauss & Giroux, 1973), p. 43.

10. An anecdote is not especially conclusive evidence for the occurrence of this phenomenon. I attempted to substantiate this practice with other patrolmen, but the results were inconclusive. What persuades me that the anecdote is not entirely far-fetched is that Jonathan Rubinstein reports a similar phenomenon; see J. Rubinstein, *City Police*, p. 450.

11. John McNamara, "Uncertainties in Police Work: The Relevance of Police Recruits' Backgrounds and Training," in *The Police: Six Sociological Essays*, ed. David Bordua, (New York: John Wiley & Sons, 1967), p. 179.

12. The dilemmas confronting police supervisors are, of course, not unique. Compare Roger Little's description of platoon leaders during wartime: "The more he participated in their activities, the more he tended to share the sentiments of the men

he commanded, and his willingness to use the sanctions available to him diminished correspondingly." The breakdown in hierarchical controls, Little observed, increased as the risk and stress on the platoon increased, but controls were reasserted when the platoon was withdrawn from combat and held in reserve. See "Buddy Relations and Combat Performance," in *The New Military,* ed. Morris Janowitz (New York: W. W. Norton & Co., 1969), pp. 208, 213. Similar pressures confront supervisors in mines; see Alvin Gouldner, *Patterns of Industrial Bureaucracy,* (New York: The Free Press, 1954), pp. 137–156.

13. Evidence presented in chapters 6 and 7 show that the field supervisors in these three departments are quite willing to tolerate abuses of due process, but are very concerned about discourtesy, rudeness, and other violations of "professional" conduct.

14. Strictly speaking one cannot compare indexes with an unequal number of items. Thus, the most important comparison in table 5.3 is between the Instrumental and Crime and Law Enforcement indexes. This restriction does not apply, however, to comparisons between departments on one index.

15. Joseph Wambaugh, *The Onion Field* (New York: Delacorte Press, 1973), p. 223.

16. There is one instance, however, where a patrolman's choices on the street have implications for advancement in the department. This is when a patrolman desires to advance to a specialized unit such as narcotics or traffic control. Here promotions often depend on demonstrated competence in the specific area, for example, in developing narcotics informants. The implications of this are discussed in connection with crime fighting in chapter 6.

17. The scale was developed with key cluster analysis, a variant of factor analysis. The two questions in the scale, which are Likert questions with values from 1 to 7, were summed; 50 was added to each individual's score, and the scores were normalized with a mean of 50 and a standard deviation of 10. See Appendix for a full discussion of the method used.

18. The question was worded as follows: "How often do the field supervisors and watch commanders in this department reprimand patrolmen for violations of rules?" The possible responses were "hardly," "not often," "sometimes," "often," or "very often." The difference between the LAPD and the two small departments is statistically significant at $P \leq .05$.

19. See Appendix for a full discussion of the method used to construct this scale.

20. I suspect that the spread of police unions since 1945, and particularly since the late 1960s, is partly a reaction to the triumph of police professionalism during this period. It is becoming increasingly clear that police unions have served in some instances to limit the impact of departmental controls, and especially the power of divisions of internal affairs. The relationship between police unions and police professionalism is a topic that deserves more detailed consideration than it so far has received. For general discussions of police unions that bear on this topic see Robert Fogelson, *Big-City Police* (Cambridge, Mass.: Harvard University Press, 1977), pp. 193–218; P. Feuille and H. A. Juris, "Police Professionalization and Police Unions," *Sociology of Work and Occupations* 3 (1976): 88–113; and Richard C. Larson, ed., *Police Accountability: Performance Measures and Unionism* (Lexington, Mass: D. C. Heath & Co., 1978).

21. Linda Wallen, in a study of the internal affairs division in the LAPD, found that after 1969 the percentage of citizen complaints for excessive force which were sustained increased from 5 to 11 percent. See Linda Wallen, "Professional and Bureaucratic Processes of Organizational Control: Internal Discipline in the Los Angeles Police Department," (Ph.D. dissertation, University of California, Los Angeles, 1976), chap. 3.

22. In a study of urban and rural police departments in England, Maureen Cain found differences in the system of authority and administrative control similar to those I have found between the LAPD and the small departments. Noting the greater importance of informal as opposed to formal assessment of a patrolman's performance in small rural departments, Cain observes: "A single mistake could ruin a man's chances [for promotion] for life. Thus there was a strong dependence on senior officers and, because the sanctions were so great, a considerable anxiety about taking risks." Things were much different in the large urban department. See Maureen Cain, "On

the Beat: Interactions and Relations in Rural and Urban Police Forces," in *Images of Deviance,* ed. Stanley Cohen (Middlesex, England: Penguin Books, 1971), pp. 62–97, especially pp. 85–86.

23. On the normative aspects of authority systems see Jay Jackson, "The Normative Regulation of Authoritative Behavior," in *The Making of Decisions,* ed. W. J. Gore and J. W. Dyson (New York: The Free Press, 1964), pp. 213–41.

Chapter 6

1. As James Q. Wilson states: "The patrolman's role is defined more by his responsibility for maintaining order than by his responsibility for enforcing the law"; *Varieties of Police Behavior: The Management of Law and Order in Eight Communities* (New York: Atheneum, 1970), pp. 16–19, and chap. 2, passim.

2. O. W. Wilson, ed., *Parker on Police* (Charles C. Thomas Publishers, 1957), pp. 101–2.

3. Lawrence P. Tiffany, Donald M. McIntyre, and Daniel L. Rotenberg, *Detection of Crime: Stopping and Questioning, Search and Seizure, Encouragement and Entrapment* (Boston: Little, Brown & Co., 1967) provides a lucid discussion of the legal issues; see pp. 6 and 41 for a discussion of probable cause.

4. For some evidence on the displacement effects of aggressive patrol see S. James Press, *Some Effects of an Increase in Police Manpower in the 20th Precinct of New York City* (New York: The New York City Rand Institute, 1971).

5. Cf., Albert Reiss, Jr., *The Police and the Public* (New Haven: Yale University Press, 1971), especially chap. 2. In addition to the greater involvement by patrolmen in crime-related incidents, the number of actions initiated by the police to control crime is much higher—43 percent compared to 20 percent—than in Reiss's study of the Chicago, Washington D.C., and Boston police departments.

6. The contemporary wisdom holds that only a very small portion of a patrolman's time is taken up with crime-related activities—most studies estimate 20 percent or less. See, for example, John A. Webster, "Police Task and Time Study," *The Journal of Criminal Law, Criminology, and Police Science* 61 (1970): 94–100. One could argue that these studies cast considerable doubt on my contention that patrolmen face a conflict in managing calls and crime fighting responsibilities. My contention is that the salience of this conflict depends on a patrolman's interpretation of his role. Even so, the objection is not convincing. The difficulty with studies such as Webster's is that they are based upon dispatches and do not take account of actions initiated by the police. Thus they underestimate the actual amount of crime-related activity undertaken by patrolmen. For a critique of time studies and an approach similar to the one used here see John C. Meyer, Jr. and Winthrop E. Taylor, "Analyzing the Nature of Police Involvements: A Research Note Concerning the Effects of Forms of Police Mobilization," *Journal of Criminal Justice* 3 (1975): 141–46.

7. David Petersen also observed an informal pattern of specialization among patrolmen in a Southern police department; see "Police Disposition of the Petty Offender," *Sociology and Social Research* (April 1972), pp. 320–30.

8. So far as I know there are no studies which have taken a close look at this question or even the broader issue of discretion in detaining and then releasing suspects. For an analysis of the relevant legal issues, see Edward L. Barrett, "Police Practices and the Law—From Arrest to Release or Charge," *California Law Review* 50 (March 1962): 11–55.

9. At a large party involving perhaps 150 to 200 people, the field sergeants in one department did take command and decided how to proceed. This, however, was the only instance where I observed a field supervisor pulling rank and taking charge.

10. Cf., Lawrence P. Tiffany et al., *Detection of Crime,* pp. 30–31. Tiffany discusses some of the legal problems with the use of the vehicle code as a source of probable cause. See also fn. 16 below.

11. The aggressiveness scale includes all questions in table 6.3 except for statement b and three statements dealing with the attitude test. See the Appendix for a description of all the items in the scale.

Notes

12. David Matza's comment is taken from Carl Werthman and Irving Piliavin, "Gang Members and the Police," in *The Police: Six Sociological Essays*, ed. David Bordua (New York: John Wiley & Sons, 1967), p. 75.

13. This of course is the nub of a long-standing controversy between the police and members of minority communities. See Werthman and Piliavin, "Gang Members and the Police," and Armando Morales, *Ando Sangrando (I Am Bleeding)* (La Puente, Calif: Perspectiva Publications, 1972) for discussions of the point of view of blacks and Mexican-Americans.

14. See Morris A. Forslund, "A Comparison of Negro and White Crime Rates," *Journal of Criminal Law, Criminology and Police Science* 61 (June 1970): 214–17; and T. N. Ferdinand and E. G. Luchterhand, "Inner-City Youth, The Police, The Juvenile Court and Justice," *Social Problems* (1969): 510–22. For an argument that the higher arrest rates for blacks are due to social class rather than race see Edward Green, "Race, Social Status, and Criminal Arrest," *American Sociological Review* 35 (June 1970): 476–90. For a dissenting view which argues that race is the crucial factor, see Bruce C. Johnson, "Taking Care of Labor: The Police in American Politics," *Theory and Society* (Spring 1976), pp. 89–117.

15. See also in this regard, William Chambliss, ed., *Crime and the Legal Process* (New York: McGraw-Hill, 1969), p. 101; and Egon Bittner, *The Functions of The Police in Modern Society* (Rockville, Maryland: National Institute of Mental Health, Center for Studies of Crime and Delinquency, 1972), p. 10, especially footnote 13. For a perceptive discussion of how such practices are rooted in the working conditions of all street-level bureaucrats, not just the police, see Michael Lipsky, *Street-level Bureaucracy: Dilemmas of the Individual in Public Services* (New York: Russell Sage Foundation, 1980), pp. 105–116.

16. After encountering a man who had committed a traffic violation, but had no identification, two patrolmen simply gave him a citation. When asked why they did not make an arrest on sec. 40302a of the Vehicle Code, they replied that it was used sparingly since abuse might lead to its being declared unconstitutional as the vagrancy statutes in California have been.

17. George L. Kelling et al., *The Kansas City Preventative Patrol Experiment: A Summary Report* (Washington, D.C.: The Police Foundation, 1974). A good summary of recent studies on the effectiveness and consequences of aggressive patrol can be found in George L. Kelling and David Fogel, "Police Patrol—Some Future Directions," in *The Future of Policing*, ed. Alvin W. Cohn (Beverly Hills: Sage Publications, 1978), pp. 151–82.

Chapter 7

1. For a lucid discussion of the "in-presence requirement" and some of its ambiguities see Wayne LaFave, *Arrest: The Decision to Take A Suspect into Custody* (Boston: Little, Brown and Co., 1965) pp. 231–44.

2. A decision not to enforce the law is sometimes based on a consideration of the evidence at hand and thus strict legal considerations. I believe that in the case of minor violations few decisions not to enforce the law are made for these reasons. Most patrolmen think, with some justification, that they do not stop people who have not committed minor violations. The difficulty of proving an offense may be considered by a patrolman, but it is not often decisive. More commonly, the lack of evidence or the anticipated action of the prosecutor or courts may be used as a pretext to cover other reasons for nonenforcement. This, as we shall see, is true of disturbances. Finally, in the incidents evaluated here the question of evidence is not in contention.

3. One other factor influences decisions not to enforce the law: a patrolman's subjective assessment of either a suspect's or a victim's personal characteristics or background. This is of greater import in disturbances and will be considered in the discussion of them. For another discussion of nonenforcement, albeit from a legal point of view, see Wayne LaFave, *Arrest*, pp. 61–164.

4. An instance of this occured during the LAPD's 1973 dragnet on prostitution. An

off-duty LAPD Captain was arrested for soliciting an undercover policewoman and drunk driving. The officers initially attempted to cover for him but they were unsuccessful, and all were disciplined by the department. See "Officer Arrested on Vice Charge Fined," *Los Angeles Times,* 4 October 1973.

5. LaFave, *Arrest,* pp. 87–89.

6. For further evidence and discussion of this phenomenon see Albert Reiss, Jr., *The Police and the Public* (New Haven: Yale University Press, 1971), pp. 48–53, and 136–40.

7. I would estimate on the basis of the field observations that the attitude test is regularly employed to exact deference by a great deal more than one-quarter of patrolmen in these departments. The wording of the statement may also have artificially depressed the extent of agreement. It is possible that if the statement had been worded "arrested or issued a citation" the percent of agreement would have been higher since a citation is regarded as less serious than an arrest. I did not word the question this way because a traffic citation is technically an arrest and I presumed it would be so interpreted. I have no way of knowing if it was or not.

8. While the evidence for this conclusion is drawn from the field observations, Raymond I. Parnas has observed a similar tendency for patrolmen to interpret their legal authority narrowly in these situations; see his "The Police Response to the Domestic Disturbance," *Wisconsin Law Review* (Fall 1967) pp. 914–60.

9. Along these lines see the discussion of nonenforcement in Sanford Kadish, "Legal Norms and Discretion in the Police and Sentencing Processes," *Harvard Law Review* 75 (March 1962): 913–14; and Joseph Goldstein, "Police Discretion Not to Invoke the Criminal Process: Low-Visibility Decisions in the Administration of Justice," *Yale Law Journal* 69 (March 1960): 573–80.

10. Wayne LaFave, *Arrest,* pp. 110–14; Kadish ("Legal Norm and Discretion," pp. 913–14) observes that "rather than overly strict enforcement against Negroes, what commonly is involved is a calculated nonenforcement of certain laws against the Negro population, justified on the ground that a lesser standard of morality prevails and that it is therefore unwise to apply the general legal standards to them."

11. Nine percent of drunkenness arrests for reasons of "drunk and disturbing" in Inglewood were made in on-view situations compared to 33 percent in calls for service. Arrests for "plain drunk," on the other hand, were more likely to be made in on-view situations (73 percent compared to 42 percent in calls for service). The data show a similar pattern in Redondo Beach. The null hypothesis that arrests for drunk and disturbing are no more likely in on-view situations than in calls for service can be rejected in both departments at a level of significance of less than .05.

12. My evidence and interpretation of these events differ greatly from those of Albert Reiss, Jr. I think on the whole patrolmen are far more manipulative than he gives them credit for being, and thus less dependent on citizens. See his *The Police and the Public,* pp. 73–88.

13. For a good, though somewhat dated, discussion of alternative ways of dealing with these problems see Raymond I. Parnas, "Police Discretion on Diversion of Incidents of Intra-Family Violence," *Law and Contemporary Problems* 36 (Autumn 1971): 539–65.

Chapter 8

1. The best discussion of decision rules or "routines" in street-level bureaucracies is Michael Lipsky, *Street-level Bureaucracy: Dilemmas of the Individual in Public Services* (New York: Russell Sage Foundation, 1980), pp. 87–158.

2. My distinctions between different types of incidents is somewhat similar to the distinction between the law enforcement and order-maintenance functions drawn by James Q. Wilson, but the use is rather different. Wilson argues that most of the variation in discretion is a result of two factors: the mode of intervention in an incident and whether it involves a law enforcement or order-maintenance problem. Here the point is that these incidents impose different constraints on patrolmen but that discretion is determined by operational style and the impact of departmental controls. See

James Q. Wilson, *Varieties of Police Behavior: The Management of Law and Order in Eight Communities* (New York: Atheneum, 1970), pp. 84–85.

3. Additional support for this typology comes from William Ker Muir's recent study of policemen and an earlier study by Susan O. White. All three studies were *conducted independently and in different departments,* and all arrived, to some degree, at remarkably similar types of policemen. White's categories are very close to mine, while two of Muir's types (the Professional and Enforcer) are almost identical to two of mine (the Old Style and Clean Beat Crime Fighters). See William Ker Muir, Jr, *Police: Streetcorner Politicians* (Chicago: University of Chicago Press, 1977), pp. 13–36; and Susan O. White, "A Perspective on Police Professionalization," *Law and Society Review* (Fall 1972): 61–85, especially pp. 70–79.

4. For a description of an Old Style Crime Fighter doing just that, see Joseph Wambaugh, *The Onion Field* (New York: Delacorte Press, 1973), pp. 229–233.

5. A few of these patrolmen are similar to those Muir has dubbed avoiders, men who simply cannot measure up to the responsibilities of police work. See Muir, *Police: Streetcorner Politicians,* pp. 31–36.

6. For a complete description of the items in each scale see chapter 6, pp. 145–146; 163–167 and Appendix. Both scales have been normalized with a mean of 50 and a standard deviation of 10.

7. Wilson, *Varieties of Police Behavior,* pp. 138–39; 230–6.

8. See chapter 5, pp. 120, 124–126 and Appendix for a full discussion of the items in each scale and the method used in constructing them.

9. The only exception to this generalization worth mentioning is that patrolmen who adopt the Service Style tend to be slightly better educated than the others. But the difference is not large and not statistically significant.

10. I do not wish to appear to be arbitrarily ruling out the importance of deeply rooted psychological traits. The significance of operational style for police discretion clearly suggests that the psychology of individual policemen, and the link between psychological traits and an operational style, ought to be investigated in more depth than it so far has been. The question must remain open for the moment, for I have neither the data nor the expertise to pursue it here. For some provocative hints along these lines see William Ker Muir, Jr., *Police: Streetcorner Politicians,* passim.

11. On the process of socialization in police departments, see John Van Maanen, "Working the Street: A Developmental View of Police Behavior," in *The Potential for Reform of Criminal Justice,* ed. Herbert Jacob (Beverly Hills: Sage Publications, 1974), pp. 83–103; and "Police Socialization: A Longitudinal Examination of Job Attitudes in an Urban Police Department," *Administrative Science Quarterly* 20 (1975): 207–28.

12. Cf., William Ker Muir, Jr., *Police: Streetcorner Politicians,* pp. 184–87; 235–57. Muir believes sergeants to be far more influential in shaping the behavior of patrolmen than I do. I do not doubt that some sergeants are influential nor do I doubt that they can be. But my observations lead me to believe that in most cases they are not terribly influential, partly because a lot of them are not interested, but mostly because of the bifurcation of internal control in police departments.

13. Such a development is entirely consistent with Van Maanen's data. See "Police Socialization: A Longitudinal Examination of Job Attitudes in an Urban Police Department," especially pp. 220 ff.

Chapter 9

1. James D. Thompson, *Organizations in Action* (New York: McGraw-Hill, 1967), pp. 117–25.

2. The most obvious reason for the lack of comparability between arrest rates, as patrolmen consistently maintain, is that no two situations are ever exactly alike. The time of day, the participants, the particulars of the situation, and the demeanor of officer and citizen will all differ. For some offenses, especially, traffic offenses, the differences may be of little consequence; but in more ambiguous situations such as drunkenness or family disputes they may matter a great deal. Moreover, when one

compares arrest rates, one really does not know with any degree of certainty exactly what it is that is being compared. It is only in a superficial sense that one can argue that by comparing arrest rates, one is actually comparing the exercise of discretion. What in fact is being compared are the formal charges preferred against a suspect— that is, the end result of a patrolman's interpretation and judgment of a situation. Thus, the comparison of arrest rates is unsatisfactory as the *only* measure of discretion since one cannot always be sure what those rates *mean*. I would argue that only when similar situations and the decision-making process in these situations are compared can one begin to explain discretion. The use of hypothetical incidents is one way to do this.

3. Ideally, the survey data should be supplemented with data on an individual patrolman's rate of arrests for various offenses, number of traffic citations, and field interrogations—in short, his "stats." Obviously such measures could be used as a test of the validity of the hypotheticals. I did not obtain such data for two reasons. First, it was unavailable in one department. And second, I faced a trade-off between attempting to obtain such data and still maintaining the confidentiality of the interviews. I opted for confidentiality.

4. See Albert Reiss, Jr., *The Police and the Public*, (New Haven: Yale University Press, 1971), pp. 53–62.

5. There is no strong relationship between operational style and the desire for a promotion in any of the departments.

6. I should note that all of the relationships reported here have been controlled for those background characteristics of patrolmen which analysis suggested might be important. These include social class, education, and service in the military. In *no* case do controls for these factors alter any of the reported relationships.

7. Since operational style, as we know, is related to the perception that discretion is limited, we might expect it to have some effect. While it is difficult to sort all these factors out with a limited number of cases, controlling for operational style *does not* change the relationship between the perceived limits on discretion and the choice in this incident. This leads me to believe that the effect of this variable in this incident is almost entirely a departmental one.

8. Redondo Beach patrolmen are more likely than those in the other departments to say that supervisors want them to stay out of trouble. See chapter 5, table 5.3 for the relevant evidence.

9. Again this effect is independent of operational style. See above, footnote 7.

10. The skeptical reader may have asked by now whether it is really size that distinguishes these three departments or rather some other factor such as the uniqueness of the LAPD. I think this is doubtful for two reasons. First, all three departments are professional departments, and all subscribe to the same broad values. There is far less difference in the values and beliefs of field supervisors than in those of patrolmen. Second, there is indirect evidence that some violations, namely assaults, are treated differently in other large and small departments. See Sidney Sonnenblum, John J. Kirlin, and John C. Ries, *How Cities Provide Services: An Evaluation of Alternative Delivery Structures* (Cambridge, Mass.: Ballinger Publishing Co., 1977), pp. 179–81.

Chapter 10

1. On the police violence in the Houston police department see Tom Curtis, "Police in Houston Pictured as Brutal and Unchecked," *Washington Post*, Section A, 13 June 1977, p. 1; on the shootings in Los Angeles see "Los Angeles County District Attorney to Probe Slaying of Nude Man," *Los Angeles Times*, 13 August 1977, Section I, p. 1; and *The Report of the Board of Police Commissioners Concerning the Shooting of Eulia Love and the Use of Deadly Force*, "Part I—The Shooting of Eulia Love," (Los Angeles Police Dept., October 1979). For an account of Arthur McDuffie's death and the actions of the Miami Police see George Lardner, Jr., "McDuffie Death: It Seemed to Be Open-Shut Case," *Washington Post*, 21 May, 1980, p. 1. See also H. Jerome Miron and Robert Wasserman, *Prevention and Control of Urban Disorders: Issues for the*

Notes

1980's (Washington D.C.: University Research Corporation, 1980) for a discussion of the aftermath of the McDuffie trial in Miami.

2. George L. Kelling and David Fogel, "Police Patrol—Some Future Directions," in *The Future of Policing*, ed. Alvin W. Cohn (Beverly Hills: Sage Publications, 1978), p. 166. The evidence, however, is not conclusive. For a critique of the major study in this area, the Kansas City Experiment, see Richard C. Larson, "What Happened to Patrol Operations in Kansas City? A Review of the Kansas City Preventive Patrol Experiment," *Journal of Criminal Justice* 3 (1975): 267–97.

3. See Kenneth R. Mladenka and Kim Quaile Hill, "The Distribution of Urban Police Services," *Journal of Politics* 40 (February 1978): pp. 112–33.

4. Armando Morales found that although a working- and lower-class Mexican-American area and a white middle-class area of Los Angeles had approximately the same incidence of alcoholism, the former had far more arrests for drunk driving than the latter. See *Ando Sangrando (I Am Bleeding)* pp. 54–55; See as well Robert Fogelson, *Big-City Police* (Cambridge, Mass.: Harvard University Press, 1977), pp. 255–60.

5. Egon Bittner, *The Functions of the Police in Modern Society*, (Rockville, Maryland: National Institute of Mental Health, Center for Studies of Crime and Delinquency, 1972) p. 112.

6. Gerald M. Caplan, "The Case for Rulemaking by Law Enforcement Agencies," *Law and Contemporary Problems* 36 (Autumn 1971): p. 500.

7. Herman Goldstein, "Police Policy Formulation: A Proposal for Improving Police Performance," *Michigan Law Review* 65 (April 1967): 1123–46; and see Goldstein's most recent statement of this perspective in his *Policing a Free Society* (Cambridge, Mass.: Ballinger Publishing Co., 1977), chap. 5.

8. Jerry V. Wilson and Geoffrey M. Alprin, "Controlling Police Conduct: Alternatives to the Exclusionary Rule," *Law and Contemporary Problems* 36 (Autumn 1971): pp. 493–94.

9. Goldstein, for one, is very much aware of these problems; see *Policing a Free Society*, pp. 111–12.

10. Herbert Kaufman, *Administrative Feedback: Monitoring Subordinates' Behavior* (Washington, D.C.: The Brookings Institution, 1973), pp. 63–73.

11. Egon Bittner, *The Functions of the Police in Modern Society*, p. 81, and chap. 11–17.

12. Ibid., p. 121.

13. Max Weber, "Science as a Vocation," in *From Max Weber: Essays in Sociology*, ed. Hans Gerth and C. Wright Mills (New York: Oxford University Press, 1946), pp. 139–45.

14. William Ker Muir, Jr., *Police: Streetcorner Politicians* (Chicago: University of Chicago Press, 1977), chap. 12, passim.

15. This is the gist of Eliot Freidson and Buford Rhea's research on professional controls; see their "Processes of Control in a Company of Equals," in *Medical Men and their Work*, ed. Eliot Freidson and Judith Lorber (Chicago: Aldine Publishing Co., 1972), pp. 185–99; and "Knowledge and Judgment in Professional Evaluations," *Administrative Science Quarterly* 10 (June 1965): 107–24.

16. For discussions of the power and autonomy of professions see Corinne Gilb, *Hidden Hierarchies* (New York: Harper & Row, 1966); Bengt Abrahamsson, *Military Professionalization and Political Power* (Beverly Hills: Sage Publications, 1972). Bittner, I might add, is very much aware of this paradox; see *The Functions of the Police in Modern Society*, p. 122.

17. Eric A. Nordlinger and Jim Hardy, "Urban Decentralization: An Evaluation of Four Models," *Public Policy* 20 (Summer 1972): p. 373.

18. The best available summary of this literature is Gordon P. Whitaker, "Does Structure Make a Difference in Police Performance?" Paper presented at the 1978 Annual Meeting of the American Political Science Association, New York.

19. James Q. Wilson, *Varieties of Police Behavior: The Management of Law and Order in Eight Communities* (New York: Atheneum, 1970), p. 283.

20. Jeffrey Pfeffer, Gerald R. Salancik, and Huseyin Leblebici, "The Effect of Uncertainty on the Use of Social Influence in Organizational Decision Making," *Administrative Science Quarterly* 21 (June 1976): 227–45.

21. For an analysis of the literature on political participation which would confirm this point, see Robert R. Alford and Roger Friedland, "Political Participation and Public Policy," *Annual Review of Sociology* vol. 1 (1975), pp. 429–79; especially pp. 450–64, which discusses citizen participation in bureaucratic agencies.

22. Peter B. Bloch and David I. Specht, *Evaluation of Operation Neighborhood* (Washington, D.C.: The Urban Institute, 1973), pp. 109–16. In TEAM 28, the forerunner to NATP in the LAPD, patrolmen were successfully confined to the team area; see Lawrence W. Sherman, et al., *Team Policing*, (Washington, D.C.: The Police Foundation, 1973) pp. 73–74; 94–96. By the fall of 1977, however, some departmental administrators in LAPD admitted that it was difficult to confine patrolmen to the assigned area.

23. Bloch and Specht, *Evaluation of Operation Neighborhood*, pp. 37–46; and 69–72.

24. Gerald Caiden, *Police Revitalization* (Lexington, Mass.: Lexington Books, 1977) pp. 275–86.

25. See the evidence in Bloch and Specht, *Evaluation of Operation Neighborhood*. pp. 119–123; Gerald Caiden, *Police Revitalization*, p. 288; and Alfred I. Schwartz and Summer N. Clarren, *The Cincinnati Team Policing Experiment: A Summary Report* (Washington, D.C.: The Police Foundation, 1977), pp. 36–38.

26. The phrase "social workers with guns" was coined by Robert DeGrazia, most recently Chief of Police of the Montgomery County Police, Montgomery County, Maryland.

Appendix

1. The computer program used to construct the attitudinal scales was developed by Carl P. Hensler. For a full discussion of the program and the method see his, "The Structure of Orientations Toward Government," (Ph.D. dissertation, M.I.T., 1972), especially chap. 3.

2. R. J. Rummel, "Understanding Factor Analysis," *Journal of Conflict Resolution* 11 (1967): 445.

3. Hensler puts it this way: "The output is an n variable by m factor loading matrix A which relates the observed variables' values Z to the hypothetical variable (factor) values: Z equals AF." "The Structure of Orientations Toward Government," p. 86.

4. Ibid., p. 67.

5. Ibid., p. 68.

Bibliography

The Police

Ban, Michael. "Local Compliance with Mapp vs. Ohio: The Power of the Supreme Court, A Case Study," Ph.D. dissertation, Harvard University, 1972.

Banton, Michael. *The Policeman in the Community.* New York: Basic Books, Inc., 1964.

Barrett, Edward L. "Police Practices and the Law—From Arrest to Release or Charge." *California Law Review* 50 (1962): 11–55.

Bayley, David H., and Mendelsohn, Harold. *Minorities and the Police: Confrontation in America.* New York: The Free Press, 1969.

Bittner, Egon. "The Police on Skid Row: A Study of Peace Keeping." *American Sociological Review* 32 (1967): 699–715.

———. *The Functions of the Police in Modern Society.* Rockville, Maryland: National Institute of Mental Health, Center for Studies of Crime and Delinquency, 1972.

Black, Donald J. "Production of Crime Rates." *American Sociological Review* 35 (1970): 733–48.

———, and Reiss, Albert, Jr. "Police Control of Juveniles," *American Sociological Review* 35 (1970): 63–77.

———, and Reiss, Albert, Jr. "Patterns of Behavior in Police and Citizen Transactions," in *Studies of Crime and Law Enforcement in Major Metropolitan Areas,* Vol. 2, Section 1. Washington, D.C.: U.S. Government Printing Office, 1967.

Cain, Maureen. "On the Beat: Interactions and Relations in Rural and Urban Police Forces," in *Images of Deviance.* Edited by Stanley Cohen. Middlesex, England. Penguin Books, 1971, pp. 62–97.

Carte, Gene E. and Carte, Elaine H. *Police Reform in the United States: The Era of August Vollmer, 1905–1932.* Berkeley: University of California Press, 1975.

———. "Technology Versus Personnel: Notes on the History of Police Professional Reform." *Journal of Police Science and Administration* 4 (1976): 285–97.

Chapman, Brian. *Police State.* New York: Praeger Publishers, 1970.

Chevigny, Paul. *Police Power.* New York: Pantheon Books, 1969.

Clark, John P. "Isolation of the Police: A Comparison of the British and American Situations." *Journal of Criminal Law, Criminology and Police Science,* 56 (1965): 307–19.

Cohen, Bernard. *Police Internal Administration of Justice in New York City.* Santa Monica: The Rand Corporation, 1970.

Cohen, Bernard, and Chaiken, Jan M. *Police Background Characteristics and Performance.* Santa Monica, Calif.: The Rand Corporation, 1972.

Conot, Robert. *Rivers of Blood, Years of Darkness.* New York: Bantam, 1967.

Cumming, Elaine; Cumming, Ian; and Edell, Laura. "Policeman as Philosopher, Guide and Friend." *Social Problems* 12 (1965): 276–86.

Douthit, Nathan. "Police Professionalism and the War Against Crime in the United States, 1920s–1930s," in *Police Forces in History.* Edited by George L. Mosse. Beverly Hills: Sage Publications, 1975, pp. 317–33.

Erie, Steven P. "The Los Angeles Police Department Budgetary Process: Politics, Power and the Public Interest." Mimeographed. Los Angeles: Institute on Law and Urban Studies, 1972.

———. "Trends in the Provision of Public Services: Los Angeles Police Expenditures and Manpower Allocations, 1930–1970." Mimeographed. Los Angeles: Institute on Law and Urban Studies, 1972.

Ferdinand, Theodore N., and Luchterhand, E. G. "Inner-City Youth, The Police, The Juvenile Court and Justice." *Social Problems* 15 (1969): 510–25.

Fisk, James G. "Some Dimensions of Police Discretion," in *The Police Community: Dimensions of an Occupational Subculture.* Edited by Jack Goldsmith and Sharon S. Goldsmith. Pacific Palisades, Calif.: Palisades Publishers, 1974, pp. 63–83.

Fogelson, Robert M. *Big-City Police.* Cambridge, Mass.: Harvard University Press, 1977.

Forslund, Morris A. "A Comparison of Negro and White Crime Rates." *Journal of Criminal Law, Criminology and Police Science* 61 (1970): 214–17.

Gardiner, John A. *Traffic and the Police: Variations in Law Enforcement Policy.* Cambridge, Mass.: Harvard University Press, 1969.

Gazell, J. A. "William H. Parker, Police Professionalization and the Public: An Assessment." *Journal of Police Science and Administration* 4 (1976): 28–37.

Goldstein, Herman. "Police Discretion: The Ideal Versus the Real," *Public Administration Review* 23 (1963): 140–48.

———. *Policing a Free Society.* Cambridge Mass.: Ballinger Publishing Co., 1977.

Goldstein, Joseph. "Police Discretion Not to Invoke the Criminal Process: Low-Visibility Decisions in the Administration of Justice." *Yale Law Journal* 69 (1960): 543–89.

Green, Edward. "Race, Social Status, and Criminal Arrest." *American Sociological Review* 35 (1970): 476–90.

Groves, W. Eugene, and Rossi, Peter H. "Police Perceptions of a Hostile Ghetto." *American Behavioral Scientist* 13 (1970): 727–44.

Grupp, Stanley E., and Lucas, Warren C. "The 'Marihuana Muddle' as Reflected in California Arrest Statistics and Dispositions." *Law and Society Review* 5 (1970): 251–70.

Haller, Mark H. "Historical Roots of Police Behavior: Chicago, 1890–1925." *Law and Society Review* 10 (1976): 303–24.

Harris, Richard N. *The Police Academy: An Inside View.* New York: John Wiley & Sons, 1973.

Hersey, John. *The Algiers Motel Incident.* New York: Bantam Books, 1968.

Hopkins, Ernest Jerome. *Our Lawless Police.* New York: The Viking Press, 1931.

Hudson, James R. "Police-Citizen Encounters that Lead to Citizen Complaints." *Social Problems.* 18 (1972): 179–93.

———. "Organizational Aspects of Internal and External Review of the Police." *Journal of Criminal Law, Criminology, and Police Science* 63 (1972): 427–33.

Johnson, Bruce C. "Taking Care of Labor: The Police in American Politics." *Theory and Society* (1976): 89–117.

Kadish, Sanford H. "Legal Norm and Discretion in the Police and Sentencing Process." *Harvard Law Review* 74 (1962): 904–31.

Kelling, George L., et al. *The Kansas City Preventive Patrol Experiment: A Summary Report.* Washington, D.C.: The Police Foundation, 1974.

———. and Fogel, David. "Police Patrol—Some Future Directions," in *The Future of Policing.* Edited by Alvin W. Cohn. Beverly Hills, Calif.: Sage Publications, 1978, pp. 151–82.

Kephart, William M. *Racial Factors and Urban Law Enforcement.* Philadelphia: University of Pennsylvania Press, 1957.

Kirlin, John J. "The Impact of Contract Services Arrangements on the Los Angeles Sheriff's Department and Law Enforcement in Los Angeles County." *Public Policy* 21 (1973): 553–83.

La Fave, Wayne R. *Arrest: The Decision to Take a Suspect into Custody.* Boston: Little, Brown and Co., 1965.

Lane, Roger. *Policing the City: Boston, 1822–1885.* Cambridge, Mass.: Harvard University Press, 1967.

Larson, Richard C. "What Happened to Patrol Operations in Kansas City? A Review of the Kansas City Preventive Patrol Experiment." *Journal of Criminal Justice* 3 (1975): 267–97.

Bibliography

Levy, Burton. "Cops in the Ghetto: A Problem of the Police System." *American Behavioral Scientist* (1968): 31–34.

Lundman, Richard J. "Routine Police Arrest Practices: A Commonweal Perspective." *Social Problems* 22 (1974): 128–40.

McDonald, Donald. *The Police: An Interview with William H. Parker, Chief of Police of Los Angeles, California.* Santa Barbara: Center for the Study of Democratic Institutions, 1962.

MacInnes, Colin. "Mr. Love and Mr. Justice," in *The London Novels of Colin MacInnes.* New York: Farrar, Straus and Giroux, 1969.

McKeachern, A. W., and Bauzer, Riva. "Factors Related to Disposition in Juvenile-Police Contacts," in *Juvenile Gangs in Context.* Edited by M. Kelin. Englewood Cliffs, N.J.: Prentice-Hall, 1967, pp. 148–160.

McNamara, John H. "Uncertainties in Police Work: The Relevance of Police Recruits' Backgrounds and Training," in *The Police: Six Sociological Essays.* Edited by David Bordua. New York: John Wiley & Sons, 1967, pp. 163–252.

Manning, Peter K. *Police Work.* Cambridge, Mass.: The M.I.T. Press, 1977.

———. "Rules in Organizational Context: Narcotics Enforcement in Two Settings." *The Sociological Quarterly* 18 (1977): 44–61.

Meyer, John C., Jr., and Taylor, Winthrop E. "Analyzing the Nature of Police Involvements: A Research Note Concerning the Effects of Forms of Police Mobilization." *Journal of Criminal Justice* 3 (1975): 141–46.

Miller, Wilbur R. "Police Authority in London and New York City, 1830–1870." *Journal of Social History* 8 (1975): 81–95.

Morales, Armando. *Ando Sangrando, (I am Bleeding.)* La Puente, Calif.: Perspectiva Publications, 1972.

Muir, William Ker, Jr. *Police: Streetcorner Politicians.* Chicago: University of Chicago Press, 1977.

Niederhoffer, Arthur. *Behind the Shield: The Police in Urban Society.* Garden City, N.Y.: Anchor Books, 1969.

Ostrom, Elinor, and Parks, Roger B. "Suburban Police Departments: Too Many and Too Small?" in *The Urbanization of the Suburbs.* Edited by Louis H. Masotti and Jeffrey K. Hadden. Vol. 7, Urban Affairs Annual Reviews. Beverly Hills, Calif.: Sage Publications, 1973, pp. 367–402.

Ostrom, Elinor, and Whitaker, Gordon P. "Does Local Community Control of Police Make A Difference? Some Preliminary Findings." *American Journal of Political Science* 17 (1973): 48–76.

———. "Community Control and Governmental Responsiveness: The Case of Police in Black Communities," in *Improving the Quality of Urban Management.* Edited by David Rogers and Willis Hawley. Vol. 8, Urban Affairs Annual Reviews. Beverly Hills, Calif.: Sage Publications, 1974, pp. 303–334.

Packer, Herbert L. *The Limits of the Criminal Sanction.* Stanford, Calif.: Stanford University Press, 1968.

Parker, William H. "The Police Challenge in Our Great Cities." *The Annals of the American Academy of Political and Social Science* 291 (1954): 5–13.

Parks, Roger B. "Police Patrol in Metropolitan Areas—Implications for Restructuring the Police," in *The Delivery of Urban Services.* Edited by Elinor Ostrom. Vol. 10, Urban Affairs Annual Reviews. Beverly Hills, Calif.: Sage Publications, 1976, pp. 261–82.

Parnas, Raymond I. "The Police Response to Domestic Disturbance." *Wisconsin Law Review,* 1967, pp. 914–60.

———. "Police Discretion and Diversion of Incidents of Intra-Family Violence." *Law and Contemporary Problems* 36 (1971): 539–65.

Petersen, David M. "Informal Norms and Police Practice: The Traffic Ticket Quota System." *Sociology and Social Research* 35 (1971): 354–62.

———. "Police Disposition of the Petty Offender." *Sociology and Social Research* 36 (1972): 320–30.

Piliavin, Irving, and Briar, Scott. "Police Encounters with Juveniles." *American Journal of Sociology* 70 (1964): 206–14.

Press, S. James. *Some Effects of An Increase in Police Manpower in the 20th*

Precinct of New York City. Santa Monica, Calif.: The Rand Corporation, 1971.

Radano, Gene. *Walking the Beat.* New York: Collier, 1969.

Reiss, Albert, Jr. "Career Orientations, Job Satisfaction, and the Assessment of Law Enforcement Problems by Police Officers," in *Studies in Crime and Law Enforcement in Major Metropolitan Areas* vol. 2, Section 2. (Washington, D.C.: U.S. Government Printing Office, 1967).

Reiss, Albert, Jr. *The Police and The Public.* New Haven: Yale University Press, 1971.

Reiss, Albert, Jr., and Bordua, David. "Environment and Organization: A Perspective on the Police," in *The Police: Six Sociological Essays.* Edited by David Bordua. New York: John Wiley & Sons, 1967, pp. 25–55.

Report of the National Advisory Commission on Civil Disorders. New York: Bantam Books, 1968.

Richardson, James F. *The New York Police: Colonial Times to 1901.* New York: Oxford University Press, 1970.

Rossi, Peter H.; Berk, Richard A.; and Eidson, Bettye K. *The Roots of Urban Discontent: Public Policy, Municipal Institutions, and the Ghetto.* New York: John Wiley & Sons, 1974.

Rubin, Jesse. "Police Identity and the Police Role," in *The Police and the Community.* Edited by Robert F. Steadman. Baltimore: John Hopkins University Press, 1972, pp. 12–50.

Rubinstein, Jonathan. *City Police.* New York: Farrar, Straus & Giroux, 1973.

Sacks, Harvey. "Notes on Police Assessment of Moral Character," in *Studies in Social Interactions.* Edited by David Sudnow. Free Press 1972, pp. 280–93.

Savitz, Leonard. "The Dimensions of Police Loyalty." *American Behavioral Scientist* 13 (1970): 693–704.

Silver, Alan. "The Demand for Order in Civil Society: A Review of Some Themes in the History of Urban Crime, Police and Riot," in *The Police: Six Sociological Essays.* Edited by David Bordua. New York: John Wiley & Sons, 1967, pp. 1–24.

Skogan, Wesley G. "Efficiency and Effectiveness in Big-City Police Departments." *Public Administration Review* 36 (1976): 278–86.

Skolnick, Jerome H. *Justice Without Trial: Law Enforcement in a Democratic Society.* 2nd ed., New York: John Wiley & Sons, 1977.

——. *The Police and the Urban Ghetto.* Chicago: American Bar Foundation, 1968.

Smith, Bruce. *Police Systems in the United States.* 2d ed., New York: Harper & Row, 1960.

Smith, Dennis C., and Ostrom, Elinor. "The Effects of Training and Education on Police Attitudes and Performance: A Preliminary Analysis," in *The Potential for Reform of Criminal Justice.* Edited by Herbert Jacob. Beverly Hills, Calif.: Sage Publications, 1974, pp. 45–81.

Stinchcombe, Arthur L. "Institutions of Privacy in the Determination of Police Administrative Practice." *American Journal of Sociology* 69 (1963): 150–160.

Stoddard, E. R. "The Informal 'Code' of Police Deviancy: A Group Approach to 'Blue Coat Crime'." *Journal of Criminal Law, Criminology and Police Science* 59 (1968): 201–13.

Sykes, Richard E., and Clark, John P. "A Theory of Deference Exchange in Police-Civilian Encounters." *American Journal of Sociology* 81 (1975): 584–600.

Task Force Report: The Police. The President's Commission on Law Enforcement and Administration of Justice, Washington, D.C.: U.S. Government Printing Office, 1967.

The Challenge of Crime in a Free Society. A Report by the President's Commission on Law Enforcement and Administration of Justice. New York: Avon Books, 1968.

"The LAPD: How Good Is It?" Special Report, *Los Angeles Times.* 18 December 1977, section VIII.

Thompson, Hunter S. *Hell's Angels.* New York: Ballantine Books, 1966.

Tiffany, Lawrence P.; McIntyre, Donald M.; and Rottenberg, Daniel L. *Detection of Crime: Stopping and Questioning, Search and Seizure, Encouragement and Entrapment.* Boston: Little, Brown & Co., 1967.

Turner, William. *The Police Establishment.* New York: Putnam's, 1968.

Uelmen, Gerald F., *Varieties of Police Policy: A Study of Police Policy Regarding the*

Bibliography

Use of Deadly Force in Los Angeles County. Beverly Hills: Institute on Law and Urban Studies, 1972.

Van Maanen, John. "Pledging the Police: A Study of Selected Aspects of Recruit Socialization in a Large, Urban Police Department," Ph.D. dissertation, University of California, Irvine, 1972.

———. "Police Socialization: A Longitudinal Examination of Job Attitudes in an Urban Police Department." *Administrative Science Quarterly* 20 (1975): 207–28.

———. "Working the Street: A Developmental View of Police Behavior," in *The Potential for Reform of Criminal Justice.* Edited by Herbert Jacob. Beverly Hills, Calif.: Sage Publications, 1974, pp. 83–130.

Vollmer, August. *The Police in Modern Society.* Berkeley, Calif.: University of California Press, 1936.

Wallen, Linda. "Professional and Bureaucratic Processes of Organizational Control: Internal Discipline in the Los Angeles Police Department," Ph.D. dissertation, University of California, Los Angeles, 1976.

Wambaugh, Joseph. *The Blue Knight.* New York: Dell Publishing Co., 1972.

———. *The Onion Field.* New York: Delacorte Press, 1973.

Webster, J. A. "Police Task and Time Study." *Journal of Criminal Law, Criminology and Police Science* 61 (1970): 94–96.

Werthman, Carl, and Piliavin, Irving. "Gang Members and the Police," in *The Police: Six Sociological Essays.* Edited by David Bordua. New York: John Wiley & Sons, 1967, pp. 56–98.

Westley, William A. *Violence and the Police: A Sociological Study of Law, Custom and Morality.* Cambridge, Mass.: The M.I.T. Press, 1970.

White, Susan O. "A Perspective on Police Professionalization." *Law and Society Review* 6 (1972): 61–85.

Wilson, James Q. "The Police and Their Problems: A Theory." *Public Policy* 12 (1963): 189–216.

———. "Dilemmas of Police Administration." *Public Administration Review* 28 (1968): 407–17.

———. "The Police and the Delinquent in Two Cities," in *City Politics and Public Policy.* Edited by James Q. Wilson. New York: John Wiley & Sons, 1968, pp. 173–196.

———. *Varieties of Police Behavior: The Management of Law and Order in Eight Communities.* Cambridge, Mass.: Harvard University Press, 1968.

———. "Police Morale, Reform, and Citizen Respect: The Chicago Case," in *The Policemen: Six Sociological Essays.* Edited by David Bordua. New York: John Wiley & Sons, 1967, pp. 137–62.

———. "The Police in the Ghetto," in *The Police and the Community.* Edited by Robert F. Steadman. Baltimore: The Johns Hopkins University Press, 1972, pp. 51–90.

——— and Barbara Boland. "The Effect of the Police on Crime." *Law and Society Review* 12 (1978): 367–90.

Wilson, Orlando W., *Police Administration.* 2d ed. New York: McGraw-Hill, 1963.

———, ed. *Parker on Police.* Springfield, Illinois: Charles C Thomas Publishers, 1957.

Woods, Arthur. *Policeman and Public.* New Haven: Yale University Press, 1919.

Woods, Joseph G. "The Progressives and the Police in Los Angeles," Ph.D. dissertation, University of California, Los Angeles, 1973.

Bureaucracy, Professionalism, and Public Policy

Abrahamson, Bengt. *Military Professionalization and Political Power.* Beverly Hills, Calif.: Sage Publications, 1972.

Albrow, Martin. *Bureaucracy.* New York: Praeger, 1970.

Allison, Graham T. *Essence of Decision: Explaining the Cuban Missile Crisis.* Boston: Little, Brown & Co., 1971.

Argyris, Chris. "Understanding Human Behavior in Organizations: One Viewpoint," in *Modern Organization Theory.* Edited by Mason Haire. New York: John Wiley & Sons, 1959, pp. 115–154.

Blau, Peter M. *The Dynamics of Bureaucracy.* Rev. ed. Chicago: University of Chicago Press, 1963.

———. "Critical Remarks on Weber's Theory of Authority." *American Political Science Review,* 57 (1963): 305–316.

Blau, Peter M., and Scott, W. Richard. *Formal Organizations: A Comparative Approach.* San Francisco: Chandler Publishing Co., 1962.

Bledstein, Burton J. *The Culture of Professionalism: The Middle Class and the Development of Higher Education in America.* New York: W. W. Norton & Co., Inc., 1976.

Blumberg, Abraham S. "The Practice of Law as Confidence Game: Organizational Cooptation of a Profession." *Law and Society Review* 1 (1967): 15–39.

Brim, Orville G., Jr., and Wheeler, Stanton. *Socialization After Childhood: Two Essays.* New York: John Wiley & Sons, 1968.

Child, John. "Predicting and Understanding Organization Structure." *Administrative Science Quarterly* 18 (1973): 168–185.

Crozier, Michel. *The Bureaucratic Phenomenon.* Chicago: University of Chicago Press, 1964.

Cyert, Richard M., and March, James G. *A Behavioral Theory of the Firm.* Englewood Cliffs, N.J.: Prentice-Hall, Inc., 1963.

Davis, Kenneth Culp. *Discretionary Justice: A Preliminary Inquiry.* Urbana: University of Illinois Press, 1964.

Derthick, Martha. "Intercity Differences in Administration of the Public Assistance Program: The Case of Massachusetts," in *City Politics and Public Policy.* Edited by James Q. Wilson. New York: John Wiley & Sons, 1968, pp. 243–266.

Downs, Anthony. *Inside Bureaucracy.* Boston: Little, Brown & Co., 1967.

Easton, David. *A Framework for Political Analysis.* Englewood Cliffs, N.J.: Prentice-Hall, 1965.

Edelman, Murray. *The Symbolic Uses of Politics.* Urbana: University of Illinois Press, 1964, pp. 22–43.

Eisenstein, James, and Jacob, Herbert. *Felony Justice: An Organizational Analysis of the Courts.* Boston: Little, Brown & Co., 1977.

Feeley, Malcom M. "Two Models of the Criminal Justice System: An Organization Perspective." *Law and Society Review* 8 (1973): 407–23.

Friedson, Eliot, and Rhea, Buford. "Knowledge and Judgment in Professional Evaluations." *Administrative Science Quarterly* 10 (1965): 107–24.

———. "Processes of Control in a Company of Equals," in *Medical Men and Their Work.* Edited by Eliot Freidson and Judith Lorber. Chicago: Aldine Publishing Co., 1972, pp. 185–199.

George, Alexander. "The 'Operational Code': A Neglected Approach to the Study of Political Leaders and Decision Making." *International Studies Quarterly* 13 (1969): 190–222.

Glib, Corinne L. *Hidden Hierarchies: The Professions and Government.* New York: Harper & Row, 1966.

Goode, William. "Community Within a Community: The Professions." *American Sociological Review* 22 (1957): 194–200.

Goss, Mary E. W. "Influence and Authority Among Physicians in an Outpatient Clinic." *American Sociological Review* 26 (1961): 39–50.

Gouldner, Alvin. *Patterns of Industrial Bureaucracy.* New York: The Free Press, 1954.

Greenwood, Ernest. "Attributes of a Profession." *Social Work* 2 (1957): 44–55.

Haber, Samuel. *Efficiency and Uplift: Scientific Management in the Progressive Era.* Chicago: University of Chicago Press, 1964.

Hage, Jerald, and Aiken, Michael. "Routine Technology, Social Structure and Organizational Goals." *Administrative Science Quarterly* 14 (1969): 366–76.

Hall, Richard H. "Professionalization and Bureaucratization." *American Sociological Review* 33 (1968): 92–104.

Bibliography

Harries-Jenkins, G. "Professionals in Organizations," in *Professions and Professionalization*. Edited by J. A. Jackson. Cambridge: Cambridge University Press, 1970, pp. 53–107.

Huntington, Samuel. *The Soldier and the State*. Cambridge, Mass.: Harvard University Press, 1957.

Jones, Bryan D., Greenberg, Saadia R., Kaufman, Clifford, and Drew, Joseph. "Service Delivery Rules and the Distribution of Local Government Services: Three Detroit Bureaucracies." *Journal of Politics* 40 (1978): 332–368.

Katz, Daniel, and Kahn, Robert. *The Social Psychology of Organizations*. New York: John Wiley & Sons, 1966.

Kaufman, Herbert. *The Forest Ranger: A Study in Administrative Behavior*. Baltimore: The Johns Hopkins University Press, 1960.

———. *Administrative Feedback: Monitoring Subordinates' Behavior*. Washington D.C.: The Brookings Institution, 1973.

Kirlin, John J. "The Impact of Increasing Lower-Status Clientele Upon City Governmental Structures: A Model From Organization Theory." *Urban Affairs Quarterly* 8 (1973): 317–43.

Levy, Frank, Meltsner, Arnold, and Wildavsky, Aaron. *Urban Outcomes: Schools, Streets, and Libraries*. Berkeley: University of California Press, 1974.

Lipsky, Michael. *Street-Level Bureaucracy: Dilemmas of the Individual in Public Services*. New York: Russell Sage Foundation, 1980.

Little, Roger W. "Buddy Relations and Combat Performance," in *The New Military*. Edited by Morris Janowitz. New York: W. W. Norton & Co., 1969, pp. 195–223.

Lynd, Kenneth S., ed. *The Professionals in America*. Boston: Beacon Press, 1965.

McCleery, Richard. "Communications Patterns as Bases of Systems of Authority and Power," in *Theoretical Studies in Social Organization of the Prison*. New York: Social Science Research Council, 1960, pp. 49–77.

March, James G., and Simon, Herbert A. *Organizations*. New York: John Wiley & Sons, 1958.

Mechanic, David. "Sources of Power of Lower Participants in Complex Organizations." *Administrative Science Quarterly* 7 (1962): 349–64.

Merton, Robert K. "Bureaucratic Structure and Personality," in Robert K. Merton, *Social Theory and Social Structure*, enlarged ed. New York: The Free Press, 1968, pp. 249–60.

Mladenka, Kenneth R. "Organizational Rules, Service Equality and Distributional Decisions in Urban Politics." *Social Science Quarterly* 59 (1978): 192–201.

——— and Hill, Kim Quaile. "The Distribution of Police Services." *Journal of Politics* 40 (1978): 112–33.

Montjoy, Robert S., and O'Toole, Laurence J., Jr. "Organization Theory and the Implementation of Policy Mandates." Paper Presented to the 1977 Annual Meeting of the American Society for Public Administration, Atlanta, Ga.

Niskanen, William A., Jr. *Bureaucracy and Representative Government*. Chicago: Aldine, 1971.

Novak, Steven J. "Professionalism and Bureaucracy: English Doctors and the Victorian Public Health Administration." *Journal of Social History* 6 (1973): 440–62.

Ostrom, Vincent. *The Intellectual Crisis in American Public Administration*. 2nd ed. University of Alabama Press, 1973.

Palumbo, Dennis J. "Power and Role Specificity in Organization Theory." *Public Administration Review* 29 (1969): 237–48.

Peabody, Robert L. *Organizational Authority: Superior-Subordinate Relationships in Three Public Service Organizations*. New York: Atherton Press, 1964.

Perlmutter, Amos. *The Military and Politics in Modern Times*. New Haven: Yale University Press, 1977.

Perrow, Charles. "A Framework for the Comparative Analysis of Organization." *American Sociological Review* 32 (1967): 194–208.

———. *Complex Organizations: A Critical Essay*. Glenview, Ill.: Scott, Foresman & Co., 1979.

Pfeffer, Jeffrey, Salancik, Gerald R., and Leblebici, Huseyin. "The Effect of Uncertainty on the Use of Social Influence in Organizational Decision Making." *Administrative Science Quarterly* 21 (1976): 227–45.

Pious, Richard. "Policy and Administration: The Legal Services Program in the War on Poverty," in *The Politics and Society Reader.* Edited by Ira Katznelson et al. New York: David McKay & Co., 1974, pp. 101–27.

Schon, Donald. *Beyond the Stable State.* New York: Random House, 1971.

Scott, W. Richard. "Professional Employees in a Bureaucratic Structure: Social Work," in *The Semi-Professions and Their Organization.* Edited by Amitai Etzioni. New York: The Free Press, 1969, pp. 82–140.

Selznick, Philip. "Foundations of the Theory of Organization." *American Sociological Review* 13 (1948): 25–35.

Simon, Herbert A. *Administrative Behavior,* 3d ed. New York: The Free Press, 1976.

Shils, Edward A., and Janowitz, Morris. "Cohesion and Disintegration in the Wehrmacht in World War II." *Public Opinion Quarterly* 12 (1948): 280–315.

Spier, Hans. *Social Order and the Risks of War.* Cambridge, Mass.: The M.I.T. Press, 1969.

Steinbruner, John. *The Cybernetic Theory of Decision.* Princeton, N.J.: Princeton University Press, 1974.

Stinchcombe, Arthur L. "Bureaucratic and Craft Administration of Production: A Comparative Study." *Administrative Science Quarterly* 4 (1959): 168–187.

Sykes, Gresham M. *The Society of Captives.* Princeton, N.J.: Princeton University Press, 1958.

Tannenbaum, Arnold S. *Control in Organizations.* New York: McGraw-Hill, 1968.

Thompson, James D. *Organizations in Action.* New York: McGraw-Hill, 1967.

Toren, Niña. "Semi-Professionalism and Social Work: A Theoretical Perspective," in *Semi-Professions and Their Organization.* Edited by Amitai Etzioni. New York: The Free Press, 1969, pp. 141–196.

Trist, Eric, and Bamforth, K. W. "Some Social and Psychological Consequences of the Longwall Method of Coal-Getting." *Human Relations* 4 (1951): 3–38.

Tullock, Gordon. *The Politics of Bureaucracy.* Washington, D.C.: The Public Affairs Press, 1965.

Vickers, Sir Geoffrey. *The Art of Judgment.* New York: Basic Books, Inc. 1965.

Vollmer, Howard M., and Mills, Donald M., eds. *Professionalization.* Englewood Cliffs, N.J.: Prentice-Hall, 1966.

Warwick, Donald P. *A Theory of Public Bureaucracy: Politics, Personality, and Organization in the State Department.* Cambridge, Mass.: Harvard University Press, 1975.

Weber, Max. *From Max Weber: Essays in Sociology.* Translated by Hans Gerth and C. Wright Mills. New York: Oxford University Press, 1946.

———. *The Theory of Social and Economic Organization.* Translated by Talcott Parsons and A. M. Henderson. New York: The Free Press, 1947.

———. *On Law in Economy and Society.* Translated by Edward Shils and Max Rheinstein. New York: Simon and Schuster, 1954.

Wiebe, Robert H. *The Search for Order: 1877–1920.* New York: Hill and Wang, 1967.

Wolin, Sheldon S. "The Age of Organization and the Sublimation of Politics," in Sheldon S. Wolin, *Politics and Vision.* Boston: Little, Brown & Co., 1960, pp. 352–434.

Governmental Reform and Democratic Control of Administration

Altshuler, Alan. *Community Control: The Black Demand for Participation in Large American Cities.* New York: Pegasus Books, 1970.

Bibliography

Banfield, Edward C., and Wilson, James Q. *City Politics*. New York: Vintage Books, 1963.

Bell, Daniel, and Held, Virginia. "The Community Revolution." *The Public Interest* 16 (1969): 142–77.

Bloch, Peter B., and Specht, David I. *Evaluation of Operation Neighborhood*. Washington, D.C.: The Urban Institute, 1973.

Caplan, Gerald M. "The Case for Rulemaking by Law Enforcement Agencies." *Law and Contemporary Problems* 36 (1971): 500–14.

Fesler, James W. "Approaches to the Understanding of Decentralization." *Journal of Politics* 27 (1965): 536–66.

Friedrich, Carl J. "Public Policy and the Nature of Administrative Responsibility," in *Bureaucratic Power in National Politics*. Edited by Francis E. Rourke. Boston: Little, Brown & Co., 1978, pp. 399–409.

Gilbert, C. E. "The Framework of Administrative Responsibility." *Journal of Politics* 21 (1959): 373–407.

Gittell, Marilyn. "Community Control of Education," in *Urban Riots: Violence and Social Change*. Edited by Robert A. Connery. New York: Random House, 1968, pp. 63–75.

Goldstein, Herman. "Police Policy Formulation: A Proposal for Improving Performance." *Michigan Law Review* 65 (1967): 1123–1146.

Hahn, Harlan. "Ghetto Assessments of Police Protection and Authority." *Law and Society Review* 6 (1971): 183–94.

Hart, David K. "Theories of Government Related to Decentralization and Citizen Participation." *Public Administration Review* 32 (1972): 603–21.

Hayes, Samuel P. "The Politics of Reform in Municipal Government in the Progressive Era." *Pacific Northwest Quarterly* 55 (1964): 157–69.

———. *Conservation and the Gospel of Efficiency: The Progressive Conservation Movement*. New York: Atheneum, 1974.

Herbert, Jacob. "Black and White Perceptions of Justice in the City." *Law and Society Review* 6 (1971): 69–90.

Hofstadter, Richard. *The Age of Reform: From Bryan to F.D.R.* New York: Vintage Books, 1955.

Hudson, James R. "Police Review Boards and Police Accountability." *Law and Contemporary Problems* 36 (1971): 515–38.

Jacobs, Paul. *Prelude to Riot: A View of Urban America From the Bottom*. New York: Vintage, 1968.

Kahn, Ronald. "Urban Reform and Police Accountability in New York City: 1950–1974," in *Urban Problems and Public Policy*. Edited by Robert Lineberry and Louis Masotti. Lexington, Mass.: D. C. Heath & Co., 1975, pp. 107–27.

Karl, Barry Dean. *Executive Reorganization and Reform in the New Deal*. Cambridge, Mass.: Harvard University Press, 1963.

Katznelson, Ira. "The Crisis of the Capitalist City: Urban Politics and Social Control," in *Theoretical Perspectives on Urban Politics*. Edited by Willis D. Hawley and Michael Lipsky. Englewood Cliffs, N.J.: Prentice-Hall, 1976, pp. 218–226.

Kaufman, Herbert. "Administrative Decentralization and Political Power." *Public Administration Review* 29 (1969): 3–14.

Lineberry, Robert L., and Fowler, Edmund P. "Reformism and Public Policies in American Cities." *American Political Science Review* 61 (1967): 701–16.

Lowi, Theodore J. "Machine Politics—Old and New." *The Public Interest*. No. 9 (1976): 83–92.

McGowan, Carl. "Rule-Making and the Police." *Michigan Law Review* 70 (1972): 659–94.

Merriam, Charles E. *Chicago: A More Intimate View of American Politics*. New York: The Macmillan Co., 1929, pp. 24–69.

Milner, Neal. "Supreme Court Effectiveness and the Police Organization." *Law and Contemporary Problems* 36 (1971): 467–87.

Nordlinger, Eric A., and Hardy, Jim. "Urban Decentralization: An Evaluation of Four Models." *Public Policy* 20 (1972): 359–96.

Ostrom, Elinor. "The Design of Institutional Arrangements and the Responsiveness of the Police," in *People vs. Government: The Responsiveness of American Institutions.* Edited by Leroy N. Rieselbach. Bloomington, Indiana: Indiana University Press, 1975, pp. 274–364.

Raine, Walter J. "The Perception of Police Brutality in South Central Los Angeles." *Los Angeles Riot Study,* Los Angeles: Institute of Government and Public Affairs, U.C.L.A., 1967.

Rothman, David J. *The Discovery of the Asylum.* Boston: Little, Brown & Co., 1971.

Schwartz, Alfred I., and Clarren, Sumner N. *The Cincinnati Team Policing Experiment: A Summary Report.* Washington, D.C.: The Police Foundation, 1977.

Sherman, Lawrence W., ed. *Team Policing: Seven Case Studies.* Washington, D.C.: The Police Foundation, 1973.

Waldo, Dwight. *The Administrative State.* New York: Ronald Press, 1948.

———. "Development of Theory of Democratic Administration." *American Political Science Review* 46 (1952): 81–103.

Waskow, Arthur. "Community Control of the Police." *Transaction* (1969): 4–7.

Weber, Max. "Politics and Government in a Reconstructed Germany," in Max Weber, *Economy and Society,* Appendix II. Edited by Guenther Roth and Claus Wittich. Berkeley, Calif.: University of California Press, 1978.

Weinstein, James. *The Corporate Ideal in the Liberal State: 1900–1918.* Boston: Beacon Press, 1968.

Whitaker, Gordon P. "Does Structure Make a Difference in Police Performance?" Paper presented to the 1978 Annual Meeting of the American Political Science Association, New York.

Wilson, Jerry V., and Alprin, Geoffrey M. "Controlling Police Conduct: Alternatives to the Exclusionary Rule." *Law and Contemporary Problems* 36 (1971): 488–99.

Yin, Robert K., and Yates, Douglas. *Street-Level Governments: Assessing Decentralization and Urban Services.* Santa Monica, Calif.: The Rand Corporation, 1974.

Index

abuses, in police work, 288, 290, 304, 321n13
accountability, 14, 42, 292–93
administration, and discretion, 8, 9, 28, 89–90, 123
administrative centralization, *see* team policing
administrative controls, 99, 247; and characteristics of structure, 277–78; and communal-professional conflict, 66; and external pressure, 127–28; police behavior, as result of, 8, 9, 96, figure 5.1 (p.100), 101, 127, 169; *see also* departmental controls
administrative discretion, 25; and implementation, 22
administrative style: and decision-making patterns, 8–9; and operational style development, 239
administrators: and aggressiveness, 242; and discipline, 98; expectations of, 96, 97, table 9.5 (p.270); and ideal patrolmen, 114; influence of, 22, 28, 99; and police-community relationship, 58, 91–92; and selectivity, 242; traffic enforcement, and attitudes of, 189
aggressiveness, 61; and administration, 169, 242, 247; of Clean Beat Crime Fighter, 223, 231, 232; modification of, 244: of Old Style Crime Fighter, 223, 225, 226, 227; in public disturbance calls, 273, table 9.7 (p.274); and service order-maintenance calls, table 9.5 (p.270), 271; of Service Style patrolmen, 223, 235; and team policing, 301–2; *see also* Los Angeles Police Department; and aggressiveness
Aggressiveness Scale, 310
aggressiveness patrol, 161, 163, table 6.3 (p.164); and court challenge, 178–79; problems of, 136–37; and threshold for action, 178
allocative decisions, 25, table 1.1 (p.30)
Alpin, Geoffrey M., 293

American society, effect on police, *xiv–xv*, 32
appearance, and evaluating citizen behavior, 162, 170, 172
apprehension, and deterrence, 136
arrests, 324n10, 325n22–326n, 327n4; and disturbance calls, 209; and team policing, 301
assault, in communities studied, table 3.1 (p.67)
attitude of patrolmen: and enforcement, 196, 197–99; and operational style, 242–43; team policing, and changes in, 302; *see also* beliefs; values
attitude test: and enforcement decision, 194–95, 196; use of, table 7.2 (p.200), 201, 324n7
authority, *see* legitimate authority; impersonal authority; moral authority
autonomy: administrative effect on, 22–23, 110, 120–27; perception of limits on, 124, table 5.7 (p.125); and professionalism, 39, 47, 56; and size of department, 29, 129; status and, 61; and team policing, 299, 300; *see also* listings under specific departments studied
avoidance, 94, table 5.7 (p.125), 126

background, and operational style, 242–43
Ban, Michael, 28
Banton, Michael, 36, 37, 39
Basic Car Plan (BCP), 300
beat cop, and community relationship, 71
beliefs, 7–8, 177; and behavior of patrolmen, 276; and discretion, 222, 266; and occupational socialization, 277; systems of (*see* operational style); *see also* attitudes; values
bifurcated system of internal controls, 98–102; and reform, 286
Bittner, Egon, 295
Bloch, Peter, 301

339

booking procedure, 160–61
boredom, 143–44, 178
Bouza, Anthony, *xiv*, 133
Bradley, Tom, 62
budget: and administrative discretion, 25; and political control, 62
bureaucracy, *xiv*, 13, 14, 275; operational styles, and attitudes toward, 240, 242; structural contradictions of, 93
burglary, table 3.1 (p.67); as narcotics-related crime, 149–50
business community, and support of LAPD, 63
"buying" a call, 143

Cain, Maureen, 321*n*22
California Penal Code (Section 415); and disturbing the peace, table 9.2*n* (p.259)
calls for service, 138, 139; disturbances and, 202; and engineering, 141–42; incidence of, table 6.1 (p.140)
Carte, Gene, 44
centralization: and nineteenth-century reform, 12; and professionalism, 44, 60
Chapman, Brian, 281–82
charge determination, 154–55, 156
chief of police: and administrative style, 239; attitudes of, 98–99; influence of, 58–59, figure 5.1 (p.100);
choices, routine, 7; *see also* discretionary choices
citizen *xi;* evaluating behavior of, 175; influence of, 57; order maintenance disputes, and protection of, 205; participation of, 13, 302
citizen's arrest: in disturbance calls, 204, 206; for misdemeanors, 183; in Redondo Beach, 259
civil liberties: and allegation of violations, 11
civil service reforms, 11, 115
class: effect of professionalism on, 57; and effect of reform, 45; and variations in law enforcement, 6, 66
Clean Beat Crime Fighter, 224, 229–32; and shift in aggressiveness, 244
clientele, ambiguity of, 77
code six, 142, 149
coercion: and abuse of power, 304; legitimate use of, 4, 6; and Old Style Crime Fighter, in police work, 48, 76, 80
coincidence, *see* happenstance
community, 12, 37, 38–39, 46, 130; and autonomy, 66, 180; and discretion, 55–56; and misdemeanors, 182–83; operational style, 238–39; size and individualism, 87; and team policing, 14, 299;

see also community relationship; size of community
community control model of reform, 292, 296–98
community relations: and aggressive patrol, 137; and department policies, 57, 58–59; and instrumental goals, 111; and nonenforcement, 251; and promotion, 116, table 5.4 (p.117), 119; of Service Style patrolman, 236
compliance, strategies to gain, 78, 80
conflict in police work, 9; between internal control systems, 76; between legitimate autonomy and crime fighting, 180; between patrolmen and supervisors, 92, 219, 247; of instrumental and substantive goals, 111–14; of Service Style patrolman with professionalism, 237, 242; source of, in police bureaucracy, 93
conformity, 15, 267, 268, 319*n*
Constitutional law, and discretion, 128
controls, 8, 88, 128–29
"corporate objectivity," and goal of professional model of reform, 295
corporate professionalism, 41, 42
crime control: and bureaucracy, 160; impetus for, 316*n*14; and patrolmen's expectations, table 5.3 (p.112); and professionalism, 42, 43; and promotional criteria, table 5.4 (p.117); and reform, 288; and team policing, 300, 302; *see also* crime fighting; crime prevention
crime fighting, 135–81; centrality of, 179; deemphasizing, 13; and operational style, 223, 236; as priority, 145, table 6.2 (p.146), 147; and reform, 285, 287–88, 303; risks and opportunities of, 265
crime prevention, 138–39; and aggressive patrol, 163; *see also* crime control; crime fighting
crime rate: 67, table 3.1 (p.68); and administrative control, 127–28; and effect on police, 55; and F.B.I. statistics, 318*n*14
crime-related indidents, and involvement in, 139, table 6.1 (p. 140)

Davis, Edward M., 61, 63, 75
Davis, Kenneth Culp, 22
decentralization: and community control model of reform, 292, 296–98; and contemporary reform, 12–13, 304; of decision making, 87; in nineteenth century, 46
decision makers, 29, table 1.1 (p.30)
decision making: decentralization of, 87;

and legalism, 201; and partners, 86; patrolmen's perception of influence over, 99–101, figure 5.1 (p.100); patterns of, 8–9; *see also* discretion; discretionary choices

decision not to arrest, 189–91

decision rules, and police discretion, 222

demographic differences between communities, 66–71

department affairs, patrolman's perception of influence over, 99–101, figure 5.1 (p.100)

departmental controls: and behavior of patrolmen, 275–79; and discretion, 276, 324*n*2; formal, 129; and hierarchical authority, 76; impact of, 248; informal, 128–29; and occupational socialization, 277; and operational style modification, 275–76; and police unions, 321*n*20

department goals, 111

department policies: and operational style development, 239; and police-community relationships, 57, 58–59

department size: and administrative control impact, 97, 128–30, 256, 277, 278; autonomy and, 279; and citizen satisfaction, 297; and conformity, 267; and discretion, 97, 126; and enforcement, 267, table 9.4 (p.268); and engineering, 142; and felony arrest, 145; and internal controls, 265; and legal authority interpretations, 256; and limits of control, 128–29; and monitoring of patrolmen, 128; and operational style, 240, 276; and perceived discretionary limits, 240, table 8.3 (p.241); and promotion, 267, table 9.4 (p.268)

detainment, and extra-legal considerations, 156–57

deterrence: and crime fighting, 135, 136; and visibility of police, 138, 139

deviant behavior: and enforcement of minor violations, 187–88; indicators of, 169–76

devotion to service, and professionalism, 39

discipline, 120–27; administrators' attitudes toward, 98; and discretion, 96, 120–27; field supervisors enforcement of, 104, table 5.1 (p.105); in large departments, 60, 129; as policy substitute, 89; and professionalism, 44, 47, 50; and training, 88, 89

discretion, 3–4, 96, 221, 222, 249–60 passim, 324*n*2; and administrators' expectations, 96; and case histories, 152–53; and case histories of disturbance calls, 212, 213; and communal-professional conflict, 66; and community expectations, 55; and crime fighting, 135; and decision to arrest, 152–53; departmental controls, and influence on, 276; and discipline, 120–27; and extra-legal consideration, 156; and hot calls, 151; and independent action, 141; and judgment, 290; limits on, and the law, 28; and misdemeanors, 183; and mood, 142–43; and operational style, 244–45; in order-maintenance calls, 218; and organizational structure, 30; patterns of, 279; perceived limits on, table 5.7 (p.125), 240, 241, table 8.3 (p.241), 266; and probable cause, 162; in professional model of reform, 295; reasons for use of, 4; and risk and opportunity assessment, 264; and selective enforcement, 158; and size of department, 126, 128; and social sanctions, 130–31; supervisors' influence over, 104, 122–23; *see also* administrative discretion; limits on discretion; police discretion

discretionary autonomy, 27–29

discretionary choices, 30; and administrative policy, 89–90; and beliefs, 266; conflicts in formation of, 31, 32; consequences of, 6–7, 246, 266; limits of constraints on, 32; and operational style, 26–27, 204; priorities, and influence on, 7; *see also* discretion; decision making

discretionary incidents: supervisors' expectations, table 9.3 (p.261); survey response to, table 9.1 (p.250)

discretionary power, 23, 31

discretionary problems, 104

disorderly juveniles, *see* public disturbance

displacement, and mood of policeman, 143

disturbance calls: and arrests, 205, 209; evaluation of 212–18; and nonenforcement decisions, 202–18, table 7.3 (pp. 210–11); *see also* order-maintenance calls; public disturbance

disturbing the peace, and California Penal Code, table 9.2*n* (p.259)

diversity among patrolmen, 8

domestic violence: police reform and, 289

drunk driving: and arrests, 191, 258, table 9.2 (p.259); case histories involving, 190–91; enforcement of, table 9.4 (p.268); and supervisors' expectations, table 9.3 (p. 261); and variations in handling of, table 9.1 (p.250); *see also* minor violations

duality, and discretionary autonomy, 29

due process, 154, 321*n*13
dynamics of organization, and choice, 23–24

education of patrolmen, table 3.2 (p.70); promotion, and effect of, table 5.5 (p.118); and Service Style patrolmen, 325*n*9
education of population, in communities studied, 69
efficiency and professionalism, 41
elderly, 69
El Sereno, and high-crime role, 70
end of watch, and minor violations, 187
enforcement: attitudes of supervisors and patrolmen compared, 260–64; and factors influencing decisions, 192; inequality of, 298; and leniency, 258; of misdemeanors, table 7.1 (p.184), 185, 186; quality of, and reform, 285; regulation of, 122
enforcement of rules, 109
engineering: and free time, 141–42; and Old Style Crime Fighter, 228
English police departments: risk and discretionary choices, 321*n*22
environmental constraints, on discretionary autonomy, 27–28, 29, table 1.1 (p.30)
ethnicity of patrolmen, table 3.2 (p.70)
evaluating patrolmen 115, 116; negative nature of, 121; and power of supervisors, 109; problems of, 80, 119
evidence, effect on nonenforcement, 323*n*2
experience: and deviant behavior indicators, 171; and limits on rationalization, 33; and power of supervisors, 109; and public disturbance call, table 9.7 (p.274); and serious order-maintenance calls, 271, table 9.6 (p.272); and vulnerability, 266
expertise, and professionalism, 39
extra-legal action: and aggressiveness, table 6.3 (pp.164–65) 166; situations necessitating, 156–59
extra-legal objectives, 192–93
extremism, of Clean Beat Crime Fighter, 231

family dispute: attitude of supervisor and patrolman compared, 263; and supervisors' expectations, table 9.3 (p.261); variations in handling of, table 9.1 (p.250); violence potential of, 77; *see also* serious order-maintenance call

felony: incidence of, table 3.1 (p.67), table 6.1 (p.140); and Old Style Crime Fighter, 225; and patrolmen, 144
felony arrest, 144–61; case histories of, 152–53, 154; and department controls, 159; discretionary choices, 151–59; and race, 153–54, 177
field incidents, table 6.1 (p.140)
field interrogations, 139, 161, 162–63; in crime prevention, 136; incidence of, table 6.1 (p.140); and Professional Style patrolmen, 232, 234; *see also* stops
field supervisors, 92, 102–10, table 5.1 (p.105); aggressiveness of, 166; and attitudes toward crime fighting, 180; attitudes toward order-maintenance calls, 208; authority of, 103–4, 107, 108; expectations of, 260–62; influence of, 99, figure 5.1 (100); and influence on priorities, 145, table 6.2 (p.146), 147; and internal control, 247; and monitoring patrolmen, 120, table 5.6 (p.121); and promotion, 116; relation to patrolmen, 101, 102, 127; and source of power, 109; upgrading, 304
Fogel, David, 288
free time, use of, 141–42, 234
frenzy of Clean Beat patrolman, 231
Friedrich, Carl, 295
frustration: of Clean Beat patrolman, 230, 232; of rookie patrolmen 320*n*21

goals: departmental, 111, 112; of reform, 291–92, 295
goal conflicts: and effect on patrolmen, 110–15; and public agencies, 33
Goldstein, Herman, 292
group conflicts, and police function, 38

happenstance, 154, 161
harrassment, use of, 156–59
"headhunting," 127
hierarchical controls, 89–90, 91, 93; breakdown of, 320*n*12–321*n*; and size of department, 97, 278; *see also* administrative controls; departmental controls
high-crime area: and aggressiveness, table 6.3 (pp.164–65), 166; and Mexican-Americans, 70; violence potential of, 78
Hollywood Race Track, and crime rate, 68
homicide, incidence of, table 3.1 (p.67)
hot calls: reaction to, 151–53; and sergeants, 159; violence potential of, 77
Hughes, Everett, 56

human frailty: and nonenforcement, 195; and patrolmen's acceptance of, in his colleagues, 115
"hunches," ability to develop, 169–70

ignoring disturbance calls, table 7.3 (pp.210–11), 214
ignoring violations, 185, 187–88
impersonal authority, and law, 38–39, 46
implementation of policy, 22, 23–24
indicators of deviant behavior, 169–76; and usefulness of, 176–77
individualism: in the police culture, 84, 85–86; of supervisors, 123
inequality, as effect of leniency, 298
informal action, and enforcement, 185
informal control, of police, 46
informants, and importance of, to promotion, 321n16; and nonenforcement, 192–93; recruitment of, 148
information, 78, 136, 171–72
Inglewood, 15, 66–71; aggressiveness in, table 6.3 (pp. 164–65), 166, 167, 169; and autonomy, 64–65, 66; attitude toward blacks, 72; chief of police's attitudes, 98, 99; crime rate in, table 3.1 (p.67), 68; felony crimes in, table 3.1 (p.67); the Forum and influence on crime rate, 68; Hollywood Race Track, and crime rate in, 68; and individualism, 87; and leniency and nonenforcement, 258; and minor violations, table 7.1 (p.184), 185, 186, 269; and perception of supervisors behavior in, table 5.6 (p.120); police-community relationship, 64–65, 72–73, 74; and priorities, 269; and promotion, 115, 269; and public disturbance calls, 257–58; and serious order-maintenance calls, 256; and size of police department, 59, 64, 65; and supervisors' expectations, 260–64, 269; see also small departments
initiative and discretion in crime fighting, 135
"inner check," and professional model of reform, 294, 296
in-presence requirement, for misdemeanors, 183, 204
instrumental goals, and patrolmen's expectations, 111, table 5.3 (p.112)
Internal Affairs Division of LAPD, 60
internal affairs units, 60, 92; and "head-hunting," 127
internal control: conflict and division in, 97–102; and field supervisor, 247; and risks and opportunities, 265; systems of, 76

interpersonal disputes, and order maintenance, 203–4, 207
intervention, and perception of supervisors' behavior, table 5.6 (p.120)
isolation of police, 49

Jacobs Plan, and financial autonomy of LAPD, 63
judgment, 33, 57, 296; in crime fighting, 137–38; and discretion, 290; of legality, 263–64; and operational style, 26–27, 233; and police culture, 82; and welfare of the community, 60
juveniles, in communities studied, 69; and legal authority of patrolmen, 273;
juvenile gangs, in Northeast division, 67

Kansas City Police Department, and effect of patrol levels on crime, 180
Kelling, George, 288

large department, see Los Angeles Police Department
latitude of discretion, 27–29, table 1.1 (p.30)
law: ambiguity of, 4, 5; and impersonal authority, 46; intent of, 5, 188
law enforcement: aggressiveness, in 163, table 6.3 (p.164–65); and allegations of discrimination, 11; and coercion, 4; and operational style, 223, 229, 232; and patrolmen's expectations, 112, table 5.3 (p.112); as priority, table 6.2 (p.146), 147; risks and opportunities in, 265; and social distinctions, 6
legal authority, and juveniles, 273
legal criteria, for field interrogation, 162
legality: and enforcement decisions, 201; and judgment of supervisors and patrolmen compared, 264; and problems in crime fighting, 136
legitimate authority, 50; and goal conflicts, 111; and moral consensus, 37; and professionalism, 46, 47; and size of department, 129–30
legitimate autonomy, and informal specialization, 147–48
leniency, 258, 270, 298
lethal force, and hot calls, 151–52
limits on discretion: minor violation, and perception of, 267, 268, table 9.4 (p.268); operational style and perception of, 326n7; in policymaking model

limits on discretion *(continued)*
of reform, 292 public disturbance calls, and perception of, 274–75, table 9.7 (p.274); and serious order-maintenance calls, 271–72; table 9.6 (p.272); small departments and perception of, 275
location of communities, and crime rate, 68
Los Angeles Police Department: and aggressive enforcement, 61, 145, table 6.3 (pp.164–65), 166, 167, 297; and arrest, 260, 272, 273; autonomy of, 60–65, 66; and avoidance, table 5.7 (p.125); and bureaucracy's influence on patrolmen, 275; chief of police's attitudes, 98; Central Area Division of, 318*n*16; changes in, *viii*; character of communities served by, 15, 66–71; crime rate in area of, table 3.1 (p.67), 68; and citizen complaints, 321*n*21; complaints within, 319*n* 3–20n; and detachment of, 72, 73; discipline in, 60; and enforcement style, 249, 258; and financial autonomy, 62, 63; and field interrogations, 145; and individualism, 87; and informant, 148; and innovative programs, 300, 301; and minor violation enforcement, 252; and misdemeanor enforcement, table 7.1 (p.184), 185, 186; Old Style Crime Fighter in, 229; operational style and arrests in, 267; perception of supervisors' behavior, table 5.6 (p.120); and Police Commission and political control of, 62; and professionalism, 60, 219; and promotion, 115–16, 118; public disturbance enforcement, 257–58, 274; and serious maintenance calls, 256; size of, 59; and supervision, 240–41, table 8.3 (p.241); and supervisors' expectations, 260–64; and team policing, 300; uncertainties in, 278; and vulnerability, 274
lower-class area, and aggressiveness, table 6.3 (pp. 164–65), 166
loyalty, 82–84, 90, 94, 3; 9*n*8

MacArthur Park, 258–59
McNamara, John, 110
Madison, James, 282
managers and supervisors, as decision makers, table 1.1 (p. 30)
manner, and supervisor-patrolman conflict, 167
Mapp v. *Ohio*, 28
mediation, 207, 208
merit system, 41
methodology of study, 15–18

Mexican-Americans, 69, 70; and drunk driving arrests, 327*n*4; and felony crimes, 67
Miami, *xi*
middle class: and police reform, 45, 298; and responsiveness of small department, 66
middle managers, and environmental constraints, 29
military service: and background of patrolmen, table 3.2 (p.70)
minorities and aggressiveness, table 6.2 (pp.164–65), 166; in communities studied, 68, 69; and criminal justice, *xi;* and effect of professionalism, 57; and opinion of police, 11–12; *see also* Mexican Americans
minor violations: attitudes of supervisors and patrolmen compared, 260; and enforcement, table 7.1 (p. 184), 191; hypothetical examples of, 249, 251; management of, 269; and operational styles, 226, 229, 234; and political implications of nonenforcement for, 202; reform influence on, 289; small departments and management of, 270; and "stockpiling," 265; variation in management of, in communities studied, 251; *see also* order-maintenance call; serious order-maintenance call; service maintenance call
misconduct, 60, 92, 122
misdemeanors, 182; arrests for, 177, 259, table 9.1 (p.259); enforcement of and policy manual, 186; and "in-presence requirement, 204
models of policing, past and present, 284
modernization, and effect on police work, 32
monitoring patrolmen, 128
mood, and effect on police work, 142–44, 192
moral authority: problems with, 37
moral choices, 78–79
moral consensus, 37, 47
Moses, Robert, *xiv*
Muir, William Ker, Jr., 296, 325*n*12
mutual role expectations, 32

narcotics enforcement, and informants, 192
narcotics investigators, and patrolman's relation to, 150
narcotics-related crime, 149–50
narcotics specialization, 148–49
narcotics violations, 67, 145
negative discipline, 103, 111

Index

Neighborhood Action Team Policing (NATP), 300, 301
neighborhood meetings, and team policing model, 300
New York Police Department, and team policing, 301
Niederhoffer, Arthur, 89
nonenforcement: case histories involving, 190–91; categories of, 185; and community relations, 251; and policymaking model of reform, 294; and professionalism, 194; reasons for, 187–202; and special groups, 193; and tolerance of carelessness, 195
Northeast Division, 67, 70

obedience, and police training, 88, 89
observation, and perception of supervisors' behavior, table 5.6 (p.120)
occupational socialization: and operational style, 243; and police action, 277
Old Style Crime Fighter, 224, 225–29; and conflict with administration, 227, 242
on-view stops, 167, table 6.4 (p.168); and arrests, 324n10; frequency of, table 6.1 (p.140), 141, 161; and Old Style Crime Fighter, 227
operational styles, 26–27, 223–25, table 8.1 (p.224), table 8.2 (p.230), 238–44; and attitude toward supervision, 240–41; comparison of, 237; and conflicts in police work, 139, 141; definition of, 223; department controls, and influence on, 276; development of, 86; and discretion, 264, 324n2, 326n7; and drunk driving incident, 267, table 9.4 (p. 268); elements of, 141–43, 223; and individualism, 86; judgment, 137; and pace, 230–31; and perception of constraint, 266; and promotion, 326n5; and psychological traits, 325n10; and public disturbance, table 9.7 (p.274); and service order-maintenance incident, table 9.5 (p.270), 271, 276; size of department and, 267, 276; and time usage, 141; see also Clean Beat Crime Fighter; Old Style Crime Fighter; Professional Style patrolman; Service Style patrolman
opinion, differences among patrolmen, 222
opportunity, 264–66; see also risk and opportunity
order-maintenance calls, 202–6, 207–9; and arrest rate, 259, table 9.2 (p.259); and citizen's arrest, 204; and field supervisors' expectations, 262–63; and interpersonal disputes, 203–4, 207; and operational style, 224, 227–28, 229, 231; and patrolmen's attitude toward, 204–5; and promotional criteria, 117; and reluctance to act, 218; see also public disturbance, service order-maintenance calls; and serious order-maintenance calls
order maintenance role, emphasis on, 13, 43
organization, and impersonal authority, 46; and operational style, 27; and professionalism, 44
organizational constraints: on discretionary autonomy, 27–28, 29, table 1.1 (p.30); limits on, 34
organizational dynamics, 23–24
organizational elite, 29, table 1.1 (p.30)
organizational goals, 32
organizational uncertainty, risks and opportunities in, 265, 266

pace, and operational style, 230–31
Parker, William H., 42, 43, 60, 62, 135, 284
particularistic values, in small departments, 298
partners, 86
patrol cars, limiting nature of, 71
patrol division, as autonomous subsystem, 88
patrolmen, 69, table 3.2 (p.70), 84–85; and administrative control, 9, 127; and attitude of citizen (see attitude test); control held by, figure 5.1 (p. 100), 101; duties of, 6; and enforcement difficulties, 182–83; expectations of, desired and perceived, table 5.3 (p.112), 113, 114; and field supervisors, 101–2, 262; and identification with supervisor, 244; misdemeanor enforcement and attitude of, table 7.1 (p.184), 185, 186; and narcotics investigator, 150; order maintenance and attitude of, 204–5, 208, table 7.3 (pp. 210–11); and perceived influence 99, 100, figure 5.1, 101; power of and hierarchical control, 90; and priorities, 145, table 6.2 (p.146), 147; prior occupations of, 319n13; promotional criteria, and effect on, 115; and regulatory decisions, 25; and statistical controls, 123–24; team policing, impact on behavior of, 301; and uncertainties, 110–27; and undermining supervisors authority, 107–9
patronage, elimination of, 41

345

Perceived Limits on Discretion Scale, 311
Perception of Supervisors' Behavior Scale, 311
Perlmutter, Amos, 41
personal authority, 38–39, 46, 65
personal characteristics of victim: disturbance calls, and influence of, 214: and nonenforcement, 323*n*3
personality, *xii*; and operational style, 27
personal pressure, and enforcement decisions, 192, 194; *see also* stress
personnel complaints, and power of supervisor, 109
police: criticism of, 11, 12; factors determining effectiveness, 38; military compared to, 88; and political control, 45; and relation to society, 34, 36–37; self-image of, 48–49; and social worker function of, 6
police brutality, allegations of, 11
Police Commission, 62
police culture, 49, 82–86; and coercion, 48; and crime fighting conflicts, 139; and discretionary requirements, 93; and peer group controls, 76; and policymaking model of reform, 294; and professionalism, 50, 128;
police department: autonomy and size of, 29; conflicts under professionalism, 49; nineteenth century, 44, 45
police discretion: and community factors, 38, 56; definition of, 3; impersonal and personal authority compared, 39; and professionalism, 47; *see also* discretion
police organizations, and limits on control, 127; and relation of police to community, 56; *see also* police union
police power, debates over use of, 11
police reform, *see* reform
police unions, and limits on departmental controls, 321*n*20
police work, 76–79, 80; as a craft, 296; intrinsic conflict in, 139; professionalism and effect on, 79; and substantive goals, 111
policy decisions, implementation of, 22, 23–24
policymaking, 5, 24–25
policymaking model of reform, 292–94
policy mandates, and change in organizational responsibility, 26
political conflict, and discretion, 34
political control: and budgetary process, 62; and relation to police, 45
political decisions, defined, 21
politics: and crime control, 43; and relation to administration, 21
predictability, 33
pretext arrest, 209

preventative patrol, and crime control, 42, 43, 288; *see also* aggressive patrol
prior information, 170, 172–73
priorities: and administrative controls, 277–78; choice of, 145, table 6.2 (p.146), 147; in crime fighting, 137; and discretionary choices, 7; and field supervisors' expectations, 262–63; in Inglewood, 269; of Service Style patrolmen, 236; and time, 141
probable cause, 162–63, 178–79, 194
procedural choices, 25
production norms, 278
professional code, 48
professionalism, 12–13, 41–44 passim; and accountability, 14; and administrative consequences, 127–31; and the attitude test, 199; and bureaucratization, 14; and civil service reform, 11; and community welfare, 60; conflicts and pressures under, 49–50; and discretion, 47; effects of, 13, 39, 79; elements of, 39, 43, 47; and hierarchical control, 93; historical origins of, 41–42; and inequalities of enforcement, 288–89; and instrumental goals, 111; and internal control conflict, 128; and legal norms, 315*n*5–316*n*; and management of misconduct, 92; minor violations, and enforcement under, 201; nonenforcement and, 194, 195, 206, 218–20; and operational styles, 229, 232, 235, 237, 241, 242; and police-community relations, 56, 57; Vollmer's view of, 43
professional model of reform, 292, 294–96
Professional Style patrolman, 224, 232–35
Progressive movement, and police professionalism, 41–42, 284
promotion, desire for: and adherence to regulations, table 5.5 (p.118); and drunk driving incident, 267, table 9.4 (p.268); and informants, 321*n*16; and nonenforcement, 268; and operational style, 326*n*5; and public disturbance, 274, table 9.7 (p.274); and serious order-maintenance call, 271, table 9.6 (p.272); and specialization, 148, 150; and supervisors' expectations, 269; and vulnerability, 266
promotional criteria, 115–19
property crimes, table 3.1 (p.67)
prosecutor, and influence on discretionary choices, 159
psychological traits, and operational style, 242–43, 325*n*10
public agencies, 33
public control, and demand for professionalism, 40

Index

public disturbance: attitude of patrolmen and supervisors compared, 263; factors determining management of, 204, 273–75; hypothetical example of, 256–57; and variation in enforcement, table 9.1 (p.250), 256, 258; and supervisors' expectations, table 9.3 (p. 261), 263
public opinion polls, 11–12
public policy, implementation of, 23
public pressure: and bureaucratic control, 93–94; and small departments, 129
public support, of Los Angeles Police Department, 63
punitiveness, and perception of supervisors' behavior, 240, table 8.3 (p.241)
Punitiveness of Supervision Scale, 312

race: and aggressiveness, 166; and arrests for minor violations, 177; attitude of police toward, 72, 313n12–14n; and discretionary choices, 153; and law enforcement, 6; and nonenforcement, 324n10; and order-maintenance dispute, 205, 208; and public disturbance calls, 214; and residential segregation, 67–71
racial crises, xiv
racial diversity of communities studied, 69
Rampart, 70; felony crimes in, table 3.1 (p.67); see also Los Angeles Police Department
rationalization of tasks, 32; limits to, 33
Redondo Beach, 15, 66–71; and aggressiveness, table 6.3 (pp.164–65), 166, 167; and autonomy, 64, 65, 66; chief of police's attitude, 98–99; and citizen's arrest, 259; community relations activities in, 65; covering action in minor violations, 253; crime rate in, table 3.1 (p.67), 68; and field supervisors' expectations, 260, 262; and identification of patrolmen with community, 72; and individualism, 87; minor violations, 249, 253, 269; and misdemeanor enforcement, table 7.1 (p.184), 185, 186; and perception of supervisors' behavior, table 5.6 (p.120); and promotional criteria, 115; public disturbance cases, 257–58; ride-along program in, 65; and serious order maintenance calls, 256; size of police department in, 59; supervisors' expectations and goals, 260–64, 326n8; and uncertainty, 269
reform, 12–13, 39, 285–93; and community control model, 292, 296–98; and conflict between professionalism and police culture, 286; and corporate

professionalism of police, 41; crime control emphasis and timing of, 316n14; decentralization and, 304; democratic control and, 287; and discipline, 47; limits to, 303–5; and policymaking model of, 292; and professional code changes, 48; and professionalism, 42; and professional model of, 292, 294–96; and rationalization, 32; and separation of police and community, 46; team policing model of, 292, 299–302
reformers, and continuity between Progressives and professionals, 316n13
regulations: adherence to, table 5.5 (p.118); enforcement of, 122
regulatory decisions, and substantive choices, 25, table 1.1 (p.30)
Reiss, Albert, Jr., 203, 265
reputation, and department size, 128
resources: and administrative control, 277; and discretion, 43; and field supervisors expectations, 262; and limits on autonomy, 64; and order maintenance problems, 271; use of, and reform, 289
responsiveness to community, and size of the department, 130
reward-performance gap, and effect on patrolment, 111, 115–20
ride-along programs, 65
risk: actual and perceived, 264–66; of aggressive patrol, 179; in English police departments, 321n22; and selection of specialization, 150
risk and opportunity: and discretion, 264–66, 267; in non-felony cases, 271–74
robbery, criteria and definition of, 318n15
role conflict, and coping, 287
role of police, 4, 37
Rubinstein, Jonathan, 108–9

scale construction, 307–9
Schon, Donald, 24
secrecy, in police culture, 83
selective enforcement, 157–58
Selectiveness of Law Enforcement Scale, 310–11
selectivity: administration attitude toward, 242; and operational style, 223, 225, 235, 236
self-protection, and discretion, 151
Selznick, Philip, 299
separation: of police and community, 46, 48, 57; of police and politics, 43
sergeants: and hot calls, 159; influence of, 325n12; role of, 103–5; statistical con-

sergeants *(continued)*
    trol, and attitude of, 124; supervision, and attitude of, 105; *see also* field supervisor
serious order-maintenance calls: factors determining management of, 271–73; and field supervisors' expectations, table 9.3 (p.261), 263; risks and opportunities in, 265; and variations of enforcement, 254–56; and vulnerability, 276; *see also* family dispute; disturbance calls; public disturbance
service, and limits of reform, 303–4
service order-maintenance calls, 251, 252; factors determining patrolman's behavior at, 270–71; and operational style, 224, 229, 234–35, 270, 276; risks and opportunities in, 265; and variations in handling of, table 9.1 (p.250), 252
service orientation, and Professional Style, 233, 234–35
service role, 13
Service Style patrolman: and conflict with administration, 242; and educational background, 325*n*9; negative group, 235–36; as operational style, 224; positive group, 236–37; and professionalism, 237, 242
sex, and disturbance calls, 214, 217
size of community: and limits on autonomy, 65; and police-community relationship, 57–58
size of police departments in communities studied, 59; *see also* department size, small departments
skill and operational style, 225–26, 230
Skolnick, Jerome, 194
small departments, 274, 275, 298; avoidance in, table 5.7 (p.125); field supervisors' expectations, 262; and leniency, 258, 270; and narrow interpretation of legal authority, 256, 273; and nonenforcement, 253, 297; and public pressure, 129; and team policing, 301; and uncertainty, 275, 278
social class, and background of patrolmen, table 3.2 (p. 70)
social objectives of laws, 5
social sanctions, and control systems, 130
social work aspect of police work, 6
solidarity, 80–82; and hierarchical control, 90, 94; and occupational pressure, 221; in police culture, 76, 80, 82; ubiquitous character of, 318*n*6
Specht, David, 301
specialization, 147–50
statistical controls, 123–24

status, as basis for autonomy, 61
"stockpiling," 265
stops: experimental nature of, 178; and hot calls, 151; and knowledge of individuals, 173; police-initiated, 167, table 6.4 (p.168); risks and opportunities in, 265; for suspicious circumstances, 173, 174, 175; uncertainties of, 172
street-level bureaucracy: administrative discretion in, 31–35; and conflicting public interest, 34; discretionary power and, 23, table 1.1 (p.30); environmental constraints on, 29; and organizational elite, 29
"street sense," of Old Style Crime Fighters, 225
stress, 77–79; and operational style, 240; of professionalism, 49
substantive decisions, 25, table 1.1 (p.30)
substantive goals, 111, 112
suburban government and community control model of reform, compared, 297
supervision: attitude toward, 104, table 5.1 (p. 105), 106, 240; perceived problems of, table 5.2 (p.106)
supervisors: abuse of due process, and toleration by, 321*n*13 and attitude test, table 7.2 (p.200), 201; behavior of, perceived by patrolmen, table 5.6 (p.120); civil service and limits of control of, 115; conflict over nonenforcement, 219; conflict with Old Style Crime Fighter, 277; constraint and expectations of, 277; and dependence on patrolmen, 91; expectations of, 260–64, table 9.3 (p.261), 277; and influence on discretion, 122–23; minor violation enforcement, and attitude of, table 7.1 (p.184), 185, 186; and observation of patrolmen, 121; operational style, and influence of, 244; order-maintenance calls, and attitude of, table 7.3 (pp.210–11), 270, table 9.5 (p. 270); perception of their function, 320*n*8; power of, 109; public disturbance incidents, and attitude of, table 9.3 (p.261), 263; punitiveness and perception of, 240, table 8.3 (p.241); relations with, and promotion, table 5.5 (p.118); and rule enforcement, 88; *see also* administrator; field supervisor
supervisor-patrolman relationship, 107, 110, 160
suspicious circumstances, and reason for field interrogation, 162, 173, 174, 175
system code, 48

Index

Tammany Hall, *xiv*

Taylor, Frederick, 41–42

team policing, 181, 300; and aggressive patrol, 171; and the community, 14, 58; as model of reform, 292, 299–302; New York Police Department and, 301; and stability, 299; Team 28 experiment and, 301

Team 28 experiment, and team policing in New York, 301

technical competence, and professional model of reform, 294

technical rationalization, and professionalism, 33, 43

tension: and hierarchical controls, 94; and internal control conflict, 97; between police culture and professionalism, 201

time, use of, 139–42, 234

traffic enforcement, and field supervisors' expectations, 262; and operational styles, 226, 234; Vollmer's views on, 43; and violations as misdemeanors, 182

training of policemen, 25, 44, 295; and emphasis on discipline and obedience, 88–89; and professionalism, 39

uncertainty, 77–79, 80; and administration controls and expectations, 266, 278; in deviant behavior detection, 171; limits of, in policymaking model of reform, 293; and negative organizational pressure, 287; and operational style, 244–45; public disturbance call and, 275; in small departments, 278

unemployment rate, in communities studied, 69

upper class, and community control model, 298

urban government decentralization, and community control model of reform, 296

values: changes in, 48, 49–50; and police-community relations, 57, 58; and police discretion, 37; *see also* attitudes; beliefs

Van Mannen, John, 319*n*8, 320*n*21

vehicle code, and field interrogation, 162

vice laws, and inattention to, 236

victim culpability, and degree of enforcement, 227, 231

victim legitimacy, 214–16

Vietnam war, *xi*, 10

violations, ranking of, and enforcement, 188

violence: and disturbance call potential, 203; and Old Style Crime Fighter, 227, 228; and Service Style patrolman, 236; unpredictability of, 77–78

violent crimes, incidence of, table 3.1 (p.67)

visibility of patrolmen, as deterrant to crime, 138, 139

Vollmer, August, 60, 114, 179; and Progressivism in police work, 42–45; and reform, 284, 285, 316*n*13

vulnerability: and constraints perceived, 266; and discretionary choices, 266–67; importance of, in order-maintenance calls, 272–74, 276

Wallen, Linda, 321*n*21

Wambaugh, Joseph, 84, 114, 229

war on poverty, 10, 21

watch commander, and attitude toward supervision, table 5.1 (p.105)

Watts revolt, 61, 62, 72

weapons possession, 145

Weber, Max, 305

Westley, William, 48, 49, 82

Wickersham Commission, *xiii*, 12; history of, 313*n*12

Wilson, James Q., 8–9, 25, 96, 298, 324*n*2

Wilson, Jerry V., 293

Wilson, O. W., 42, 77, 96, 284

women, and order maintenance disputes, 205

Woods, Arthur, 4

work controls, and police discretion, 96

work environment, and limits on discretion, 28; and limits on rationalization, 34

working-class immigrants, and nineteenth-century police, 45

work-related problems, and perceived supervisory problems, 104, 105, table 5.2 (p.106)

Yorty, Sam (Mayor), 62